Her Mind SCREAMS MURDER

Titles also by Jenny Mac
'The Australian Outback Series'
April Rain (Book 1)
Cheyla (Book 2)

'Australian Narratives'
Australiana 'POEMS' Ocean to the Outback

Jenny Mac

Jenny Mac, born in the Outback Country of Central Australia, now lives close to the ocean on The Central Coast of New South Wales Australia with her husband, and is mother to three grown sons.

As an Author she is now fortunate enough to pursue her passion for writing Fiction Novels about the Country she loves, Australia.

Her Mind SCREAMS MURDER ...A CRIME FICTION NOVEL...
'Murder/Mystery ... Deceit/Romance'

Some towns, places, or areas in this Novel, are fictional.
All products devised within the Author's imagination.
Characters are fictional, and bear no reference to anyone.

Her Mind SCREAMS MURDER

The Detectives Notebook

Jenny Mac

Copyright © 2024 Jenny Mac
All rights reserved.
ISBN 978 0 6483536 7 6 (Paperback)

No part of this publication may be reproduced or transmitted in any form or by any means, without permission in writing from Author: Jenny Mac

Prologue

Deep within the shadows of her mind, bright stars materialized to partially cloud her vision, then altered spasmodically though it was day, to become a white blinding light that pierced her senses.

Hazy distorted scenes flashed before her, portraying a forgotten past long buried, as sharp rays of light stabbed at her eyes.

Her head hurt with such ferocious pain she fell to her knees.

The staircase was plunged into darkness …but she could see…

As if by magic a scene appeared …There was a body… cold and lifeless …dead eyes staring… There was blood …much blood…

She screamed a silent scream in revulsion as she recognized the body. Memories of her lost life came alive, and she relived the true horror of it. She could recall the screams in the darkest hour urging her to creep along the balcony to the steps, but just one missing step proved fatal, then she was falling to the treacherous rocks below.

Was it all real? …A cruel prank… Or, could it be a fact?
Shock was taking over, but some influence forced her to face reality! Her body trembled to shake uncontrollably as she sobbed. Then she noticed people, just shadows really, peering at her. *Who were they?*

Jenna Temple stared around in desperation with un-seeing eyes as confusion took over, but her heart cried another emotion … *FEAR!* It consumed her, she felt threatened and sensed the deadly danger.

Her Mind SCREAMS MURDER

Chapter One

Richard Temple stepped off the train onto the platform. Took a flight of steps down to a lower level, walked up to the turnstile to insert his ticket then he weaved a pathway through the throng of people towards the exit, and stepped out into the busy street below.

It was only a two-block walk to the function center, and he really felt the need to stretch out after his long day. Besides he planned on having a few ales tonight to celebrate the year's end of another very successful business year in his globally operated textile company.

However, his curiosity spiked an interest to meet the mysterious new wife of sole business partner George Delvin, who only recently had secretly married, in his very late fifties too. That was a blinder of a news flash, but the decider to leave his car at the station in 'Blue Bay,' a little Australian fishing village on the coast, his home town.

Richard resided on a semi-rural property named 'Oceanview,' seventy acres, just outside the village. He usually commuted from there to the city by car, but chose the train ride just for convenience. *I shall get a cab home, or whatever!* he thought. *I'm really not too fussed!*

But later, much later. If at all! he decided, as he walked along.

There really isn't anyone to rush home to anymore, is there? Jenna is home. *But Jenna can certainly look after herself!* he chuckled. Besides! We do have permanent staff and we employ a house maid, a stableman, yardman, and cook! he thought to himself absently.

Of course, his wife Julia resided there, but she didn't participate in caring for anyone at all. Instead, she was obsessed with herself, and consumed by her own self-pity. She openly detested everyone in the world around her. *No! There is no need to rush home! Any love they had was long gone.* Julia had certainly made sure of that. It was impossible to converse with her as their arguments turned sour.

Although Richard knew in his heart it wasn't only her actions, it was his own. He simply found her so repulsive now he could not imagine being close to her again. He had come to hate her, that is how it was with them in this so-called marriage since the accident.

I can't go on. I must do something about it!

He had found her writhing in pain on the kitchen floor some two years ago now. Her head, fully alight with flames caused from a gas burner which erupted in her face, and her hair on fire. Richard had just stared as the huge flames engulfed her face, and neck as he fought through veils of shock to regain his wits, before rushing to her aid to extinguish the flames, but it was too late. Way too late!

She had been hospitalized for three months in the intensive care unit. They didn't expect her to pull through, but miraculously she did. Several attempts were made by plastic surgeons to restore her scalp, her face and neck to her former self, but every operation had complications, so she ultimately remained with permanent scaring and such horrific injuries of the worst kind that portrayed her as a monster. A living, breathing monster, who soon became consumed by hate for a world that really didn't want to see her, or know her.

His recollection of the day he collected her from the hospital to bring her home was an awakening. From that day she immediately became a twisted, withdrawn, and bitter person, simply wallowing in self-pity, and she pushed him away to the point of no return.

Once again, he could feel his gorge rising from that well-known worm deep in his gut that always tested him as the guilt rose in his throat threatening to choke him, and he tugged at his collar trying to relieve the heat so he could breathe. Though deep in his mind he relived the accident that had ultimately changed both their lives.

Guilt! I continuously live with guilt, always mindful of what I say! I just want a full life! The need to feel love again with some-one who will love me back, but there is no hope for that now, is there? Not with Julia anyway. *No, there's no going back!* he thought sadly.

He desperately tried to push all these thoughts aside to prepare himself for the busy night to come, but now he had thought about it and it was all fresh in his mind, he realized finally. His home life, and his marriage for that matter, was just a shambles. He knew it most definitely now. He was just so tired of endlessly hiding things, pretending all was fine. *But it wasn't! Was it?* he questioned himself. All his lies, his cheating, affairs experienced, was in desperation for some contact, that only seemed to bide his time. Fill in a gap or sate his appetite for the love and attention he so needed for a while, but he felt no love! He had that once with his wife, and guessed he still cared for her, but he didn't love her how she was now. Just a crazy, hateful person, bent on some revenge for her horrendous injuries.

Julia seemed only a memory now of their past life together.

Some-how, some-time it has to change! he promised himself.

Suddenly, right there in front of him, a huge building captivated his attention, and he walked closer. Then he paused to look up at it reaching to the sky. The function center had many facilities to offer, and it was the hub of activity for this part of the city. A huge variety of events were held in there. He guessed it appropriate he had been fortunate enough to secure this booking for their annual party. He walked up the stairs, then headed towards the double doors. They swung open at his approach, so he passed on through, strode across the tiled floor, then took an elevator to the top floor. Thick, carpeted floor cushioned his step as he moved out into the hallway, then he walked down towards the check-in counter that he knew would be at the entrance to the room he had reserved.

Hillary West sat behind a lavish desk looking impossibly busy, but just so elegant in her chic outfit that defined her status. She was Richard's secretary. *My right-hand girl!* he thought absently, as he slowly ambled towards her, although his gaze began unashamedly undressing her as he scrutinized her long shapely legs, and his eyes caressed her perfect figure clad in the tight-fitting outfit. But it was the red hair that always done it for him, and he sighed with lust.

I guess she is much more than just my secretary in certain situations! he thought to himself. But he smiled secretly as visions of her young body pressing up against him came to mind, and already he wanted her. But Hillary West was, he knew for certain, always professional in every sense. *She knew her place!* and he liked it that way.

"Mister Temple!" she gushed. Then a blush rose to highlight her cheeks when she sensed his presence before her. Her honey-colored eyes widened as she looked up at him in surprise, then she added.

"Good evening, sir!" she managed to express, with a wry smile.

"Good evening, Hillary! You are looking as beautiful as ever I see, and how is it all going? Is everyone here?"

She blushed once again in reply. "Thank you, sir! Yes, I do think they are all here now, so it is good timing on your part, and might I add." she leaned over to whisper. "You look quite spiffy also sir!"

Richard chuckled. "Thanks, Hill! But aren't I always?" he teased.

"Yes! I guess you are Mister Temple." she said in annoyance. "Maybe I shall take back my compliment, and get back to work! So would you sign here please Mister Temple?" she asked, back to her professional self, as she slid the guest book and pen over to him, with just a hint of a smile creasing her lips.

He smiled as he ran his finger down the guest list searching for a name. His hand paused at the most unknown one. *Miranda! Hmm!* he mused. *An interesting name!* He bent down to sign in then pushed the guest book back towards Hillary, as he looked up.

"Guess I'll head on in then Hill, shall I see you after?" he asked with a question in his voice, and she blushed again with her reply.

"Yes, it would please me a lot sir! I will be here until the finish!"
"Good! I shall see you later then Hill!" he stated, then he walked towards the doors, and Hillary gazed longingly after him as he left.

Such a gorgeous hunk of a man he is! she thought to herself. Their intimate relationship was to be strictly confidential. She had agreed to a pact on that, *and she was to be professional in the public eye.*

Richard stood momentarily in the doorway scanning the room, then he saw her, and he grinned. It was not difficult to identify her amongst all the guests in the crowded room. She simply stood out from them, blooming like a rose in a sandy desert. She was laughing out loud now, others laughed with her. Then slowly she turned her head to look around. Her eyes passed over him, but were quick to return to then hold his gaze. Seemingly they smoldered as they bore into him. He simply gasped, unable to tear his eyes away from her. *Just what colour are those eyes?* he wondered. *They are just so dark, and so tantalizing, h*e was mesmerized by them.

Good god! Seriously? This woman cannot be George Delvin's wife? he questioned himself in amazement. George was getting on now! He had never married, too obsessed with his job and was a good friend.

George owned a home high on the bluff at the edge of the city.

He cast his eyes upon George. He was vocal with laughter now.

Deep wrinkles etched his brow as a result. He moved his fingers through his thinned, brown hair which was showing signs of a bald spot, and greying at his temples, as he attempted some explanation.

He would have to be at least fifteen years her senior, besides he is not a fit man, and his waistline has thickened. He's good looking enough, but I really don't see a connection with these two. *So! What could be the attraction, and why George Delvin of all people?* he puzzled, in total confusion, as he looked at Miranda who seemed just in her element.

Something churned inside his gut as he watched her. The black chiffon dress swirling about her exposed bare shoulders. Platinum hair, so very shortly cropped, fell softly against her lovely face. Her ivory skin seemed flawless, and her full breasts peeked out over the top of her bodice as she laughed, only now she was not laughing as another expression had captivated her face, transforming her into a seductress. *She is simply exquisite! Beautiful beyond doubt!* he noted, as he slowly walked towards where she stood beside George.

People addressed him or tried to strive for attention as he strode through the crowd, and he earnestly made an effort to acknowledge each one of them as he passed by, or paused even to speak to others, but his eyes never left the face of the mysterious Miranda.

Miranda's smile had disappeared as she watched this hunk of a man cross the room, and walk towards them. He was tall. His body seemed so muscular under the flimsy shirt, though he was so lean, and toned like a panther and she could imagine the feel of him up against her as that familiar ache gripped her, making her forget for the moment she was un-obtainable, and so very recently married.

Still, she looked unashamedly at his handsome, suntanned face which was chiseled to perfection, framed by jet-black hair that was swept back at the sides. *He is so slick, and he knows it.* she thought.

But it was his teasing blue eyes which had captivated her mostly, as he held her own smoldering gaze. She shivered with excitement.

Well, well, huge handsome one! Just what rock did you crawl out from under. I wonder? Though more importantly I fear that I should know! *Just what is your business here, sir?* she silently asked herself.

"Are you alright Miranda?" her husband asked. "You seem just a little distracted!" Immediately her face altered as she looked up to present him with her best smile, then she replied to him sweetly.

"Distracted? No, not at all George, my love! I am fine my darling. I was just looking around the room at all your dear friends, and yes, it hit me then, as I realized what a great man you must be!"

George chuckled to himself. *Gee whiz! What a lucky man I am!* he thought. *I have just married the most beautiful woman in the whole world.* He almost had to pinch himself to believe it still. Just thanks to the good lord I attended that particular charity luncheon on that specific day. *It was the day when I first met Miranda.* Surprisingly, his invitation delivered direct to his office was a hand written one in a flowing text and almost personal. He didn't think anything of it at the time, but noted that a lot of business executives from different companies in the vicinity were attending the fund raiser as per the guest list attached and all the confirmations. So, he assumed then it must be an important event to be invited to, and relaxed to join in.

He was greeted at the front door by Miranda James herself. She was the sole organizer for the fund raiser. She then pointed towards the donation box as she introduced herself. He was so taken by her beauty that he immediately dug deep into his wallet for some cash. Money was irrelevant! So, he slid a wad of notes into the slot.

She smiled a sweet smile, as she thanked him for his donation.

That smile makes it all worthwhile. he realized, as he listened while she explained all the events on for the luncheon.

She was decidedly more glamorous than any woman he'd ever known, she intrigued him. So, he was more than a little tongue-tied.

Then with a turn of her hips she beckoned him to follow her.

He responded numbly with a nod of his head, then she retrieved the box, and closed the doors behind them as they passed through. Upon entering the room, he observed all the host of guests, so it did look to be a successful function. But George, he was more intent on Miranda and trailed along behind in awe of her, but keeping her in sight, just watching her, and her hips as they swayed before him. Then he was being presented to his table where the place settings read to be George Delvin, and Miranda James. He looked up at her in surprise. "Yes George! I shall be dining with you today. That is of course unless you don't wish me to?" she stated questioning him.

"Oh! Oh yes please do so!" he stammered. She smiled a knowing smile, as he rushed to pull out the chair for her, and then she seated herself so elegantly. He sat in the seat opposite to her, and looked directly into her smoldering eyes which seemed simply to consume him, but then he sensed the waiter hovering near him, and started.

"Wine Sir?" the waiter asked, as he produced a red, and a white.

"I prefer red!" he stammered. "And you Miranda, red or white?"

"Red will do me fine thank you George darling." Then there was that smile again, and his heart lurched, his chest constricted tightly.

"Would you be a dear and order lunch for both of us George!" she was saying. "I must greet my guests now. I am, after all, the hostess, you know!" she smiled, and her laugh was a tinkle.

Order? I don't even know her, or what she likes! he stressed.

He learned over lunch that she was now a widow. Had been for a short time, though she didn't appear to show any signs of grief. On the contrary, her smiles were that of a very happy person, her laughter like the tinkling of a bell. Her husband Des James, was his name apparently, had fallen overboard during their long overseas journey whilst on a cruise ship, and his body had never, ever been recovered he believed. Or rather, it was Miranda who had told him, quite matter-of-factly as if the subject was of second nature.

George found it no problem to play the consoler if the occasion arose, and was not indifferent to adopt the role of protector, though he didn't think she needed protecting at all. Being in her prime in her early forties he guessed that Miranda was very confident, and capable. A seasoned traveler, her heritage was of France he learned. She was strong and very beautiful. He was struggling to believe she was showing such an interest in him! He was smitten by her after that luncheon, but more so later when he lay beside her stark naked in a monstrous motel room bed in the city. They made love like he'd never known sex before. *It was just so exotic!* He couldn't believe her abandonment to reality. Her sense of freedom was her release to be a wild thing, and so carefree! *So, there was nothing!* ...he noted... *Not one thing!* ...*She didn't know about pleasing a man!*
He was simply obsessed with her! Miranda was a perfectionist in every way. Luckily, he was on leave for two weeks, so they dated. However, after only four dates, and simply on a whim, he proposed to her, and to his astonishment she agreed to his marriage offer. So, they eloped to be married on a secret island. It was what Miranda wanted, and suggested to him, and he had agreed with her.

Suddenly a deep voice spoke out just in front of him momentarily cheating him of his little reverie, and he tried to re-focus.

" Good evening, all! George, are you with us or still stargazing?" George turned to come face to face with Richard Temple. "Well, it's about time Richard! Finally, you decide to arrive, and we were all beginning to think you were a no show! But no, my good friend, I wasn't stargazing at all! I was just so deep in thought. I do have a lot on my mind now you know Richard!" he stammered.

Richard gave him a knowing look, and chuckled to himself.

"Yes, I could imagine!" he replied, his face pulling up into a wide grin as he turned towards Miranda, then gazed deep into her eyes. He felt the contrast of her huge dark violet eyes against the paleness of her skin was simply devastating. *My God, her eyes seem to consume, and control.* he thought as he prepared himself for the introduction, but then decided to take the initiative. "Well, you must be the beautiful Miranda I have been hearing so much about. My name is Richard Temple, George's partner! I am very pleased to meet you!" he stated, as he held out his hand to her. She took his hand in her velvet one. It was a brief handshake, though he felt the sensation of a static vibration just by her touch.

Miranda felt it too but she smiled her best smile as she shook his hand. "It is such a pleasure to meet you also Richard Temple." she replied, with just a hint of an accent that appealed to him.

"I have to warn you Miranda, that George hasn't stopped talking about you, and naturally we have all been anxious to meet you. So, congratulations Missus Delvin, and congrats George!" he offered. "It is time you made a stand, my man, so well done!" as he reached out to take George's hand, and they shook hands, then he leaned in to take Miranda's hand once again to place his lips softly upon it.

"Thank you, Richard for the wishes, but first things first. Let us not delude my new wife into an illusion that I am a full partner in the business, that would be stretching the point a little. I only have a small percentage remember?" stated George, as he laughed it off.

Quickly Miranda withdrew her hand from Richard in surprise. *"But I thought...* Miranda's voice trailed off, and Richard looked at her just as a shadow clouded her beautiful violet eyes.

He was confused, but couldn't be sure why, but some emotion was there in those eyes, he felt as he sensed Miranda's tension.

George did too. "What is it, Miranda?"

Quickly Miranda recouped. She smiled sweetly at him to reply.

"I was about to say to you George, I thought you knew the others already had told me about that. But I didn't want to talk out of school so to speak, if you didn't know they had already told me!"

"Oh! I see Miranda! I have a loyal wife, Richard." he chuckled. Richard chuckled too, but he was not too sure about that. "Still, a solid partner George! For many, many years now and a great friend too!" replied Richard, and he looked back at Miranda who quickly cast her eyes down, and he wondered why. *She definitely seems quite perplexed. Of that, I am sure, but what about? I simply know what I saw in her eyes just now.* So, I don't buy that explanation one little bit. However, he decided to ignore it, and changed direction.

"Ok George! We had better get this party started. Time for idle chit-chat later I'm afraid old mate. How about we set Miranda up at our table with our friends who she is acquainted with now, while we get things organized, then you will have time to introduce her around just before dinner, and then we will celebrate old buddy?"

"Sounds like a plan Richard. Are you fine with that Miranda?"

"Yes of course, darling, you go on ahead!" replied Miranda, back to her usual flippant self, as she flashed him her best smile, then she squeezed his hand for reassurance.

"Love you!" George muttered, as he planted a kiss on her cheek.

"Love you more!" she teased, as she pushed him away. "Now go as Richard said!"

Richard looked hard at them both, but he turned his attention solely on Miranda, and their eyes made contact. He expected her to be submissive, but what he saw there shocked him to the core, just to totally confuse him once again. *Surely not! But yes! I do think she is playing with me! Steady on Miranda! That, is playing with fire! Just how resilient is she I wonder?* He turned away from her just as quickly to address his friends, and to interrupt their conversation.

"Sorry to barge in guys, but George and I have things to do! Jim, I was wondering if you and your wife Anne, would mind taking Miranda under your wing for a short while? Maybe you could find where we are seated, we shouldn't be too long!"

"Sure Richard! I realize that you and George have much to do. Miranda will be in safe hands with us!" he chuckled. "Actually, we were thinking of doing just that anyway so, you may come along with us now Miranda if you wish?" he urged. "It is time to move on to find our seating. Are you ready to join us now Miranda?"

Richard, and George turned together. Richard wrapped his arm around his shoulder as they left the group, but as he walked away, he heard Miranda reply. "Yes Jim, I am ready now, thank you!"

But he could feel her eyes eating into his back.

Miranda was feeling annoyed. They had located their table, and were seated, but she contributed to the conversation with the circle of friends only under sufferance so, after a short while she made a petty excuse to leave the table. As she stood with drink in hand, the men at the table rose from their seats in respect. "Thank you, gents!" she responded. She smiled that sweet smile at them as she excused herself, and left them to return to their seats. She was going outside, but had to pass closely to where Richard, and George were both very busy, their heads locked on a computer screen. She turned her head slightly, then walked past them. But at the balcony door she paused a little while simply to look back over her shoulder and smiled a knowing smile. Miranda knew that Richard would be watching her, and as their eyes met across the room, she could feel his were undressing her as his steady gaze caressed each part of her body from the tip of her head, down to her toes, and a shiver went through her in response to his scrutiny. She held his gaze steadily, and steadfastly, as her own eyes smoldered with lust for him. She stared blatantly at his face in defiance, but with a precedent of her intentions. Then she was gone.

Richard could not take his eyes off her and he watched longingly with total interest as she seductively un-maned him to stare straight at him. *That was an invitation if I ever did see one!* he pondered, as he watched her disappear through double doors of the outer balcony. *But it is such a hopeless one!* he stressed. She has just married my best friend, and partner. So, *what am I thinking? But he knew exactly what he was thinking.* Even though he felt so ashamed, he could not still the stirring in his loins. It was taking a really huge effort on his part to stop from rushing outside onto the balcony, to gather her into his arms, *to take her then, and there, and very quickly.*

He grabbed a quick sideways glance at George beside him, just thinking maybe he could tell, but noted George was still engrossed deeply in work. He was in his own little world, and oblivious to the events taking place between him, and Miranda. Richard made his decision right then on the spot. *I just have to talk to her, and it must be right now, preferably this minute!* he promised himself. His gut ached, something in his chest was squeezing it tight, and because of the affect she had on him, he found he was in a some-what awkward state, which could erupt at any time. There was no doubt Miranda had her hooks into him already, and surprisingly enough with only just a few short sentences. He couldn't last until another meeting with her occurred, nor knew when that would be? he pondered.

No, I have to do it now!

"That just about wraps it up George!" he offered. "You finish up what we were doing, then it's time for introductions at dinner. I just noticed Miranda going outside to the balcony over there, so I shall go and collect her for you. We will both meet you back at our table in the dining room if you like! Is that ok with you George?"

George nodded his head, still so intent on what he was doing.

"Sounds like a good plan old friend!" he replied absently, when he finally spoke, and didn't even look up from the computer screen.

Richard looked hard at him then he simply replied. "Ok! See you inside shortly! Then let's get this party started George." he added.

"Yeah! Sure Richard, go ahead, I won't be long!"

He twisted through the tables of guests, politely acknowledging some of them with a nod of his head, but ultimately making a bee-line towards the balcony doors. Once at the doors, he momentarily paused to look through the glass panels at Miranda standing there. *Impossible it may seem.* Or an impromptu time even! *But it's definitely not one to be denied,* or idly discarded either! *However, right there is a real picture of perfection!* He groaned so softly to himself, as he took in all the beauty of her. *Whatever is wrong with me all of a sudden? No woman I have ever met before has affected me in this way!*

Then he gulped in sheer disbelief, as he stared.

A breeze stirred up outside to lift her chiffon dress high to swirl about her like a mysterious cloud was enveloping her, but leaving absolutely nothing to the imagination when it swept upwards, and he caught a close-up glimpse of her perfect thighs. He gasped. The intake of breath he subconsciously held, soon turned into a throaty groan of pure pain, *as he noticed she was wearing no underwear.*

He opened the door latch quietly, pushed both doors out, then stepped through silently to the balcony tiled floor, and closed them behind him so gently, as he tried his hardest to make his entrance a surprise to her, but suddenly he had an urge just to watch her. Her elegance was something to behold. Her platinum hair swept across her face in the breeze, her body petite but taller than most, was one of perfection. Her breasts lifted almost from her bodice as she drew heavily on a cigarette, then she exhaled swiftly to be seemingly lost in a cloud of smoke, and he was cheated momentarily of his vision until the breeze quickly dispersed it, and swept it away.

M iranda was really so angry with herself. When she was in this mood, she became confused and anxious, indecisive even. So, she indulged in a cigarette, or two just to calm her nerves. Now she stood unsettled on the balcony trying to justify her decisions.

I have made a big mistake! she thought. *A huge mistake, and I don't make mistakes, ever!* Lesson one Miranda. Do your research well! She tossed it over in her mind. *How could she know the company director George Delvin,* whom she had married, *was not the major share-holder in the business? Oh, damn it!* But never mind! I have overcome far worse before, and survived! *I will simply alter my plans a little.*

"Penny for them?"

She jumped as the voice startled her. Then turned, and there he was just standing there with a big smirk upon his face like he could read her thoughts. *This incredible hunk of a man, Richard Temple!*

"Oh Richard, I was miles away, please forgive me?" she pleaded. Richard was surprised to see she could compose herself so quickly.

"Of course, but all good! I could tell you were deep in thought, also smoking I see! I sensed you were a little uneasy inside, so I do hope nothing has upset you. But nothing to forgive that I can see. I am so sorry for startling you! It wasn't my intention at all Miranda!"

She looked him squarely in the face. Her violet eyes seemed to darken more if that was at all possible. They smoldered as they met his. Then surprisingly she moved closer to him to speak very softly. "Well! What is your intention Mister Richard Temple? I think at this stage I really need to know that, so please explain sir!"

He laughed out loud as he gaped at her. *Has she no shame?* She is just so irresistibly tantalizing this woman, and so close I can almost feel her. *Round one might be Miranda's* he mused before replying.

"My intentions Miranda you will find are really quite honorable my lady! I am guessing you would like to hear the truth!"

"If you don't mind!" came her husky reply.

"Alrighty! I simply must have you all to myself, though it seems that horse has bolted. You are married, but so am I! I take it you do love George Delvin, Miranda? However! I shall remain open to all suggestions! Who knows which way the wind may blow! I guess it really depends on you Miranda!" he stated, as he grinned broadly. His smile teased her as he looked at her searchingly, still wondering if that was enough to win his bout. Then came the tinkle of laughter preceding her reply which felt agonizingly cruel, and just like a slap in the face, so he didn't seem to think so.

Apparently, he would need more than that to win a bout with Miranda!

Oh! He is so cheeky, and I like that! she thought. Her laugh became a tinkle, then she smiled her sweetest smile at him as she moved to a table to set her bag down, then made a big event of finding some stick-on-notes, and a pen, and began writing down a number.

When she finally spoke, she looked him square in the eyes, with hers blazing. "Of course, I do love George! He is my husband now Richard. How could you ask that question? Though I could simply guess why. But pray do tell me, what of your wife Richard Temple, your relationship? Do you love your wife?" she asked inquisitively. Richard stepped closer and she smelt a manly presence as he spoke.

"My wife is an invalid, so there is no love between us anymore Miranda! We don't share the same bed, or even a room. I have never felt love for a long time, not until today. You may call it lust, and I guess it is in a way, but I know love, how it feels to love! It is taking all my restraint to stop from claiming your pink lips, though at the same time I would be betraying my friends trust, and I don't take that lightly. So, you look me in the eyes Miranda, and tell me you don't feel the same as me, because I just know you do! I can feel it. So, if you do! There will be no future with George on my terms!"

There it is. My cards are all on the table! he thought seriously.

Yes! he mused. *Second bout won by yours truly! Or was it?*

Because then so suddenly, her composure changed as she stared directly at him, her voice was almost husky-like when she spoke.

"Your terms! Ah, ah! That is for me to know, and you to find out Mister Richard Temple!" she uttered seductively, as her violet eyes darkened. "There may be a little spark there worth pursuing, but then who really knows? Who tells us the future Richard? To me, it can change on a whim to be played or snuffed out just like a candle! So, what about our future you so blatantly ask me Richard Temple? Hmm! What say we both indulge in a little experiment, simply just to find out? You should call me sometime Richard!" she stated, as she produced the note, and pressed it deeply into his hand.

Her hips swayed as she departed to leave him there gaping, but then turned and stood in the doorway smiling her best smile as she spoke seductively. "By the way mister Richard Temple! If you must know, I indulge in a cigarette if I am anxious or confused!"

Richard was still gaping as he watched her hips sway as she left. Then he listened to her throaty voice, so teasing, and so sexy, it was tempting him as she paused at the door. He shook his head in sheer disbelief. *She is just so brazen, but so tantalizingly beautiful she is doing my head in and the rest of me is in no better state!* I bet that she already knows she has me wound around her little finger, and I think she is quite used to these similar situations, though she does seem very intelligent. I must remember to retain the upper hand in future.
After all, that is what I am used to and she needs to realize that! We must play by my rules! So, now I will be more assertive, and not wear my heart on my sleeve like I just did, because it is quite out of character for me, but she really got to me, got under my skin!

God, I just have to have her! I simply must! Or I may explode. So, until then, but only then when I claim her, will I decide if I keep her? *Though I could not imagine why I wouldn't.* As it seems to me there is more than what meets the eye with this Missus Miranda Delvin! *I will need to be so much more positive!* More definite in making certain decisions that will encourage her do some second guessing. To coax her to seek me out, hunt for me, instead of the other way around, or she will totally control me. I am usually always in total control with any of my relationships, but now? *She has un-maned me a little, but that won't happen again!* Oh! No sir-re! Uh! Uh! *Miranda! You simply won't know what hit you lovely lady!* Hmm! This does pose to be a very testy, but interesting situation! he chuckled to himself. *So, Miranda Delvin, do let the games begin!* he schemed. However, though he had only just met her, he sensed a deep affinity with her, which could only mean one thing really. Secretly he was guessing, that they were so much alike it was uncanny.

It was just a matter of who was going to break first.

Slowly he re-couped, then followed her into the dining room, which he noticed as he walked through the double doors, was all set out as per his instructions, and decorated beautifully. He knew where their table would be, as it would head the others for when the speeches started, so he headed over there. He noticed Miranda had already found George, so now they were laughing and chatting away, but more noticeable to him was the shun as he joined them, when she turned her head away, oblivious to his existence.

Hmm! *Looks like I may need a concrete plan, as now the pretty lady is playing hard to get.* Richard thought in bewilderment. *What cheek she has!* She seems to change on a whim. *Well two can play that little game my lovely!* He made a huge point of ignoring her as he took his place at the head of the table to be seated, and most conveniently several others were immediately striving for his attention, so he immersed himself in a deep conversation with them all, before looking across the table to acknowledge George.

"So, did you get it all done George?" he queried.

"Yep! All wound up for another year Richard. All our overseas clients are solid so, we can sit back and relax tonight. I need a break though, a get-away from it all. It's been a long year!" he chuckled. Suddenly a brilliant idea hit Richard, it just seemed to gel nicely, so as not to seem unusual. He smiled broadly at George, and mused. *This is just perfect!* he thought to himself. *I should have thought of this idea sooner!* He chuckled to himself, and relished the idea before he spoke up, so resulting in a wide grin that spread his lips.

"Well George! I aim to please, that you know already! But there is something that you don't know my dear friend so I guess I should explain. It so happens people, I have further plans, to discuss with you all, that I was keeping for a special surprise later! Only now, I find I have to spill the beans a little earlier as per George's request, so now is as good a time as any I suppose!"

He hadn't at all! There had been no surprise to tell of, or special plan before. But now Richard made out it was a plan already pre-arranged. Only trouble now was, he would have to excuse himself so that he could make a few quick phone-calls to get the wheels in motion. *Or there really would be no plan!*

George spoke first. "Do tell Richard, what special surprise?"

Richard laughed. "Ah! You will have to wait a little longer my friend, there are a couple of pressing issues I must deal with before dinner!" So, with that announced he rose from his seat then nodded to everyone as he left the table to walk briskly across the room. Hillary looked up in surprise as he approached her. "What is it sir?"

"Hi Hill! I just remembered I had to call Jenna. Could you put my call through, and then you may go inside to dinner!"

"Of course, sir! Right away sir!" she said, and dialed the number. He grabbed the handset from her, and spoke urgently with Jenna to explain his requirements for eight extra guests for two days, and to tell Pablo to get horses in, and consult with the cook about food.

R ichard Temple smiled when he replaced the receiver. *Just as well Jenna is there.* She is so reliable, and as tough as nails so, *she will get the job done!* he thought, as he headed towards the dining room feeling mighty pleased with himself. Then he sauntered confidently across the dining room floor to their table, and his grin widened as he sat down and looked at his guests.

All chatter ceased as they expected him to speak, and he chuckled.

"Well! As I was saying before lovely people, I have a surprise in store for you all. Just had to make sure all was in order at home, but Jenna has everything in hand, so, it is a goer. Starting tomorrow at 8 a.m. sharp, my staff will be serving breakfast on the lawns for you all. Just a beginning for a two-day stop-over at 'Oceanview.' So, you are all invited to stay over for Saturday, and Sunday. It is just a little mini holiday for your hard work so-to-speak as George requested! I have so much organized to treat you all. Music, dancing, tennis, horse-riding or swimming. If it takes your fancy, it will be at home!"

Richard couldn't help notice the raised eyebrows of Miranda's. Finally, he had her attention, and he chuckled as he looked directly at her, then his grin became much more of a challenge as he spoke.

"So, what is your fancy Miranda, do you like riding horses?"

Her eyes brightened as she stared wide-eyed back at him, and at first, he thought maybe she wasn't going to reply, but suddenly her demeanor changed as she became a little girl again, and then came her trademark smile as she turned to George and gushed.

"Oh, George did you hear? Horses. Oh! I do love horses Richard! I love going out on trail-rides! I used to do that back home, but then I had my own horses. However since, I haven't had a chance to go riding. Oh! I do hope we can attend. May we George?" she pleaded.

"Of course, my love! Richard has organized a weekend get-away for us all, so we will all attend. You will love it at his place. He has everything you could imagine. But horse riding! I will not be doing that my love! I can't ride a horse, but you may go out with Richard, he will look after you, and we will be well catered for at the house!"

"Oh! How exciting this is going to be George! Thank you so very much my love!" Miranda squealed. Then she kissed him full on the lips, but her searching eyes were fixed on Richard Temple.

Richard returned her gaze, and immediately realized that a plan was forming on its own, in a way so he could finally get her on her own. *Yes, just perfect!* I couldn't have organized better. he thought to himself, then gave her a cheeky grin as he spoke. "Don't you worry Miranda! I am an experienced rider! So, I shall take good care of you!" he grinned, to tease her as he addressed the others. "Now, is everyone in?" he asked. "I need a head count?"

Everyone at the table laughed at the absurdity of it, then one by one they accepted his offer by a raise of hands, and then started to chat excitedly amongst themselves, exploring all avenues available.

Richard chuckled. *Seems I have struck a chord with them!*
He looked to Miranda again, his eyes teasing, challenging her. She seemed to squirm in her seat if that was possible, until once again surprised him as she approached him on a different tack.

Miranda smiled sweetly. "So! Tell me Richard. Who is this Jenna, that you give so much responsibility to?" she asked sweetly.

He was floored. Out of everything they had been speaking about it was the mention of Jenna she picked up on, so he couldn't help but wonder why. A puzzled frown creased his brow as he replied. "Jenna is my only daughter Miranda, and in my absence, she has full reign of the household and staff, and looks after her mother!"

Hmm! I never figured on a daughter. thought Miranda.

"I see! Just how old is this daughter who takes on such a lot of responsibility, Richard?" she asked sweetly.

Richard glared at her in annoyance, wondering why the sudden interest in Jenna? Then he chuckled as a thought crossed his mind.

"You may be interested to know that she is quite old enough I fear Miranda. You see, Jenna is just sixteen going onto twenty-six I would say!" he said bluntly, and smiled at her.

Miranda laughed, that tinkling laugh that sent shivers up his spine.

"Just sixteen? I find that hard to believe. It is simply so ridiculous for one so young to have all that control and power! Don't you think so George my love?" she asked her husband.

George stared firstly at Richard, then momentarily at Miranda. "Well! How should I put it? I guess it is simply that you don't know Jenna yet Miranda dear! You will understand when you meet her!" A smile disappeared from Miranda's face as she stared at Richard.

"Umm! Seems to me you have an interesting daughter Richard. Such accolades I find hard to believe, so I cannot wait to meet her. Maybe she shares your nature, Richard!" she said, smiling sweetly.

"Well, tomorrow you shall find out for yourself Miranda. Now enough about my daughter let's get this party started and let's eat!"

"Yes, but of course Richard!" Miranda replied instantly as she watched him change moods yet again.

Richard snapped his fingers and at once a band started playing. He waved at the idle doorman, and as if by magic trays of food were being brought out by the staff, and immediately placed along the tables, as waiters attended the guests at the tables with drinks. "Good, finally. It is about time! Let's get this show on the road!" He raised his glass to his guests. "A big congrats for a job well done for this year everyone. So, cheers, and enjoy all!" he stated.

Miranda simply stared at him in awe, as his power of leadership mesmerized her, his control over people consumed her thoughts. She sat quietly, to puzzle over her dilemma. She hadn't counted on Mister Richard Temple, or his daughter Jenna either for that matter.

Don't underestimate this one Miranda. she reminded herself.

Chapter Two

Jenna Temple climbed the stairs up to their private rooms, and her dense auburn hair bounced in a mass of curls as she hurried.

She stepped onto the thick carpeted hall-way covering the length of the top floors, her foot-falls cushioned as she headed towards her mother's bedroom to inquire if she needed anything before dinner, when suddenly in the quietness, she became aware of raised voices. She could hear people yelling out loudly, and when she got closer to her mother's room, all the arguing and crude cursing became so much more increased in volume, that she rushed forward to grab for the door handle at the same time as Melita Sanchez', their long-standing housemaid burst angrily through the doorway and almost knocked her over as she slammed the door shut behind her, yelling back over her shoulder in Spanish, oblivious to Jenna's presence.

Jenna stood back to stare at her, and became aware that it wasn't the yelling that was the only concern, it was the look of pure hatred in Melita's dark eyes that shocked her so much, and her angry face.

What on earth is going on here?

She was about to demand an answer of explanation as to what had taken place when a shrill peel broke the silence as the telephone rang loudly to stop her, and she had to go downstairs to answer it.

She stared at Melita quickly who was now glaring at her. "I shall speak with you later about this Melita!" she promised her matter-of-factly, then raced down the hallway to the stairs. She mused on it all absently as she rushed across the foyer to pick up the receiver.

Jenna had just turned sixteen, but she had learnt to grow up very quickly ever since her mother's accident and had taken on the role of protector and sole manager of the homestead and staff years ago.

Her father worked in the city, so when she answered the phone and listened to her father's request, it came as no surprise to her.

"Yes father, I understand your needs! I'll do that straight away! Don't worry, I'll have it all presentable for your guests tomorrow!"

She put down the receiver to the usual thanks from her father, she had grown so used to for many times now. There wasn't much Jenna couldn't do, she was an Aussie. She knew her father relied on her heavily, but was used to it all now, it was second nature to her.

Jenna soon realized that she had a lot of work to do, and seeing that she was already downstairs she thought it best to speak with their cook first, and turned to go that way, as she thought to herself.

Just as well it is school holidays, a lot of preparation is needed for the morrow! Jenna walked into the kitchen, and looked over at the cook, Paula Hastings standing at the stove stirring something in a huge pot with those massive arms. She was a huge lady, so tall, and very overweight. Her hair was dark, but dampened from the heat.

Paula had been initially employed by her father some years ago as the permanent cook for the homestead. Her husband Ted also worked for them as yardman and handyman for 'Oceanview.' They lived and rented one of the small cabins available on the property.

She must be at least forty-five now. Jenna thought as she spoke to her. "Something smells good Missus Hastings!"

"Oh Jenna, you startled me!" replied Paula as she jumped a little. Then wiped the sweat from her brow, and wiped her hands on the apron around her waist as she gazed at Jenna with beady grey eyes.

"Thought we might have steak and kidney pie for dinner Jenna. I do hope that is suitable for everyone, but I intend to cook some vegetables of course! What brings you in the kitchen so late?"

"Yes, that is fine for dinner thanks Missus Hastings! I have had a phone-call from my father. He is inviting eight guests out for the weekend! They will all be arriving for breakfast, and I shall invite one guest. So maybe the usual Missus Hastings. Fruit, cereal, juices, pancakes with the extras, and of course bacon, eggs, and damper!"

"For lunch? A bar-be-que, but also cold meats for sandwiches. I thought we may have a pig on the spit for dinner. Whatever stores you need let me know tonight, as I will be sending an email to the butcher for the pig, and they will deliver it as usual in the morning. Same for the grocer, so order nibblies too. I shall order drinks!'

"Food for Sunday? Maybe a hot and cold lunch, and something pleasant for a sit-down dinner that night. I shall leave it up to you to decide. I shall talk to Melita, and if you would set up the outside as usual for the guests, please! That would be good! Just bring in two extra casuals to help with the serving. Is that okay with you?"

"Yes, we will manage Jenna! Ted will start with the outside area in the morning. Trust your father to leave things to the last minute!"

Jenna frowned at that remark, but decided to let it slide for the moment, and continued on speaking. "Ok! Make a list, and give it to me at dinner Missus Hastings. You may need to go up and speak to mother about her dinner requirements for tonight as well!" she added. "Now I must speak with Melita, then go to find Pablo. So thank you, Missus Hastings. If you need me, I won't be far away!"

She began walking towards the door just as Paula spoke.

"Jenna about your mother. I can't go into her room anymore!"

Jenna stopped dead, to turn with a surprised look on her face. "I wasn't aware of that Missus Hastings!" she replied. "Also, I am not sure I understand the meaning, or reason behind it either?"

"It is just what your mother said Jenna! I am not allowed to go to her room. If she wants food, she'll come down to get it, or I will send one of the girls upstairs with her dinner, but they must knock on her door! Your mother is sick in the head, I think! She is so angry all the time, and is being damn hard to live with. I can tell you! She is lashing out at us all, trying to lay blame for the fire on any one of us you know! I am quite certain of that because she screamed at me with her eyes blazing in accusation when I was up there only this morning, and the others are getting similar treatment!"

Jenna's green eyes smoldered in anger; her reply was very curt.

"You are aware that you are speaking badly about my mother, Missus Hastings! I won't have my mother spoken about like that, as it is not your place to judge here! Is that clear? My mother needs special care and love, not arguments. You are employed here by my father to cook, not to judge people here, and if my mother wishes that you don't enter her room, then please don't! It is her house after all! So, be very careful what you say here, and I suggest you listen in future. So please do not argue with her, you have no right to do so! Are you quite certain you understand that?" Jenna questioned.

"Yes Jenna, quite clear. I understand!" replied Paula.

Paula turned away, as a scowl crossed her face she thought. Like mother like daughter. *Only now, this kid gives me my orders!*

But Jenna did not miss the ugly scowl or sly look crossing her face and for some reason she felt slightly threatened but put it aside.

"I was just on my way up to see mother when the phone rang, so I shall talk to her about this Missus Hastings, we shall talk later!"

"Yeah sure, whatever! Won't do no good Jenna!"

"Oh, yes it will Missus Hastings if you just do as you are told!" Jenna decided to leave it there before she really lost her temper. She had only this very minute, reprimanded the woman for speaking out against her mother, but already Paula was saying things Jenna didn't like to hear, but also Jenna sensed some underlying tension, so she turned, and walked out of the room in search of Melita.

This could be yet another staff problem I must deal with! she guessed as she walked up the staircase.

Melita ducked her head back in the linen cupboard as she saw Jenna emerge at the top of the stairs, but Jenna had already seen her. "A word if you please Melita!" she uttered, as she opened the door of the cupboard. Melita jumped, and turned to face her.

Her hair was jet black, but her dark eyes were guilt-ridden as she glared directly at Jenna. She was not so tall, but muscley in stature, especially her arms. Her body appeared to be very muscle toned for a forty-year-old woman used to heavy lifting.

"I shall give you a chance to explain your behaviour earlier, when you so rudely left mother's room Melita! Just the truth please, I will stand for no lies!" stated Jenna.

Melita stared at her defiantly. She had crossed paths with Jenna before, and knew she was young, but a force to be reckoned with.

"Well! I was in ya mother's room ta clean and change tha linen, an then I stopped ta look through the rows of books out in tha other room. Ya mother she be screamin at me. Tellin me not ta touch her things, and not ta come to her room ever again, and that she would change her own linen, an also clean her own room. Then she started blaming us workers fer the fire, saying we at fault fer the accident, and told me ta get out of her room. So, I guess that made me angry with her, and I yelled back." she said, and hung her head.

Jenna took a deep breath, and once again spoke with authority.

"Listen to me very carefully Melita, as I will never repeat this to you again. This is my mother's house and estate! You are employed here to serve her employ, and what my mother says is what you do, it is your job after all! Is that quite clear?" she demanded.

"Yes Jenna, it is clear!" answered Melita.

"Good, then we shouldn't have any more problems! If mother wants to clean her rooms, and change her own linen, then you make sure she has fresh linen when you are changing the others. Arrange a table outside her room to place it on, and have a basket there so she can put her soiled linen in so you can wash it! As far as the cleaning goes, I am sure mother can find anything she needs in the cupboards. She is not a cripple you know Melita, she just needs love and understanding, and you yelling at her will not help her much at all. I am not happy about this Melita, so don't let it happen again. Also! Mother needs her own privacy, so please respect that, and don't enter her room again. If you have a key, give it to me now, or I will collect it later. You have to adhere to mother's wishes if she doesn't want anyone in her room! Is that clear?"

"Yeah sure, here be tha key!" Melita said sharply, as she dug for it in her tunic, then handed it over.

Jenna took the key from her and slipped it into her pocket, then as an afterthought she looked at her. "Please clean, and set up the single room down from mine Melita as I will be inviting a guest to stay over. Father is inviting eight guests to stay over for two nights, and they will arrive for breakfast, so you will need to set up four double rooms downstairs., and also you will need to help Paula set up the lawns outside ready for the guests in the morning, and the remainder of their stay. That is all, are you clear on everything?"

"Yes Jenna, it won't be a problem!" replied Melita.

"Good, thank you Melita. No doubt it will be a busy two days!"

"Is Pablo at the stables now, or is he elsewhere?" asked Jenna.

"I think he may be still over there, or he was an hour ago!"

"Thank you, Melita! I must speak to Pablo also! Just make sure all the rooms are ready by tonight, and leave all keys in the doors."

"It will be done Jenna!" said Melita.

Jenna nodded. "Thank you, so carry on Melita. I will overlook what you have done just for this time, but please take it as a warning that I won't accept that type of behavior again!" she said, watching her.

Melita immediately turned away just as the deep frown creased her forehead. She was angry and was trying hard not to show it but then she started shaking with frustration, as she thought. *I have this young kid tellin me what I have to do, as usual!* So, what else is new? *It is so hard to take, but this kid is a tough nut to crack.*

It was beautiful weather outside Jenna noticed when she strolled across to the stables. *Father could not have selected any other better weekend to invite guests over.* She had watched the weather report on the television the night before, they said it was meant to be excellent weather, and clear sunny days. *Good riding weather!* she thought.

It was so quiet over at the stables that it seemed almost deserted, so Jenna walked through to the back yards where she noticed Pablo was tending to the horses in the yards.

"Hi Pablo!" she called out as she got closer. "Good! I see you have some horses close by! We are in need of them tomorrow!"

Pablo looked up in question. "Hi Jenna, what is up?"

"Father rang. He is having eight guests staying for two days this weekend, and I shall invite one guest, so we need sufficient horses in, including our own, and for you to have them saddled and ready by early-morning tomorrow. Is that possible?"

"Yeah, it won't be a problem, Jenna!"

"Excellent, you may also need to help Ted set up the lawns."

"Ask him to set up the marque. Just the usual set-up outside on the lawns with tables, chairs, bar-be-que, etc., and have him light the spit early, and clean the pool, as the guests will be here for breakfast at 8.am. You know what to do don't you Pablo?"

Pablo smirked at that. *Of course, I do know what to do young one!* he thought, but decided not to say a word. He too had crossed paths with Jenna before, and hadn't won any arguments with her.

"Yeah! Sure Jenna, no problems. It'll be an early start tomorrow but I might get some things done in the shed before it gets too dark today, so don't you worry, I'll have it all ready for you by breakfast. Most of the horses are in, and the others are in the first paddock, so no problems. I will speak to Ted later." he replied.

Jenna smiled at him. "Thank you so much Pablo. Sorry about the short notice as I only just found out myself. So let Ted know that!"

"Not to worry Jenna, all is ok! So will do!"

Confident in her organization Jenna decided to make a phone call.

Jack picked up the call very quickly as he was already inside his parent's house when the phone rang, and Jenna laughed.

"What's so funny?"

"Oh nothing, I guess! I simply thought you must have been sitting beside the phone to answer so quickly."

"No! Doing jobs for mum inside, so I was close. What's up?"

"I am organizing a two-day party, and stop-over for some guests of fathers, so I would like you to come over and stay as well, if you would like to, that is?" Jenna queried.

"Riding?"

"Yes, riding!" Jenna laughed at his question. "Or swimming, fishing, hiking, whatever you would like to do!" "Our breakfast is at 6.15am so, you'll need to be here about 6.00am, because we will have breakfast before the other guests, maybe up on the top balcony overlooking the ocean. So, are you coming Jack?"

"Sounds like a plan, of course I am coming! See you then Jenna. I have to go now!" and the line went dead.

Jenna smiled, then made another phone call. Her father picked up straight away. "What is it, Jenna?"

"Hi father, I just had a thought. So, I wanted to know if I should arrange a bus to pick up your guests to come out in the morning?"

"You are amazing Jenna! Thanks for thinking of that, just send me a text to confirm that the booking is made, and I will endeavor to inform them all tonight during dinner!"

"Ok, you can consider it done, but I will text you, and by the way all arrangements have been made with the staff for the morrow!"

"You are a legend Jenna, my girl. I can't thank you enough!"

Jenna sighed as she ended the call. She called the bus terminal to secure the booking, then sent a text to her father as she walked over towards the house, anxious now to speak to her mother of the change in events for the weekend.

She noticed that a hallway table was set up outside her mother's room as she knocked on the door. *Well at least Melita is doing what I asked* she thought with huge relief, and called out as she entered her mother's suites. She found her mother standing at the bay window seats in her second room, which to her was the entertainment room, where a small dining area was artfully set up simply to capture the magnificent view of the ocean. A living room was a separate section for her lounges and T.V. and bookshelves heavily laden with books of all ages, and genres led the way to an office and small kitchenette.

Jenna noticed her mother fussing with the plants along the sills each side of the window seats as she peered outside the window at the failing light, so she paused at the doorway to look at her first as she knew only too well that sometimes her moods would sway and she could become quite vicious with her speech.

Some repercussion the experts say, a result of the accident, as the fire caused severe burns to the head area that had damaged nerves, and with her thought process, sometimes her mind wandered. No-one could detect her current moods, as they changed momentarily. One minute she was talking freely, the next she would go into a violent rage. Her injuries were so severe, grotesque even. Livid raw scars remained on her scalp, face, neck, arms and chest, but tactfully covered by a long scarf swathed across to hide them.

"Hello mother!" uttered Jenna, as she moved over closer to her. "What are you doing there?" she asked.

Julia Temple turned her head very slowly. She had always been an attractive woman, Jenna remembered. But now, she was just a shell of her former self. Just to look upon her was heart-breaking to Jenna as her mother tried to widen her sad, green eyes in reply.

"Oh, Jenna, it is so good to see you. I am tending to my orchids Jenna! I make sure I fertilize and water them, aren't they beautiful? Just look at all those colours! This is the best place for them, on the window sill. It is where they grow best!" she said excitedly.

Jenna looked at them, and agreed. "They are so beautiful I must admit mother. I guess it is safe to say this is their favourite place if they grow better here!" she replied with a chuckle.

Her mother tried to laugh, but instead looked at her seriously. "Please note this, Jenna, as it will be important for you to know, but right here is my favourite place also, with special things around me. Remember Jenna! It is my most favourite place in the whole world! Now, what did you do today?" she asked, changing the subject.

"I won't forget mother. I know you love this window setting! As for today? Well, it ended up a very busy day, but I have everything in hand. You may want to know I am aware you have had problems with the staff, but trust me I have spoken to them all quite sternly!"

"So, they will respect your privacy in future. Is there anything else I may need to know mother? I only heard their side of the story!"

"Only that I don't trust any of them Jenna! Is all you need to know!"

"Ok, say no more! You will find a hall table just outside where your linen will be left, and a basket put there for your soiled linen to be washed. Are you quite sure you want to clean your own rooms?"

Julia became agitated. Green eyes blazed as she spat her reply. "Why, of course I shall clean my own rooms, Jenna! I plan to do just that. I am not a cripple you know, so don't treat me like one!"

"I know that mother, I was making sure I had the story correct!"

"It is definitely correct! No-one except you is to come in here!"

"Ok! Now on a much lighter note mother! We will be expecting guests for the weekend. Father asked me to organize everything for him, and I have arranged to get the horses available for a trail ride. How would you like to come out riding with me? I'm inviting Jack to stay over, so he will be coming riding with us also!" Jenna stated.

Her mother's demeanour changed at once as she looked fondly at her daughter. "Ah, such a clever woman you have become young Jenna. Quite the lady of the house now! Your father is very lucky to have you here to carry out his instructions to the extent you do. You have developed into quite the organizer, and I am so proud of you! You have great strength Jenna! I am so pleased of that. But you are only young yet so it will hold you in good stead for things to come!"

"Thank you, Mother, but what things to come?"

Julia shook her head. "No, not today, Jenna! However, there will come a day we shall talk in depth, but not today. Especially since you have generously found time to tend to your mother's needs!"

Jenna shook her head. "If you say so mother!"

"You are such a good girl Jenna, so thank you for the invitation to go out. I haven't been horse-riding for quite some time now, and you know how I love it, and the sunshine will be so good for me!"

"So, I will say yes! I would love to go riding! But only with you, and Jack. I do not want to go out with the others. Please make sure of that Jenna! You must promise me that" she stressed.

"I will mother, just trust me. I am pleased you decided to come!"

"You, I do trust Jenna! But no-one else!" her mother replied.

Jenna sighed. It was pointless arguing with her when she was in this mood and so set in her ways. "If you ever want to talk mother, on any subject for that matter. I am here at any time, you know!"

"Yes, Jenna. I do know that, but let it go for now!"

"As you wish! How would you like breakfast out on the balcony tomorrow? I can set up a table for us. It is meant to be a lovely day!"

"Sounds ideal Jenna. I will look forward to tomorrow then!"

"Good, I shall have breakfast sent up for 6.15.a.m for three of us, and dinner tonight? Is steak and kidney pie ok with you mother?"

"Yes please, I do like that meal." Julia replied.

"Right, I will bring it up later. Do you need anything else now?"

"No Jenna, I have all I need here. I will see you later!"

"That's fine mother, I shall be back later." Jenna said, as she bent over to place a peck on her mother's covered cheek.

Her mother pulled away from her embrace, and Jenna winced. She had to keep reminding herself that touch offended her mother. Quickly she left the room, walked briskly down the hallway to the stairs, and went through to the kitchen. As she walked in the cook was getting pies from the oven, and the aroma filled the room.

"Hello Missus Hastings. Dinner sure smells wonderful. Would you serve mine, and mother's dinner for 6.30pm, and I will take it up to her? I have spoken to her about your conflicts, so in the future just ring her phone to ask what she wants for meals please, and have the girls take it up to her. They will find a table outside to put a tray on. Tell them not to go inside her rooms, just to knock on the door, but let her know it is there!"

"Ok, I am pleased that's settled thank you, Jenna!" Paula replied.

"You're welcome. I take it all is rectified now. Is that correct?" Paula's eyes clouded over as she thought on that. *Sure, until the next time!* but she replied. "Yes Jenna, we will manage."

"Excellent! Now Missus Hastings, about in the morning. Would you ask Melita to set up the balcony table upstairs for three of us. Mother, myself, and Jack! So please serve our breakfast up there at 6.15.am, and well before the guests who are to be served at 8.am. as I will have many things to do before the guests arrive!"

"Yes Jenna, it will be done!"

"Good! Now, do you have the list for me for food yet? As I have to get the orders in as soon as possible."

Paula dug into her apron pocket, then handed the list to Jenna.

"All done Jenna!" she said. "I think I have covered it all!"

"Excellent, thank you for that Missus Hastings. I shall endeavor to do that now." she stated, then turned, and walked briskly out to the office with a million things on her mind.

Jenna could hear the motorcycle revving from her room. It was a sign. A definite threat to the silence breaking and a start to a new day. She glanced at her watch and grinned to herself.

Right on time Jack! Is he never late? she wondered, as she raced for the doors to the outside balcony, and opened them to go outside, then walked towards the very end where she could see the carpark.

She waved as Jack got off the bike and looked up, and he waved back. Jenna knew he would take the trail down to the beach and use the back staircase to come up to the balcony so she turned to go and check on her mother. Her mother's rooms were closest to the stairs so Jenna knocked on the balcony door. "Are you up yet mother?" she called, and Julia Temple opened the doors and spoke.

"I certainly am Jenna. Good morning, and what a nice day it is!"

"Good morning mother, yes it sure is. You look great today, all dressed for riding I see. Oh! You have your favourite necklace on!"

Julia smiled, and looked down at it. "Yes, it is my most favourite one Jenna! It was my mother's! So, I never take it off, only to bathe!"

"I have noticed mother! It matches the colour of your eyes! Now, we must hurry as breakfast is ready! I have been down to check, and our table is set up in the usual place. They have placed our food in heating trays ready to serve, also the coffee, and tea on hotplates. I am pleased of that as I will be pressed for time this morning. So, just go down at your own pace as I will wait at the top of the stairs for Jack, he has just arrived. You most probably heard the noise up in your room from his motorbike." she laughed. "I won't be long!"

Julia tried to manage a laugh as her face twisted up. "I did hear the bike, Jenna. A rude awakening, but at least it got me moving. You run along then, that's fine as I just have to organize a few things inside, then I shall go down. Maybe I could set up our places, and pour some juice and coffee if you like!" offered Julia.

"Please do, that would be excellent thanks mother!"

"Anyone up there?" came an exerted voice from the stairs.

"That would be Jack now!" Jenna laughed. "It didn't take him long to get up here, he's keen! I shall go down the end to meet him." she said, leaving her mother's side. Then she laughed as she looked down at him, and then of his antics. His face was reddening with exertion but he seemed oblivious of it as he flicked hair out of his eyes annoyingly, and it seemed to her he was relishing the effort it took to make the climb. *He is a true country boy in every sense!* she thought, as she heard him chuckle with each leap. "Morning Jack, we are waiting, just come on up! Breakfast is ready on the balcony!"

Jenna heard him grunting, then came his reply.

"Morning Jenna! Got your instructions. Am on my way, so over and out!" he gasped with the effort. "Am almost there!" he gushed.

Jack Rickard was taking the wide steps two at a time and he was laughing at the effort. Golden, sun-bleached hair fell across his face to temporarily hide his deep green eyes. His strenuous effort showing evidence of muscle in his legs and biceps as he progressed, and Jenna took a deep breath as she watched him with fascination.

She had always been drawn to Jack. Best friends ever since they were little kids. Aussie kids, now in their teens. But lately, she was looking at Jack in a completely different way as she sometimes daydreamed of him feeling the same way about her, especially at times when he teased her. *She wondered how close they would become.*

He was incredibly handsome, and much taller than her now. *He is just filling out in all directions!* she noticed, especially in his tight-fitting riding jodhpurs. *But, so am I!* she suddenly realized. *Must be the country air.* "Hi Jack!" she said as he neared the top step.

"Hi Jenna! What a magic day." He looked at her approvingly as he scrutinized her outfit. "Wow! Look at Jenna Temple, all dressed for riding I see, and looking so beautiful too, as usual." he teased.

Jenna blushed, but replied. "Thank you, Jack! However, it seems to me that you don't look so bad yourself my friend. Thank you for being prompt as usual. Come along don't dally, breakfast is ready!"

Jack smiled at that quip, and secretly glanced sideways at her as she turned to walk away, her auburn hair bouncing with each step.

He had many opinions about Jenna Temple, if she only knew.

If only I could summon up the courage to tell her.

It seemed they had known each other forever. He had taken on the role of protector only because he was older. *Though Jenna never ever needed protecting at all, did she?* he chuckled to himself.

He always liked to think he was dictating to her since he was the eldest by almost two years, but he knew Jenna so well, and she was far too difficult to fool. *Jenna was definitely her own person, and very intelligent, confident and strong, but such fun to be with,* he knew that.

He guessed that was why he loved her so much!
Love? Oh yes! Jack Rickard knew that he had loved Jenna Temple from the first day he could say her name! *She was a true Aussie mate!*

"Great timing Jenna, I am starving!" replied Jack as he followed, then paced in step with her as they walked along the balcony.

"So, how was the bike-ride?"

"Absolutely love it, Jenna. I wish I could go everywhere on it. Oh, I can't wish my life away. I will be old enough soon though!"

"Yes, I do know your eighteenth birthday is soon Jack, but you may get caught before it! It is breaking the law!" she pointed out.

"Only a tiny bit Jenna. I am not a law-breaker, quite the opposite in fact. I only use the bike on our land and to ride over here, Surely, that is not so bad, is it? Besides, I will have my license in a week!"

"You be the judge my friend, but I am not going to visit you on the inside, looking out. Besides you could use your push-bike!"

"Seriously Jenna! Do you realize how many hills I have to climb to get here? It's not an easy ride, even on a motor bike. So, my dear friend this one time we disagree, trust you to be so self-righteous!"

"I am not self-righteous!"

"You are too!" Jack replied, as they finally reached the table.

"Surely even you must do something wrong sometime Jenna!"

"No! Not really. Or, not that I am aware of! Jack!"

Julia Temple looked from one to the other as Jenna and Jack stood in front of her at the table. "Oh! Good morning, Jack. Please sit, I have taken the liberty of pouring drinks, it is good to see you."

"So, is this little morning banter just to get the day started I hear? What joy! May I offer an opinion to settle this debate?" she asked.

Jack pulled out a chair and smiled as he replied. "Good morning, Missus Temple! It is good to see you again also. What a great day we have before us, I do hope you enjoy it, and yes, maybe you can settle this debate. I was telling Jenna that she was so self-righteous as she frowned on me riding the motorbike here without a license!"

"Ah, I see! Then I must agree with you Jack. There is no harm in that considering you don't use any main roads, and yes! I do know that Jenna is self-righteous. My fault actually! It is the way I raised her. She doesn't understand grey areas or want to know about them either, do you Jenna my love?" she asked, as she looked at Jenna.

Jenna laughed. "Well, I guess you are both right. I do tend to be very definite in my decisions. Sorry Jack, and sorry mother for our argument. I wasn't about to give in as you know, so please forgive!"

Jack chuckled, and looked at her before he spoke. "You can say that again Jenna, you are so determined, but really there is nothing to forgive! It is who you are! That is why you are loved because you have certain beliefs, and I wouldn't want you to change that!"

Julia smiled at that comment. She really liked this boy, Jack.

"Please sit down now you two, all is forgiven, so let us eat. Just look at that view! Isn't it breathtaking? It makes you proud to be an Australian! Don't you agree?" she gushed.

"It sure does mother! I am pleased to share it with you and Jack!"

Breakfast proved an enjoyable time, some serious discussions on the weather, then idle chatter about who was invited to stay over.

"Now the important part!" questioned Julia. "What time do you think would be suitable to go riding Jenna? I need time to prepare!"

"Well mother, we do have plenty of time to chat while we have an enjoyable breakfast, but after that, I think I shall need some time to organize everything with the staff, and greet the guests. So, I am guessing about 8.30am to 9.00am. You shall have time to do what you want. I will organize a thermos and snacks for morning tea and cut sandwiches and drinks for lunch. We will need to go reasonably early to beat the heat. What is your opinion, Jack?"

"Sounds good to me Jenna!" he replied.

Julia smiled at her daughter. "That is excellent Jenna. You know young lady you do think of everything! Now, just to let you know, I may go over to the stables while you are busy. I want to make sure Pablo has everything I need for riding." added Julia.

"Whatever you decide mother. Jack and I will meet you outside the kitchen at 8.45 am. with our horses. I will check all the mounts are ready for the guests who are riding, while we are at the stables!"

"That is perfect Jenna so, I shall meet you both there! Now! Enough about that. I now would like to discuss a few things with you both while we are together." and she looked directly at Jack.

"Jack, you both are in high-school now and as you already know I want Jenna to study law, but she may have to go to the city to complete that, we are not sure yet, it all depends on the university. But what about you Jack? What is your plan, if any, for the future?"

Jack looked at her with a very serious expression upon his face as he replied. "Well, missus Temple. I haven't even spoke to Jenna about it yet! As I have only just found out the requirements, so I've decided most definitely that I want to become a policeman, though I have just broken the law!" he joked and stared at Jenna. However, I don't plan on being just any policeman. I'd like to be a Homicide Detective one day in the future. I guess that stems from I was a kid!"

Jenna just stared at him. "Really Jack, I had no idea? That is most interesting, a huge expectation. What is really involved though?"

"Firstly, Jenna. I will need hands-on experience as a policeman. So, I plan to send in an application for a policeman position to Blue Bay Police Station when I turn eighteen and have all qualifications. If by chance I do get accepted for a position, I will leave school, and continue my night classes at university. Just hoping my course is a stepping stone, and caters for the levels I need, otherwise, I too will have to go to the city to complete my course to obtain my goals!"

"Oh Jack, this is huge. Are you really sure that is what you want to do? It would take specialized training to obtain that goal of being a detective, and not to mention, many years of study!"

"Time is what I have Jenna! Lots of time! It is the main reason why I'm acting now, so I have everything completed, and still be young. So yes, most definitely Jenna, this is what I want to do with my life!"

Jenna had never seen Jack so sure of anything before, and it did look like he had done his research, but she wanted to make sure.

"So, what exactly are these qualifications you need Jack?"

"I would need to complete a hands-on police job for preliminary training, as well as obtaining the all-important 2:2 under-graduate college degree, either at the university in Blue Bay or the city. Then if luck is on my side and my results good, maybe, and I say maybe! With hard work I could climb the ladder to obtain a detective status as a direction to the field I want to work in, which is in homicide!"

Jenna gaped. "That is a long road, Jack! But you can do it. I just know you can, and besides breaking the law just now, I think you will make a great policeman, and an even better detective one day!"

Jack laughed at her quip, but did so want her approval. "Thanks Jenna, that means a lot to me. I am pleased you have my back!"

"Plus, I have your back too Jack. I'm so proud of you!" said Julia.

"Thank you so much Missus Temple, that means a lot." he said.

Jenna took this reprieve to think more about what Jack had said.

She stared out over the ocean. Australia was a sight to be seen at this early hour as the sun rose higher above the horizon into a clear blue sky, and she felt such pride. Its rays seemed to dance upon the water, highlighting the whitewater of the waves as they fell, then rolled into the shore. Seagulls played on the pristine sand, the beach deserted except for all nature to see as crabs scurried along heedless of the task, they had set themselves and huge pelicans circled above ready to disclose to all, the presence of fish in their search for food.

Jenna sighed as she breathed in the sea-air deeply. Suddenly, she was in another world, and deep in thought as the prospect of Jack not being around, was something she hadn't planned on. Or rather to be exact, it was something she didn't foresee in their future, and more or less, she had taken it for granted that he would always be in Blue Bay, and close to her. She didn't want to hold him back, but they had never discussed the future, she really didn't know where her dreams may lead her either. She may even have to leave home as well, and that was frightening because she didn't want to leave Jack behind. So now, this news was a rude awakening, but also an insight into the future, and how things could change so quickly.

"Hello there?" came a voice in question to interrupt her thoughts.

"Oh, sorry Jack! I was miles away. I guess your news has shaken me up a little. I simply thought we had forever to enjoy each other's company, but I guess we have had that, and we have grown close. So, in saying that, I can only advise that whatever you decide is best for you and your future, I can only wish you the very best of luck!"

Jack glanced over at Julia Temple, then looked seriously at Jenna before he spoke. *It is now or never Jack!* he thought.

"Jenna… he stumbled. "Jenna, there is something I really must say now! Something I have been meaning to speak about for a long time now, but couldn't gain the courage to do so before. I do know that we are only young yet, but I don't need any more convincing! So, this little something is simply this! I love you, Jenna Temple! I always have. I just love everything about you, and I would like to think that whatever future I choose, that you would be a part of it too, because one day when I have reached my goals, I will be asking you to marry me, Jenna!" he said sheepishly, as their eyes locked.

"So, I am guessing you have a while to think on that! But at least you will have an answer to my question ready when I ask you to be my wife one day!" he laughed, trying to pass it off as a joke.

Jenna gulped, then stared at him in disbelief. *He does have the same feelings for me as I do for him!* she noted in bewilderment, then she looked straight at her mother who was smiling at them.

"Jack Rickard how dare you say these things in front of mother! Though I am pleased you did, as I have the same feelings for you!"

Jack gaped at her. "You do?" he questioned in wonder.

"Of course, I do, silly! You've always been the one. I love you too!"

"Really!" he gushed, as he rose up from his seat. "Shall we seal it with a kiss then, Jenna Temple?" and before she could reply, he had taken her hand, then she was in his arms with his lips on hers.

It was their first kiss, and so tender and loving that Jenna melted in his arms and blotches of red crept up her neck in embarrassment.

Julia's face twisted as she looked at them and laughed. "Oh Jack! What joy! You have made my day. Now Jenna, instead of planning a life for yourself, you can make plans with Jack. Yes! An excellent match if I ever saw one. You two deserve to be together one day!"

They all laughed. But as Jenna looked directly at Jack, she knew it was unmistakable what she saw in his deep green eyes. His love unashamedly portrayed in them, was so obvious it sent tingles up her spine. For some reason she had a new lease on life. Her young life was seeming to fade into the background, as now new direction formed, life would be good when they both achieved their goals.

Jack was lost in her huge smokey green eyes. *But he knew from this moment on, their relationship would change,* and he couldn't wait.

"You know what mother, I couldn't agree with you more, and I am so pleased you are here to share our news today, however right now. I really hate to break up the party so to speak, but duty calls! I must check everything is organized. Then I'll be busy over at the stables! Are you coming Jack?" she asked, and rose from her seat.

"Yep, right with you Jenna. Catch you soon missus Temple!"

"Yes, you most certainly will Jack!" replied Julia.

Julia certainly had a lot to think about as she watched them leave. *Yes, a great match they will be, those two.* It is so nice to know that someone like Jack will be Jenna's future. She rose from the table and looked out over the ocean reminiscing until she finally realized she had some things to prepare in her room for the day. She was very meticulous about what she needed to have with her when riding, so she grabbed her walking stick, and ambled down to her room.

It was still early when she left to walk over to the stables. As she walked in Pablo was just finishing the saddling up of her horse. She shook her head angrily as she walked awkwardly over to him.

It is just as well I came over to check! she thought. Then she became agitated, so her voice was raised as she started to tear strips off him.

Pablo looked up to the sound of her raised voice as she walked in. "Good morning missus. I have just finished your horse!" he said, then he noted the scowl on her face, and her tone of voice.

"That is not suitable Pablo! But what is more annoying to me, is that you already know that, don't you?" she screeched.

Pablo looked bewildered, and became angry. His voice raised in reply. "What do you mean? I already know what? I do have a lot of horses to saddle, so what is the problem with your horse missus?"

"My horse has the wrong saddle, and blanket, that is what! How many times do I have to repeat it to you!" she yelled. "I need the thick saddle and blanket I always have, as it is cushioned better for me, and for the horse too. So, a simple fix. Just change it please! Or you will pay the consequences young man!"

"What damn consequences?" he yelled.

Pablo was far too busy, and now he was getting riled up. "No! I won't be changing it. I have spent too much time on it now!"

"You will change it, or you won't have a job, Pablo!"

"What? Crazy person. You can't fire me!" he spat back at her.

"I can, and I will if you push me further Pablo!"

His dark eyes glared angrily at her. *Hateful woman this one be!* he thought, as he glared at her angrily. "Don't you threaten me with dismissal missus because you can't do that. Mister Richard Temple hired me, only he can fire me. So, if you don't like it, you can change the saddle yourself." he yelled.

"Now! You listen to me very carefully Pablo, or you will not work here much longer. You are stretching my patience now! You have been hired only under my authorization, as a request from Mister Temple to employ you. This is my property, it has always been my property, and it is certainly not mister Temple's property! He has no authority to hire, or fire anyone without my say-so! What I say here goes, I am afraid. Do you understand? Is that quite clear? I will not repeat it to you again, Pablo!" she yelled.

Pablo just gaped at her, not knowing what to say. This piece of information was news to him. This is not what he was told at the time he was hired, and what of the promises made to him? *Do the other staff know of this?* he wondered. *He seemed to think not.*

We were all hired by Mister Richard Temple. *But now I must ask mother if she and the others know all about this?* he mused, though his reply was purposely very blunt just the same as he thought she was bluffing, and so, he looked defiantly at Julia Temple when he spoke.

"If I have time later, then I will do it. Otherwise, it's not going to get done I'm afraid Missus Temple!" and he smirked at her.

Julia detected the snarl on his face which immediately made her angry. "Later, is not good enough Pablo!" she countered. "We will be the first people to leave the homestead, so my horse had better be saddled with my saddle and cloth ready, otherwise you can find another job! Can you please get that through your thick scull, and do what you are told!"

Pablo just laughed at her antics as the anger and frustrations on her face caused her features to crinkle and crack like a worn mask.

Jenna could hear the loud yelling as she neared the stables, and yes, one was her mother's voice. *What now?* she wondered.

She listened quietly at the door trying to take in the situation but now knew why they were arguing. As she walked inside it was very obvious a heated argument was paramount between the two, and she noted her mother's stress.

"Enough now!" Jenna called, and both their eyes flew wide with surprise as they turned to face her.

Pablo stared at her, his mouth gaping.

"Do not ever, yell at my mother Pablo!" she said firmly. "Just you wait right here! I'll speak to you next and turned to face her mother.

"Oh Jenna! I...Her mother tried to say but Jenna interrupted her.

"Mother, you are getting so upset. Please go back to the house now, and I shall handle this!" "But Jenna.... I only wanted....

Jenna held up a hand to her. "It is ok mother! I know what you need. Trust me please!" she said, as she took her arm to lead her to the door. Then she returned to stand firmly before Pablo.

Jenna stood and glared at him before she spoke.

"Really Pablo! You have made me very angry, and disappointed. How dare you speak to my mother in that way! Do you realize just what you are doing, and how much disrespect you are showing to my mother? It disgusts me! Especially to the one person you should obey, that is the hand who feeds you! Now young man, you strip that saddle off and do as my mother asks of you, or you leave this property right this minute, and I will have someone to replace you within the hour!"

Pablo glared. "What hand that feeds me?" he spat in question.

"Meaning mother's hand! Your employer, the person who pays your wages out of her estate! I think a little more respect is needed!"

Pablo gulped. "I see! I guess I could fix that saddle right now!"

"Yes, of course you can, and I shall be back to check!" said Jenna.

Chapter Three

Richard Temple parked in the driveway at Oceanview, climbed out of his car to lock it, then quickly walked to the side entrance to his rooms, rather than use the front door.

It was early. Just 6.15 am. and he didn't want to wake the whole household, but as he reached his balcony doors, he detected activity happening up on the top deck.

Sounds like Jenna is up and about and that is Jack's bike parked out front, *so I assume Jenna invited him over.* he realized.

He was in a hurry, but could not help but savor the memories of his long night in the city when he had stayed overnight with Hillary West, as he had left her bed not long ago. He could still feel her long shapely legs, and his hands caressing each secret part of her perfect body. Her flaming red hair was tussled, and fanned out as her head was thrown back, as she arched her body to scream out in ecstasy.

Ah, yes! That sex with Hill had been so very good! Hillary knew from all their previous experiences exactly what he liked, how to release his tensions. *She was used to doing that!* he knew.

He had left the city on the first train to Blue Bay, then located his car at the station where he left it, to drive home. But this minute, he had to shower and change before the bus arrived with his guests.

Richard rather liked having his own privacy. Being on the lower level gave him the freedom he desired by adding the benefit for him to come and go when he pleased without disturbing the household. When he finally moved down there, he re-structured three rooms to incorporate an en-suite specifically to suit his own needs.

So now! All dressed for the day in jeans, and silk shirt, he felt anxious for the day to begin. He walked through the house to the clatter, and noise in the kitchen, but shunned that to continue out to the lawns in search for Jenna, as the visions of how the day would unfold consumed him. He noticed the staff were running around to complete their jobs, and right in the mix of them was Jenna giving instructions, pointing to things undetected by them. He shook his head, and chuckled, but stopped short to the blast of the bus's horn.

He looked towards Jenna as her head lifted. She too, had heard the bus arrive, and he waved to her. She waved back, then gave him the thumbs up, but waved him away so he could greet his guests.

Just unbelievable this girl is, she is just a kid really! he pondered as he returned an *ok sign,* then turned to walk towards the front gates.

As the bus doors opened, they started filing out with excitement etched on their faces, and the bus-driver climbed down and opened the luggage department, and began lifting out their luggage.

Richard called a welcome to them all, and began speaking with the driver. "Hi John! Thanks for being on time and for bringing out my guests. I am guessing you could return about 8.30 am Monday!"

"Hi Richard. Not a problem. Everyone was ready and waiting to be picked up, so no hold-ups. See you on Monday!" he said, as he grabbed the last piece of luggage, and waved to the guests.

"Enjoy your weekend everyone, see you all on Monday morning!"

"Thanks John!" offered George on behalf of everyone, as he was first one off the bus, though they all called out thank you to John.

Richard smiled as he stepped forward to shake George's hand. "Welcome George! I'll have you know my man, that everything you could possibly want, I have this weekend. Where is Miranda?"

"Morning Richard! I just bet you have! Miranda is somewhere here. We both find being in a different environment is a shot in the arm, and perfect weather, so looking forward to relaxing a little!"

"Well, it is a break well earnt George!" Richard said, then moved to mingle with some of his guests. He shook hands with the men, and chatted with their wives. There seemed plenty of friendly banter amongst them as they relaxed, so he went to stand beside George.

He casually looked around for Miranda, then noticed she was at the very back, standing on the top step of the bus waiting to get off. Her eyes were alive with excitement as she gazed over the property, but he couldn't help but notice the different expressions on her face.

Miranda was excited as she took in the grandeur of the property. *My goodness it is huge, and so majestic. I shudder to think how many bedrooms, and bathrooms that house contains.* she wondered. She needed a royal tour just to satisfy her inquisitive mind as she knew for certain that the other side of the house, where it sat on the cliff-face was facing the ocean, because she had caught a glimpse of that when the bus had climbed the escarpment on their final trek to the carpark. *Just the land alone is worth a fortune!* she thought, as her eyes took in the grounds, and also the immaculate gardens trimmed to perfection. A massive marque stood grandly on the lawns claiming possession of the surrounds, graced by the floral blooms on display from the many gardens around. Her eyes shifted beyond towards the fully fenced tennis courts, and adjacent was a pool area to die for. She could tell much preparation had taken place for their visit.

Then her eyes fell on the instigator of that preparation. A young girl who seemed taller than most young girls she imagined, and she was obviously dictating to the staff as she pointed to certain areas.

She was really very pretty, and her creamy flawless skin seemed to shine with health, as did her auburn hair which fell around her face in a dense mass of curls. Miranda was about to look away when the girl looked up, and she gasped as their eyes locked. Deep green eyes seemed to search Miranda's soul so she could not look away.

Jenna looked up to see if the guests were all out of the bus, when her eyes fell on just one person who stood out from the rest like a rose amongst the thorns. She was an absolutely beautiful woman, and from where Jenna stood, she could sense some undercurrent, a vibe even, that emanated from her and Jenna felt something she had never experienced before in her life, as an uneasiness overcome her.

She felt the dark smoldering eyes searching her. *But for what, she didn't know.* So, for that instant, for some unknown reason she held her gaze. But deep inside something was telling Jenna to beware.

Quickly as if it was her intention, Jenna broke their eye contact. Then she walked across the lawns and over to the entrance to stand beside George and her father. She placed a pec on her father's cheek as she spoke. "Morning father, and good morning, Mister Delvin!'

"Hi Jenna! But, please call me George. I always tell you that!"

"Ok! George it is, from this moment on Mister Delvin!" she said, and they all laughed at her quip.

Richard continued to smile as he looked at her. "Good morning, Jenna!" he replied. "Looks like you have outdone yourself this time young lady!" he uttered with a chuckle as they were waiting for the remainder of the guests to file through the gates to welcome them.

"But you haven't seen anything yet to pass an opinion father!"

"I have seen enough, and I am mighty pleased, so thank you!"

"You are most welcome and yes, I know I have done a good job!"

Richard laughed at her cheek, as the last of his guests reached them, then they were both caught up in conversation.

Jenna smiled, but could not help but notice the scrutiny from the lady standing in the back row. Who then, all of a sudden, started to move forward! Then she was walking towards them.

Her perfume preceded her, turning all heads in her direction as they were greeted by her trademark smile.

"Good morning, all!" she bubbled as she reached them.

Richard had to stifle a gasp as he looked at her. His eyes roamed over her body. Her breasts captured his attention. As she spoke, they threatened to burst over the top her blouse. However, it was a tight-fitting riding skirt that done his head in, as he noticed the two very long slits up each leg almost to her thighs. Her legs were bare, and exposed with each step, leaving nothing to the imagination. *If at all possible, she is more beautiful in daylight!* he realized.

"Ah, there you are Miranda, good morning! Where have you been hiding?" asked Richard. "You must meet my daughter Jenna!"

"Good morning, Richard! Oh, I was in no rush. I was simply just admiring the view to be truthful, and what a lovely place you have here!" she smiled. "So, finally! This must be the lovely young girl I have heard so much about!" and she held out her gloved hand.

"Jenna please greet George's wife, Missus Miranda Delvin!" stated Richard. "Miranda, this is my daughter, Jenna!"

Jenna smiled at the beautiful creature before her, and shook her hand, though it felt limp in her own. "A big welcome to our home, 'Oceanview' Missus Delvin, and a huge congratulations to both of you, George and Missus Delvin on your recent marriage!" she said.

Miranda was a little confused. *This girl is no little girl!* she mused. Instead, she acts more like an adult, *not one just turned sixteen*. She is so polite, and respectful, *but speaks as if she is the owner of this place!*

Would that be a possibility? Hmm! I must find out! Could she be a threat to me at such a tender age? *Surely not, I don't think so.* Miranda looked at her now awaiting a reply, so she summoned up her best smile. But for some odd reason, this once, she felt out of her depth, and at a loss for words if possible, so that her reply was guarded.

"I simply can't thank you enough Jenna, that is so thoughtful of you. Isn't that sweet George?" she turned to involve her husband.

"It certainly is Miranda, but that is Jenna. Always so thoughtful. Thank you so much for your wishes, Jenna!" George responded.

"You are welcome, Mister and Missus Delvin!" came the reply.

Richard sensed some tension between Miranda and Jenna, so he ceased the conversation. "Sorry to interrupt guys, but we have to move on, so Jenna will take over now with some information!"

"Thank you so much, father!" Jenna responded, then she smiled broadly, and stepped forward to address the guests.

"A big welcome to Oceanview everyone!" she started. "Anyone who hasn't been here before may wish to explore the grounds, and inside the house. So, we shall organize a mini tour after breakfast if that suits you all, and she looked directly at Miranda.

Miranda squirmed. *Is she reading my mind now?* she wondered.

Jenna continued. "Though we won't be taking you through our private rooms. My mother is up and about this morning and she is coming out riding with Jack Rickard, my friend, and myself. If you need anything at all during your stay, please just ask any member of our staff, my father or myself!" Everyone clapped, and smiled.

"Firstly, your accommodation. It is all on the lower level, and I have asked our housemaid Melita to leave your room keys in the doors. You should have enough time now to put your belongings inside the rooms, and maybe freshen up for breakfast which will be served in the marque at 8 a.m. Could I have a show of hands to tell me who plans on riding today, so I can arrange your mounts with

Her Mind SCREAMS MURDER

our stable-man Pablo?" She quickly noted the hands raised. "Thank you! Now because we have a bar-be-que arranged for lunch, if any of you should plan to be out riding, please advise the staff before you leave, and they will provide drinks and sandwiches to take out. Now, more about your rooms!"

"George! I have arranged for you, and your wife to be in the first room opposite the staircase. It has an ensuite, and access out to the deck overlooking the ocean! I do hope you enjoy your stay!"

"Thank you, Jenna, we certainly will!" said George.

Miranda stood gaping at Jenna and mesmerized by her skills in organization. *She just called my husband George! Surely not!*

"You are most welcome George!" came Jenna's reply.

There it is again! Miranda realized, as Jenna continued.

"Now, for our remaining guests! You shall find that the rooms on the lower floor are identical, and all have balconies overlooking the ocean. Mister, and Missus Collins, next room along. Mister, and Missus Worth, the third room down, and Mister, and Missus Felon, the fourth. There are two double bathrooms to service these rooms! Enjoy your stay everyone. I will leave you all in the hands of Melita who is waiting for you at the stairs as I have to check on breakfast!"

They all thanked Jenna, and when she departed, they picked up their belongings to stroll across to the house, but Miranda noticed that Richard had lagged behind, and she fell in step with him.

"Aren't you going over to the house Richard?"

"No, Miranda. I had better give Jenna a hand, as no doubt she will want me to check the spit. I will join you for breakfast in a bit. Are you coming out riding with me?" he asked as he searched her face.

Her eyes flew wide to twinkle in her reply. "I certainly am Mister Richard Temple, that is a must do! Now, would there be any chance of me going over to see the horses now, where ever the stables are?"

"Well, I would go with you, but right now I fear I have things to do, but you could go over to the stables before breakfast if you like. Pablo will be there. I shall ask George to take your luggage over to your room, and get your key. See that double gate down there!" he pointed. "Go through that, and follow the track to the stables!"

"Oh, that is excellent! Thank you, Richard, you are most kind. I won't be too long. Be a dear and tell George for me!" she pleaded.

"No problems Miranda! I shall check on Pablo after breakfast."

As an after-thought, she smiled up at him and her head lolled to one side in question. "One other thing Richard? I also heard Jenna say that your wife is going out riding today! So, tell me? Why hasn't she come down to greet your guests? I think that is a little rude!"

Richard's eyes darkened as a scowl curled his lips, so his reply was quite short. "Don't you think I know that, Miranda! There is no need to remind me of the fact. Though, I really have no interest in what my wife is doing, and I have already explained our situation to you. However, to answer your question as best I can. Definitely, no! She won't be coming down. She is not interested in my guests, or anyone else for that matter. Jenna will take her out riding today, and I believe she has invited her friend Jack Rickard over as well."

"I see! Then we may meet them on the trail?" stated Miranda.

"Probably not, they will go a different route to us."

"How can you be so sure Richard?"

"I just know. Trust me, Miranda! My wife will not go anywhere where my guests are, and she certainly doesn't need me with her, and I don't need her either. That ship has sailed! She has Jenna!"

Miranda laughed that tinkle of a laugh, then she turned to walk away, but lingered to step back a little simply to look him square in the eyes with her violet eyes smoldering as she spoke so very softly.

"Well, things can change Richard! *So why do it?* she whispered. *Why go on at all when it's a simple fix! Just get rid of her then!*" she said.

Richard gawked as he watched her walk away. *Get rid of her? What did she mean?* he wondered. He had thought many times of doing just that, though he didn't know how, but to have it spoken to him so bluntly really made him think, and several ideas came to mind.

No, she can't mean that surely! Maybe I am reading too much into her statement? She may have simply meant just to leave my wife! I could certainly do that I'm rich enough in my own right, but 'Oceanview!' It is so special to me, it is home. *No, I could never leave this property!* he thought decidedly as deep thoughts now stirred his imagination as he walked across the lawn to take a servant's door to the kitchen.

"Hi Paula!" he said to the cook as he walked in to approach her.

"Oh, good morning, Mister Temple. Breakfast will be on time for you, and your guests." offered Paula Hastings with a smile.

"Good, it looks like you have all that we may need. I really need to speak to Jenna! Do you know where she is?" he asked.

"Jenna went over to speak to Pablo about the horses for yourselves, and your guests today. She is back now though, as she was just here checking on breakfast, and putting in her request for food and drinks for their ride, and I believe she was going out to see Ted about getting the pig on the spit, and start cooking it.

"Ok, good to hear. I was hoping Jenna had arranged to get meat for the spit in for dinner? Guess I will go out and give them a hand!"

"Yes, Mister Temple! Jenna ordered a full pig. Ted fired the pit this morning, and just came in to collect the pig to put on the spit."

"Excellent, nobody seems to need my help." Richard chuckled.

"However, I will go out to speak with Jenna and Ted. Would you arrange drinks, and lunch for two. For me, and my guest, for when we go riding after breakfast? We have advised the others to ask you the same request, so you will know who is left here for lunch."

"Will do Mister Temple, I hope you enjoy your day!"

"Sure will, thanks Paula! Maybe dinner at 7.30pm?" he queried.

"Yes, we should be ready by that time I think Mister Temple!" said Paula. "I will let you know when you come back in."

"Thanks for your help!" said Richard, then he walked across the kitchen floor, and disappeared through the door.

Miranda noticed the veiled figure walking on a track towards the house as she was making her way down towards the stables.

That must be the wife, Julia Temple. she realized.

Oh! There is Jenna also, following just a little behind her.

As she approached the stable doors Miranda paused outside as she could hear someone speaking, and she listened to the distressed voice. She quickly peeked around the door, and noted a young boy walking around, waving his hands in the air explaining a situation as he spoke on his mobile phone, and she ducked her head back.

"But mother this is news to me, and all of us. Now we could be dismissed any time! You know what Mister Temple promised us!"

He listened, then replied back. "What! Are you serious? I guess I could, seeing you are so adamant! But are you sure we have to do that?" his face paled at the reply, but answered. "Ok, I will do it!"

Miranda peeked again to see him end the call, then to pull a knife from his scabbard and sidle over to a honey-coloured mare. *Whatever is he doing?* she wondered as she crept closer. *Ah, I see now!* she mused as she grabbed her phone to take a couple of photos. She waited for a while then called loudly as she stepped into the stables.

"Is anyone there?"

Pablo's head flew up, and she could see guilt written clearly on his face. "Oh! You startled me Missus. I am Pablo, the stable boy!"

"Good morning, Pablo. You are just the person I need to see. My name is Miranda Delvin, a guest here of Mister Richard Temple's. I shall be riding with him today, and I have permission from him to look at the horses, and choose mine!' and she smiled her best smile.

"Sure. I will show you the horses that are for Mister Temple and his family. If you are riding with him, then you may choose your mount from the rest of the horses if you like!" and Miranda smiled.

"I do like! So, lead the way, Pablo."

He beckoned to her. "This is Miss Jenna's horse, and one I have picked out for her friend Jack. The honey-coloured mare is for her mother, Missus Temple. I have just re-saddled it to her liking!"

Pablo looked at Miranda and smiled awkwardly at her when he spoke. "I am so sorry Missus Delvin, I am a little pushed for time, so while you are looking at these horses, I will go and bring the rest up to the yards so you can choose your mount while you are here. Oh! Mister Temple will be riding the black over there." he pointed.

Miranda moved amongst the saddled horses, and waved him to go. "That is fine, thank you Pablo!" she replied, and when she was sure he had left, she moved closer to the honey-coloured mare.

Now! I must see what Pablo has done? She patted the horse to calm it down. All seemed in order, but she knew what to look for, so she bent down low and her eyes fell on the girth strap at a place almost hidden from sight. She gasped as her thoughts ran wild imagining the repercussions it would cause, but quicky took a close-up photo.

Someone has a huge grudge to bear no doubt! Interesting. *But this is just perfect.* she realized. *An opportunity arises.* But they usually do. *Well, with me anyway!* she chuckled, as she delved deeply into her hand-bag in search for what she needed to add her little touch.

Miranda laughed. *Things do happen for a reason.* she mused, and she was feeling quite smug with herself, so that when Pablo had returned, she wasted no more time there, but quickly selected a horse to ride, and pleading that it was now time for breakfast, she thanked him, and quickly left to make her way back to the lawns.

Breakfast was being bought out on trays, and placed in the food warmers, just as she returned. *What good timing!* she thought.

Miranda congratulated herself as she located where George was and walked over to him. *What an eventful morning it's been.*

"Oh, you made it back just in time Miranda." George whispered, as he pulled out a seat for her, and she folded her legs elegantly as she sat down, and smiled her best smile at him.

"Oh, George you should see the horses. They are of the best stock and I can't wait to go riding. Wish you were coming!" she gushed. "Riding horses? No, not me my love. I shall be quite content here. I have news for you also." he said, and leaned in closer to whisper.

"You will think we're on our honeymoon tonight!" he chuckled.

"What do you mean George?" Miranda giggled a reply.

"Well, you just wait until you see our room. It is to die for! I have taken the liberty to hang our clothes, and I will hold the key seeing you are going out riding. Is that, ok?"

"Of course, thank you darling. That was very thoughtful."

Miranda jumped a little to the sound of the gong.

"I guess that is breakfast." George muttered. "Thank goodness, I am starving, and right on time too!" he said, as he glanced at his watch. "Shall we Miranda?" he asked, as he held out a hand for her.

Everyone seemed to converge at the same time at the trestle table groaning with the abundance of food, their appreciation obvious as conversations were struck up as they filed along the table.

Richard moved in close to George and Miranda. He inhaled the fragrance of her perfume to savor it for a moment before he spoke.

"Looks like a good spread George! I am beginning to think that I am better off not being here!" he joked.

"It certainly is a feast to brag about Richard, as usual Jenna has done you proud! You should pay her more." he chuckled.

Miranda looked quickly at Richard. "So, you pay your daughter to work here Richard?" she queried.

"Well actually I don't! Jenna just volunteers." he chuckled.

"But now that I think more about it, I guess a Christmas bonus is in order! I must talk to Julia!" he added. Though knowing quite well that Jenna was already subsidized from the estate.

But no-one else needed to know that. he thought.

"Yes, but from what I have seen, I'm sure Jenna would think she is worth more than a Christmas bonus Richard!" argued Miranda.

"Hmm! Really, you think so? Maybe! We shall see! What did you think of the horses Miranda?" he said trying to change the subject.

"Oh, Richard. You do have good taste in horses, I give you that!"

Jenna, and Jack led the horses from the stables down towards the kitchens, and Jenna went in to get their lunches and drinks. Jack helped her stow them in the saddlebags, just as Julia arrived.

"Good timing mother. I have checked your horse and all is good! I guess we only have to decide now on which route we take?"

Julia was hell-bent on trying out the jumps, and Jenna was also. So, it was a unanimous decision when Jack agreed wholeheartedly, and they set off, deciding to take the trek up to the cliffs overlooking the ocean, then to head inland towards the paddock that was set up for horse-jumping. They would have their lunch there.

Jenna led the way as the winding track was narrow to start, and they followed it up to the cliff-tops. Julia Temple rode close to her, and Jack trailed behind them.

"Comfortable mother?" Jenna asked, as she turned to speak.

"I certainly am Jenna, though just as well I have my thick saddle and blanket, it does cushion the ride, and when we get to the jumps, I will be pleased I have it then!"

As they reached the summit, the track widened, so Julia and Jack moved their mounts up to ride beside Jenna, and when they topped the rise the brilliance of the ocean captivated them. Julia gasped.

"Oh, what joy! How wonderful I haven't been here for some time."

"Now, that is what I call a top view!" uttered Jack in amazement. "How lucky you are to live here. It really is beautiful up here!"

"It is one of our best views Jack, which is why we rode this way first. Just look at the different colours of the ocean, and how big the waves are today. You can see the coastline for miles up here! We will follow it a short way before the turn-off, and you shall find the beauty does not stop here Jack! So, if everyone agrees we will take a break soon to have a cuppa before heading inland, and it will give you a chance to rest for a while mother!"

"Thank you, Jenna, it has been quite a while since I have ridden. So yes, a break will be greatly appreciated." stated Julia.

Jack was enjoying the ride immensely, but when they came upon a secluded place by a stream, he thought it was perfect there to have morning tea. "How about we stop here Jenna?"

"It is perfect here, with logs to sit also, so yes, it will be fine Jack!"

Jack dismounted, and firstly helped Julia down from her horse.

"Thank you, Jack, you are so thoughtful." Julia uttered.

He smiled at Jenna as he took the reins from her, and she smiled back. Then he led all the horses to the stream to drink while Jenna attended to the food. After relaxing they left taking the inland track.

Back at the homestead though. With breakfast finally exhausted, Richard was trying hard to get the couples organized who were going out riding with him and Miranda. He was getting anxious to get away now. He had been very patient, and had gone through the motions of idle conversation. But, right now, this minute, there was only one thing on his mind, and that was to finally have some alone time with the exquisite Missus Miranda Delvin. "Hurry along now people!" he urged. "We should have been at the stables by now! We haven't even selected our horses yet, and the day is getting away!" he stressed, as he cast his eyes on Miranda.

She was all aglow with pure excitement, and it was infectious amongst the others. "Are you ready to leave Miranda?" he asked. "Absolutely, let us go Richard! Ever since I saw the horses before breakfast, I've been anxious and can't wait to ride the one I picked!"

He chuckled, then he turned to speak to George. "Come on, walk with us George, and tell us what your plans are for the day?"

George smiled. "Yeah sure! Well, we have all decided on a tennis match before lunch. Then maybe a swim later, then we will settle down to a game of poker. I think Henry is looking forward to that!"

"Good, you are all sorted then!" Finally at the stables, Richard watched his guests Jim and Anne Collins, Charles and Betty Worth select their mounts, then Pablo led the black, and appaloosa stallion over. He nodded at Pablo, and spoke. "Are you sure you want this horse, Miranda? How well do you ride? He tends to get frisky!"

She laughed, that throaty laugh, thrilling in the confrontation as her eyes menaced his in reply. "Yes, I know! It's always the stallions who get frisky Richard! That is no worries to me, I can handle it!"

He gulped, and looked to the others but they were talking, and didn't hear Miranda, and he sighed with relief as looked back at the cheeky grin on Miranda's face. Already she was teasing him. *This is going to be some interesting day, I bet. You won't know what hit you, Miranda Delvin!* he thought and chuckled as he smiled back at her.

It was a lovely trail they took through the bushland, and Richard pointed out some topics of interest of birds nesting, and he pointed out the wildflowers in bloom, then they were at a crossroad where there was a cave to explore, and his guests dismounted.

"Jim!" said Richard. "You guys can explore the cave here, there are torches in your saddlebags, and then continue along this trail. It takes a swoop around, then back to the stables. You have been here many times before so you know which way to go but Miranda hasn't been here before, and there is something I want to show her!"

"We will visit the cave on the way back and catch up with you, but if you are not there, we meet back at the homestead. So, we will be taking the other path on a different route. Are you ok with that?"

"Sure Richard! You should take Miranda down to the creek to show her the falls if you like, we may be here a while. We may even have morning tea here after we have searched inside the cave! Anne is interested in doing that." replied Jim.

"Great, it sounds like a plan! Strangely, but I intend doing just that. Come Miranda, we go this way!" he urged, as he pointed the way.

Richard set the pace at a trot but Miranda urged her mount into a canter. The stallion reared, but she controlled it effortlessly and laughed as he pulled strongly to canter past, and shot into the lead.

"Have a care!" Richard called out. "You don't know that horse!" But it fell on deaf ears as Miranda just laughed, and urged the horse on even more so. She sat up very straight in the saddle, and the only movements were her commands to guide the horse. Richard could not help but admire the way she rode. *She looks quite at home on that stallion. I'll bet she learnt to ride as a child.* he suddenly realized.

He urged his own mount on now, so as to not lag behind, but he was really enjoying just watching her. In no time they reached the bank of the creek, and he rode up alongside her. "Follow me down Miranda!" he said. "There is a small path down to water's edge, but it is hard to find, but I want to show you something special."

He reined in on a sandy bank, dismounted and tied his reins to a large tree branch, then he took her reins and led her horse over to tie the reins. He chuckled as he stood beside her horse.

"That was quite a display of horsemanship then Miranda! I am very impressed. You must tell me later, how you acquired that talent?"

She tossed her head back to laugh at him. "Ah! Mister Richard Temple, there are many qualities I possess that may interest you!"

Richard grinned broadly. "I just bet there is, and I can't wait to find out! But come now, you won't want to miss this my lady!"

He lifted his arms up to help her down. As she raised a leg over the pommel, the slits in her skirt widened to reveal her pure, ivory smooth skin up to her thighs. He gulped as realization hit him.

There would be no underwear under that skirt, he just knew it! He was completely thrown. His mind was momentarily distracted for that instant. Then she was jumping down into his arms.

His legs buckled, and he thought he was going over, but luckily, he regained his footing to hold on to her strongly, pulling her close to his chest. Her closeness was the one thing he had dreamed about as her perfume filled his nostrils. Just to touch her was too much as he searched her beautiful face, and looked into her deep violet eyes, then her mouth was so very close, her red lips inviting with a wide-open smile, and he could feel her warm breath on his cheek.

He lowered his head a little and nuzzled her neck, then instantly his lips claimed hers quickly as he pulled her closer to him still. *Her lips are like velvet, so soft and just like rose petals!* he thought. Then in his urgency he became more demanding, and rougher still, as his tongue slipped intimately inside of her mouth, teasing and probing.

Richard was completely lost now in this moment of passion, and lifted her up higher. He held her very easily with one arm, his other hand unfastened the ribbons on her bodice and her breasts fell, free.

He lowered his head to suckle one nipple. Tenderly pulling, and tugging at it until he heard her groan but when she arched her back, his mouth covered her other nipple, nipping it gently until it stood proud. He expected her to speak. But no, instead she was gasping, and moaning with pleasure. So, his hand searched for the slit in her skirt and slipped his hand inside to caress the softness of her skin. He tugged frantically at the skirt trying to raise it over her thighs, but gasped when it pulled free. *I knew it, there is nothing underneath!*

His body stiffened, his urgency ten-fold now as he cupped her taut buttock in his hand and squeezed, but it was not near enough to sate his appetite, so he crept a hand between her thighs to softly stroke her most secret parts, then his fingers slipped inside her.

Richard immediately sensed her urgency, and his was more than matching hers so he gently lowered her to the sand. He stripped off his shirt and threw it on the sand, and lay Miranda on to it. Quickly, he discarded his boots and jeans, then with an enormous thrust he didn't think he possessed, he was mounting her with not only brute force, but with a desire of pure want that stunned him to the core, as he slipped inside her to a different world. It was a world of love, that he so needed, a closeness and bond he so lacked, as feelings of pure ecstasy washed over him, and he never wanted it to end. Then they both screamed out as one, their pain and passion combined.

He folded his arms tightly about her, trying to savor the feelings as he sort out her tender lips, and this time his passion was gentler.

Miranda stirred as the long kiss ended, and looked into the eyes of the handsome man hovering over her, and she shivered. Feelings that she thought had been long buried, had now re-surfaced. Their love-making was fierce, brutal even, with a wild passion portraying each other's needs. An obvious attraction between them eventually needing to be stilled as their appetites were fully sated. However, there was such tenderness as well, and something else she was not used to. *She knew for sure he felt the same as she felt right now.* It was a shock for Miranda to realize she simply hadn't loved before. All her relationships were pre-planned, and her need was not of love, but of money, and how she could prosper from the relationship. She never let anything get in the way of her plans, but now? She was in foreign territory, and really didn't know how to play this game. She knew she felt love for this man, and it frightened her.

Now, just one minute Miranda! she reprimanded herself.

Stick to the plan as usual and all will be good! Then she thought to herself. *But there is no harm in experiencing a little love along the way!* It could be an asset, and will make the task so much easier.

So, with that thought in mind she smiled her best smile, and her voice was a little husky when she spoke.

"Well, well! Who would have thought it? Such passion! You don't woo a lady first Richard Temple! You simply just take! But I do like a man who can take control!" she said, as she laughed.

Her laughter was a tinkle, another thing he loved about her.

"Now, just a minute lady. I didn't exactly hear you say stop!"

Her smile became cheeky, her voice husky with lust. "Oh! But I didn't want it to stop Richard. Let us say that we jelled well, and I wouldn't mind experiencing that again right this minute! That is, if you could summon up the energy?" she said, as she tilted her head.

He laughed at her cheek. "Are you serious?"

"I never say anything I don't mean Richard Temple!"

He shook his head in disbelief. "I just knew that we would be on the same page Miranda!" he stated in wonder before continuing.

"There is a small waterfall to explore, though there seems to be something much more appealing and of more urgency, I would like to explore a whole lot more! Come! I will take you somewhere more private Miranda." he uttered, as he held out a hand to pull her up.

She smiled that sweet smile at him as she took his outstretched hand, and he led her to a secluded area close to the falls.

"It really is beautiful!" stressed Miranda as she stood watching the water tumbling down over huge boulders into the creek.
"Hmm! I told you so. However! You my lovely, are the beautiful one, so all else pales in comparison! But do come along, time is of the essence. You see, I haven't had my fill of you just yet my lady!" Richard gushed as he pulled her close and kissed her demandingly.

Miranda seemed to melt into his embrace and kissed him back with the same urgency as he gently stripped off her remaining clothing until she was completely naked. He quickly made a place for them to lay down, and gently lowered her to the ground as he stripped off his clothing and lay across her body, and she could feel the hardness of him. She pulled him closer still as his hands roamed over her taut body, touching and squeezing gently, but his mouth was seeking the sanction of her aroused nipples, and he sucked.

She groaned and arched her body rigidly as it tingled with some alien feelings washing over her, and she relinquished all reality as she couldn't help but succumb to the sheer thrill of it all. She glided her fingers down his torso and urgently took him in her hands.

Their love making was repetitive. Each one trying to still the fires burning inside them, to sate an appetite that evolved between them. But it wasn't until much later when they had ridden their horses back to the cave entrance, dismounted to secure the reins to a post, and entered by the torch light, that the real conversations began.

They sat close together on a bench seat. Richard draped his arm around her shoulders, and he pulled her very close as he spoke.

"So, what now Miranda? You must know how I feel about you? I love you, and my mind is set on having you all for myself. There is just one problem. George, and your marriage! What will you do?"

Miranda squirmed, not liking to be put on the spot. If she learnt anything, it was not to disclose her feelings so she almost dismissed the question with her remark. "I will think of something!"

"Maybe, I should talk to George!" Richard offered.

Her eyes blazed in the darkness. "No, you will not. I will handle George and my marriage, myself Richard! Just leave it to me!"

"You had better do it, Miranda! As I am not sharing you. So, you must end it with George! Is that clear!" he stated in desperation.

"Crystal clear Mister Richard Temple!" she replied.

He wished that he could see her face as the remark seemed to be somewhat short, and he felt uncertain of her intentions. He had to make certain. Surely what they both just experienced was enough. However, he seemed to sense that Miranda's reply was guarded in some way, as to not disclose her intentions, and that worried him.

Richard was committed now, and when he committed, he never quit. Not on any subject, but this was different. This was about love! He had found love, and he wanted Miranda at any cost. He did not know her really, well not yet, though what they shared was enough proof for him. It was what he had been searching for. But for her? He wasn't sure! So now, he just needed a full commitment from her.

He looked her way, though he couldn't see her, but he was about to pursue the issue much further to find out her intentions, just as his mobile phone rang. So annoyed, he grabbed it quickly from his pocket, and looked at the screen. "It's Jenna!" he said absently.

"How strange for her to call me, I had better answer it!"

His face paled as he listened to Jenna in distress during the call.

"Good god Jenna are you serious, what needs to be done?"

He listened intently. "So, you have called them already! Good, what should I do?" he listened again. "Yes, I can do that! I will go straight away. I am at the cave, so it won't take me long to ride back, but make sure you don't move her. I will ring you when they arrive. What's that you say? Yes, a good idea. I will ring him, bye!"

Richard snapped the phone shut, and spoke hastily to Miranda.

"You are not going to believe this Miranda, but there has been a very bad accident, so I have to get back to the house pronto to meet the ambulance, but I must ring Pablo first!"

"Really Richard, what type of accident?" queried Miranda.

"It is my wife! She has fallen badly from her horse while clearing a jump, and she is unconscious. Jenna has called the ambulance, but I have to meet them at the house and direct them to the paddock."

Richard paused to take a breath before continuing. "Though right now, I must call Pablo to tell him to ride out and find her horse, as it has bolted from the jumping area with the saddle half hanging off it! God knows what damage has been done!"

Miranda smiled in the darkness. It came as no surprise to her at all, as a matter of fact she was expecting it, and she felt the sense of achievement that she always got after a successful outcome.

Then she spoke. "Oh dear, poor thing. Horses do tend to get hurt from such accidents, so you must act soon, and poor Julia too. You must go quickly Richard. So, don't you worry about the phone call. I shall call Pablo and explain what he has to do. You can't afford to damage such a fine horse. Just text me his number, and I just need to know where Jenna and Julia were at the time of the accident?"

"That is exactly right! You are a gem, so thank you Miranda. Just tell Pablo they were riding in the paddock where the jumps are. He will know where to go! I must rush, but will text you the number now. I'll catch you later at the house maybe!" then turned to leave.

"Yes, sure Richard!" she replied as she watched him mount up.

She couldn't stop smiling. Her little plans were coming together, just as they usually do, and she relished the task before her. *How conveniently this has panned out. Now to set a little fear into the heart of one Pablo Sanchez!* thought Miranda, as she scrolled for his number, and saved it. Then she laughed as she dialed his number.

Pablo picked up straight away. He listened as he heard the news. At first there was silence from him before he finally stammered a reply, but his face soon paled as he listened to Miranda speak. Then it twisted up in agony at the accusations she firmly stated, and his body started to shake with the sheer dread of it all of being exposed.

"Do as I say Pablo and it will remain our little secret! So, just take a different girth strap with you! Use it to replace the damaged one, and bury that out there. It is damaging evidence to you." she added.

Chapter Four

Jenna laughed as they cantered along. She could see the jumps all set out in the paddock but they were all anxious to get started so, when they reached the shaded seating area, no time was lost in dismounting. All they had to decide was, who was going first.

"If you don't mind Jenna and Jack, I would like to jump first, it's been so long. I guess you could say I am a little excited." said Julia.

"Of course, you can mother, what do you think Jack?"

"Fine with me Jenna." replied Jack.

"Excellent Jack! You will see an expert rider out there in action as mother used to compete in horse events before her accident."

"Away you go Missus Temple, you could put on a show for us!"

Julia laughed as she mounted her horse. "I will do my best Jack, but I guess it's like riding a bike after a long time, you never forget."

"Just watch her closely Jack. Mother is a professional, so she will circle the whole track first and look closely at the jumps, and when she decides to go, she will spring into action quickly."

"Wow, I guess we are in for a treat." offered Jack.

They stood side by side, and Jack put an arm around Jenna, and she leaned back against him. He turned her towards him and kissed her tenderly. She kissed him back with a passion she didn't know existed inside her, then suddenly she was easing him away gently.

"We are supposed to be watching, Jack!" she said, as she smiled.

He nuzzled her neck. "Yes, I know. Just making up for lost time. Look, your mother is half way around, doing just what you said!"

Jenna giggled from his touch. Then, at the precise moment she sensed her mother was ready, she stepped forward to look closer.

"What is it, Jenna?"

"I am not sure, but the saddle. Something doesn't look right!"

Julia was in a full canter now with the first jump looming. Each bound was altering her position on the horse, and Jenna screamed.

"Don't jump mother! Wait, just don't jump!" but her screams fell on deaf ears, as in her excitement Julia was urging her mount to lift. Then they were airborne, clearing the railings effortlessly. But that was where everything went wrong as the saddle slipped sideways, the horse bucked, and bolted, throwing Julia mercilessly to ground.

Jenna was frantic, and screamed. She climbed the fence and ran across the paddock, only to stop short near where her mother lay in a crumbled heap, bleeding from her wounds, and unconscious.

Jack was beside her in no time. "My god, is she alive?"

As Jenna knelt beside her mother, she breathed a sigh of relief as she felt a pulse, she looked at Jack. "Barely! But we do nothing Jack, don't touch her. I shall call for an ambulance, and she dug into her pocket for her mobile, dialed, and began speaking to someone.

"Ok, all done! They are on their way!" she said, as she completed the call. "But now I must call my father so he can direct them to us, and she dialed again. She was shaking, but she spoke intently with her father, being very precise, and trying to cover all issues.

Jack stared in awe, realizing there was a lot more to Jenna Temple.

Julia still lay unconscious out in the paddock. As Jenna crouched down close to her to check for a pulse once more, she sighed with relief when she found it. As she looked on helplessly, she couldn't help but notice her twisted body that was at an awkward angle.

Just how much pain can one person endure? she wondered. *Surely mother has been through quite enough already!* She realized then that if she pulled through this time, it would be a miracle. It seemed to her that this time, this accident has caused multiple issues, and who is to know exactly what is going on internally. Her thoughts faded as she spied the ambulance coming down the track, and she waved.

Richard was first out when the driver stopped the van.

"Whatever happened Jenna? It is not like Julia to fall." he asked, as soon as he walked up beside her.

"I am not sure father! But I did notice something strange about the saddle just as mother was about to jump. It just didn't look right. It was crooked as if it was slipping sideways, or something."

"I see! Well, you will have to get that checked when Pablo brings it back with the horse. Miranda is calling Pablo to go and get them."

Jenna stood and faced her father. "Even so father, I think mother would sense something wrong with the saddle, and if a loose girth strap, she would have knowledge on that too I am sure, and how to handle the situation. It has to be more than that, maybe the horse! I must question Pablo thoroughly! I am grabbing at straws here!"

"I tend to agree Jenna. In that case you had better check it out, and the horse too. You just never know! Now how is your mother?"

"Will do! It is not looking good for mother at present I'm afraid. She is still unconscious, so an obvious head injury from the look of that cut, or it could be concussion, and she could also have multiple fractures. Let's hope there is no internal bleeding." replied Jenna.

"I see! I had better go with her in the ambulance, unless of course you want to go, but I must tell my guests what has happened here!"

"I will have to cancel their stay for tomorrow, so I shall need to contact the bus driver to collect them in the morning." Richard said.

"Jack and I will go with mother in the ambulance father. Maybe you could come and collect us at the hospital afterwards, that way you can stay to notify your guests of the events, and the bus driver"

"Yes, that will be the best idea, Jenna. I will be there in a couple of hours. Is that okay? It will give me time to organize everyone."

"That will be just fine, but don't rush. Spend a little time with your guests, as there will be a lot of tests to be done no doubt."

Richard watched as the paramedics lifted Julia onto a stretcher and eased her into the van. His mind was racing. *What if she does not survive?* A wicked thought crossed his mind though he dismissed it quickly as something else disturbed him. *If she doesn't make it, then what happens?* Suddenly, he realized for the first time that he didn't even know if Julia had made a current will. If so, where the hell was it kept? But more importantly, would he be on it? That was the big question considering their circumstances. The Estate passed down to Julia from her family. She had made sure it was in her name only.

He just had to find out, but how? Julia was a very private person, and she would go to great lengths to conceal that information. *I must look into that!* he decided, then he looked up to signal to the ambulance driver to wait as he noticed they were ready to pull out.

He opened the door to climb into the spare seat. "Drop me up at the house please mate, I'll drive to the hospital later." he muttered.

"Yeah sure!" said the driver.

At the house Richard got out quickly, then he waved to Jenna through the back window before he left to speak with his guests.

He spoke to them all as one to inform them of the accident, and of his plans to shorten their stay. Everyone was so understanding, and offered their best wishes to him and Jenna, and offered to assist in any way, but Richard thanked them, and said that all was sorted.

Then he looked to where Miranda was standing with George, so he walked towards them, and he could not escape the smoldering eyes of Miranda as she searched his face. He could still feel her body close to him, and could smell the sweetness of her breath on his face and her perfume seemed to linger like a memory in his nostrils, and his body stirred with the want of her. He spoke to George first as he walked up beside them. "Hi George, I can't tell you how sorry I am about this. I know how you were looking forward to the break, so you will have to make the most of today and tonight old mate!"

"I feel so sorry for poor Julia, she really has enough to cope with as it is, but this will set her back some. Can I help?" George asked.

"Yes, it will George! That is if she survives, and we won't know any results for some time, so I must go into the hospital soon to find out what is happening, and to bring Jenna and Jack back home. So, seeing you have offered, could you babysit this lot for me, and also check with cook about dinner? Maybe ask her to put meals away for myself, Jenna and Jack. I must leave in a while George!" he said.

"Certainly Richard, I am only too pleased to help out, that will be an easy task. I shall go in and speak to the cook now if you like?"

"Good man, that's a good idea!" answered Richard.

"Right, I'll be on my way right now Richard, and good luck at the hospital." he said, as leaned in to kiss Miranda. "I won't be too long Miranda, just need to get our dinner sorted, and I'll be back!"

"No rush George darling, Richard will leave me with the others! Won't you Richard?" she asked him as she produced her best smile.

Richard grinned at her, then replied to George. "Yes, go George. Miranda will be fine. I am sure the others will take care of her!"

He waited until George left, then moved in close, and whispered to Miranda. "You must break all ties with George now Miranda!"

Miranda glared at him. "Leave it be Richard. I have ideas, so I'll handle George my own way, in my own time. Don't hassle me!"

His mouth widened in response, hoping she meant that. "I am not hassling you, Miranda. I just want it fixed so it's over and done with. Just how will you handle it my lovely, prey tell?" he queried.

Miranda smiled broadly. "Oh, that is for you to find out Richard! So, just leave that to me. I have a special way of dealing with critical situations Mister Temple! I have just attended to one crisis for you!"

"You have? How do you mean? I don't follow your meaning!"

"Well, you wouldn't Richard, because you didn't see! However, I did! I certainly did!" she chuckled. "Now it has been dealt with in my own special way. You will be thanking me later, that's for sure!"

"I'm still not with you Miranda! Just what did you see? What is the crisis that you dealt with, and why will I be thanking you?"

"My, My! A lot of questions Richard! Never mind, I shall tell you simply this now. You shall have no more problems in future with Pablo Sanchez. You see, it was Pablo who slashed the girth strap to cause Julia's accident, and I actually saw him do it! So, I guess you could say we had a heated discussion, but now he is beholding to me. He'll do whatever I say to keep me from disclosing his actions!"

Richard's face turned red as he spluttered his reply. "It was? Are you serious Miranda? These are bad allegations, so criminal too!"

"Very serious Richard! I never joke of my discoveries! However, you can be assured I have dealt with it in the most severe way!"

Richard could not believe the ruthlessness of the woman, though he had to admire her tenacity, and he wanted to know more now.

"So, tell me about it, Miranda!"

"Ok! When I went to the stables to select my horse for the ride, I heard Pablo on the phone taking orders, then I saw him use a knife on the girth strap. Later I checked the damage and took photos. You told me to call him after the accident, so I enlightened him, and said if he does what I say it remains our little secret! To replace the girth strap, and bury the damaged one as its damaging evidence to him!"

Richard gaped at her. "You done what Miranda? That my dear, is blackmail. I would think to sack him instead of stooping to that!"

Her laugh was a tinkle, as she looked up at him and replied, but her eyes were deadly serious. "Oh! It is only a little blackmail dear Richard, but worthwhile in the long run. I wouldn't be sacking him at all, rather using him to your advantage. You will find I am right!"

He couldn't help smiling, her laugh had that effect on him, and it was her devious ways that got to him, but he could see her point, and he pondered on it, a while. "Hmm! Yes, you could just be right Miranda! I'll go along with that for now. Maybe we should inform the police of his involvement. It is attempted murder after all!"

"No! No police Richard. Just leave Pablo Sanchez to me, and you will find he will do anything you ask of him!"

Richard suddenly looked serious. "Anything?"

"Definitely, I would bet on it, Richard! So, do we have a deal?"

"I guess we do Miranda!" he whispered as he pulled her close.

She snuggled into him as he claimed her lips, but her mind was working overtime. *Oh! My goodness me Miranda. You do have special talents.* she thought. Then the kiss ended, and he held her back and his eyes seemed to crinkle at the corners as a smirk spread his lips.

"You do realize Miranda? This deal concretes our relationship!"

Her laugh was a tinkle with her reply. "Then lock it in Richard!"

Once again Julia Temple defied all odds to regain consciousness, and survive, to be alive and as well as could be expected despite her severe injuries. As Jenna listened to the doctor explain what the tests showed, she shook her head in disbelief. A broken collar-bone, broken pelvis, a broken ankle, and severe concussion. Her internal organs were fine with no bleeding, the head scan showed nothing only a deep cut to her head needed stitches. She was still concussed, but the doctor was optimistic for a full recovery in time.

"Thank you doctor!" Jenna said, as she turned to Jack. "Can you believe that Jack? Mother is going to be alright! It will just take her a while to recover from her injuries, and I guess she will be in a lot of pain, but at least she has survived another accident once again!"

Jack smiled. "I guess she is one tough lady Jenna. But you know what? I think you too are of a similar nature, and you have the same resilience. Both very strong women, and I admire that!" he said. "It is what I love about you most. Your strength and resilience!"

"Why, thank you Jack. I will take the compliment, though I don't see the need for it. It is just how I was brought up, so no big deal!"

"It may not be a big deal to you, as you say. But Jenna, it is a very important part of your demeanor, and most people recognize that."

"Yes, I do realize that, Jack. I can sense when I am being studied. I felt it today, especially when I met missus Miranda Delvin. There is something about that woman I haven't quite worked out yet, but I will in time, that is for sure. I am usually good at judging people!"

A knock on the door turned their heads, and Richard entered.

"Hope I am not interrupting, is it alright to come in now?"

"Hi father. Yes, come in., the doctor has just left us."

"So, how is the patient doing now, any results yet?" he asked.

"I guess you could say that we have good news." replied Jenna, as she explained to her father what the doctor had told them. "It will be a long road, but mother is expected to make a full recovery."

"Excellent news. All the best Julia!" he said as he looked at her. Julia gazed at him through groggy eyes, but there came no reply.

Richard shuffled his feet in embarrassment for the shun, but he managed a smile as he added. "You must be exhausted Julia so God speed. I won't hang around then, but, if you need anything, just let me know." Once again, he experienced that feeling of hate in the pit of his stomach, but tried to ignore it, and turned to Jenna instead.

"I have much that needs to be done, and guests to entertain!"

"Are you both ready to go home with me now Jenna?" he asked.

"Yes, certainly father. Mother will probably sleep now as she has had her dinner and medication and we are both hungry because we didn't get any lunch today! I will say goodnight for now mother, and I will return tomorrow with some clothes for you." said Jenna as she tapped her hand. It was pointless to try and kiss her, as she knew her mother felt bad about anyone touching her face.

On arrival at the homestead again, Richard noticed that in his absence, his guests had been helping with the dinner arrangements, and as he walked into the kitchen George smiled as he spotted him.

"Oh, you are back. Good timing, I must say Richard. Cook is just about to serve, so I am waiting for them to take the platters outside, and I am to serve the drinks. I am the newly appointed bar-tender, would you believe it?" he laughed. "We are all organized here, and the girls are putting on a little music, so it looks like we will party tonight. How is Julia, is she conscious? Nothing too serious I hope?"

"Sounds great George, so pleased you are enjoying yourself, and yes! Julia has rallied once again! She is awake now. So, if all is ok, I will go out to speak to the others, and see you out there!"

Once outside Richard noticed Miranda and headed her way. "I am sorry about the shortened stay, but I will make it up to you!"

Pablo was in an absolute mess. His whole body was shaking, and as he faced his mother, he was finding it hard to concentrate. So, the predicament he was in as he tried to relate it, became a stutter.

"Get a grip on yourself boy!" scolded Melita as she stared at him.

"But mother, you don't understand! I did what you asked, and now it has caused a very bad accident, and the horse has bolted!"

"Good! Then she got what she deserved then. Stupid old cow!"

"But she could be hurt really badly!"

"Tough!" spat Melita. "Remember we get nothing if she rules!"

Pablo frowned at that, but summoned up the courage to explain further. He knew his mother would be furious. "We have one small problem mother. I was seen!" he said timidly. "Somebody saw me!"

"What! Who saw you?" his mother screamed. "You stupid boy!"

He looked up in fear of her. "One of the guests saw what I did, and I know it is true what she says, because she explained it exactly how, and where it was done. So, now she is blackmailing me, and threatening to tell someone if I don't do as she asks!" he whined.

Melita was furious, and she glared at Pablo. "Stupid, stupid boy. Who is this person? What is it she wants you to do?" she asked.

"I have to go and find the horse, and bring it and the saddle back, but I know what state the saddle will be in. She suggested I would have to replace the girth strap with another, and bury the damaged one. She said it would be our secret. Do I trust her, or what? What if she tells? I think her name is Miranda a guest of Mister Temple's."

"Well, it seems very straight forward to me Pablo. What she says is exactly what you have to do! Now stop looking so guilty, and go and get the job done! We'll deal with this Miranda at a later date! She won't tell! Do you know why? Because it sounds as if Miranda may have dabbled in foul play herself to stoop to blackmail. It does seem so strange that she wants to cover up your involvement in the incident! *But, why is the question?* We shall have to find out Pablo!"

"Do you really think so mother?" Pablo questioned. "She looked like a really nice lady and so very pretty. That is why I found it hard to believe the words she spoke on the phone. Then her demands, so blatant, as if she has a hold on me somehow, and I feel threatened."

"Ah! Don't be fooled by a pretty face Pablo. They are the worst! So, yes! I really believe she has done this before, and we should play her game for now, but things will change, you will see! Besides you are going to get blamed for the accident anyway! But the girth strap is damaging evidence, so you must get rid of it, then replace it."

"They will come to check the saddle you know! So, have specific answers ready my boy, as there will be questions" Melita replied.

"Oh! My god, I didn't think of that." said Pablo in distress.

"Who the hell will question me mother? Not the police I hope?"

"No, it most likely will be Jenna or Mister Temple. So, just show them evidence of the horse and the saddle with the replaced girth strap. Do not mention the damaged one, and act ignorant! That will be our secret Pablo, the damage to the girth strap! So, as you bury it take particular notice if any further damage was done to the girth strap. I would bet on it, then report only to me as soon as possible."

"Pablo! It will be our only evidence against Miranda Delvin!"

Two weeks later came news George Delvin was dead. "A tragic accident!" reported a police officer as he spoke to Richard in his company's office. "His brakes must have failed! Or maybe he just lost control on the bend going around the cliff because the car was hurled over the crest then burst into flames. Nothing remaining of George Delvin I am afraid sir! But luckily, we could still read the number-plate from his car to know who it belonged to, so we went up to his house to notify his wife. She is rather in a bit of a state now Mister Temple, but she told me to contact you at this company, and said George worked here with you. Do you think you could go up and visit her, as I don't think she has any family, or anyone to care for her?" asked the constable.

"Yeah sure! I'll go to visit her. I really can't understand as George is meticulous about his car. Doesn't even get anyone to service it, as he does it all himself. So, I don't think there would be a problem with his brakes, and as for George losing control, that is strange. He has lived on that cliff-top for many, many years and he is the most reliable and careful driver I know, so he wouldn't be speeding, just the opposite in fact as he knows the road so well!"

"Odd! But thank you Mister Temple. If there is further evidence then I will let you know. Someone will be going out to scour around the site today, and to try and get to the remains of the deceased, but we don't suspect any foul play at this stage, just bad luck I think, but something might turn up. You just never know. Now I must get back to the station, excuse me mister Temple!" said the constable.

Richard watched him until he had walked through the doors, and disappeared, then he grabbed his jacket and left his office, and took the elevator down to the carpark. As he unlocked his car and got in, his thoughts turned to George. *Such a good friend he was.* He missed him already, but something gnawed at his stomach as he couldn't help but think there was a good reason for his death, but what? Then he thought of Miranda and the words she had said.

"Leave it be Richard. I have ideas so I'll handle George my own way, in my own time. Don't hassle me!"

How would she handle it? By leaving him of course, what else? He sat very still, but deep in thought, as he imagined other ways.

Surely not, no not Miranda! No way would she be involved. What a preposterous thought! *She is his wife for god's sake!* So, how could I even think that? *What the hell is wrong with me lately?* he wondered as he gunned the engine to drive out of the car-park.

He drove towards the highest peak and wondered why on earth George liked living there. As he drove around the tight bends he noted where the accident took place as it was police taped up. So, he stopped to get out of the car, and looked over the edge. He shook his head sadly. *What a loss, such a damn shame!* As he drove on to the house, he realized. *There'll be no evidence from that wreckage!*

Miranda slid the drapes aside so she could look out, then noticed the car approaching the driveway. She knew exactly who it was, so she closed the drapes and desperately tried to compose herself. Her plan was to play innocent, and that role was no foreign trait of hers.

She purposely stalled until the doorbell had peeled three times, then she made sure her eyes were misting over before she opened the door. It was something that always worked for her. She just had to remember a certain unpleasant time in her life that immediately brought tears to her eyes. It happened like clock-work every time.

"Oh Richard! Thank God you are here!" she exclaimed, sobbing uncontrollably as she rushed into his arms. "I am not coping at all!"

Richard held her close, and he could feel her body trembling, so at once he made his decision. "Go and pack your bag Miranda, you are coming to live with me! We will talk later when you get settled."

Miranda couldn't believe her luck. *This is so much better than my plan as now I don't even have to explain anything.* she realized.
She looked up sadly, then meekly asked. "For how long Richard?"

"This my love, will be a permanent arrangement! 'Oceanview' will be your home in future, and you will love it there!" he replied.

Six weeks after the accident Julia Temple was finally discharged from the hospital, and the taxi driver helped her into the cab.

She had graduated to a walking stick, so gone were the crutches, her body was healing, but she suffered pain and an awkward limp.

Jenna had opened her balcony windows and doors to air out her room. Now she walked across the lawns, then paused to wait inside the gates for her arrival. She was concerned, as a lot had happened at 'Oceanview' in her mother's absence, and Jenna wanted to break the news to her gently. George Delvin was deceased now, taken by a tragic car accident, and her father had arranged his funeral some weeks ago. George was no longer a partner in her father's business as in his demise all his property, house and his shares in her father's business had gone to his wife Miranda. But that was not the half of it, and she knew her mother would not approve with what she had to tell her. Especially the news of Miranda Delvin living there with her father permanently, and was making her presence felt too from what she could make out by the occurrence in the kitchen earlier.

She could not believe the cheek of the woman. Jenna had been in the foyer, but could hear the very loud arguing going on in the kitchen between Miranda Delvin and the cook Paula Hastings.

Miranda was laying down the law to Paula, and demanding that her personal preferences be made, however Paula was so adamant, and was standing her ground, and Jenna heard her quite clearly.

"I don't think that will be happening Missus Delvin. However, I shall check with Jenna if that pleases you!" offered Paula.

"No, you will not check with Jenna, cook. You will do as I say!"

"What is going on here Missus Hastings?" asked Jenna sharply as she walked into the kitchen. "Missus Delvin would you leave the kitchen please, but just wait in the foyer as I want to speak to you!"

Miranda stared at her. "No, I will not wait in the foyer to speak to you Jenna. I came in here to order the food I like, so anything you would like to say to me, you may say it to me right here. I am here with authorization from your father, I will have you know!"

Paula looked embarrassed. "Sorry Jenna." she said. "But... she tried to continue, but Jenna interrupted her.

"It is alright Missus Hastings! I'll speak to you later!" Then she turned to face Miranda Delvin, and spoke. "I don't usually discuss staff issues in their presence Missus Delvin, but as you wish!"

"Firstly! You have no place at all in this kitchen! You are a guest here. Guests do not enter this kitchen and they certainly do not have a say in what is cooked here. That is my job! I will not have outside interference with my staff! Is that understood?" Jenna stressed.

"You will not tell me what I can, and cannot do!" said Miranda.

"I can, and I certainly will Missus Delvin! Simply because I have total control in running this household and also my staff! This is my home, not yours! So don't think you can come in here to change it!"

Her Mind SCREAMS MURDER

Miranda's eyes smoldered. She glared and shot daggers at Jenna. She opened her mouth to complain again, but Jenna carried on.

"Which brings me to my second point! My father has no interest in running this property, and has left any decisions up to me, and that is how it works here. 'Oceanview' has been run by me for quite a long, long time, especially since my mother's accident. It is my mother's property after all so, what she says goes. My father has no authorization to send you in here making demands! Is that quite clear? So, that concludes our discussion Missus Delvin! Please leave the kitchen, and do not come in here again. You know the way out!"

Miranda gaped in disbelief. *Really? Her mother's property she just said.* "You are so undesirable after all Miss Jenna Temple, but you be warned, this is far from settled. I shall speak with your father!"

"You do what you like Missus Delvin, but it won't change anything! I would also like to warn you as well that I will be speaking to my mother about you. However, if you are the instigator of any further problems here, I'll have you removed from the premises!"

Miranda was furious, and not used to being put in her place, so she wheeled around and stomped out, cursing madly as she left.

Jenna ignored her, and turned to face Paula Hastings whose face had blanched a little from Jenna's fury as she began to speak to her.

"Carry on Missus Hastings, so pay no attention to her. You have only one boss, that is me. Just remember that please!" said Jenna. "Just let me know if you have further problems, and I will settle it!"

I just bet you will young Jenna Temple! thought Paula, as she gaped at her squarely. She couldn't believe what she just witnessed. *I had better tell the others about this. They will know in future not to take on Jenna! She is as ruthless as!* she mused, as she replied.

"It is as I thought it would be Jenna, so no problems. I will know what to do if there is a next time! Though, I really do doubt it." she chuckled, and Jenna smiled as she looked at her.

"Now, on a lighter note Missus Hastings! My mother is coming home from hospital today! So, I would require something suitable cooked for a celebration lunch. Just for her, and myself please. Let's say, about 12.30pm, and served up on her balcony!"

"Consider it done Jenna!"

"Thank you, Missus Hastings." she said, and smiled as she left.

Julia's cab pulled into the driveway, and Jenna was thankful for the distraction from her thoughts, so she opened the front gates and waited until the driver had helped her mother out of the cab, then she hugged her. "Welcome home mother. It is so very good to see you recovering. You had me worried for a while there. Come, I have lunch organized for us up on the balcony. I have much to tell you!"

"Hello Jenna. I must say it is good to be home, and lunch sounds good, especially a home cooked lunch. I am recovering quite well actually, my doctor is pleased with my progress, and I have had the best of care. Everyone fussed, and a physio worked with me daily. However, I am now anxious to talk to you also Jenna!" she replied. "I have had some time to think things through, and I have come to a huge decision. So, I will need your full co-operation my dear!"

Miranda Delvin was definitely not one to let things lie. Rather she preferred to have the upper-hand at all times, and now she sat frustrated in her room adjoining Richard's. She looked around the room in desperation not knowing which way to turn, and thought. My god mister Richard Temple *you have some explaining to do. This isn't your property at all!* Rather, it is your wife's estate, though you would be on her will as beneficiary, or would you? *I must find out!* As your daughter seems to rule here with an upper hand! She is so ruthless! It'll take all my finest efforts to best her. *But your turn will come Jenna Temple!* Her mind was in turmoil then it came to her. She jumped-up. *Of course, the will!* she laughed. There'll be paperwork somewhere, *and I bet I know just where?* Then she raced out the door.

She took the outside flight of stairs up to the balcony above, and she knew exactly which room it was because Richard had told her it was the first one opposite the staircase down to the beach.

Miranda took in the surroundings and noticed all the windows were open, but were screened, and the French doors were ajar with the screen door pulled across. She just couldn't believe her luck. All was quiet, so she tried the screen knob and it slid across. Slowly she slipped inside the room, and looked around quickly as she listened for any movement, but there was none. There was a bay window where orchids grew in planters on the window sills, complimented by a full table setting to take in the views. This incorporated a living room and an extensive library with rows and rows of books and an office. But it was the other room opposite that she wanted, the bedroom. She moved across the floor effortlessly and having done this before, she would be swift, but thorough as she knew where to look, but each place was empty of all paperwork, and every drawer was locked. She went back into the office, and the huge drawers in the desk were locked, and solid. Miranda knew exactly what tools she would need, and made a mental note to come back again when no-one was home. Then she slipped out to the balcony.

"Who the hell are you?" came the screech, and Miranda froze. A frail veiled figure with an awkward gait used a walking stick to edge towards her. "You were in my room!" came the accusation.

"Sorry, I was just seeing if anyone was home. Richard said you lived up here. We are friends and he has generously let me stay here since my husband was killed in the car crash. I thought you must have been inside when the door was open, I wanted to meet you!"

"Well, I certainly do not want to meet you!"

"I am so sorry for the intrusion!" Miranda said sweetly.

"Nobody goes into my room, not ever! Do you get that?"

Julia Temple yelled at her in question. "What did you steal?"

"Oh, I didn't steal, see!" and she placed her hands palms up, and added. "But yes! I do get that. I am so very sorry, but they told me you were handicapped, and coming home from hospital" she lied.

Julia pointed to the stairs with her walking stick. "Go now! Or I call the police! Furthermore! Any hussies of Richard's don't belong here in my homestead, especially sneaky, sly ones. So, I really don't need to know you. Just get off my balcony, and get out of my house! I do hope that is quite clear!" she stated as Miranda smirked.

Miranda was not having a good morning. This was twice in one morning she had been dressed down, and basically told where to go, and both times by two generations of 'Temple' women. *Ah, but we will see who has the last laugh ladies.* she promised herself.

Julia watched her leave, then she turned painfully to limp back towards the lunch table she had left when she heard a noise down the balcony. She eased herself into the soft cushions, and sighed as she stood her walking stick up behind her seat. Jenna had just gone down to check on their lunch so she would be back any time. Julia thought more about the woman. She did recall seeing her at their property on the day of her accident, but it was only very briefly in passing. It was when she was walking back from the stables to the house, she had noticed her going in the direction of the stables. She didn't know who she was, only that she would have been a guest of Richard's. *Hmm! She was alone, so I wonder why she was going to the stables?* What would her purpose be? *Who said she could?*

Julia was puzzled as she knew the woman had not been to their property before, so if she was going out riding then she would have assumed that Richard or Jenna had organized the mounts, so there would be no need for a stranger to go to the stables.

Hmm! I think that is a bit odd, and cheeky really! Her thoughts were squashed when Melita approached the table with a huge tray.

"Lunch is ready missus!" came her voice in interruption. Melita seemed to be avoiding any eye contact with Julia. Her eyes were downcast when she spoke, Julia noticed, and she wondered why.

Obviously, there is no welcome home for me then. she thought. I can guess Melita still holds a grudge from our last argument no doubt, but before she could reply, Jenna spoke up from behind.

"Just put it all on the side table please Melita, and I will serve!"

"Ok!" said Melita in relief, and she put the tray down quickly, not wanting to converse with Julia Temple or Jenna, especially not about Julia's accident. Melita knew too much now. She was waiting on Pablo to report if there was other damage to the girth strap. If so, the tables would turn and proof against the dangerous Miranda.

"Oh Jenna! Thank goodness you are here now, as I have just had the worst confrontation with a woman called Miranda Delvin."

"Not you too mother! I had an issue with her this morning when she was giving orders to cook in the kitchen. I told her she had no business doing that, and I had to be quite adamant with her as I told her not to go in the kitchen again, but she wouldn't take no for an answer. So, what has she done now?" asked Jenna.

Julia looked at Jenna. "I caught her coming out of my room!"
"Are you serious? That is preposterous. I left your room open to air out. So, did you check your room for anything missing mother?"
"I was too shaken! Would you check for me? There is something else Jenna. I saw her going to the stables the day of my accident!"

Jenna looked thoughtful as if she was processing it all. "That is strange. I am not really liking this Miranda Delvin at all, as there is something more to her that I can't quite fathom out yet! You do realize she is George's wife mother? George was killed by having a very untimely accident, his car going over the crest not far from his house. Father arranged his funeral some time back now!"

"Oh dear, poor George! He is one person I liked a lot, how sad. But this wife of his. I also don't like her Jenna, and I told her to get off my property. I don't know what Richard will think of that seeing she is a friend in need, but I really don't care. I made my decision!"

"But a good one too I think mother as you will find she is more than a friend in need to father! I am so sorry, but you must know!"

Julia wasn't fazed at all. "Jenna, at this stage of my life, nothing would surprise me at all about your father. I do know of his affairs. I am sorry to have to tell you that, but I guess you already know?"

Jenna hung her head. "Yes, I do know, and too much I'm sorry!"

"Let us have our lunch Jenna before it gets cold. I have come to accept your father's infidelity for your sake, but now it is out in the open, I think things need to change. When we have eaten, I would like us both to go down to my room, and you can check it out. Then there are some very important things I need to discuss with you!"

"But firstly Jenna, while it is fresh on my mind. "On the day of my accident did you check my horse for injuries, and also especially my saddle for any damage or wear and tear?" asked Julia.

"Definitely mother! I went straight across to see Pablo when he brought your horse in and luckily no damage to your mare, and the saddle? Well, I was very meticulous with that as I needed answers to my questions also. Only because just as you were about to jump the hurdle, I yelled out not to jump as I noticed some malfunction as the saddle was slipping off. Strangely enough there was not one thing wrong with it, or the girth strap, so that remains a mystery! On the other hand, I just can't put my finger on it, but the girth strap looked different somehow to me. Strange, but I can't imagine why? However, I did give Pablo warning and a dressing down as he had saddled your mare, and I accused him of negligence, though I think his mistake was the girth strap wasn't tightened enough! That is the only reasonable thing I can think of, and Pablo was no help."

"Hmm! I am not so sure about that Jenna. As you know, I check my mount myself, and that girth strap was firm and intact, as were the other fittings. No! There has to be some explanation, and I think I know what Jenna! That is why now, this instant we need to talk!"

They sat in silence while they consumed their lunch, and then suddenly Julia grabbed her stick and stood up. "Follow me, Jenna!" she urged, then she limped badly down the balcony to her room.

Seated in Julia's best seating by the bay window, the orchids on display were magnificent blooms and Jenna realized why it was her favourite place, as she looked out at the ocean in all its splendor. She gasped with relish from the pure perfection of it all, as the sun played on the water, and the waves rolled into shore.

"Such beauty mother, the view is endless from up here!"

Julia sighed. "Yes Jenna, true. I have learnt to appreciate it every day however I have no way of knowing how long I can do that for!"

"Why not mother? It is the perfect place for you to recuperate, to be strong again. In no time you will be going down to the ocean!"

Julia looked hard at her daughter, and knew what she had to say would be very hard for her. *But she is also tough.* she thought.

"Jenna, what I have to talk about is quite serious so, I want you to pay attention. One day you may need to recall this information!"

"Mother, you are scaring me now. What is wrong, whatever are you thinking? What is it all about?" pleaded Jenna. "Just tell me!"

Jenna sensed something sinister was about to be revealed when their eyes met, and she looked deeply into her mother's green eyes.

Then her mother spoke so softly, she had to lean over to hear.

"Someone in this house is trying hard to kill me!" she whispered. "Please don't brush it off lightly Jenna! I can sense the vibes. If you think about it, each one of them may have good reason to get rid of me. I have had two serious accidents now, though this last one was no accident! Someone deliberately tampered with the girth strap!"

Jenna's face paled as she realized how serious this conversation was. "Goodness me mother, are you certain? Having an accident is one thing! But murder, from someone in this house! I am finding that a little hard to digest. Maybe you just need to rest!" she offered.

"Sorry Jenna, but my mind is made up, and I must get my affairs in order. Please listen carefully, as I will cover many topics, ok?"

"Yes mother, I hear you, so you have my full attention now!"

"Good! First things first. I plan to set it up tomorrow. You, Jenna, will become sole owner of 'Oceanview!' That includes all holdings, and all monies, as soon as you turn eighteen. My trustworthy city solicitor shall pen a letter to you at a city postal-box that I shall open for you, and also inform my bank of the same by letter. I will write a new will too and there will be two copies Jenna, he will hold one! For now, I shall continue to run things here, but should anything at all happen to me, then my solicitor will have my written authority to freeze all assets and monies until you are eighteen! Is that clear?"

Jenna gaped. "You can't be serious mother? What about father?"

"I am! I'm sorry Jenna, but I will be telling Richard and his hussy to move out. It will be in my will also. I have that right as I inherited this estate from my parents. Your father's signature relinquished all his rights, so it is solely in my name, but it will be yours one day! I don't trust a bank or a solicitor here to do the right thing if I am not here, and Richard may try to over-rule my will, so this is it!"

"Now, just hold on a minute mother. You have only come home from hospital today, and you are not strong enough!"

"Trust me Jenna, it must be done, and as soon as possible! All I need is for you to get me on that train, and I shall arrange it so that he picks me up in the city, and on my return to put me on the train. I'll get a cab home, if need be, then it will be done, and I can rest!"

"No way! I'll organize a cab for us to and from the station! Better still I could go into the city with you. It is the best idea after all!"

Julia frowned. "Definitely not Jenna! It must be kept a secret. The less you know is safer as it could be used against you. So, I can't tell you all you must know, not even the P.O. Box No., My plan is best!"

"A secret, and a plan! So, I can't tell anyone at all?" Jenna asked.

"No, Jenna you can't, I'm sorry! It will jeopardize your safety!"

"You're making it sound quite ominous mother. Are you sure it is necessary? What of the second copy of the will, where will it be?"

Julia smiled. "The other copy is for you Jenna, but not now! You will know when you turn eighteen that the time is right to try and find it! Then you must play a game, a treasure hunt if you like!"

Jenna laughed. "Oh! Come on mother, are you serious?"

"I never joke about money or of my estate Jenna. It will surprise you to see the worms come out of the woodwork wanting a share! So, as I have planned, it will be smoothly organized for you to take over. This is what you must do! So, are you ready for instructions?"

"I guess so mother, thank you! Providing this is what you want, but I can't imagine anyone wanting to kill you." she said hesitantly.

"Good, thanks accepted! However, I have this gut feeling Jenna, and I must act now, just in case. You can be assured I have thought this out Jenna, please follow me now!" Julia grabbed her stick, and stood up. She beckoned Jenna to follow her, then ambled to the very end of the bookshelves where she plucked a novel from its home.

"This is the oldest book I own Jenna but one you must remember as there will be no paper trail to prompt you. Only two things are most vital to remember Jenna! This book, and my favourite one!"

"The Tale of Two Cities!" said Jenna, as her mother held it up. "I know it well, and of course I know your favourite one!" she added.

"I know you do but The Tale of Two Cities, remember well! You must look for it when the time comes. Inside I'll leave a clue to the next hiding place revealing a clue to your final quest…To find a key that unlocks a post-box containing deeds to the house and my will!"

They left home early the next morning as soon as the cab arrived to take them to the rail station at Blue Bay. Jenna noticed that the train was already at the station, and she made sure her mother was safely on the train and comfortable before she left her compartment.

"Just ring me when you are returning mother. I will be staying in Blue Bay for the day to wait for you." she said on leaving.

"Yes, Jenna I will. I shall hope to get on the next train back. What I have to do won't take long. See you then!" she said, and waved.

Jenna strolled down to the pier where she found a coffee shop, so she went inside to order breakfast. They only had time for coffee earlier, but Julia had packed food, and drink for herself.

As she sat by the window looking out over the Bay, millions of thoughts flitted through her mind. *What if my mother is correct?* she mused. *So, am I in danger too? Oh, surely not!* No-one at 'Oceanview' could be so bad, *or could they? There have been nasty arguments.*

But murder? That is something that happens to other people, isn't it?

She thought of Jack. They had become so close lately. *So, how was she to keep the secrets from him,* when every living minute they had to spare, they were together. They were planning a big outing for the following week, and Jenna couldn't wait. Jack had plans in place to obtain a job at the police station, and wanted to discuss future plans with her. Seems his idea of being a policeman was paramount, his stepping stone towards an ultimate dream to be a detective. *Hmm! Missus Jenna Rickard has a nice ring to it.* she thought, and smiled.

Her daydreaming held the bad thoughts at bay momentarily but deep down, Jenna felt a little scared for her mother as the more it crossed her mind, the more she realized that she could be right. She would have to be very vigilant in trying to protect her. *But how? She couldn't be with her every minute.* she sighed. *Things will work out, they usually do,* and my mother could be taking all these precautions for no reason at all. *Yes, that's it for sure!* she thought.

Chapter Five

Jenna was laying on her bed, just staring up at the ceiling. Covers discarded, her sheets all twisted from tossing and turning about, but sleep would not come… She was distraught… *Jack was coming early! He was never late!* she stressed. This was an important day. H*is eighteenth Birthday*, and they had so much to discuss. It could be a turning point in their lives, so they had planned a special day to go out horse riding, and the cook had packed a picnic lunch for them.

She punched her pillow in desperation as her eyes were drawn towards the bright shafts of the moonlight streaming in through the windows and keeping her awake, so she rose to draw the drapes. It was at that precise moment she heard it. A loud crack, outside in the stillness like timber falling or breaking, and a scream…though faint on the breeze, drifted up to her clearly…and she froze…

Slowly she inched the balcony doors ajar to peek out just as yet another cry echoed out. She froze again, and waited patiently until there was silence out there in the darkness before she crept furtively along the balcony towards the steps leading down to the beach.

Moonlight lit the wide steps. Cautiously, she paused on top of the stairs on the alert for any activity, but there was none. All was quiet, so she stepped down slowly. Then with more confidence her pace increased some-what though subconsciously she counted each step like always as she slid across on bare feet until her foot reached for the fifth step. *Or where it was supposed to be! For strangely she felt no purchase there.* Her body hovered momentarily, then swayed in momentum, unable to go backwards so, she then toppled forward.

Jenna realized her predicament too late, and screamed as she fell through the gap in the steps, to be hurled into oblivion and beyond.

So aware of the dangerous rocks below she curled herself into a tight ball as she fell, then cringed as she dreaded the hit. But to her surprise she felt her landing was cushioned by something, and she immediately struggled to rise in confusion, but in the moonlight her gaze fell upon a figure and the stone-cold lifeless eyes staring at her.

She screamed out loudly from the horror of it. *There is so much blood, too much blood!* were her thoughts, as she backed away, not wanting to be close to the body, as recognition gripped her. To look upon the body was just too painful to bear, so she stood rigid in the moonlight shaking and sobbing, then willed herself to look again.

Deep inside, great sorrow consumed her as she then confronted the body in disbelief. She shivered as the familiar eyes stared up at her, but then noticed something not quite right about the body. It was twisted at an awkward angle but something else also…*Oh no!*

There was torn skin with ragged edges and those well-known dead eyes stared up at her from the roughly severed head which lay slightly askew to the remaining corpse but a majority of body parts completely severed and hacked off badly were lying beside. she realized. She gagged.

Hot liquid rose up from her gut into her throat, and filled her mouth, but it all spurted out in a spray when she began to sob. Big, heart-breaking sobs, as she tried to distance herself on legs of jelly.

Silence ruled the night. Just one unmistakable sound, the surge of the ocean as huge waves broke, and rushed into shore.

It was a moonlit night, and the steps were bathed in its glow. But below, down amongst the deadly rocks, two figures stood arguing.

"Now! What to do with the witch? We can't bury her here, and it's a struggle to get up that steep hill to the carpark. We could be seen soon too! You took far too long getting her to the steps!"

"Wasn't my fault! It wasn't easy, she struggled like a demon!"

Julia Temple opened her eyes and painfully tried to move her legs, but they wouldn't move, and helplessly she groaned in pain.

"Wait! Look there, she is alive!"

Julia felt cold as darkness took over, when a shadow fell over her.

"She won't live long!" came the reply as a hand fell on a hatchet and it was lifted high. "Damn it! I thought she was dead!" and the hatchet buried deep into Julia's neck. There was no remorse, just a grunt and a curse. "Die!" as her bloody head lolled sideways.

"Nooo! No. How could you?" and the sobbing started.

"Don't be a such a cry-baby, she was a damn witch anyway! But we must move, and now we are forced to bag her. It is just as well I brought bags. You do that while I go and replace the step!"

"What did you just say? What the hell do you mean? Bag her?"

"Use the hatchet, chop her limbs off and bag her, easier to bury!"

"Oh no, I won't do that!" *I can't do that!*

"Well, you had better learn awfully quickly. Just be finished by the time I return from replacing that big step. It will be an effort to get the bolts in but a vital part of the plan so, it must be done right!"

"I could have done the step!" was the retort in frustration as the hashing and thrashing began, and blood spurted everywhere. So now, an additional sound to the surging of the ocean in the night was of the hatchet chopping, and mincing bone and flesh, and the sound of vomiting in the sand as a rosy hint of night sky threatened.

"Good god get a grip…the voice was suddenly cut off by some racket of a crashing noise above them, then came a scream. So, they rushed into the shadows just as a body fell from way up high.

"Now we've got more trouble! Someone else has fallen. My god, but it's Jenna! Oh Nooo! What will we do now?"

"So what? It's better still, we kill two birds with one stone! It just makes two of them to get rid of that's all, however it's proving to be an almost impossible task as time is getting away! In no time it will be light! So, just shut up, and let me think!"

"Yeah sure, you think you know everything! But what the hell are you doing now, what's with the rock? Oh no! Not that! Nooo!"

"Have to! Must finish the job here and later I'll work out a plan!" Jenna was stunned though her fall seemed to be cushioned, and she backed away in confusion wondering why, until the total horror of it set in as she witnessed the scene of the body before her. A shadow loomed to block out the moonlight as it closed in on her but she was unaware of being bathed in darkness as scalding tears blinded her.

Suddenly, she felt ill. She was totally consumed by sorrow now, devastated and stricken with grief. Her hands shook uncontrollably from shock, and she almost fainted as she vomited in the sand. So, ultimately, she was far too distressed and slow to realize there was movement right beside her. She was openly vulnerable as her tears forbade clear sight, and alerted far too late as she looked up to see a dark shadow looming beside her, and something solid came from no-where to smash heavily into her forehead to crack it wide open.

She reeled from the brute force of it as blood spurted profusely from her head, and her body swayed on lifeless legs. Suddenly she toppled forward, then collapsed in a heap as she fell heavily to the ground amongst the treacherous rocks.

Then the darkness closed in on her.

"Oh! You've killed her!" came the retort, but ignorantly ignored.

"Listen, we must stick to the plan it's important! Just finish your job! Then take the bags up past the water line to the dunes and bury them separate but deep, and have them buried by the time I return. It is vital I get that step back in place, we'll work out the rest later!"

"Yeah, sure we will, just go then and leave the dirty work to me!" Such was the extent of the gruesome task at hand, as if in a dream with bowed head and tears welling in repent with every strike to continue, until the labored breath behind proved reality once again.

"Damn, what a huge struggle to get that step back in! Just as well I had help. Not much time left 'til dawn so, we must move quickly! But what a right mess, so much blood around. You made a hash of that job! But more importantly, did you get all the bags buried?"

"Yep, done! Found a gap in a dune, led to a cave to dig holes in!"

"Better still! It will be harder to find anything there. Good work! Oh, hell no, what else can happen? Just look down the beach there!" In the semi-darkness but closing in, bright headlights lit up the sand along the water's edge as some vehicle slowly edged towards them.

"Quickly! Kick lots of sand over the blood! We don't have time to waste now as someone is coming! Run as best you can up that damn hill to the carpark with some gear! I'll bring the rest and the tools! Our driver better be there. Later it will still be early enough to return. So, if all is clear down here, then we will deal with Jenna!"

... *But when they returned. Jenna's body was gone!* ...

"What the hell? So, was she still alive then? Maybe we should have checked! Damn it all, where could she be? Maybe the house? Look! Police are combing the beach! Guess we'll find out soon enough!"

"I suppose so, but the not knowing is killing me! What the hell will we do if she tells someone what she saw? But I guess she didn't see us, so it may be in our favour to act normally, and innocently!"

"Exactly! So, that is what we must do. Now let's get out of here, as we still have some cleaning up to do!"

Billy Faraday was excited. It was his first day's work at The Blue Bay Surf Club and his enthusiasm was second to none having arrived an hour early for his shift, but no-one seemed to mind at all, instead they all laughed at his obvious commitment, and the joke seemed to set the mood for his new employment.

"Welcome Billy!" said his boss, Jock. "Seeing you are keen, your first job is to rake sand on the beach down to the lighthouse! Come, I'll give you a run-down how to operate the sand buggy machine!"

Daylight was not far off, but still dark as he left the clubhouse, so Billy used the headlights, and drove on firm sand at the water's edge as required. He was enjoying the drive so went further down the beach than asked to as he was admiring the mansions up on the cliffs. Though they were bathed in semi-darkness, he noticed their splendor, but a flight of timber steps grabbed his attention as they snaked down to a private sandy beach and he turned towards them.

In the headlights he noticed faint lights in the house above, but under the steps amongst treacherous rocks, something was there. He knew not what, but the buggy lights shone on something white.

Gently he braked, then gingerly he climbed from the buggy. *It could just be white rocks?* he muttered to himself. Though he thought otherwise, because to him, it was simply the way it looked, and he thought. *Yes! It definitely appears much softer than rocks.* Like a pile of crumpled clothes maybe. *But, why are they there if it is clothes?* So, subconsciously he had then made the decision to take a better view as it puzzled him. Taking a torch from the glove compartment, he started to walk towards the crumbled items he had seen before.

He shone the torch ahead but when he closed in, he stifled a gasp as his eyes could not comprehend what he was seeing, as the white crumbled items had materialized into the form of a body. His own body trembled, and his legs felt weak. He didn't know what to do, as the body, which he realized now was a young girl, looked dead.

Quickly he realized that he had to check, so he bent down to feel for her pulse. His heart skipped a beat as he felt the faint pulse, but her face was badly cut up and her head was bleeding profusely. She was losing blood fast and he simply had to do something. He didn't want to move her, so he wondered what was the best thing to do.

He looked at the landscape, and up at the steep hill, and realized an ambulance wouldn't get down to where he was. He grabbed his phone to make a call to the ambulance station, then explained the situation, telling them it was urgent as the girl was barely alive, and he suggested they go straight to the Surf Club at Blue Bay, that they would provide a sand vehicle for them there. He was told by the paramedic to call the police, and he did so. Then called his boss Jock to inform him what he had come upon, and steps he had taken.

"You've done well Billy. It must come as shock to you, first day on the job and all. Can't say we've ever had this happen before! Just need your exact location, but you stay put. I'll meet the ambulance out front and lead them to you. Just don't move the girl Billy as she may have neck injuries as well!"

Billy looked at the girl. "Better be quick Jock. I fear for this girl's life. She is losing too much blood!" he uttered as his body trembled.

"Oh! I see! You must look inside the buggy, Billy. There should be a towel under the seat. Try and place it over her head injury, and you might have to hold it there firmly. That should compress it, to still the bleeding until we can get there, but don't move her head!"

"Ok I will try that, Jock. Please don't be long then." he whispered as he ended the call, closed his phone then went back to the buggy.

Billy located the towel quick enough, just where he was told to look for it, then he headed back to the girl.

Her breathing was very faint, he had to bend over close to her to feel her breath on his cheek. Then, so cautiously he folded the towel, and placed it lightly across the gaping wound in her head.

Billy gasped as blood immediately soaked through the towel. He was shaking, but decided to place his hand flat upon the towel, and apply a little pressure, and soon the blood flow eased up a little.

He was so thankful for that, and prayed to the lord above as he diligently kept the same pressure on it.

Please hurry. he thought. *I don't want this girl to die here.*

How awful would it be on my first day's work? he wondered.

His thoughts were consumed with possibilities so that when the sand vehicles finally approached, he was unaware. Then suddenly, there were people everywhere, and paramedics praising his efforts.

Then quickly and professionally, they had the girl set up with a drip, fitted a neck brace, and then lifted her on to a stretcher.

Jock looked at Billy who was in a daze and he put an arm around him. "Well done young fellow. You may have just saved that young girl's life. Great thinking for a young bloke, so well done, Billy. I will drive your buggy back to the club, and you can ride in the sand groper with your patient if you prefer." he stated.

Billy focused. "Yes, I would like that Jock, so, thank you!"

"You are welcome, Billy." replied Jock.

Jack arrived at the house on time, but was puzzled by the fact that Jenna wasn't at the front gate waiting to meet him as arranged, it was his birthday after all. Instead, another factor worried him as well when he parked next to the line of police cars in the car park.

He walked across to the edge of the cliff, and looked over, only to notice police officers swarming the private beach area. He shook his head. *Guess I will find out later what is going on.* he mused.

Shunning the front door access to the house, he turned towards the side steps that led up to the top balcony, and climbed swiftly. As he passed Julia Temple's room, he noticed the door was ajar, and he found that odd as Missus Temple was very particular about her privacy, and always kept her doors locked. He knocked on the door and it swung in. It was then that he noticed the broken lock and he called out to her, but there was no reply. Now he was concerned so, he called out again, much louder, as he stepped inside her room.

There was evidence of a struggle. He noted items strewn across the floor, her walking stick, chairs tipped over, and the bed linen in disarray, a bed-side light still burned. He quickly searched all her rooms, making sure he didn't disturb anything as he had a distinct feeling something sinister had happened. *Could it be Julia Temple was kidnapped.* She wouldn't be out at night, and wouldn't attempt the steps without aid of the walking stick that she ambled along with.

He raced from the room and down to Jenna's room as something squeezed his gut tight. A premonition maybe but he felt uneasy so, he called out franticly as he reached her room. "You there Jenna?"

Jenna's door was open. He knocked, and called again, but there was no reply. He stepped inside the room, but it was deserted, and her bed linen was all tossed about. *The stables! That is where she will be.* he thought, as he retreated. Then raced down the internal steps of the house. He checked the kitchen first, but no Jenna, and at the stables no-one was there, and Jenna wasn't there either. *Where the hell is she, and where are all the staff?* he wondered, as he raced across the lawns. He noticed Richard Temple's car was still in the car-park, obviously he hadn't left for work, so Jack needed to speak to him.

He turned the corner to Mister Temple's rooms, and realized he wouldn't have to go banging on his door as two police officers were there doing just that. Jack paused just as Richard opened the door.

"Senior Constable Jenkins, Blue Bay Police!" the officer in charge was saying. "I must speak to the owner of the property?" he stated.

"Yes, that is me! Richard Temple!" replied Richard, as he ran his fingers through his hair. "Me, and my wife's, actually. What's up?"

"There has been an accident of some sort down under the steps towards the beach. A young girl has been taken to the hospital in an extremely bad way. An ambulance driver seemed to know her! Jenna Temple, he named her, and thinks she lives in this house!"

"That's impossible! Are you certain, as Jenna is my daughter? As far as I know, she is upstairs in her room!" Richard replied.

"Then, I suggest we have a look Mister Temple!" said the officer.

Jack couldn't help himself. His heart was in his mouth, as words gushed out. "Sorry to interrupt Constable, but I am Jack Rickard, and Jenna is my girlfriend. I was to meet her out front this morning, but she wasn't there or in her room, nor in the house, or the stables, and there was no-one around to ask, so I was coming to see Mister Temple but that's not all Constable there's more you should know!"

"Jenna's mother, Missus Julia Temple is missing also, and she is handicapped so she wouldn't attempt the stairs. Her room has been broken into as the door lock is broken! I was just up there, and both the rooms are deserted. The ambulance driver would actually know Jenna, as her mother had an accident about six weeks ago. A fall off a horse, and she was taken into the hospital, and Jenna rode to the hospital in the ambulance. My god, I can't believe this! Are you sure it's Jenna, Constable? If it is, I must go to the hospital to see her!"

The Constable looked at the boy's face in sympathy. "Hmm! This is all very interesting, thank you for that information, Jack. At this stage, I am not sure if it is Jenna in the hospital but we will see."

Richard frowned deeply as he interrupted. "Now! Don't confuse the officer, Jack. I'll take over now!" he said curtly, and stepped out of the doorway to face the Constable. "No-one here is missing!"

"Ah! Not quite Mister Temple, at least not until we investigate further!" Senior Constable said, then he stared to look past Richard.

Miranda had appeared in the doorway. "Who is there, Richard? Oh!" she exclaimed, when she eyed the officer staring at her.

Her Mind SCREAMS MURDER

Richard looked somewhat uneasy, but introduced Miranda as a visitor. "Miranda Delvin's husband has only recently passed away, and I have offered her a place to recuperate!" he explained.

"Hmm! I see!" came the reply, then the Constable added. "If this new information is valid, your wife could well be a missing person Mister Temple, and the young girl's accident is a mystery as yet. So, we must thank Jack for his input into the situation! Thanks Jack!"

"You are most welcome Senior Constable Jenkins!" replied Jack.

"I don't see the need for that." Richard offered. "Julia Temple is my wife, officer, and we share this property. But I assure you she is upstairs! Or she was, the last time I saw her, which was yesterday. She prefers her own space since the fire you know!"

"A fire, and a horse accident!" repeated the Constable. "Hmm!" he pondered, as he directed his gaze towards Jack.
Richard's face darkened in annoyance as the Constable persisted.

"I will require you to show me what you have detected upstairs Jack! Nothing has been touched I hope?" asked the Constable.

"No sir!" replied Jack.

"Good man!" he said then looked at Richard Temple.

"So, Mister Temple! Let us investigate these two rooms please, but only you and Jack for now!" he stressed, as he stared at Miranda hovering behind Richard. I will interview you both there!"

Miranda's frown at being left out, did not go undetected.

"One other vital thing Mister Temple!" he stated. "Later, I would appreciate it if you would arrange all the house members and staff to meet me in your living room for interviews at 11.00am please!" Maybe Jack could ride in to town, and back here again with me, as I need the girl to be identified by someone as soon as possible if I can. Would you accompany me for an ID at the hospital, Jack?"

"Most definitely, Constable Jenkins!"

Are you alright with that Mister Temple?" he asked.

"Yes, sure officer. It is fine by me. I may need some extra time to get everyone together anyway." he replied.

"Good! So, for now. Please be advised that both the rooms are out of bounds, and are to be locked. Please notify everyone of that, and if you have a spare lock anywhere Mister Temple, please bring it with you. Also, I shall require any room keys you may have for both rooms please. Except for my men! No-one, including yourself Mister Temple, will be allowed in these two rooms. When I leave, they will be locked, and taped up. Is that quite clear?" he asked.

"Yes officer! If you think that is required, then I understand."

Richard walked back in the room, and opened a desk drawer to retrieve a lock and keys, then handed them to the officer and spoke.

"Just follow me now officer, we will go up by the side stairs!"

"Come along Jack, show us what you have discovered! I will talk to you both briefly, and take your statements while we are there. Then, I must go downstairs to the accident site and take some notes. You would be most welcome to come along if you wish to Jack, it might be a good experience for you! We will go into the hospital to identify the victim after that Jack. I believe you made enquiries how to apply for a position as a policeman. There are numerous tests to pass, but if you get through, you may work with us in the future!"

"I hope so Constable! I'm guessing the tests are the worst, then the wait for a result and study. I will come down to the beach with you sir. I noticed all the officers there this morning when I arrived!"

"Good man. Well, you must have arrived very early Jack?"

"Yes, I did sir! Jenna and I had special plans for today to go out after daylight. It is my birthday and she told me she'd prepare food for us and wait at the front gate for me, but not this morning. That was the first warning for me, sent shivers up my spine actually!"

"Thanks for that info, Jack and Happy Birthday!"

"You are welcome, Constable Jenkins, and thank you!"

Jack stared at Jenna laying very still on the hospital bed. "Yes! It is definitely Jenna, Constable Jenkins! Only, I thought she would be awake at least! Is there a way to get information on her injuries?"

"So, it is Jenna Temple then! Yes, it looks like something may be wrong for her to still be unconscious. I am quite sure someone here can help us by answering a few questions. So, just wait here please Jack!" said the Constable. Then he was away in search for someone, and with him when he returned was a friendly nurse in tow, with Jenna's patient chart in her hand as she approached the bed. "You must be Jack, the patient's friend? Constable Jenkins told me of you and that this young girl is Jenna Temple! I'll help if I can. I'm Anne!"

They both acknowledged her, and then Jack spoke out first. "Hi Anne, my name is Jack Rickard and I'm Jenna's boyfriend. We! The, Constable and I, require information on Jenna's condition please?"

"I see! Well Jenna was admitted unconscious, and has undergone rather extensive tests. An MRI head scan showed bleeding on her brain and damage to the skull of her forehead so doctor ordered to place her into an induced coma, meaning we will purposely keep her unconscious in case there is a problem and to reduce any risks! It's the usual way to treat this injury the healing process is lengthy!"

"How long will she be in this state of unconsciousness Anne?" asked Constable Jenkins. "I need to speak to her urgently!"

"Well, in these cases, it could be days, weeks, or longer. We don't know for sure, but the doctor will advise us. You can visit any time, but I can't guarantee she will be awake!" replied Anne.

"Ok, thank you! But is there any way you could notify the police station if she wakes up. I think she may hold vital information that could help with this mystery?" inquired Constable Jenkins.

"I will make a note of that Constable Jenkins, but I am certain it won't be a problem so, you will be notified in due time."

"Would you like a call also Jack?" she asked.

"No, thank you Anne, I plan on being here personally every day to visit so, I will check in with you then, if that is ok with you?"

Anne pondered the question. "That's good Jack, but don't expect any miracles in the near future or even for some time. I simply don't want you getting disappointed, but you may also need to know that in these cases, most times the patient is transferred to the city, as they have far better facilities there, and rehabilitation usually takes some time, and specialists are required!" Anne explained.

Jack looked a little dejected, but replied as best he could, though his heart was racing. "Thank you, Anne! I really didn't expect that. Would you notify me if that happens?" he asked.

"I really don't think I could do that, Jack. It is hospital policy to only notify the next of kin and we are yet to obtain that information. However, there is no reason why you shouldn't ask the next of kin for details, when we find them."

"I see! Don't worry then, I could do that if Jenna is transferred to the city. I will just deal with it one day at a time!"

"That is really all you can do for now Jack!" replied Anne.

"Yes, I guess so!" replied Jack.

Anne turned to face The Constable to speak. "Since we are talking about this, Constable Jenkins, would you happen to know if Jenna has any parents, or a next of kin I could notify?"

"Yes Anne! I know she has only one, her father Richard Temple. He lives at 'Oceanview,' that is where Jenna's accident took place. I will inform him if you like!" replied the Constable

"Appreciated! Thank you, Constable Jenkins! She made a note on the chart before she added. "I shall endeavor to contact you to keep you updated on Jenna's progress. I'll see you both next visit!"

"Excellent, thank you for your help, Anne." said The Constable.

"Thank you, Anne." said Jack.

Chapter Six

Miranda was angry. *How dare they?* she fretted. *I must know what is going on* She thought of going up the side stairs to the balcony to listen at the door, but discarded that idea in case The Constable discovered her there. *That wouldn't look good at all* she thought. So, she submitted to waiting. *Not something she was good at* she realized.

She was beside herself with concern as she sat there thinking and could not wait for Richard to return to the room to inform her what was said. So, when he finally strolled in the door, she just felt like screeching at him but instead, she smiled and sighed with relief.

"Oh, thank goodness you are back Richard! I am not partial to being left out of things so, what did The Constable find out, or ask?"

Richard stared at her anxious face momentarily, then he replied. "Sorry, Miranda! He asked a lot of questions about Julia, because of the state of her room. He stated she is either missing, or murdered so, no-one is to enter her room any time during the investigations!"

"You are kidding me, I hope sir?" questioned Miranda.

"No, I am not kidding! But without Julia's body, she is missing!"

Miranda seemed perplexed as she glared angrily at Richard.

"There is something I have been meaning to ask you Richard, so I guess now is a good time. It has been brought to my notice, that Jenna has a lot of pull with organization here, so who is actually the beneficiary of this property in the event that Julia does not return?"

Richard's face fell, and he looked just a little uncomfortable with his reply. "That is just it, Miranda. I do not really know for sure! I have never thought about it until just now, and I wanted to search Julia's room to look for a copy of her will, but my plan to access the room is squashed now! So, you know as much as I do!"

"Well maybe a little more Richard!" said Miranda with a smirk.

"What do you mean?" asked Richard.

"I mean that I have thought ahead. Sorry, I haven't mentioned it before but it was when Jenna threatened to have me removed from the property for going into the kitchen and requesting meals to my taste. That did not sit lightly with me. I was angry! So, I had to find out for myself who rules here. I have been up to Julia's rooms when the doors were left open in search of the same document, her will. But Julia caught me red-handed. She told me to leave her property, but not before I realized where to look. I had come up with nothing, but now I know where to look if you can get us inside her rooms!"

Richard gaped at her. "That may not be possible now! You can be quite devious Miranda. I must keep a close eye on you in future!"

"Please do!" she offered as she sidled up against him.

"He folded his arms around her, and they kissed passionately until Miranda eased him away to say. "You do not honestly believe that Julia would leave this property to Jenna, do you? She is just the daughter. You, the husband, should be the beneficiary!"

"I honestly don't know Miranda! I did sign papers giving away my rights when we married, but now we are separated. I'm not sure how that pans out if she doesn't return, or if I am even in her will?"

"So, nothing definite about Jenna either, unless Jack confirms the victim in hospital is Jenna? We'll know more when they return. Oh, you must attend the living room for questioning at 11.00am!"

"That is a worry, what will I say! This is all very inconvenient! How will we ever get a chance to search for the will now Richard?"

There was chaos in the kitchen when Richard informed Paula and Melita that there was to be a police investigation regarding the disappearance of Julia Temple, and if indeed the girl at the hospital is actually Jenna Temple, then answers will be required to the many questions police have, and therefore, must be asked firstly of those closest to Jenna, and in the household. "So!" said Richard. "I expect you both to have all staff present and accounted for by 11.00am."

Paula's face was ashen as the platter slipped from her hands and clattered as it hit the floor, and splattered the contents everywhere.

"Get a grip woman!" snapped Richard. "Clean it up quickly and go out and find the others, and get back to the living room pronto!"

Melita stood quietly. Suddenly she possessed a vacant look, her stare blankly altering her features. Her head spun as Richard tried to stress the need to contact the casual workers, as they had to be brought in as well, but Melita's mind was suddenly elsewhere.

She was recalling conversations she had with Pablo. *I am being threatened!* he had said, and again after the incident, she requested of Pablo to look for any other damage to the honey-coloured mare's girth strap before burying it, and he had burst into her work station upstairs with great elation on his face exclaiming excitedly.

"You will not believe this mother, but you were so right about Miranda Delvin! What she did to that girth strap, added to what I did caused the most damage, and a fatal accident!"

Melita had smiled a knowing smile. She was usually right about certain characters, especially those who blackmailed people.

"Well, that's great news Pablo. I did expect it so just keep it to yourself! If we do need evidence, you know where to get the girth strap if the accident is investigated any time or questions are asked, but it proves we must be wary and conscious of the fact. Miranda Delvin may stoop to low tactics and try to lay blame on you!"

"Oh no, do you think she would?"

"I certainly do if she has something to hide, but rest assured Pablo, now we hold the trump card so, we can expose her for the damage of the girth strap, but we have the proof, and she doesn't!"

"Will you do it Melita?... Melita!" Richard was asking anxiously.

Melita snapped out of it. Her head pounded with uncertainty, but she came to her senses as the reality of the present hit her. *My god we must stick to the plan!* she mused as she replied to him.

"Yeah, sure Mister Temple. I can do that for you!"

"Good, then we all meet in the living room at 11.00am."

"Yes sir, Mister Temple!" Melita and Paula mumbled in unison, and he grunted, and wheeled around to leave.

Miranda was perched elegantly on the settee in the living room he noticed as he walked through, and he chuckled as he took in her appearance. She just looked so beautiful in her polka-dot dress. If they weren't so pressed for time, he had an urge to take her right there and then, but instead he sat beside her and kissed her.

"Why so amorous Richard? Is there no end to your needs?" she asked when their lips parted. "But now is bad timing my love!"

"Why are you here now Miranda? Interviews start at 11.00am!" She smiled her best smile as she looked at him. Then came the tinkle of her laugh. "I am quite aware of that Richard, but I do like to be prepared, and I want to have the best vantage point to speak from!"

He couldn't help but chuckle along with her as he gazed upon her beauty. "Only if you say so Miranda, though I really could think of something else much more interesting to fill in the time while we wait, but stay if you must. I do have a couple of pressing things to take care of, but I won't be long, and I will be back!"

"Do you have any ideas at all what questions will be asked, and if it includes the other accidents Julia had?" Miranda queried.

"I really don't have any idea, except common sense tells me the Constable will want to know times, our whereabouts at the time of Julia's disappearance, and the mystery surrounding Jenna. Maybe we will both say we were in the common room downstairs for the entire night watching movies until you retired quite late. Say from 4.00am - 5.00am, but don't bring up past accidents unless he asks. I guess then we will have to answer his questions to the best of our knowledge. Anyway, Julia's horse accident is the only one you are aware of, but just act ignorant of the facts. So, are you ok with that?"

"Yes of course!" Miranda snapped, then waved him away. "Off you go then!" She then looked around the room in despair. Already she was lost deep in her thoughts until she sensed someone enter the room, and she lifted her head to look towards the entry just as Melita walked in. She was not smiling, nor did she speak, but just stood there with a smirk upon her face which seemed to unsettle Miranda more than the dark brooding eyes that challenged her.

Miranda was almost about to say something, but thought better of it. *What does she have to smirk about?* she mused. *Maybe Melita knows more about the horse accident than they are letting on,* as it was Pablo, her son, who went out to get the horse and saddle.

She wondered what excuses they'd conjure up, of their whereabouts around the time of Julia's disappearance, and then Jenna's accident, that is if it is Jenna in hospital. *That would be interesting.*

However, if they're pressured and decide to speak up first, *they may point a finger at her for any incidents at all,* if they were devious enough to lay blame on her. *Loose ends! Loose ends to deal with.*

But Melita doesn't realize who she is dealing with either does she? Hmm! But that girth strap is a worry if questions are asked.

She didn't trust Melita, and those deadly eyes. She didn't like those menacing eyes of hers! Not for one moment. she realized.

Then there was movement by the doorway as the workers filed into the room. Miranda took particular notice of Ted Hastings who looked at no-one, and hung his head low as if he needed to inspect his boots, as he walked a little behind Paula his wife, who strutted down the far end of the room not bothering to talk to anyone either.

Ted was tall and thin, with scraggy hair pulled back and tied in a throng at the back of his head. He was still dressed in his work clothes that were all shabby, and covered in grease. Though it was his over-sized heavy boots completely covered with clods of mud that Miranda noticed mostly as she stared at the carpet where a trail of mud was falling off as he passed, and shuffled along after Paula.

He could at least have changed his clothes, and his boots! she thought, as she herself sat in waiting looking immaculate.

Suddenly a booming voice echoed in the room, causing Miranda to jump in her seat. Richard had returned, but she stared at his face as she turned. It was set like a mask, and a deep frown creased his forehead. This worried look he wore, she had never seen that type of look before as he commenced doing a quick head count, then he spoke out loudly, and sharply to everyone filing through the door.

"Good, just as well you are all prompt!" he looked at his watch.

"Expect the Constable and his assistant to arrive in ten minutes!"

Melita quickly took the opportunity to turn around, and hurried across to the other end of the room to take a seat just as Richard was satisfied everyone was accounted for, before he addressed them.

There was whispering amongst the staff when Richard said they were gathered together for questioning by Senior Constable Jenkins regarding the disappearances last night of his wife Julia Temple or any information on Jenna, as she could be missing also!"

There was a hush in the room as he continued.

"Be prepared to be interviewed individually as a lot of questions will be asked of each of you! Times of your whereabouts etc."

Pablo hung his head as Richard seemed to glare directly at him, then continued. "So! A young girl was found under the steps to the beach in the early hours of this morning. She was injured, and in a critical state and was taken by ambulance to the hospital. Police are combing the area now. We don't know for certain yet whether the injured girl in hospital is Jenna, or not? However, the Constable will inform us of that when he gets here. If it is Jenna, he'll explain her injuries, but you know what the big question will be?" *What reason would Jenna have for being underneath the steps in the dark hours of the morning?* "That is the big question, and remains a mystery!"

"If the girl is not her, I think Jenna will be a missing person!"

Miranda noticed at once, at the mention in the brief about Julia, and Jenna, that all eyes of the staff flitted to each other's faces. They all seemed nervous to her. Their eyes glazed over, and strange as it may seem, she detected guilt displayed on each of their faces.

Amateurs! she thought. How are they going to hold up when the questioning begins? *Such hopeless people I am involved with!*

Then the doorbell rang, and Richard stated as he walked across the room. "That will be the police now I am guessing!"
He opened the front door to usual greetings from Senior Constable Jenkins, his assisting officer and Jack Rickard, and they entered.

Jack stepped aside. Then slowly, he peered around the room at the people as Richard began introducing Constable Jenkins, and his assisting officer Mervin Peters, to the staff, and Miranda Delvin. Then without further ado, Constable Jenkins instantly took over. "Good morning, all! Thank you for attending. First things first!"

"We have two issues to cover today and it will take some time! Individual statements will be taken by my officer, Peters!" he then turned to Richard. "Could we use a private room Mister Temple?"

Richard spoke out. "Yes, you may use my study, Constable. It is through those doors!" he pointed. "They lock from the inside!!"

"Perfect! We interview one person at a time, a lengthy process!"

"So, everyone please be aware. We have a mystery surrounding Julia Temple! There is a lot of blood at the crime scene. It could be hers, but too much sand to determine that, and we don't have her body! So, she remains as missing, and Jenna Temple is indeed the girl in the hospital. She is now fighting for her life! We are treating Jenna's case as an attempted murder. This is a very serious charge!"

Gasps came in unison from his audience.

Jack stood puzzled. These were all people he knew very well. All of them except for Miranda Delvin, whom he only previously met on the day of Missus Temple's horse accident, some time back. He looked across at her now, then particularly noted, she was the only person in the entire room who was smiling. It was that sweet smile only she possessed. He thought it odd, and out of place so to speak.

He was thinking wildly now. He had visited Jenna and knew the extent of her injuries. Jack realized in that instant someone had tried to kill her! *Why, who would want to hurt Jenna? It made no sense!*

Could a real murderer be present in this very room? Jack stressed. *Impossible!* he shivered as he peered at the sullen faces. Some guilt ridden he felt, but it could have been another emotion. *Or was it?*

Nothing added up. *What really happened to Jenna Temple?*

There seemed to be a mystery regarding Jenna's injuries. Sure, there was lots of blood around under the steps, that had astounded him when he visited the crime scene with Constable Jenkins. *All the blood couldn't be Jenna's surely? Or, it could be Julia Temple's!* he didn't even know if they had alternate ways for testing in Blue Bay.

Jack was deep in thought as Constable Jenkin's voice droned on continuing to explain about Jenna Temple's condition to the people.

So, what really happened? Did Jenna, walk down the steps, or fall over the railings or, was she pushed? he wished he knew.

Constable Jenkins seemed to think the latter because there was no damage to the steps, they were intact. He assumed she either fell over the railing, or was pushed, as there was evidence of where she fell below. However, he felt the rocks below were not the cause of the damage to her head, rather a large rock found covered in blood.

Jack still procrastinated. *Maybe she walked down the steps, but why on earth would she?* It was dark, and way before daylight. *No, she'd never be out at that time!* It was impossible for him to think that Jenna fell over the railings. *Jenna Temple could descend those steps blindfolded if she had to! Of that I am certain!* he thought.

Or! Was she really pushed? *But, how do they prove that?*

Now the Constable stated that the rock they found covered in her blood was what caused her head injury, and they had proof of that, as blood samples taken confirmed it being Jenna's blood! Also, scans from the doctor proved the indentation on Jenna's forehead, was a match with the shape of the deadly rock identically.

Eyebrows were raised, a few odd shuffles on the seats. But no-one uttered a word. Instead, you could have heard a pin drop.

Jack listened. Maybe that is correct! *But still, the reason why she was out that late in the first place just didn't sit right with him.*

There was much to process, and for the first time Jack accepted that this is what he'd chosen for a career path. *Investigating!* That part of it was awesome, but there was also the gruesome side at the same time. However deep inside his gut with everything combined, came the thrill of it, as something urged him on to succeed, and to figure it out. *So, he knew what he had chosen was his true calling.*

Then his mind snapped back to the issues at hand.

What of all the other blood? Maybe it was Missus Temple's blood as The Constable suggested, *if she was hurt badly*. Though they class her as missing so, she *could have been kidnapped?* He knew she would put up a fight, and by the look of the state of her room, it appeared to him as if it had started there. *But, if so! Where was she?* Where was Missus Julia Temple? he wondered. *Where did the struggle end?* Was it in her room, or up on the balcony? Missus Julia Temple may not have been down under the steps on the beach at all.

Just maybe? he pondered on the possibility a while. *However, if so, all the blood splattered on the sand might be Jenna's after all.* Maybe some-thing more sinister may have happened to Julia Temple! *But if correct, where was her body?* She just can't disappear, *or could she?*

Jack's head ached as he tried to sort it out, but it was hopeless!

Best left to the professionals for now! he thought. *No doubt I will hear first-hand, how investigations are going if I secure this job.* It seemed so surreal to him that as soon as next week he could be making a start in his chosen career, he couldn't stand the wait.

He looked up as Constable Jenkins finished speaking. So, now the interrogations would begin. Officer Peters stood up and handed each person a form, and pen to fill out their personal details. Then, with a tap on the shoulder, he selected one person to follow him.

Paula Hastings was nervous, and her hand shook as she held the form. She rose from her seat and followed the officer into the study.

No need for me to stay, I have given my statement to Constable Jenkins! Jack realized, and moved in closer to the Constable to shake hands.

"Thank you, sir I'll be off now!"

"Right you are, Jack. Best wishes in your tests and application. Just remember that commonsense rules, and good luck Jack!"

Jack smiled at The Constable, then he replied. "Thank you, sir. I do appreciate your advice! But, be assured, I will do my very best!"

Chapter Seven

It had been a worrisome week for Jack Rickard. Jenna's condition hadn't changed, and he was getting worried. His birthday was a non-event, and the worst day of his life. There were no celebrations, not even with his parents, even though he had just turned eighteen.

However, some things had changed. With his father's guidance and tutoring, he obtained his license and was learning to drive. He also sat for the test examination and completed his application for a job as a policeman. So, it was a waiting game for the outcome, that was the worst part. *Someone has my life in their hands.* he knew.

Though finally when word came, it was so unexpected that Jack didn't realize the letter he was opening contained a chapter into his life he so needed now. He was beside himself and jumped up for joy, wanting to share his news with someone, but knew his parents were out. Immediately he saw visions of Jenna, then sadly he sank down onto the couch, hands cupped his face as he cried for the first time in his life as he realized. *He couldn't tell her!* He now had a start for their future plans they wanted …But… *He couldn't even tell her.*

It was a whole new world for Jack Rickard. So much to learn, and though he didn't know it at that time, he was paving the way to success beyond his wildest dreams. New friendships he made on the force were forged, to be friends for life. He was the new kid on the block but he fit like a glove. His enthusiasm well noted amongst the officers who took to him straight way, and offered their advice.

Jack relished being accepted into the real world as a policeman, and took on board every piece of advice on offer. He became like a sponge, just soaking up as much knowledge as he could muster. He had just experienced the thrill of the chase momentarily, but to him it was only a taste of excitement for what was really to come with his ambitions, what he wanted to do when he reached his pinnacle.

He became so popular, especially to those who got in close, and got to know him well, and he grew with them. They soon learnt of his dreams and ambitions. A university study program he attended at university for night courses that he changed and updated to three times a week simply to obtain his ultimate goal and direction in life. Others admired him for his tenacity, his insight and commitment at such a young age, and they all pitched it to help him.

However, three-week days were taxing and long ones for Jack.

After eight hours at the station learning the ropes by picking up the simplest of tasks first, until his progression became well noted by his superiors, and soon he mastered anything that his chief gave him, but his days continued on every afternoon after work when he religiously caught a bus to visit Jenna in the hospital. He always felt down after he left there as she was still in a coma, so all he could do was sit there, and hold her hand. He talked, but didn't know if she could hear him, he felt so helpless and his confidence waned. Going home was a quick visit. A shower, and dinner, a chat to his parents about work, and Jenna was all he had time for. They always seemed to cheer him up, and give him some hope that things would change.

He held that thought, but deep down he simply didn't like what was happening with Jenna, day after day with no change. *If I could only help her!* he wished. Then he had to leave to catch another bus to attend the all-important night, tutoring classes at the university. *This is where I must excel.* he thought to himself as he stepped off the bus. *It will be for our future.* Then he walked through the gates, eager for the night to begin, and the learning to continue.

It was almost a month to the day when Jack decided he had to speak with Constable Jenkins. It was a while since he had updates on the investigations involving Jenna and her mother, Julia Temple, so, he walked up to his office and knocked on the Constable's door.

"Enter!" came the call from within.

"Good morning, Constable Jenkins." said Jack, as he opened the door, and walked inside.

"Ah! Jack. I have been hearing good things of you lad. Come in and take a seat Jack." he pointed to the chair opposite himself, and Jack walked across the room, and sat down.

"No need to ask Jack, it's written all over your face that you need updates on the investigations for your girlfriend, and her mother!"

"Yes, thank you, sir! Any information at all will be helpful to me. I visit Jenna every day but there is no change and it's worrying me!"

"I think it is worrying the doctors too Jack! I took it upon myself to visit the hospital this morning, as like you, it is worrying me also. You see, Jenna holds all the vital information about her attack, and could possibly even know her attacker! Also, she may have some knowledge on her mother's disappearance. However, because she is in a coma we can't question her, and are no further advanced! So, I spoke to her doctor, and then privately to the young nurse we met, Anne. I asked her what further treatment is scheduled for Jenna. I don't think she was meant to say, but she said they would wait two more days, then Jenna would be transferred to a city hospital!"

Constable Jenkins looked directly at Jack before he continued. "Depending on what the specialists say there, Jack. But she may have to undergo an operation, as apparently, she has a hemorrhage on the brain so it is very serious, they are monitoring her closely!"

"My god! Damn it all. I was just there last night after work, as I am every night but no-one has told me that! I have noticed they were keeping a close eye on her, but I didn't get to speak to Anne!"

"It might be they only tell the next of kin, Jack. So, that would be Richard Temple. Maybe you should talk to him for information?"

"Yes, it could be. I might go out to see him on the weekend! So, what is happening with the investigation? Do you have any leads?"

"Wish it was that simple Jack. Our only positive lead to date, is that Jenna was definitely attacked, as we have identified her blood on rocks, on sand, and the fatal rock which caused her main injury, but by whom, or why she would be under the steps, still remains a mystery. We are treating her case as attempted murder but we can't seem to get to the bottom of things! If only she was conscious, we may have a better chance of finding out. However, Julia Temple's disappearance is baffling too, and proving to be quite a mystery as well. All other blood scattered in the sand can't be tested here as we don't have correct equipment to do it. We have no body to say it is murder, and everything seems to lead us to a dead end. We have no prints, only un-readable footprints, because the shoes must have been covered. We dug up the whole beach area, and under the steps looking for a body but no luck there, just some green shafts of stone! Blood samples, and all findings were sent to the city branch!"

"Did the household members and staff reveal anything to you?"

"I can't really lay blame on any one person in the household as they all seem to have solid alibies Jack, and mainly with each other, which is a bit suspect, but that is how it is, we can't prove otherwise, so, after extensive questioning with them we are none the wiser!"

"But if you could lay blame on two persons Constable Jenkins?" The Constable's head flew up from his paperwork, and then stared directly at Jack before he spoke.

"Strange you should ask that question, Jack! I thought the same thing, but what is your theory behind that statement?"

Jack looked straight at him, then spoke. "Well, it seems to me it would take more than one person to carry out a murder in that area, and then retreat up that hill with a body. Just my thoughts! Unless Missus Temple was kidnapped, but still may require two people!"

"Really? That was exactly my theory too Jack. So much so, that until something unfolds, I have taken the liberty of replacing both door locks on the two rooms in question at 'Oceanview' and have a safe deposit box here at the station for keys. No-one can enter those two rooms now we have declared Julia Temple a missing person!"

"That is good to hear, as they both have private things up there!"

Constable Jenkins eyed Jack thoughtfully. "You know Jack, that is clever thinking. I think you will make a good detective one day!"

Jack stood proudly, and chuckled. "Well, I have been giving it a lot of thought. Besides, my course studies at university are showing me a whole new way of thinking, and it does help!"

"Hmm! I think it may be time to up your workload. Maybe some hands-on shifts out on a beat in town with senior officer Keans. What are your thoughts on that Jack? Do you think you're ready?"

Jack beamed at being given a chance, and a simple step upwards.

"Yes Sir!" he replied. "That is exactly what I need, I am ready!"

"Good, I would suggest you continue with your course study. You will probably find there is a follow up course you must do!"

"Yes, there is Constable Jenkins! Though I am not too sure at this stage whether I can do it here, or if I have to go to the city!"

"Well, keep me posted Jack. I will do all I can to help out!"

"I will, thank you, sir!" Jack replied.

Finally Jack realized he was getting somewhere, and working outdoors was what he wanted to do, it reminded him of Jenna. He realized the importance of the job, and looked at the Constable, and he said seriously. "I won't let you down sir!"

Constable Jenkins smiled, and replied. "I know that Jack, that is why you have the job. Now, on another note, back to 'Oceanview.' I have more information of interest for you. "Apparently, the sole owner of the property 'Oceanview' is Julia Temple. We received the confirmation of that from a city firm as soon as she was reported a missing person, surprise! Also, a letter from her bank came to say her money and assets would be frozen. She can be a missing person for several years you know Jack if we don't find her body!"

Jack processed that information before replying. "Hmm! I hadn't expected that, sir. I naturally assumed Mister Temple would be part owner of 'Oceanview.' There has to be another explanation!"

"Yes, there is Jack! But, best to keep it under your hat though!"

"Of course, totally Constable Jenkins!"

"As for Mister Temple being a joint owner? Not so, according to the source of the firm practice in the city, you may be interested to know Jack! I thought that a little strange. Almost as if Julia Temple didn't trust anyone here. Apparently, 'Oceanview' was her family's estate and in turn, as rich families often do, it then passed down to her. When she married Richard, he relinquished all his rights of ownership, and of all monies concerning 'Oceanview,' by signing an indemnity clause in their marriage arrangement. I have it all in writing from a city firm, the solicitors name not disclosed, he leaves no stone unturned this guy. Julia Temple was wise to employ him!"

"Maybe she had reason to believe she needed secrecy? Having said that, several years is a long time to tie up an estate if Missus Temple is not found, or her body recovered even. What will happen to the property, and who will pay the staff if everything is frozen?"

"Some of them live there, and it is Jenna's home after all, and I am sure she wouldn't want it to lay dormant! Will you tell her?"

"I must say, Jack. You do pose some interesting points. Another indication that you will surely make detective, one day! Firstly, this has just landed in my lap, so it is very hush, hush, please Jack. I do imagine Richard Temple will be informed as well. However, until he knows then we have to keep a lid on it! Our investigations will still go on, but I really must say whoever committed these crimes is testing us all. Now, as for Jenna. Of course, I would tell her of this information, but that is where my problem lies. The doctor told me only this morning, that even if Jenna wakes up, she may suffer some memory loss. It has been far too long now! So, how to communicate with her may be a huge problem if she doesn't know who she is!"

"My god, things seem to be going from bad to worse! Poor Jenna, I feel so helpless. So, this could really change her whole life. To be left in limbo would be the worst thing to happen!" Jack paled under this new information, and in his mind flashed all the plans they had for their future. *A future that may never happen.* he thought.

Constable Jenkins felt sorry for him, and gently rested his hand on Jack's shoulder. "She is alive Jack! Hold on to that thought!"

Jack shook his head in embarrassment, he felt like crying again.

"Thank you, sir! I shall try to remember that! It's really all I have to cling to. I must go now! Will you excuse me? I have much to do!"

"Of course, Jack. I will get the wheels in motion for you to start working with Keans on Monday. Thank you for a great chat, and if you need me, well you know where I am!" said the Constable as he watched Jack nod, and offered a thank you before turning to walk away, then he disappeared through the doorway.

Jack's shoulders slumped in defeat! His eyes suddenly blinded by tears as they rolled down his cheeks. *This seems to be becoming a habit.* he thought, as he ambled down the hall to his work station.

Suddenly he felt depressed. *If I can just get through this day?* he thought as he sat down at his desk. Things cannot get any worse, *however there might be some brighter news when I see Jenna later.* he was hoping. *But, no! If she is not awake, they won't tell me anything.*

He realized in that instant that Constable Jenkins was so correct, and that he would have to go out and visit Richard Temple in the morning. *Surely Mister Temple would attempt to shed some light on Jenna's treatment for him.* He would have been told! he thought.

It was the main topic during dinner with his parents when he explained Jenna's situation that evening.

"Jack, these things happen for a reason, and I think the doctors have done the right thing by keeping her in a coma. Otherwise, she may have died. Now you are saying she is hemorrhaging and they may need to operate. I wouldn't beat yourself up about it, Jack, the doctors will look after her, and Richard Temple may tell you more!"

His father stood up and placed a hand on his shoulder. "Your mother is right Jack. You can drive my car out tomorrow!"

Jack had mixed feelings, and felt really strange as he opened the door of his father's car to get out at the gates of 'Oceanview.' He dared not look over the edge of the mighty cliff-face which dwarfed the strip of beach below it. Instead, he shuddered with dread, and fumbled with the latch on the gate then walked inside the grounds.

He had noticed Mister Temple's car in the car-park, so knew he was home, and decided to go straight across the lawn to his rooms. He stepped up onto the porch, and was about to knock when he heard raised voices within. He hesitated, then stood rooted to the spot as he heard the conversation clearly. There was no mistaking the two voices of Richard Temple and Miranda Delvin arguing.

He winced as he heard the sound of something hitting furniture inside, and the continuous cursing of Miranda Delvin.

"These keys won't fit Richard!" she yelled as the keys clattered onto a table. "What is going on, what have you done, and why on earth did you let them change the locks to the rooms! How the hell am I supposed to get into the rooms. I'll never find that will now! Besides, I was thinking of moving into your wife's room. She won't need it now, will she? It is so much nicer up there than your rooms!"

Richard coughed. "Well! I was waiting for the right time to tell you! These came in the mail yesterday!" he handed her two letters, then added. "Julia may be dead, Miranda, but that doesn't give us the right to move into her rooms! You had better read the letters!"

"I can't see why not! They are the best rooms. After all, it is your house, and Julia is not here now. So, I wish to live upstairs Mister Richard Temple!" suddenly she stared blankly at him, as it sunk in what he had just said. "What do you mean by that... Julia may be dead???" she stiffened as she wondered. *What is he not saying?*

Richard's face reddened. "Well, I... well, I!" he stuttered, then continued. "What I meant to say was! She could be dead, and until a body is found she can be a missing person for several years, and cannot be declared dead, so it is pointless worrying about her will! Read the letters of the latest development, and you will know!"

Miranda glared at him, not sure if he was telling the truth, as she snatched the letters from him, and her face paled when she read the contents of the first one. "I just can't believe it Richard, but you have let things get out of hand now!" she screeched. "Because Constable Jenkins has declared Julia a missing person legally now, a city firm is involved, and has stated in this letter that Julia Temple is the sole owner of 'Oceanview.' That is a news-flash! You have been lying to me Richard! I was to understand that you were part owner with her in 'Oceanview' and you were only worried whether or not Julia had left the property to you in her will because you are living apart!"

"Excuse me! I told you I signed papers giving away my rights!"

"What papers?" she snapped.

"Papers of an indemnity clause that I signed within the marriage arrangement between Julia and I, this city firm would have a copy!"

Miranda frowned. "I see! But still, if she is missing or dead, you should still be the beneficiary, should you not?" she asked.

"Only if it is written in her will, but we won't know that now! Please, just read the other letter Miranda, as there are more issues!"

She glared at him, and mumbled to herself. *Issues he says, what issues?* She ripped out the other letter from its envelope and began to read. Anger rose like a living thing in her throat as she stared up at Richard, and her face reddened as she began to shriek.

"This is from the bank Richard, Julia's bank!"

"Yes, I know!"

"They are freezing all assets!" she screamed. "All money too, so who pays the bills? There'll be no staff, we will have to move out!"

Richard yelled back at her. "Don't be stupid woman. There is no way I am moving from 'Oceanview.' Not ever! It is my home! I have lived here too long now to give it away. No, I will fight for it!"

Suddenly Richard paused to place one finger over his lips. "Shush, Miranda. Did you hear that? I think someone is outside the door listening. I definitely heard something like a thump, just outside!"

Jack had heard enough. So much so, that he was shaking. *There is really too much to digest.* he realized, as he turned quickly to exit. Now he just wanted to get away as quietly as he could, but his shoe caught on the edge of the door-mat, and he tripped and fell heavily to the floor, and there he lay sprawling, as the door was flung open.

An ugly scowl graced Richard's brow to wrinkle it deeply as he quickly opened the door and flung it back to emerge in the doorway ready to frighten off whoever was there and he stared down at Jack.

"What the hell are you doing there, Jack?" he yelled.

Jack took a moment to compose himself as he painfully got to his feet. "Sorry Mister Temple! I didn't mean to disturb you. I know it is Saturday, and your day off work, but I just came out to ask you if you have any information about Jenna? However, before I could knock on the door my shoe got caught up in the mat, and I tripped, and fell over. Now I've got a bruised hip you can bet!"

Richard glared at him to see if there was any truth in that. *Did he hear our conversation?* he wondered. *But he was laying on the floor, and he does look hurt, so maybe he is telling the truth.*

"You know what Jack? You could have phoned, as I don't like being disturbed in my private time. So don't come out here again, just a phone-call will suffice, but I haven't got anything to tell you anyway as Jenna is still in a coma, and they are monitoring her!"

Jack had never seen Richard Temple in this type of mood, but he certainly was in one now he noted. "Yes, of course Mister Temple, I will phone next time. It is just Constable Jenkins told me she has a brain hemorrhage now, they will only monitor her for two days and plan to transfer her to a city hospital for an operation, and that is tomorrow! Could you confirm that, and where they will send her?"

Richard thought hard as he looked at Jack's stressed face. *I must nip this in the bud now, this boy is never going to give up!* he realized.

He chuckled. "Well, that is news to me Jack! A bit outlandish I must say as no such thing is happening. Jenna will be woken soon!"

"I don't think that is correct sir, the Constable said he spoke to the doctor, and one of the nurses. I go to visit Jenna every day, and I can't get information on her treatment as I am not the next of kin!"

"Are you questioning my judgement Jack?" asked Richard.

Jack paled under his scrutiny. "Well, no sir! I mean yes sir I guess I am! I would have thought you would have the latest information about Jenna and her treatment, and if she is being moved. Surely you would want me to know seeing Jenna is my girlfriend!"

Richard wasn't about to trade secrets with any boyfriend. *I will have to deal with this.* he thought. Then, quite deliberately he spoke rather abruptly to Jack. "Jack, I have a lot on my mind, and I am in the middle of an important discussion. I have told you all I know, so I am afraid our talk is over. Besides, you will need to forget about any relationship with Jenna. I will be taking care of her interests in future, and they won't be including you I am afraid. See your own way out, and don't come out here again!" he said matter of factly, as he turned on his heel walked through the doorway and slammed the door, leaving Jack standing there open-mouthed in disbelief.

Forget Jenna he had just said! I do not think so Mister Richard Temple. What-ever is wrong with you? he wondered. Jack simply could not believe the conversation that just took place, and he wondered why. Sadly, he turned to walk down the stairs, then crossed the lawns to the gate out to the carpark. He stood for a while dumbfounded, as he looked over the beautiful property 'Oceanview' for the last time, and tears welled to run freely down his face. *What will I do?* he questioned himself. *Maybe I will get answers this afternoon!* But when he visited her hospital bed though, Jenna was gone. *A nurse told him Jenna was transferred to the city urgently but she wouldn't say where to.*

Miranda was quick to speak as soon as Richard closed the door. By no means had she finished their conversation so she wanted answers right away. But to hear him speak so bluntly to someone whom he knew, especially Jack Rickard, puzzled her more so.

"We have unfinished business Richard, so we need to talk now! But what was going on out there with Jack Rickard? You did talk to him rather abruptly, and why should he forget about Jenna?"

"Well, Jenna is in real trouble and I don't want him pestering me about her treatment, or where she is. That is not his business now!"

"If you say so but I thought it would be up to them to decide that!"

"Not any more it isn't!"

"Why not, and what trouble is Jenna in to bring this on?"

"I had a phone call from her doctor earlier. They are transferring her to a specialist in the city today. No doubt Jack will find that out when he visits the hospital, but I am not giving him information! I don't want him here. That is why I told him to forget about Jenna!"

Ah, I see! she mused but then attacked him on a different topic. "Well, you handle it! But pray tell what we do about 'Oceanview? Do we have to move? We could move to George's and my house."

"Defiantly not Miranda! The way I see it is, we move on now! 'Oceanview' is my home, and I don't plan on leaving here! You may not realize it, but I am very rich in my own right, and I will pay for all expenses to keep it running, you can help with staff if you wish!"

Miranda smiled that sweet smile again. "Help with the staff?"

"I will keep all the staff and pay their wages, and you my love, can run the household. Would you like to do that?" he asked.

"You would give me total control of running the household and the staff? Is that correct Richard?" she inquired.

"Certainly!" he declared. "We are together now, we are one!"

Miranda couldn't keep the smile off her face. Suddenly all things were shaping up nicely. "In that case, Richard Temple, you can bet I'll do just that! I shall begin on Monday, soon you will see results!"

Richard shook his head, and smiled. "I have no doubt about that at all beautiful lady!" he replied as he pulled her close, then roughly claimed her lips. But she seemed to respond with a similar urgency as she tugged at his trousers to loosen his belt, and melted into his embrace. Richard chuckled as he lifted her effortlessly, then carried her to the bedroom. "We do make a perfect team Miranda!" he said, as he laid her gently upon the bed. Then he shed his clothes to cover her body with his own, and began to remove her clothing and kiss her bare skin. "We'll be lovers and partners in everything my love!"

She lay naked and writhing beneath him as she pulled down his head to place her breast in his mouth. She gasped as he suckled her, but managed a reply. "We could be partners in crime my love!"

He lifted his head to look at her and smiled a cheeky smile. "That we could be Miranda, that we could be!" and he nipped at both her nipples until they rose like red rubies and he sucked them. Then his head slowly moved down to seek her belly-button where he kissed her softly. His head spun, and he groaned as he parted her legs and discovered such tenderness between her inner thighs where his lips caressed each and every part of her. His tongue began probing and teasing, searching as he couldn't get enough of such perfection, but then found the heart of her. She screamed out in ecstasy as she felt it and shivered in shock as his mouth covered her most secret parts.

Much later Richard lay propped up on pillows while he secretly watched her sleep. She was so unbelievably beautiful, and had been negligent of a gown, so he took in all the pleasure of her nakedness.

I have George's accident to thank for that! he realized as his mind wandered to George, his accident, and other conversations he had with Miranda, and a frown crossed his brow. He had urged her to break all ties with George, and she had glared at him when she spoke. "Leave it be Richard. I have ideas, so I'll handle George my own way, in my own time. Don't hassle me!" *Hmm!* he thought.

Richard stared at her body knowing he would have her forever, and his loins stirred at the thought of it, but he couldn't still the thoughts and certain questions he needed answered. *I really know so little about her.* he thought. *But, does it really matter though?*

It suddenly hit him that he had never, ever questioned her about George, it seemed irrelevant at the time. Only now her words had come back to haunt him. "I will handle George and my marriage, myself Richard! Just leave it to me!" *What did she mean by that?*

How would she handle George? What ideas did she have to end their marriage? *But that's not all!* He remembered when they first spoke about Julia she had said. "It's a simple fix, *just get rid of her!*"

Get rid of her? he wondered about that but had shrugged it off at the time, as he did with Pablo's incident? What did she just say?"

"We could be partners in crime my love!"

What would she know of crime, has she committed any crime?

Then as if on cue, he noticed her eyes slowly opening, and she smiled that lusty smile at him that he loved.

"Ah! The lady wakes." he said. "I just had the craziest thoughts. I was thinking of George, and how he died. Can't believe his brakes failed! Can you Miranda? You must have noticed how fastidious he was with that car, surely you must have questioned that?" he asked.

Immediately he noticed the reaction on her face just before she quickly raised her hands to her eyes and rubbed them, and yawned before answering him. "Oh, poor George! I do miss him. I am sorry you mentioned him as it has made me feel quite sad. But yes! I do remember him changing his brake pads just the day before he died, he was going on about his safety, the road around the cliffs and all!"

"So, you were with him the day he done that?" asked Richard.

Miranda chuckled. "Yes, of course I was with him that day. I was always with him. He was explaining to me all about the brakes, and brake lines, to be conscious of the importance of maintaining a car!"

"You're a quick learner too Miranda! So now you'd be able to do similar to your car, if need be, wouldn't you?" he asked evasively.

"Of course, silly!" Miranda gushed. Then a hand went up to her mouth as she realized she had said too much. She turned her head away quickly, but already fuming with herself that she had been so stupid to allow Richard to trick her into that conversation.

Richard watched her closely, expecting a full confession. But her next reaction was what totally flawed him as she turned to face him brazenly, completely in control of her emotions now, as if the words hadn't been said. He gaped as she quickly resumed composure.

"I find this conversation so tedious Richard, and petty even! But I shall pretend it never happened!" she said firmly, as she flung her legs over the bed and stood to glare at him. Her violet eyes seemed to darken more, if possible, but the daggers shot, were meant solely for him as she added. "Let us not speak of it again as it upsets me! Let us move on!" then she started pulling on her clothes angrily.

Richard became concerned, he didn't like it at all when Miranda was angry so he tried to apologize. "Oh, Miranda please forgive me darling, I didn't mean to be insensitive! Yes, we should move on!"

But she wasn't listening, instead she began talking again.

"Besides, I have other more important things to do now. I have changed my mind. I intend on going to see the staff, and have them all meet with me this afternoon so I can give them all instructions rather than wait until Monday, if that is alright? Will you join us?"

"Hmm! A good idea. I did tell you to run the household, so what you say, goes now! Though, I would prefer to speak alone with the staff after you are done talking, just to get some facts straight!"

"Excellent that is fine with me! So, I must change now Richard!"

"Ok! Actually, speaking about Monday, I may leave work earlier to visit the hospital. I must find out about Jenna and her treatment!"

"Hmm!" she replied. "Go if you must, but we need to know!"

Miranda made an entrance as if she owned the place when she entered the kitchen. She was immaculately dressed in her best riding outfit and the purple vest seemed to darken her violet eyes.

"Morning cook, pay attention, I wish to speak to you!" she said.

Paula Hastings was at the stove, and she turned to face her. "Oh, it's you!" she said abruptly. "My name is Paula, so call me that in future, and really, you shouldn't be in here!" she offered.

Miranda laughed, and it gave her much pleasure to continue.

"Cook will do! So, I'll call you that! Now! I will speak briefly as I am quite busy. I am the newly appointed household manager for 'Oceanview' cook! So, if you wish to remain working here, I would suggest you listen to me in future!" and she smiled that sweet smile.

Paula's face reddened as the blood rushed to her head, and she gaped at her. "I want Mister Temple to confirm that!" she stated.

"Then ask him, he will be talking to the staff after me! However, nothing will change, I am your boss now cook. So, you will answer to me, and only me! Is that understood?" she asked, as she smiled.

Paula stood rooted to the spot, but did not reply.

"Have it your way cook, but it will cost you one way or another! I shall return at precisely 1p.m. So, I will expect you to make certain you have assembled all the staff for a meeting with me in the living room at that time, and you can regard that as your first duty under my management, and my orders! No need to contact Pablo. I plan to go riding, so I will tell him myself when I go over to the stables!" With that said, she turned to walk spritely from the kitchen, to leave Paula staring after her, as she crossed the foyer to the front doors.

Miranda chuckled as she crossed the lawns. *That felt good!* she relished the thought with satisfaction. *So, what goes around, usually comes around!* she mused. Then she smiled as she stepped onto the path leading to the stables. She was on an important mission now, and nothing would deter her. *Things need to be set right!* she realized.

At the stable doors she paused to gather herself for a second, then boldly pushed the doors in, and walked towards the noises being made out back where Pablo was busy hammering something.

"Good morning!" Miranda said, as she greeted him with a smile.

Pablo started at the voice, and dropped his hammer as he stared at her standing there. There was something about this woman that had always scared him, she put fear in him to make him vulnerable.

"First things first Pablo! I am the newly appointed Manager for 'Oceanview!' So, that means I'm your boss now. I am holding a staff meeting at 1 p.m. today and I will expect you there. Understand?"

"Yes missus!" he replied shakily, and hung his head.

"Good! Now, do you have two horses close by?" she queried.

Pablo looked up, but could not look into those devilish eyes, so he looked out the window. "Yep, just outside. I planned to do some shoeing today, so there are four horses in the stables!"

"Excellent, you go and get two horses, and saddle them up, and I shall wait here. Do you have a coffee making facility here?"

"Yep, just inside there." Pablo pointed.

"Good! I'll have a coffee while I am waiting, so you can go now!"

He paled as he looked at her quickly. "Yes Missus!" he mumbled meekly, then dropped what he was doing to walk quickly to door.

Miranda stood in the doorway drinking her coffee, and watched as Pablo saddled up the two horses then walked them to the railing. She set her coffee down to walk outside. "All ready?" she asked.

"Yes missus! So, who is the other horse for?"

Miranda stared into his eyes and he cringed as she spoke. "For you Pablo! So, mount up. We are going for a little ride as I need you to show me something. Oh, and bring a shovel!" she added.

"What for?" asked Pablo shakily. Then he gaped at her reply.

"Just a security issue we must address Pablo, a little matter of a girth strap to attend to! So, we need to recover it. Come along now!"

Just the last few swirls of smoke drifted away on the wind when Miranda stepped forward to inspect the remnants. Only a pile of ashes remained where once was a girth strap, and Miranda smiled.

"Good job Pablo, now there is no evidence out there to convict you, and your secret will be safe with me!"

Pablo stared at her bewildered. *She has a nerve.* he thought.

"But, missus. What about your involvement? I checked the girth strap when I brought it back you know, and there was another cut!"

"Another cut you say? Not that your cut had torn to get bigger? Really Pablo? You expect me to accept that, where is your proof?"

"Proof? Just that there is another cut!" he replied quite puzzled. "But we can check the girth strap and I will soon show you missus!" then he turned quite pale as he said. "My god, we just burnt it!"

Miranda chuckled. "Yes! We did indeed, Pablo. So, I take it you have no proof of your accusations, but just to stress my point once more. I didn't have any involvement with the girth strap Pablo, and you can't prove that I did! On the other hand, I witnessed what you did to the girth strap and the big knife you used, and unlike you, I do have the proof as I took several photos! No Pablo, Julia Temple's unfortunate accident was caused solely by you, and if I have to use my evidence, then I will. You may go back to work now, just be at the meeting in the living room at 1 p.m. It is most important, and Mister Temple wants to talk to you all as well after me!"

Pablo's eyes clouded over to hear that, but his blood boiled. He wanted to strike her, and made a move forward. "Stop threatening me!" he said in anger as he stepped towards her with clenched fists.

"I wouldn't if I was you, Pablo! Do not ever threaten me, or you will end up in jail! I know too much about you. What you did was criminal, so your life remains still in my hands. You placed yourself in a corner to be at my beck and call then, or any time I choose. You must pay for your mistakes as I will fire you if you don't obey me!"

Miranda glared squarely at him. "I am your boss now, after all!"

Pablo stepped back as realization sank in. *I have been so stupid. How do I face Mother's fury and wrath,* what the hell do I tell her?

He backed away, his face haunted with the look of defeat and he didn't know which way to turn. *So much had happened,* he was at his wits end *trying to find a way out of this evil woman's clutches.*

That wasn't his only worry now, was it? he realized as he stumbled over to his horse, then mounted up and rode back to the stables.

It was five minutes to 1p.m when he walked into the living room to the glare of Miranda Delvin who had already began speaking to the other staff. They were all there he noted as he hung his head so he didn't have to make eye contact with her, then he sat at the back.

"Thank you for joining us, Pablo!" offered Miranda abruptly but produced her best smile as she continued. "I was just telling your colleges what you already know Pablo. So, in future, any decisions about the running of the household, wages, rosters, purchases etc., will be made by me. So, any time you need something for the house or stables, you must bring it to my attention! Is that understood?"

She looked around the room to a show of nodding heads, but no-one spoke! Not one word, and they didn't look too happy, but she felt a certain amount of satisfaction in that, and continued on.

"Well, that is all for now. I shall give you all new instructions on Monday. So, you must be here at 7am sharp!" she stressed. "Now, everyone wait here as Mister Temple wants to address you all."

There were some whispers, and all heads looked to the doorway as he breezed through to announce his arrival, then came silence.

Richard gave them all a passing glance, then he joined Miranda.

"What have you done to them all Miranda?" he asked, as he gave a chuckle. "They do look a gloomy lot! So! Are you all done here?"

Miranda smiled. "They're all yours Richard, I am going riding!" she pecked his cheek and spoke. "See you later!" then she was gone.

Richard turned to face the staff. "I'll be quick. In light of events things have changed. You all still have jobs, but with no benefits!"

Paula rose to her feet. "You can't do that you promised us more!" Pablo's eyes blazed when he spoke. "We have done things for you!"

Richard's eyes seemed to rest on Pablo and he glared. "Anyone who doesn't like that can leave now, that is all!" and he walked out.

Chapter Eight

Through the pain, she slowly forced her eyes to open. There were shadows close by, and she tried desperately to focus. *Where was she, and what was happening?* she wondered. She tried to rise, but the effort proved too much as the pain forced her back down again. She raised a hand to her aching head only to find it was wrapped up in bandages, just to make her more confused, but she turned her head to the sound of voices and the shadows at the end of the bed moved.

"Look, she is waking up doctor!" whispered a nurse.

"Excellent, thank goodness! Speak to her nurse Kelly! You may tell her she had an operation, but no details please. I shall come back to speak to her of that once she is recovered and I have her results!"

"Certainly doctor!" said the nurse, and moved in closer. "Jenna! I am nurse Kelly. Can you hear me? Lift a finger if you do, please!"

Jenna noticed a shadow move, then sensed someone beside her. A voice spoke to ask her a question so, slowly she raised her finger.

"That is great Jenna! I am nurse Kelly, and you are in a hospital."

"Why a hospital and why do you call me Jenna?" came the reply.

Nurse Kelly frowned at that remark and she made a note on her chart. "Well Jenna, we've been told by Richard Temple that you are his daughter, and your name is listed as Jenna Temple on our chart! You were transferred from Blue Bay to The City Memorial Hospital and you have undergone an operation. Do you recall your name?"

"No, I don't recall that name, and why did I have an operation?"

Nurse Kelly knew the doctor said she may have some memory loss, so she just made notes of their conversation, then she spoke.

"Doctor Eric Wilson is a specialist surgeon here. He performed your operation, and he is your treating doctor. He is aware that you are awake now, and will be back when you are properly recovered to speak with you about your operation. It is best if you wait to get your results from the doctor Jenna! He will have more up-to-date information for you. I shall go out to order some food, and a cup of tea for you now if you feel up to that?"

"I guess so." replied Jenna vaguely.

Richard had been advised on arrival at the hospital by reception where Jenna Temple's room was, so he was sitting in the waiting room outside Jenna's room when nurse Kelly opened the door and walked out. He stood up quickly to approach her. "Good afternoon nurse, my name is Richard Temple. I was told this is my daughter's room, and I was to wait here in hope to see her. Is that possible as I have no idea what is happening!" he asked as he stepped forward. "Any information would be helpful." he added.

"Good morning, Mister Temple. Yes, this room belongs to Jenna Temple, but unfortunately you can't see her yet. All I can tell you is that she has undergone an operation, she is awake now but waiting for the specialist to visit her. I am about to get Jenna up to eat and drink in preparation. You may wait until the doctor has spoken to her, but it could be a while if any further tests are needed!"

"Thank goodness she is awake, but what about the operation? They did tell me in Blue Bay that she may need to have an operation when they transferred her here so I signed papers for that purpose, but now I don't know what the operation was for, or even if it was a success? Can you enlighten me at all, and tell me that at least?"

"I cannot talk of the operation Mister Temple, doctor's orders. Just be patient, I am sure he will want to speak to you later."

"I see! Will I be able to speak to Jenna at some point?"

"Of course! We just need the doctor to go over a few things with her first and there may be further tests, so bear with us for now."

"Oh! I didn't realize, sorry nurse. I will wait here for your call!"

"Thank you for understanding." she said and scurried away.

Richard watched her, then made a decision, so he pulled out his mobile and dialed. "Hi Hill!" he said when he heard her answer. "Change of plans, book me off work today. I will be at the hospital!"

Hillary replied, and he closed his phone. *It could be a long day.* he thought. *I'll call Miranda too,* so he made the call, then sat waiting.

In no time he noticed a doctor enter the room and he felt anxious.

Doctor Eric Wilson entered Jenna's room. Once inside he smiled at her. "Morning Jenna, so good to see you in recovery. I am Doctor Eric Wilson. Do you feel up to discussing your operation with me?"

Jenna was propped up with pillows now. Her vision had cleared and she looked directly at the doctor. He was in his mid-thirties she guessed. His sandy hair fell loosely about his face, and she gazed into his soft blue eyes. He had a trusting smile, and Jenna warmed to him straight away. She smiled, and spoke. "Yes, please doctor, I have a million questions so I guess you'll explain what happened!"

He smiled and pulled up a chair to sit beside her. "You are a very lucky girl, young lady. You have been in an induced coma for some time now since your accident in Blue Bay. Some hemorrhaging was detected but further tests showed a tumor so you were sent here!"

Jenna stared at him. "I had an accident?" she asked. "I don't recall that. What type of accident was it, and where is Blue Bay?"

A frown creased the doctor's brow. He had expected some loss of memory but now he had to find out exactly to what extent it was.

He smiled before he spoke. "First things first Jenna. Your home is some seventy acres, an estate just outside of Blue Bay which is a town west of the city. Do you recall your home 'Oceanview' at all?"

Jenna frowned as she looked at him. "No doctor! I don't seem to have any recollection of home, or the town Blue Bay. Why is that?"

"Well, that would be from the severity of your accident Jenna. Now a little incite to your injuries prior to coming here. Apparently, you were at your home when you were attacked so severely that it almost cost you your life, but many thanks to the excellent staff at Blue Bay Hospital they were able to treat you by stabilizing you in an induced coma, and probably saved your life. Then with further developments it was a rush to transfer you to a better facility, so now you are in The City Memorial Hospital. I have just operated to remove the tumor and managed to resolve the hemorrhaging. I am confident the operation was a success and do expect a full recovery. There will be some set-backs, and that of course refers to memory loss! Now, about your operation! Because of where the tumor was positioned the operation was quite delicate! So, I did expect you could suffer some memory loss, but I did expect that to recede as time goes on. But knowing you suffered some trauma, to regain all your memory may be lengthy. So, we monitor you! Tell us exactly what you can, or can't remember, it is most vital to your recovery!"

"Yes, of course doctor! Just how long will I be in hospital?"

"There is no suggestion of time at this stage Jenna, as you have been through this trauma, I would expect you to be here for quite some time, but we will do a daily check on your improvements!"

"Oh, I see!" muttered Jenna, and she hung her head.

Doctor Wilson noticed she seemed uneasy about that so he tried to explain further. "Don't be deterred by that information Jenna. It is in your best interest to stay here until we can determine which part of your memory you have lost. I expect in a week, I should be able to tell you that and whether any further operations are needed. Then we will discuss a recovery plan for you, so at this stage, it is early days, but be patient as in time, I do expect a full recovery!"

Jenna tried to smile and looked him in the eyes. "Well, I will take your advice Doctor Wilson. I do hope you are correct as I must have a life out there, but right now it doesn't seem to exist I'm afraid!"

"Understandable my dear, but we shall get you back on track! Oh! By the way, you have a visitor outside. Are you up for a visit?"

"Well, if you think so, but who is it?"

"Your father! I believe his name is Richard Temple. If you do not mind, I will ask nurse Kelly to accompany him in your room so she can take notes during the visit! Is that alright with you?" he asked.

"If that is what you want doctor, then so be it!" replied Jenna.

"Excellent, any change in your condition needs to be monitored closely, so it will help us get you better much sooner. I will come and see you this afternoon, and again in the morning. I guess that will probably be our sessions until we have more information on you, so I will ask nurse Kelly to bring your father in, is that alright?"

"Yes doctor, I am ready, I am anxious to meet any family!"

Doctor Wilson rose, and Jenna watched as he crossed the room and stopped at the door, he waved. "See you later today. Jenna!"

Jenna waved back. "I'll look forward to that, thank you doctor!" Jenna felt anxious for some unknown reason, and the silence in the room was suffocating. She fiddled with her hands in her lap but her eyes kept flicking to the doorway with the expectation of her visitor arriving, her father. *Why can't I remember having a father?* she queried herself, but then recalled the doctor's words.

So, when at last the door opened, she was un-prepared, and just stared at the handsome man trailing behind nurse Kelly. He was tall, but muscular, with shiny jet-black hair. Though her immediate concern was his captivating blue eyes. So alien, to her eyes of green.

Nurse Kelly spoke first. "So nice you have a visitor, Jenna. Your father has spoken to the doctor so he is aware of your operation!"

Immediately the man moved closer to her bed. "Oh, Jenna! It is so good to see you awake finally, and good news of your operation. I have missed you." he said, and leaned over to kiss her cheek.

Jenna's face flushed. She stared at nurse Kelly with desperation in her eyes, and called out. "No!" as she roughly pushed him away. "Please don't, I don't even know you! You can't just come in here pretending to be my father, and try to kiss me!" she said. "Who are you? I don't remember you so, I need more proof first!" she gasped.

Richard was shocked, and took a step backwards to look hard at his daughter. *She really doesn't know me!* he realized.

Nurse Kelly stepped in quickly. She placed a hand on Jenna's arm. "It is alright Jenna, and I know you are confused. It may be a while before you start to remember things, however, trust me when I say that this man is your father as we have had him checked out, and it would probably be in your best interest to get to know him. Just chat, and find out your roots from him. Something may trigger your memory, so anything would be helpful to your recovery."

She turned to Richard. "Mister Temple, I am very sorry, but you do understand the problem as the doctor has explained it. Please keep in mind that Jenna does not know where she has come from, so I would suggest you talk openly about her family and her home, where she lives, and try to paint a picture for her! But try not to get too personal at this stage until she remembers you. Is that alright?"

"Yes, of course nurse, I understand. I am so sorry Jenna! We will take it slowly. Do you mind if I sit by your bed to speak with you?"

Jenna's eyes widened to stare at nurse Kelly who nodded to her. So, she looked at Richard Temple, and replied. "Well, I guess that would be alright. There are a lot of questions I have, so yes, please sit, but only for a short while today!"

Richard looked at nurse Kelly and then spoke to Jenna. "I won't tire you, Jenna! So firstly, your home 'Oceanview,' is an estate not far from Blue Bay, which is a short train ride from the city. You were born in Blue Bay and go to a high school there, and are in your third year. You are an only child and practically run the household in my absence since your mother's accident. You are so clever young lady, and with your grades your mother was wanting you to study law!"

Jenna straightened. "My mother?" she exclaimed. "Why has she not been mentioned, why isn't she here to visit me?" was her first question as she stared straight at the man beside her. It was in that instant his face paled, and she detected some emotion appear there.

What was that? she wondered. *Was it to do with my mother?* I know his eyes definitely clouded over just before he lowered his head, but then he seemed to regain composure to prepare his reply.

Richard looked at Jenna. Her green eyes deepening into a stare unsettled him. *What-ever will I say?* he wondered, then he spoke up.

"Your mother? I was hoping to hold that information, but I have to tell you Jenna. Your mother is incapacitated, so she won't be able to visit you here. She had a nasty horse accident, and is not long out of hospital. So, you see, she is still recuperating at home!" he lied.

"Oh, I see. I hope she is ok!" said Jenna, then added "So, because mother had a horse accident, I've been helping out in the household is that correct?" There was that look again before his reply.

"Well, not exactly. You have run the household for well over two years Jenna since the accident which left your mother disfigured as she was engulfed in flames. The horse accident was just recently!"

"Are you saying mother has suffered two accidents?" she asked.

Richard was not comfortable talking about the accidents, and he had held back vital information about their current situation, so quickly he tried to change the subject hoping Jenna wouldn't notice.

"Oh, I must tell you Jenna, before I forget to mention it. We hire a full staff. A cook, Paula Hastings, and her husband Ted who looks after the grounds, and is our handyman. They live on our property in a cabin. We also employ a full-time housemaid Melita Sanchez, and her son Pablo is the stable hand. We require a lot of stables to cater for the many horses we have, and you do love riding horses Jenna. You ride extremely well I must say!" he chuckled.

Jenna frowned, and she was not in the joking mood. "That is all very well, but it was my mother I wanted to know more about?"

Her question startled Richard, and he seemed to stumble on his next words. "Ye...s. Yes of course you do, I a...am so sorry! What was the question, Jenna?" he asked sheepishly. *My god, what a mess!*

Jenna looked hard at him. He is struggling to inform me, *and for some reason I sense he is lying to me! But why, what is he hiding?* "I was asking if mother had suffered two accidents? If you could answer that question, it would be good, but firstly there's something I shall require you to do if you will?" and she turned to nurse Kelly.

"Would you have a notebook and pen please nurse?" she asked.

Nurse Kelly smiled at her. She could detect some friction in the room and she wondered why, but she replied to Jenna's question promptly. "Of course, Jenna. I happen to have those with me." and she dug into her canvas bag and handed Jenna a notebook and pen.

"Oh excellent, thank you nurse Kelly!" Jenna smiled and handed them to Richard Temple. "First things first please! Would you mind writing down the answer to my question and following questions? I may not be able to remember later what you told me!" she stated.

"Richard grabbed the notebook. "Yes, of course, how silly of me prattling on, that is no problem, so fire away!" he joked.

Her Mind SCREAMS MURDER

"Now! Start with my mother's full name if you would."

Richard gasped. *This girl is definitely interrogating me!* he realized. He recouped quickly, but eyed Jenna momentarily before he then wrote as he spoke. "Julia Rose Temple is your mother's full name!"

Jenna felt as if someone had punched her in the chest. Somehow, that name seemed to send signals to her brain. *I know that name, but how?* she wondered, then tried to disguise her feelings. For some unknown reason she wanted to keep it to herself, and she certainly didn't want the nurse, or her father to know she recalled something.

Nurse Kelly stared at Jenna. She detected something different in her manner, but couldn't understand the emotion she had seen.

Jenna was going on. "Thank you! Now I require her age, and full address, as I would like to write to her seeing she is not well!"

Richard gulped, and began writing. *This is beginning to feel like a nightmare.* he thought. *I will have to make sure I get all those letters!*

"Now a little about me if you could. My age, date of birth, home phone number, where I attend school and my year, please, as I need information of my personal files and grades sent to me personally!"

Richard stared, but continued writing. *Jenna may have lost all her memory, but she hasn't lost any of her grit, that's for sure!*

"I don't seem to have any stationery though, and nothing else as far as I know!" Jenna was saying. Any suggestions on how to obtain things for writing and posting letters?" she asked nurse Kelly.

Richard interrupted. "Don't worry Jenna, I shall bring you some clothes and personal items back tonight as I have to go away for a short while, so I shall leave ample amount of money with the nurse now for any expenses you may incur if that's allowed nurse Kelly?"

"Certainly, Mister Temple. I can purchase Jenna's requirements at the shop here, they sell stamps, and we have a post-box on site!"

"Great, then you are all sorted my lady." he said to Jenna.

Jenna felt at ease and she looked at them. "Thank you both!"

"However, there are a couple of things I seem to be missing!"

Richard frowned. He thought all discussions were finished, but he forced a smile, and asked Jenna what her requirements were.

Jenna noticed that he seemed to be perplexed by something, but she continued. "I would like detailed directions from the city, to our home, if you would? How to get there? How long the journey takes, and the full address and postcode please! I would also require full instructions on how to get to my room. I am assuming I have one?"

Richard chuckled. "Of course, you have your own room, Jenna!"

"That's good to know! Also, please add a list of employee names, the location of yours, and mother's room, so I can find you both!"

Richard gulped but kept his head down. *My god, this is so tacky!* Jenna continued. "Only one more thing for now, but an important one. I'd like to know of any friends I may have had from school?"

Richard stopped writing. *I won't be telling her about Jack, that is for sure, I will leave him out!* He wrote all the notes, gave them to Jenna and stood. "Done! I'll leave now, I can't tire you. So, until tonight!"

Nurse Kelly approached Jenna's bed furtively when he left. "Do you feel ok Jenna, or has something upset you?" she queried.

Jenna looked at her squarely before she spoke. Surprisingly, she felt in total control. Her present memory seemed to be perfect. She could remember all the conversation just past, her discussions with nurse Kelly, and her conversation with Doctor Eric Wilson and now she was eager to speak to him again this afternoon. However, it was her home-life she couldn't recall, and all the people in her life.

"I am fine nurse Kelly! Nothing upset me at all, on the contrary, I now have information which will be helpful to me!" she replied, as she tucked the notebook under her pillow. Now, with the money father gave you, would you be as kind to buy some stationery, pens, stamps, and I'd like a lockable diary if that is possible?"

"Certainly Jenna. I shall do it immediately, and get them to you!"

Richard couldn't wait to get out of there, he had made some lame excuse about tiring her, and that he had to go back to the office.

It wasn't until he was in the privacy of the lift that he reached for a handkerchief to dab at his brow. He was shaken, and as he rode down to the ground floor his mind was in a turmoil. So much has happened. *How could I tell her about her mother?* How could I say that at this very minute *a police investigation was in full operation about the attack on her,* and *the police had classed her mother as a missing person, or a possible murder case even.* That is, if they could find her body! So far police were baffled by both scenarios.

Richard was thankful when he finally reached 'Oceanview,' and climbed wearily out of his car. But still, he walked over to the edge of the cliff face and looked down before approaching the gates. Sure enough, they were still there scouring the beach. It was in a mess. He shook his head as a shiver went through him. *What next? They have just about dug the beach up for a sixty-meter radius.* he thought.

He walked slowly across the lawns deep in thought, and a worry line creased his brow as he stepped up onto the deck outside his rooms. *Damn fools!* he thought, as he paused at the door, attempting to insert the key, when the door opened, and Miranda stood there.

"Why so grim Mister Temple?" she asked, as she looked at him. "It appears to me that you bear the weight of the whole world on your shoulders, so prey tell all?" she asked, and smiled that sweet smile only she possessed, only this time it had no effect on Richard.

"Not now Miranda, I have had enough for one day!" he said, as he pushed past her to walk inside where he slumped on the lounge.

"Oh dear, you are ruffled Mister Richard Temple! So, did you go to the hospital? Is that why you are in this mood?" she asked.

He looked up at her with a vacant look of disbelief on his face.

"She doesn't even know me Miranda and didn't recognize me!"

"Do you mean Jenna?" Miranda asked with interest.

"Of course, Jenna! Who else would I be talking of?" he snapped. "Miranda's face darkened. "Now, just a minute Richard, I am not a mind-reader, you know. If you had of answered my question, if you went to the hospital, then I would know! Wouldn't I?" she quipped.

He looked at her sadly. "Sorry Miranda, come sit beside me." he said, as he patted the couch beside him. "I guess it has shaken me, but Jenna has no memory what so-ever. The specialist has removed a tumor from her brain, so it was a very serious operation, but she is awake now, and though she has no memory, she still has that fire, and grit she always had, and it was that which shocked me more.

Miranda chuckled. "Yes, that would be Jenna!"

"I even gave money to the nurse to buy stationery for her, so she could write to her mother of all people! Then to her school. I don't know what she is cooking up, but I guess I will find out later."

"So, you didn't tell her, did you?"

"No, of course not. How could I? She has been asleep for ages!"

Miranda's own mixed feelings hounded her, then she answered. "Look on the bright side Richard! At least she is awake now, and obviously must understand her illness. She will take control now!"

Richard's eyes flew wide and he stared at her. "Control! Exactly, you are right on the button there! I think that is what she plans to do. Her plans won't involve me at all. Though she may not know it she will be on her mother's will, and that is a problem. No Miranda there's no bright side to this at all! Especially if she remembers!"

"You are making too much of this Richard. We will deal with it all when the time comes, in the meantime what do you have to do?"

"Just take some clothes and personal items up to the hospital for her tonight then wait and see, I guess. Luckily, I told her I was going away for work for a while. I just couldn't face more questions."

"Well, seems to me you have it all sorted anyway Mister Temple. Could I help by packing a small bag for her?" she smiled.

"Thanks Miranda, that would help a lot, and I'm sorry."

"Not a problem, apology accepted!" she giggled, and smiled as she reached for him with no question of what her intentions were.

He grinned, and reached for her just as a knock came to the door. Richard cursed in aggravation as he rose to answer the door and he flung it back, and Melita their housemaid stood there submissively.

Melita had been listening outside the door for about ten minutes before she decided to knock. So, she had heard every word spoken, and the hairs stood up on her neck as she shivered with realization of what this turn of events meant to everyone at 'Oceanview,' and she jumped in fright when Richard spoke abruptly to her.

"What the hell is it, Melita? It's after lunch, so what's up?"

"Sorry Mister Temple, I didn't realize you were home from work yet, but I just wanted to tell Missus Miranda that I will be here right on 9.00am tomorrow morning as arranged, to clean your rooms!"

Miranda called out as she rose from the chair. "Excellent, thanks Melita. Just let yourself in, I will leave my key under the mat. After breakfast I'll go riding. Mister Temple will be left for work by then!"

"Thank you, missus!" called Melita, then nodded to Richard as she turned to leave, and walked briskly down the deck.

Richard closed the door abruptly, then turned to face Miranda with a sardonic smile. "Well, well! The lady seems to have all the staff wound around her little finger. Good for you Miranda, well done!"

Miranda smiled her best smile as she sidled up to him. "Ah! But it hasn't been easy my love. These people are so set in their ways that any suggestion at all is an education to them. So, you see, it has been persistence on my part, a lot of it, but eventually perseverance and consistency have won through. Now, I feel I am finally getting through to them, where at first, they hated taking orders from me!"

"Hmm, I see!" he pulled her close to nuzzle her neck, and she giggled. "Where were we before we were rudely interrupted love?"

Melita hurried into the house, and almost ran across the floor and into the kitchen where Paula Hastings was at the stove cooking.

"Paula, we must talk!" she called. But Paula kept stirring at the stove. Melita grabbed her hand to spin her around, and looked into her beady grey eyes. "Listen Paula for god's sake this is important!"

Paula stared into Melita's anxious eyes. "What is so important?" she asked, as she returned to the pot she was stirring.

"I need your full co-operation Paula, because this concerns Jenna Temple!" said Melita. "Please face me, and talk to me!"

As the name was mentioned, Paula stopped stirring, and slowly turned. Jenna Temple's name had not been mentioned for a long, time at 'Oceanview,' and the hair at the base of her scalp bristled. Paula stared at Melita who was obviously in distress. "So, what is it about Jenna that you have to discuss, and why now?" she asked.

Melita leaned forward, and whispered. "I just overheard Mister Temple, and the monster Miranda talking in their room. They said quite clearly Jenna was in a city hospital and has had an operation!"

"That is perfect Melita, the furthest away she is, the better. So, it is nothing to do with us! Why the drama, I don't get it? Jenna isn't here in Blue Bay anymore, and we report to you know who now!"

"But that's not all Paula!"

Paula was getting tired of the conversation. "Just get on with it, Melita! I have food to cook, and surely you have work to do!"

Melita was annoyed. "I do have work to do! However, I thought just the simple fact that Jenna Temple is awake now, and no longer in a coma that it might spark an interest in you!!" Melita muttered.

"How would you know that, Melita?" spat Paula.

"Because, I heard them say that too, that's why! I listened to it all outside the door. I am guessing now it will only be a matter of time before Jenna is home stirring trouble. What if she remembers? There'll be more questions when she knows about her mother!"

"Maybe the police will come out here again, and we will have to answer more questions!" stressed Melita.

"So, what is wrong with that. Just deal with it!" said Paula.

"I would if I could remember exactly what I said before, but it is all becoming quite hazy now, and the questions stress me out!"

Paula gazed out the window. She had visions of how it could all pan out, she shuddered, but her mind was made up. She would be tough, and ready for anything they threw at her. She was wary now of everyone's lack of trust. She could feel it, they were all on edge, and just grabbing at straws. "You are so hopeless Melita. I thought you had more gumption than that. A few more questions will not resolve anything, or harm anyone. So, just get a grip woman!"

Melita grinned. "Yes, of course I have nothing to hide, do I? Anyway if I don't answer the questions the same again, then who cares? Thanks for the chat, I will be fine now. Just got anxious, that's all!"

Paula stared her down. She didn't expect that response at all. Still the questions sat on everyone's lips. *If they find Julia Temple's body, or question Jenna,* what then? *Do they find out a possible murderer is in this household,* as everyone here was a suspect. They were all so wary, and walking on eggshells. *Paula sensed it, and felt the vibes.*

"You do what you have to do Melita, and I will do what I always do, and that is look out for number one! Now, don't bother me with your tales, I will find out for myself in due course!"

Melita glared at Paula. One time they had become quite close, friends even, but since the drama on the beach at 'Oceanview,' *a hint of uncertainty hounded the staff.* Everyone put up a wall, kept to themselves instead of backing each other so, now Paula Hastings was stubborn, and standoffish. *It was everyone for themselves.*

Well, two can play that game Paula Hastings. You think you are so smart, but you know nothing, nothing! Melita turned to walk out, and threw a remark over her shoulder. "Just tell the others then!"

Jack was exhausted and looking forward to the coming weekend when he could have a well-earnt break. He sat at a computer in his work station of the police station, and stared regretfully at the pile of paper-work he had to do, and his mind went blank.

Suddenly he was thinking of Jenna. *I have to try and find her, but how?* he wondered. *It is pointless going out to see Mister Temple.* She is obviously somewhere at one of the big city hospitals. *So, I will just go to them all until I find her.* If only I didn't have so much to do here. I really can't get away, as I would need at least a week, who knows? *How is she, is she still in a coma? Did she need to have the operation?* All things I have never been informed of.! *Over a year has passed* and I've been consumed with my new job. He stressed, as there was a knock on his door. "Yes, the door is open, come in." he called.

Senior officer Keans entered the room with a huge smile on his face, and stared at Jack. He could sense he was under stress, but he let it go and instead, spoke to him. "Hi Jack, I was going to take you out with me today but Constable Jenkins advised me that he wants a word with you. I think you may like what he has to say too young fellow. You look like you need cheering up!" he chuckled.

"Really, right now?" asked Jack.

"Yes, right this minute. So, leave what you are doing, and go on down, he is expecting you!" said officer Keans.

Jack pushed his chair out, and a smile creased his lips as he stood and looked at officer Keans. "Thank you, sir, I will head off now!"

As he walked down the hallway, he wondered why he had been called in? *What could be so important now?* As he reached The Senior Constable's office, he knocked on the door.

"Come in Jack!" came the call from within.

Jack opened the door and went inside, then he closed the door behind him. "You wanted to speak to me sir?" he asked.

"Yes Jack, and rather urgently too, take a seat young man!"

Jack wasn't sure if he was in trouble or what, so a frown crossed his brow as he seated himself opposite the Constable.

Constable Jenkins noted the anxious look, and chuckled. "Be at ease Jack, you are not in any strife at all. On the contrary, rather the opposite, I feel. I have in my possession an email which I feel relates to you. Well rather, you were the first person I thought of when I read it. I shall try and get to the point so as to put you at ease."

"Thank you, sir! I am no too sure what to think just yet."

Constable Jenkins smiled at him. "Right, but keep in mind Jack, this is great news for you, so hear me out. Now, this information I have is a random email I feel, sent to all police departments. It could even go to many areas, so it is with great urgency that we need to address this asap. It is a once-only lifetime opportunity for a young person like yourself and I feel it is the right direction for you to take.

He looked Jack in the eyes. "This email is from our head office in The City Branch, sent by a well-known, and successful Homicide Detective who has his own suites, and operates his own business from head office! Homicide Detective Jeremy Woods. I know him personally, we attended the same university, and even then, I knew he would be a great Detective one day. Just as I sense that in you Jack, which is why we are having this conversation. Jeremy was all about helping his fellow colleagues, and supporting up and coming youngsters. So, he is now offering to train an assistant for himself to become a Detective, and work beside him. He could hire anyone, but prefers to get someone he can train personally from scratch, and you fit that bill, Jack! It is the offer of a lifetime. What do you think?"

Jack was gob smacked. He couldn't take the smile off his face. It seemed too unreal to be true. Everything he had ever wanted was down that pathway, and then he frowned as he replied. "It is the most exciting news I have heard Constable Jenkins! However, I am only a new-comer, still studying, and wouldn't get the job!"

Constable Jenkins made sure he had Jack's full attention before he spoke. "Listen very carefully Jack. All I need is confirmation from you that you can leave Blue Bay within the week, and you will get that position Jack. I will make sure of it! I don't care how many are in for it, I know this position will be the makings of you, and I can bet for certain that Jeremy will take my advice when I send him my recommendation and information on you. Your records here, your school, and of course the university that you attend, and your grades. I will leave no stone unturned, and I will back you all the way Jack. I have that faith in you. You have a great future, and I am going to make that happen for you. Ha, ha! When you become a big-shot Detective, you can come back and solve our cases for us!"

Jack laughed at the absurdity of it, but said. "Is that possible sir?"

"Of course! This is your home town. When your goal is reached you will be your own boss, and I think Blue Bay may like that also."

"You know my answer sir, it has to be a big yes! I am just sorry to have to leave here. I will miss this department and the colleagues I have befriended here, and of course yourself sir. You have been my rock. I won't forget that. I hope to re-pay you one day."

"Nonsense Jack. It's been my pleasure and I wouldn't be doing this if I didn't think you deserved it. People relate to you because of your attitude, kindness, teamwork and determination. Don't lose that Jack. Always be true to yourself and you will go a long way!"

"I will, thank you sir. I guess you could put my application in!"

Constable Jenkins nodded. I will be making phone calls to your school and Uni so, as soon as I have all your details, I will send the email, and I will ring Jeremy personally to have a chat about you!"

"I can't thank you enough sir. My parents will get a shock, but I am not telling them yet until I actually get the job, and then all hell will break loose getting ready to leave, and getting a place to live."

"Ah, about that. Leave living details up to me. I will sort that!"

"Are you sure sir. I mean, you have done enough already!"

"Don't concern yourself Jack. I know the city, and I want you to be safe, so if you don't mind, I would like to find the right place for you so I can assure your parents you will be alright."

"Yes, I guess you are correct, thank you again sir."

"No problems, now take the rest of today off to reflect on what I've said, and I will phone you late this afternoon. Keep in mind if you get the position, you must continue your studies at university, but don't worry I will handle the transfers for you to the best facility I know of in the city. You'll only have to say your goodbyes here."

Jack shook his head as he stood to leave and answered. "You are unreal Constable Jenkins. I will look forward to your call later."

"All good Jack, now go and relax!"

As Jack walked back to his work station he was in a daze. *What just happened? My whole life could be turned upside down,* but I am so ready for it. Besides, I'll be closer to Jenna wherever she is?

That was one thought he cherished, also the fact that he would be trained by the best Homicide Detective in the City, that was the big plus. *Did he deserve it?* he was beside himself with elation.

He was in a daze for the rest of that day. Later at home he felt edgy waiting for the all-important phone call, and when his phone rang, he jumped. Quickly he answered it knowing who it would be.

He thought all his birthdays had come at once when Constable Jenkins told him he had scored the position. He felt like jumping for joy, but patiently listened as he explained the finer details. He would have to be ready to leave the following Sunday. That only gave him another three days at home. *Just three days, and I will be off to start a new life. I cannot believe it.* he pondered. Constable Jenkins wanted him to come into his office the next day. He had contacted his university and made the appropriate transfers for his study to continue, and he had arranged accommodation for him in the city.

Jack wouldn't have to go to work or attend university at Blue Bay anymore. He would resume all study when he started his new job on Wednesday next week, giving him ample time to settle into his lodgings. Apparently, Constable Jenkins had an Aunty living in the city who was going to rent out a cabin to him on her property.

He would have his own privacy, but could attend her house for meals if he wished to, otherwise he had his own cooking facilities.

Oh, it is just perfect! thought Jack. *How fortunate I am.* He only had to obtain all the information, addresses, phone numbers and train ticket already booked to the city for Sunday morning by Constable Jenkins on the morrow. He also had an introductory note for him to give to Homicide Detective Jeremy Woods when they met.

Detective Woods would send someone to collect him from the railway station on Sunday. They would have a brief meeting and a quick chat about Wednesday, his first work day, then he would be taken to meet Constable Jenkins's Aunty, and move into the cabin.

Jack shook his head as they ended the phone conversation, and he raced into the living to tell his parents. They were amazed when Jack explained the finer details, but congratulated him on obtaining the position. It was a celebration dinner his mother cooked for him, and they talked for hours, but that night Jack tossed and turned in bed, not able to sleep. He could not wait for the morning to come.

It was senior officer Keans who greeted him next morning in the foyer. "Morning Jack! Big day, eh? Follow me young fellow."

Jack trailed along behind, and replied as he tried to keep pace.

"Yes, it could be officer Keans, I am to meet Constable Jenkins!"

"I am aware of that! He is expecting you. Come along now."

He took him down to the conference room, and knocked on the door. As the door opened, he urged Jack to go in. Jack entered to shouts of *Surprise!* and *Congratulations!* from his fellow workers.

Constable Jenkins came forward. "Congratulations on your new post, Jack! I couldn't help but give you a send-off. I do hope you keep in touch. We all would like to know how you are getting on, and we will miss you here. Just enjoy your party with your mates and we will get to the final details later if that is alright with you."

"Of course, sir, and thank you sir for everything you've done for me. I will make you proud of me one day, just wait and see!"

"We are all proud of you here already Jack, which is why you have this most generously offered position, and to put it mildly. It didn't take much convincing on my part that you were the right person for the job with Jeremy Woods. But to hear that you make Detective one day will be our bonus." he chuckled. "Now join in, they all want to say their goodbyes, and wish you well Jack!"

Many conversations took place as snacks and coffee was served. Jack's head was spinning with all the advice, but he spoke to each and every one of them, and they joked about different things. But a couple of hours slipped by quickly, and then Constable Jenkins was breaking up the party. It was time to go he realized as the Constable was beckoning him to follow to his office.

Jack said his goodbyes, and followed. In the office the Constable was most efficient with the paperwork. All was in order Jack noted, even phone numbers written in a book for him. Jack offered to pay for the train ticket, but the Constable refused. "No, Jack. It was my idea so I'm proud to shout you this trip. Remember, your university grades and papers have been forwarded to the city. You have the name and contact phone numbers in that notebook. Also, all your certificates, and studies you do at university, have all been emailed to Detective Woods. A most pleasant fellow you will find, and of course, a very well-educated man. I'll travel out to see you and your parents at some point tomorrow, just to reassure them!"

"Thank you, sir! I'm sure they will appreciate that. They do tend to worry, and leaving home at such short notice is mindboggling!"

Doctor Eric Wilson breezed into Jenna's room with a big smile on his face. He was running late with his rounds and was just ahead of the girls bringing the dinner trays down the hallway.

Jenna was busy transferring notes into her new diary that nurse Kelly had bought for her with stationery and pens. As she finished, she took the ribbon from around her neck which the key was tied to, and as she locked the diary something in her mind flashed.

There was a figure, but she could not see the face...*Why?* She jumped in fright from the voice in her head. *Remember, you must find the key Jenna!* and she stared at the key. *It is just a key!* she pondered. *What is it about a key that I must remember?* she wondered, and she searched her brain for an answer, but there was nothing she could remember about a key, and then...There it was again, the voice so clear. *Right here is my favourite place in the whole world, Jenna!* and she shuddered. Because somehow, she knew it was her mother's voice, and she strained to see her, but she couldn't.

She looked up in surprise as she noticed the doctor entering her room, and for some reason she felt guilty as the voice was still fresh in her mind, but she didn't want anyone to know that. She wasn't sure why, only she just couldn't tell. She wasn't sure if the doctor noticed her reaction, she hoped not as she wasn't quite sure how she would answer any questions, but when he spoke her mind was put at ease as he didn't even notice her stress. She felt certain that he wasn't coming to visit her so late this afternoon and she had been feeling disappointed earlier as she had wanted to speak to him.

"Oh, good. You are awake Jenna. Sorry, but I am running a little late, we had an emergency upstairs. Anyway, good news already my girl! All your tests are clear, and no further operation is needed at this stage! So, we just need to monitor you and make sure you keep improving. A lot of rest, and TLC is what this doctor orders!"

Jenna smiled. "Thank you doctor Wilson, that is a huge relief!"

"He smiled back, then his brow creased. "However, Jenna. With reference to recent tests on your current memory, I have discussed this with nurse Kelly, and we see clearly that your present memory is intact, and that is a very good sign, but your past memory seems somewhat blocked. Nurse Kelly has filled me in. She told me you didn't recognize your father this morning, is that so?" he queried.

"Yes doctor, I have no recollection of home, parents or friends, but I seem to be coping in everyday things like writing and math's.

Doctor Wilson frowned, but said. "Some good, some bad Jenna! It is not unusual for the trauma you have been through! However, I do feel that will change in time. Time is what we need Jenna as it is strange, so I will monitor you further while you remain here!"

"Just a question if I may please doctor as I would like to continue my school studies. So, when the time suits, would it be possible to be transferred to a hospital where I have access to university?"

"I know just the place Jenna, but be patient, give it some time!"

"Can I at least ask you to give me the paperwork so father can sign authority tonight while he is here, I believe he's going away!"

"By all means Jenna, I'll get nurse Kelly to get them for you!"

"Thank you so much Doctor Wilson. I know it is a bit premature, but I am not sure how long my father will be away. So, if he signs the papers, then it is all done and I just need to get better now!"

"That you do young lady. Now I must go. I shall see you bright and early in the morning, and we may get you up for a little walk."

"Oh, that does sound wonderful. I shall look forward to you coming early, and to go out in the sunshine will be a blessing."

"Keep in mind Jenna, I did say a little walk. Most of the time you will be in a wheelchair, but still in the sunshine." he chuckled.

Jenna didn't appreciate his jest, but at the same time realized the repercussions if she was to fall, so she smiled and then spoke.

"Thank you, Doctor Wilson. I do understand, so I do agree!"

Dinner had been served ages ago, so now Jenna sat propped up on the pillows waiting anxiously. Every now and then, her eyes flicked towards the doorway, but no-one was there. *Maybe my father isn't coming tonight.* she stressed. Then she pulled out her drawer, and grabbed a book that nurse Kelly had given her to read.

She looked at the book. It's edges all tattered and torn. *A well, read book.* she thought. *It must be an old book!* She jumped as the voice whispered to her. *This is the oldest book I own Jenna, but one you must remember.* Jenna started shaking. What is happening to me? *Why am I hearing this voice,* but not being able to identify who is speaking? *It is a little scary!* she thought. She was sure it must be her mother but why? *Why not come up and see me in the hospital and talk?*

Just then her door opened, and Richard Temple walked in. "Hi Jenna, how are you feeling?" he asked as he approached her bed. "I have some clothing and personal items in this bag, so I'll just leave it under your table and nurse Kelly can put it all away for you! Did you get the stationery items you needed?"

"I am well thanks. Nurse Kelly has purchased all my stationery requirements, so I'll be writing letters tomorrow. How is mother?"

Richard didn't expect a change in conversation, and the mention of her mother threw him a little so once again he stammered a reply.

"Ah! Well yes, your mother is slowing progressing. I imagine she'll be pleased to hear from you. What was the doctor's report?"

"It has been some time. Mother should be well enough to visit me!" said Jenna, she sensed that undercurrent again, but continued.

"The doctor is pleased with my tests, so no more operations. I asked to be transferred to another facility close to Uni. He agreed!"

"What the hell for Jenna?" queried Richard.

"To study law! So, in time Nurse Kelly is to arrange it if you sign the release, and authorization forms today before you go away!"

"Away? Oh, yes! I could be away a month. I'll fix it up for you!"

Chapter Nine

Two months later Jenna was transferred to a private clinic at the edge of the city, but more importantly for her was the fact that the university was just one block away. Her discussions with her specialist, doctor Wilson, were lengthy before he gave clearance for her to leave the hospital, and he would still be her treating doctor, but could only visit her twice a week. They covered everything, and her education, so now she was enrolled, and able to leave the clinic on said days to continue with her studies at the university. In the meantime, doctor Evan Hall would be caring for her at the clinic.

She was now able to fend for herself. Doctor Wilson was pleased with her progress, and healing after the operation. She was pleased to hear she was functioning normally on a day-to-day basis and her current memory was intact as she had to undergo very specific tests at the hospital to get that result, and her clearance. Also, according to a letter for the university from her school principal advised that apparently, she was quite clever according to her grades.

It will be good to put that to the test at university.

However, one thing clouded her present joy was the fact that after writing several letters, she still hadn't received a response from her mother, and that was so disappointing to her and she wondered why? *Maybe, I have done something wrong?* she worried, as her father had not returned to visit her again before she left hospital.

She tried to put it out of her mind, but the voice continued in her head. She thought of going home just to see her mother, but decided against it as all things important to her at this time, like her ongoing treatment and her education, were in the city. So, she had made the decision to go her own way, and do what she thought was right for her. Besides, she wanted to make her mother proud. It had stuck in her mind when she heard that her mother wanted her to become a lawyer, and at this stage, she was just thankful to be alive and able to pursue that avenue. *I do hope I am good enough?* she thought.

So, it was a long road for Jenna Temple. Initially, three days in a week at the university tired her out completely. She felt spent, and became weary easily, but she never complained. She had set herself a goal, and she would achieve that. Soon, it became second-nature to her, especially when she received accolades from her tutors. So, it was rewarding for her to discover after all she had been through, that she could understand the lessons, and actually do the work, and that most times her results were in the top two of her group.

Time slipped away like a prolonged episode, an endless passage into a new world. Days blurred into long weeks that soon became months. Her seventeenth birthday was a non-event, but they made an effort at the clinic to provide a birthday cake, and a fine present of a leather journal with her name printed on it. She did love that, and utilized it at university. Then, the whole year had passed. Most students went home for the break, but Jenna had no plans, and she had received no contact from home at all so, she stayed at the clinic instead. Until came an invite from Missus Fay Wilson, and family.

Jenna was so surprised when they said she had a phone call. She had never met her doctor's wife, and now they spoke on the phone, and even laughed together. Jenna could tell just by her voice alone, that she was a really nice, and caring person, but to invite her into their home for the holidays was more than what Jenna expected.

She needn't have worried. For, as from the first instant they met, something clicked between them and Jenna instantly liked her, and Jenna found that the whole family, even doctor Wilson, were all the same. All, good, caring people. Even the children warmed to Jenna, and she felt something she hadn't had for a long time. To be part of a family, so missing in her life. She felt wanted and that was special.

There were no discussions of her treatment and her health, more so of her studies at university, and what progress she was making there. Jenna was pleased with the fact that doctor Wilson kept her hospital results of her injuries as a private thing, and that pleased her. She talked to his wife about many things, but mostly of her pet loves like flower arranging and horse riding. Jenna told her that her father said she was a good horse rider, and that she loved horses.

"Well Eric! Did you hear that? It looks like a day out with the horses would be a good outing for Jenna!" she said to her husband.

"I did! So, I agree Fay! What say we get organized for tomorrow, and we could have a picnic down by the river." Eric replied.

"That sounds wonderful. How do you feel about that Jenna? If the doctor agrees then it is up to you?" Fay asked her.

"You have horses here?" asked Jenna in surprise.

"We sure do! My husband prides himself with our horse stock, and the children both compete in gymkhanas. We have approximately forty acres to run the horses so, ample space to ride, and especially the trail down to the river, you will love it, Jenna!"

"It sounds so wonderful. I would love a day out riding! Thank you both so much for the invite!" said Jenna excitedly.

Jenna was up bright and early the next morning, or at least she thought so until she went downstairs and noticed everyone was dressed in riding clothes, and doctor Wilson was helping Fay cook.

She smiled as she hadn't seen doctor Wilson in casual clothes other than what he wore at the hospital. "Good morning, everyone! May I help at all?" she asked, as she entered the kitchen.

"Morning Jenna, just take a seat with the girls. It is a beautiful day for a ride. We are almost done here, so breakfast is on its way!"

"Good morning, Jenna! Did you sleep well?"

"Like a baby Missus Wilson, thank you!" said Jenna as she was moving towards the table to greet the girls. They were excited too.

"Call me Fay if you wish, Jenna. We don't have formalities here, and for Eric, you may call him Eric, or Doc!" and she laughed.

"If that is alright with you both, then I will do that Fay!"

She struck up a conversation with the girls, Emma and Jill, and found out that they were avid horse riders, and had jumps down in the back paddock. They also played basketball and asked Jenna if she would like to come and watch them play tomorrow night.

Jenna agreed as long as their mother, or father was taking them.

"Oh, of course they will both be coming!" they both chimed in.

Jenna chuckled, and somehow a closeness with this family came over her. *Yes, a family! Someone to love you, for you to love back!* During breakfast they all chatted happily, and then Fay asked Jenna if she would like to help her make the sandwiches for their lunch.

Without any time wasted over idle chatter, breakfast was over, and plates were being whisked away. Everyone pitched in to clean up, then they grabbed the food and drink, and their hats and urged Jenna to follow. Eric Wilson waited at the door. "Just a word Jenna. I don't want you galloping, or using the jumps today. Just a trot, or a slow canter for this first time, ok? Any fall could be fatal! Savvy?"

Jenna chuckled. "Yes, savvy doc, and thank you for caring!"

"No problems Jenna, but there will be things in your life that you must learn yourself. Give your body a chance to heal, and whatever it is you are doing, do it at half pace. I hope you understand?"

"Yes sir, I do! But sometimes I think I am being over cautious."

"It will get easier Jenna. It's been a while now, but that does not mean you have to be on edge, just be yourself, but take care for just a while longer. Better that, then going back to hospital! Come along now we are lagging behind, and the others do love our horse days. Ah, wait! While I have your attention. I noted you didn't choose to go home for the holidays. Is there any reason for that?" he asked.

Jenna was surprised by the question, and blabbered on. "Ah, no Doc…I mean yes Doc. My father hasn't visited, I've written several letters to mother but no reply! I may have done something wrong!"

He frowned. "I find that hard to believe Jenna, but I was going to tell you since all tests are final, that going home might be just the thing you need to jog your memory, just my opinion of course!"

He strode away towards the garage, and Jenna felt a closeness to this kind man who was now a friend, but his words cut deep.

Strange! she thought. *That he should say that now!* She was a little down about a lot of things, but she did realize what was missing. Mainly, her home, family and friends. She shrugged the feelings off in annoyance, and walked quickly towards the car, and got inside.

The Wilson's block of land was not near the homestead, Jenna noted as they drove through the main gates, and onto the road. But, rather, it was off a winding track just adjacent, and as they climbed the hills Jenna could see the ocean. The sun playing upon the water made it look like glass as it shone down brightly upon it. "It is so beautiful up here." she commented. "Sunset must be a sight to see!"

"Ah!" said Fay. "Such a great idea Jenna, as it is very beautiful, so we shall come up here on the way home so you can witness it!"

"Thank you so much Fay, and a great way to complete our day."

Finally the big day arrived for Jack. Sunday was a perfect day, the sun shone brightly and he was extremely excited. It was after all, the turning point in his life. There was much fuss from his parents making sure he had everything he needed, then a short drive to the station with lectures during the trip about him keeping in contact. Then they were saying their goodbyes, and he boarded the train.

As the train rattled along Jack became mesmerized by its rhythm and he stared out the window at nothing in particular as suddenly his mind was blank of all thoughts. In the calm of it all, he realized.

I have nothing to do, except just to enjoy this journey, but so much has happened, it is blowing my mind. It has been a rollercoaster ride.

He smiled as he looked out the window with new interest. *So, I intend to do just that.* Senior Constable Jenkins has saved me all the hard work by organizing not only my transport and lodgings, but a job worth more than anything I have ever been offered in my life, and one thing is for sure. I will be doing my utmost to succeed!

Every moment of every day is a treasure, and a new experience!

Jack had never been away from Blue Bay, not even into the city, so it would all be foreign territory to him, and every day, something new to learn, but a challenge is what he wanted, he couldn't wait.

Suddenly his thoughts turned to Jenna. He sat up straight, and day-dreamed. *Finally, after all this time I have a chance to look for Jenna in the city!* Today I meet up with Homicide Detective Jeremy Woods for a briefing about my position, and to meet his staff, but I won't start work with him until Wednesday, and later today I check into my lodgings as well, but tomorrow, and maybe Tuesday as well? *So, yes tomorrow, most definitely! I'll start by visiting all hospitals in the city in search for Jenna. I should be able to get a bus to most of them.* he chuckled, as he sat back in his seat to think about it.

Yes! Jack my boy. he laughed. *It is all happening for you right now. A new life, a new job, a new place to live, and then to find Jenna!*

As the train pulled into the station, Jack couldn't help but notice all the noise. There were people rushing everywhere. Cars going in all directions, and the smell of exhaust fumes and pollution in the air filled his nostrils with an alien sense he had never experienced.

Slowly the train rolled towards the entrance of the station, and came to halt. Jack stuck his head out the window, and sure enough there was a young man holding a sign up with his name on it. Jack was relieved, but he knew that Senior Constable Joe Jenkins would be spot-on with all his arrangements. *I must remember to phone him later and let him know I am here, and to thank him.* thought Jack.

He grabbed his belongings, and started to make his way down the aisle towards the exit doors. He waited as people filed through ahead of him, and then it was his turn, and he stepped down to the platform. It was a magic day, the sun shone brightly as he walked towards the fellow he was to meet. He smiled as he got closer, then stopped, and held out his hand. "Good morning! My name is Jack Rickard from Blue Bay, so I am guessing you are to meet me!" he said, as he pointed to the sign.

Instantly the young man face lit up, and he smiled. "Sure thing, Jack, and welcome to the city!" he said, as he took Jack's hand in a handshake. "Detective Jeremy Woods requested that I meet your train as you probably realize. I work for him, my name is William Finch, just call me Will, most others do. It's good to meet you, Jack!"

"Pleased to meet you also Will." replied Jack.

"We'll be in the same office Jack, and shall work together, and I am looking forward to working with someone around my age. You will find him a great man, and boss, and an even better Detective, the absolute best, so we are very fortunate cadets, but I'll leave you to form your own opinion. We are to go back for morning tea to the office where you will meet the other staff members, and then you will have a one-on-one briefing with Detective Woods in his office!"

"We have our own offices just adjoining The City Branch Police Department." he was saying, as he grabbed Jack's suitcase. "If you are all set, we will get going Jack! Can't keep the man waiting."

"Yep, I am ready, just lead the way Will!"

They chatted as they walked through the station and out to the carpark where William walked briskly down the thoroughfare of cars, then stopped when he came to a tan-coloured sedan. "This is it, Jack. My pride and joy, bought with my first paycheck with the curtesy, and help from my friendly banker." he chuckled, and Jack laughed too. "No top-notch car, but it gets me from A to B!"

Morning tea was a casual affair as Jack mingled with his future workmates, then came the summons to enter the Detective's office.

Meeting a Homicide Detective for the first time in his life was an honour which left Jack in awe of the man who stood before him. He was a big man, but solid as a rock as if he worked out regularly.

His face looked calm, serene even, as Jack stared into eyes of the deepest blue, then they seemed to darken in thought as if he was used to searching people's souls. *He definitely achieved that for sure!* thought Jack, as he trembled and paled under his scrutiny. *I will be an open book.* worried Jack. *He will see right through me!* But his dire thoughts receded when the mouth widened into a huge smile, and his voice so deep, boomed out a welcome. "Ah, Jack Rickard! A nice strong name for an up-and-coming Detective. Welcome lad! I hear nothing but good words about you Jack. Such accolades for your work ethics and manner from Senior Constable Joe Jenkins, and his colleagues from Blue Bay. Two things that are most important to me if I am going to spend my time tutoring you to be a professional in every sense of the word! So, you should know that you owe this opportunity to him. I would hope that you thank him accordingly."

Jack was flawed. *How do I reply to so many statements in just one sentence?* he wondered, as he shook like a leaf. Then stood straight to calm himself so he could offer an appropriate answer. He looked the Detective square in the eyes before replying with earnest.

"Good morning, sir, and thank you for your welcome. I can tell you that the pleasure is all mine just by being here. I do realize I have Senior Constable Joe Jenkins to thank for nominating me so, I definitely won't be forgetting him for this huge opportunity. Thank you too sir, this means the world to me, and for your comments! I hope I live up to them, but I will give it my best shot, that you can bet on! I cannot fully express my feelings correctly enough for such an honour, but just to meet you, and to be in your employ is huge. I assure you sir, that I will not let you down. I am here to learn, and I will relish the knowledge you have to share. You can count on me! That is all I can think of to say!" Jack's smile turned into a wide grin.

Detective Woods smiled back. "I think you managed quite well Jack, and well said too I might add. A good speech goes a long, long way in this job, especially a practiced one!" he chuckled.

"But sir! You don't understand… Jack retorted. "That there was no practiced speech. It just sort-of come out!"

"Oh! But I do understand Jack, so much more than you realize! Sorry, but I was having my usual jest with you Jack, my apologies! I find you speak from the heart, and I like that. You remind me a little of me when I was your age, and just starting out. Though I had no-one to teach me the ropes so, I done the hard yards to get where I am. However, nothing was going to stand in my way, and I sense that in you. So, yes Jack! We are going to get along just fine! Also, Jack, forget the sir! Detective Woods will do, or Detective! I am not fussed with formality, but I earnt that tag, and I'm hoping you will also! Now, down to business! I take it you will resume study here at university? Be here on Wednesday, your first day, at 8 a.m. sharp, we will discuss other options. Now go and check your lodgings!"

Jack smiled. "Yes Detective, thank you!" he said feeling relieved.

Richard opened the door to his rooms, and pushed it back wide. His feet seemed to drag as he walked into his room and flopped on the bed. He felt weird, and wild thoughts were plaguing him. Too much consumed him, and so deep were his thoughts, he didn't even notice as Miranda walked into the room, then sat next to him.

"Well, someone is grim and as tense as! What's wrong Richard?"

"You won't believe half of what I've been through Miranda!"

"Well, enlighten me. Is it Jenna? Is she not recovering well?"

"Of course, it is Jenna, who else? She is well all right, and making demands left, right, and center. I haven't been back to the hospital for days, not since I had to sign release, and transfer forms for her!"

"Whatever for? Where is she being transferred to, and why?"

"Nothing is too good for our Jenna it seems. She has checked herself into a private clinic. It is a rehab center where she is closer to the University so she can study, and practice law. Her specialist plans to visit her there twice a week. He approved all this, pending the signing I've done. She could even be there now for all I know!"

"Why the University of all places. How can she study if she has lost her memory? Don't be so daft Richard. Why doesn't she stay in hospital to be treated, or come home if she is well enough."

"That's just it, Miranda. Jenna's current memory can't be faulted by the doctors. It's just her home, her family and friends she seems to have blocked out. She still doesn't recognize me, and she doesn't want to come home yet until she sees her mother, and how do you suppose that is going to happen hey? I am so angry, so frustrated, but guess what? Who pays for her bills? Yours truly, that's who!"

Miranda hid a smile as she turned her head. She couldn't help but be thankful that Jenna wasn't coming home, but she looked at Richard, and replied. "Hmm! I see your problem. Things are getting a little tacky. So, what do you plan to do Richard?"

"Tacky just skims the surface as there is nothing to do. It's done!"

He kicked a chair across the room, and ranted and raved. He was mumbling something under his breath over and over, and Miranda thought he had lost the plot. She swore she heard him say. *Trust me to stuff it up, this wasn't supposed to happen!* She wasn't sure, as each curse seemed to snuff out the next one. She was grabbing at straws.

She stared at him. His face was red and flushed with anger. She had never seen this side of him, and she wondered why this was all so upsetting to him, why not just accept it? It suited her perfectly.

Miranda moved in close to him then she spoke to him softly.

"You know what I think Richard? You must calm down so you can think clearly. You are creating more problems for yourself by acting this way, just be done with it! If Jenna wants to stay away, well I think that would benefit both of us, don't you agree?"

There was silence. Then suddenly he lifted his head, and looked at her. *He knew that Miranda and Jenna would never get on,* and he thought about that, *and the circumstances involving her attack,* before he spoke. *Hmm! If Jenna regains all her memory there may be hell to play here.* Even a new investigation from police, and questions.

"Exactly Miranda! Why didn't I think it through? Jenna coming home would create problems, and now? Well, it's a perfect solution her being in university, and we my love, can carry on as normal! I only have one regret, and that is having to pay her bills. Her mother used to do all that, and these staff I have cost too much money!"

"Then get rid of some of them, and you could sell the estate too!"

"Sell my home? No, never! Lots of things I'll rid myself of before 'Oceanview,' but staff? Thanks for your input it has helped. Guess I should thank you properly." he said as he pulled her down to him.

She giggled as she rolled onto the bed, and pulled him over her. "Hmm! Seems you do have some making up to do Mister Temple!"

Richard grabbed her, then he bent down to press his lips against hers. He reveled in the taste of her as the kiss soon became amorous.

Melita couldn't concentrate on her job at all so, she shoved the trolly into the cupboard, pulled off her protective clothes and threw them inside, then slammed the doors furiously. She was so uptight, that every muscle in her neck and shoulders stood out with tension and strain. She was angry and so frustrated after her talk with Paula Hastings, the cook. *She just doesn't seem to care!* Or she's putting on a very good front. Hmm! *I wonder?* she thought.

She needed more information, and she knew just where to get it. By chance she had just noticed Richard Temple drive into the car-park. She especially noted as he got out of the car that he was not looking very happy. *I must find out what is happening, they will both be talking* she thought, as she hurried through the house and walked along the deck to his rooms where she stood very quietly outside with her ear against the door.

Melita wasn't satisfied with what she had heard before, but now luckily, she had another opportunity to get an update. If someone opened the door, she would simply say she had come over to check with Miranda about their room cleaning.

She gasped as she listened to them talking. *Hmm!* she thought.

Jenna is being transferred to a private clinic, and she will study at a university! Well, I guess she won't be home soon, and that is good, no more police questions. But it sounds as if she has lost part of her memory, better still! *How could she study then? That is strange.*

She pressed her ear closer to the door to hear the next part. *Oh! Jenna doesn't know her mother is missing yet!* Why would that be kept from her I wonder? Now Mister Temple is getting angry, *says he might sack some staff.* That was something Melita didn't want to hear, so she slipped away quietly. It seems, I must be missing some vital information involving the house, and the estate since the absence of Julia Temple! *Our jobs are not secure after all,* and he is paying the bills, he just said. *What the hell is going on?*

Jack had risen bright and early the next day. He was all settled in his cabin, so he was liking his new home well enough. He talked with his new landlord Mary Wilkins after dinner the previous night for ages, and they had hit it off straight away. He was thankful once again for the input from Constable Jenkins, as Mary was his aunt.

Mary had given him the addresses of all the hospitals within the city limits, and the bus schedules. She travelled by bus all the time, and she had a convenient bus stop just outside her house.

Now Jack sat on the bench at the bus stop outside, and waited patiently for the bus to arrive. He had decided today he would visit the main city hospital in his search for Jenna. His heart thumped in his chest with anticipation. Now he was here, he just couldn't seem to settle down. He felt so sure he would find Jenna, but he only had two days, so today, he was hoping for a breakthrough.

As he day-dreamed he neglected to notice the bus approaching, and jumped up when it came to a screeching halt in front of him, but as the doors opened, he climbed the steps, paid the driver and located a seat at the back. Now he had the schedule he realized that getting around the city would be easy for him. He had been worried about that, getting to work, and the university, but now he was set.

When the bus pulled into the stop opposite the huge hospital, Jack gulped. *This is it then, please let her be there!* he thought, as he quickly rose from his seat and threaded his way down the aisle to the doors. They seemed to open as he approached them, and he stepped down to the sidewalk and began the long walk towards the entrance of the hospital. Something lurched inside his stomach as he nervously made his way over to the reception desk, his thoughts running wild. He realized it was rather a long time since Jenna was transferred to a city hospital in a coma, and the talk of an operation.

But she hadn't returned to 'Oceanview' as yet so, obviously she has not recovered, she must still be here! he tried convincing himself.

A female person behind the reception desk was typing, but she sensed his presence, and looked up at Jack as she smiled. "Good morning!" she said, as she removed her glasses, moved a lock of hair from her face and stood before him. "Can I help you sir?"

Jack chuckled his reply at being called sir. "I do hope so missus!"

"Oh, that would be miss, actually! Jane, is my name." she added.

He grinned. He hadn't really taken much notice of the person at all, but now as he looked at her, he could see quite clearly a trim, taut figure, manicured nails and soft blonde hair. Her brown eyes seemed to mock him from a face so angelic, and surprisingly young.

"I'm so sorry Jane! I wasn't really paying attention. I have too much on my mind I guess, but it is nice to meet you. I hope you can help. My name is Jack Rickard from Blue Bay. I am new to the city."

She laughed. He liked her laugh, and listened as she spoke.

"Well, that explains it, Jack Rickard! You are a country boy."

"Meaning?" he inquired.

"Meaning, us city people are quite different to you, country folk! Even though we are all Australians, we tend to take more notice of things. We have to you see, or in the street we would be run over!"

He laughed. "Oh, you do make a good point Jane." he agreed. "I concede!" he said, his hands raised in defense. "But, yes, I get your meaning, seeing you put it that way. In the country we have more important things to do like greeting the sunrise, enjoying the views, and in the evening simply watching the sun set over the bay. It's a tough life, but someone has to do it, and the only chance we have of getting run over is if someone stampeded the horses."

She laughed. "It must be very beautiful to see that every day. I envy you Jack Rickard. Maybe I need a trip out to the country, what brings you to the city, and to the hospital of all places?"

"You should do that Jane, and my visit here is a personal one!"

"Are you visiting someone here? I could direct you if you like!"

Jack looked directly at her. She was only young, but surely, she would understand his dilemma, so he tried to explain.

"If it were that simple Jane, then you have made my day, and I would like very much to visit a certain person if she is here, but she was transferred to the city from Blue Bay quite a long time ago now, so I am not sure if she was sent here or elsewhere. Her name is Jenna Temple, and she was in a coma. They say she may have to have an operation, and that is all I know. They wouldn't tell me, you see."

Jane stared at him. The concern was in her voice when she spoke.

"Oh! I am so sorry Jack. I guess you are not related to this person named Jenna Temple, and you would be referring to hospital policy which is standard I'm afraid if you are not the next of kin. However, unless she is in intensive care, or on the restricted list I see no reason why a visit from you would hurt! I will do all I can to help you!"

Jack's face lit up. It was the first time that anyone would even listen to his plight. "Oh! Really Jane, thank you so much. You have restored my confidence in the hospital system." he replied.

Jane smiled at him. "Don't get yourself too excited yet Jack. I am not promising anything yet, only that I will try and help you locate your friend, but I need to check a lot of records, so first things first, and I will check the current patients admitted here!" and she turned to the computer on the desk, and start to type.

Jenna Temple! she repeated to herself, as she scrolled through the patients. It seemed no time at all and she was looking sadly at Jack.

"Well Jack, she has not been admitted to the hospital lately, and I have no Jenna Temple admitted for the past eighteen months either. But, just wait one moment while I check patients on the restricted list, and then those sent here in a coma. That could be a little harder to get that information, but I shall try." she smiled.

"Thanks Jane. You are doing more than anyone has done before. I can't tell you how much I appreciate what you are doing!"

She smiled at him. "Thank you, Jack. I know Doctor Eric Wilson is a specialist here at the hospital who usually takes over the coma patients. I am just checking his notes. Hmm! It seems there are more patients than you realize, that were sent here in a coma, but not one named Jenna Temple, or at least not the ones I can see. However, I believe Doctor Wilson has private patients, and I don't have access to those patients. I am so sorry Jack, as they are confidential. I have gone back almost two years past to look for her, so it would be safe to say that Jenna Temple wasn't sent here Jack! Unless of course she is a private patient! But even so, if she was a patient currently being treated in the hospital, it would show up. I can't help you after all!"

Disappointment showed on Jack's face as he hung his head, but then he looked up and tried to smile. "Thank you, Jane. It is a long time ago too, and I don't have specific dates to offer you, so thanks."

With deep regret Jack left the hospital, but he was not done yet.

As he sat on a bench at the bus stop, he rescued the slip of paper from his pocket and looked over the list Mary had given him, and realized at once there were two more hospitals in the vicinity of the city center, and he was determined to visit both of those today. He tugged at his top pocket and grabbed the bus schedule from within and noted he had to wait an hour for the next bus so he crossed the street and then entered a café he had noticed, slipped into a booth and ordered some food and coffee. *It is going to be a very long day.* he thought as he sat there eating, and waiting for the bus.

Everything went smoothly for him. He had no problems getting around the city by bus and he was rather enjoying seeing the sights but his mood changed quickly at the next hospital, and then again at the one after. Luck was simply not on his side, but Jack wouldn't face defeat so quickly. He tried in earnest by even visiting another hospital, though he found it was a little remote, and he had to walk a few blocks to locate the hospital entrance behind the tall trees.

That night after dinner with Mary when he went out to his newly acquired quarters, he pondered on the day's events. He simply had to face the facts. It didn't matter where he went to, which hospital, or who he pleaded with, they all had the same story to tell.

Jenna Temple just didn't seem to exist. All he could hope for was that she was out of a coma and recovered enough to leave hospital, *but where was she?* Was she back home now, or where?

Something he knew now for certain. *Jenna was lost to him now!* he realized, as his gut twisted in pain at the thought. He had tried his best to find her, and failed. He just wished she knew that.

All he could do now is what he came to the city for. *His career.* He would have to knuckle down now and concentrate on his new job, his tuition and his studies. Everything he could possibly do to propel himself into the role of Detective one day, he would do. He knew he had a lot on his plate, but that was his decision, and total commitment, that he would follow though until he achieved that, and Jenna? Sadly, would have to take second place now, and that saddened him. *I just can't forget her! She was to be my wife!*

There is only one person in this whole world who could have helped me! he sobbed. *Richard Temple!* All he had to do was stand by me, speak out for me, and support me! Instead, he shut me out for some reason by not giving me any updates or information on Jenna, and Jack knew not why! *Why the sudden turn-around?*

Why in god's name would he do that to me? What's gotten into him? He knew that Jenna and I were serious about each other, but still Richard Temple was a closed book where she was concerned. *Well, he was to me!* remembered Jack. *He knew no-one else could tell me!*

As his mind still lingered on Jenna, one thing became apparent to him. It was a slap in the face, but *Jack realized he would never, ever forget, or forgive Richard Temple for doing that to him!*

Jack hung his head in his cupped hands and cried, and cried.

Jenna was loving life. She enjoyed so much more freedom now, and just to get out of the clinic was a bonus as she felt she was in her element at university. She couldn't believe herself how easily the lessons seemed to her, where others struggled. In a short space of time, she was moved up a level. She realized then, she had made the right choice, she loved the course and certainly her results also.

Still, she felt puzzled by the fact that her homelife lay dormant to her, and often she could still hear the words uttered to her from her specialist quite some time ago. *Going home might be just the thing you need to jog your memory, Jenna! It is just my opinion of course!"* he had said. In the process of settling into the clinic, then starting university, her thoughts of home had receded somewhat but subconsciously she had never forgotten those words, and she knew her doctor was right, but she wanted to wait for the right time.

Was there ever a right time? she wondered.

Her father hadn't even visited her since she moved to the new clinic, and her mother certainly hadn't either. She still hadn't even bothered to reply to her letters, and that saddened Jenna. *What is wrong with this family of mine?* she wondered. *Do I simply just go home unannounced when the time comes?* She did have the directions in her diary, and that is all she knew about her home. *But surely someone will pick me up if I want!* she thought. *I am simply over-reacting.*

As her thoughts turned to her mother, the voice returned in her head and clearly stated. *You will know when you turn eighteen that the time is right Jenna!* she jumped with fright as she always did when she heard the voice, but she was getting so used to it now, even if she didn't understand the messages. However, this message felt strange to her, because in her mind she had subconsciously decided to wait until after her eighteenth birthday before she visited home, and guessed the term break for the holidays might be a good time.

Why think of that time? she wondered. *It could be next term even.*

Why is the voice giving me directions? It is starting to freak me out, but now it seems to be what I am thinking anyway! I definitely need to go home to see my mother. *I could tell her of the messages in my head,* and there will be an explanation, *so don't stress Jenna.*

She fiddled with the ribbon around her neck and her fingers fell on the key to her diary, and she stared at it. *A key! I am to find a key the voice had echoed? But what is the key for?* Why would my mother's voice be telling me things when she could tell me herself, and why is she not coming to see me? Something gripped her chest, and for some reason she felt sad. *What is wrong with me?* I just wish I had someone close to talk to. Maybe my mother is hurt more than my father is saying, but I guess she can explain that when I see her.

With that sorted in her mind she could now concentrate on her grades and co-operate more with the doctor, and nurses at the clinic to work towards a full recovery, so she could get clearance to travel.

Travel? she thought to herself. *Hmm! No doubt it will be daunting, but rewarding as well.* What could possibly go wrong? I shall only be going from the city to my home, and of course, once there we could celebrate my recovery. I could even take my mother out for walks if she is not well. *Yep! It will be fun, a great time.* she thought.

She realized that she probably wouldn't recognize anyone, but that didn't deter her, as she hoped things may change for her as she built up strength to leave. Anyway, her mind was made up now.

Doctor Evan Hall interrupted her thoughts as he walked into her room. "Penny for your thoughts, Jenna?" he asked jokingly.

Jenna looked up at him, and smiled. He was a short, pudgy little man, and wore his spectacles on the edge of his nose, so with his eyes clearly visible, they twinkled as he spoke. "Oh! Doctor Hall. I am pleased you stopped by. I was about to ask to see you. I have just realized it has been a while since I have been home, and Doctor Wilson did suggest that it might be helpful with my recovery."

"Ah! I see. So that is what all they day-dreaming was about. I too think a return to familiar ground will be an asset, however. There are a few more items in your treatment plan that I would like you to complete first. When did you want to go home for a visit?"

"Oh! Not now. I plan to wait until end of term, or next term even if it's alright? I just wanted your opinion, Doctor Hall!"

"Well, in that case young lady, I would say it is a very good idea, but keep in mind that travel will take a lot out of you, but if we are in no rush, then towards the latter term would be perfect timing. It will give us time to make certain you are fit, and well, and ready to travel when you leave. It might be an idea to speak to the tutors at university as well. Sometimes there are parts of your program like papers and tests that you could do on-line if you have a computer?"

Jenna's eyes widened. "Oh, that is the best information, Doctor Hall. I shall definitely be speaking to the principal, and all my tutors about that tomorrow just to ask the question to see what is possible. Thank you so much for your insight. I do like to have a plan, and it has been worrying me what I should do if I need more time at home as my mother is not well. I don't have a computer here, but when I get home, I am sure there will be one there. If not, I shall get one!"

"That is good to hear Jenna, so we shall work together towards a later date. Depending on your tutors, and your progress, you may be able to leave as early as mid-term, next year!"

"Really Doctor?"

"Most definitely Jenna. We will raise the bar a little with your treatment, starting now if you like. I'll organize a more advanced physio session for you after lunch if you feel up to it? But don't be hesitant Jenna, we shall watch you closely so you don't overdo it!"

"Oh, I won't be hesitant at all! It is a definite yes!" replied Jenna. "I am so ready, and I am going to work much harder with you, and the nurses from now on. You shall see Doctor Hall!" she joked.

Chapter Ten

As the train pulled into the station at Blue Bay, something tugged at her memory, bringing Jenna to the edge of her seat.

She peered out the window at the Historic Railway Station, and beyond, the deep blue of the ocean seemed to beckon. Huge waves climbed high, then tumbled to crash down into a silhouette of blue-green and white foams as it rolled into shore only to rush up on the sandy beach. It was so beautiful Jenna felt a certain affinity with it.

Something inside her heart leapt with joy, and she smiled as she looked at the people on the beach and the boats in the small bay. *A fishing village.* she realized as she spied some men hauling big nets from a trawler, and their catch, an array of fish captured inside it.

She grabbed her small bag in haste, but waited patiently for the train to stop completely. Then the doors opened automatically, and she stepped out to the platform into full sunshine, and a sky so clear and blue, it seemed like paradise. Feelings overcome her, confused her, she knew not what, but a closeness even, like she had been here before. She was told it was where she was born. *It was her home.*

Her recollection though, was somewhat different to reality as she looked around through the eyes of a stranger. Everything else was blocked out as if it never happened. She sensed maybe she was second-guessing her return now, but with determination, she tried to suppress the muddling thoughts creeping into her mind, and so instead, began concentrating on the tasks she had set herself.

She hadn't told anyone that she was returning as she wanted to surprise them. But now, she wondered if that was such a good idea to have no-one to meet her at the station? She felt all alone now.

Stop it, Jenna! she reprimanded herself. *You have directions to the address. Just hire a car and get on with it!* You have a license.

Well, luckily, I do. she realized.

She had spent her nineteenth birthday with The Wilson's. It was there she obtained her driving license, thanks to Doctor Eric Wilson who helped in this aspect also. He suggested she may need to drive at some point when they talked of her going home. He arranged it, drove her to the appointment, and offered his car for the road test.

He was right about that too. she thought. *Yes, I owe so much to Doctor Eric Wilson,* such a great man he is, and a great family. I owe them all really, they have helped me so much!

It was summer, and the heat was making its presence felt as she stood pondering, and her reverie ended. She grabbed her luggage, then left the station to look for a taxi. Her plan was to go directly to a car-hire place and she was sure the cab driver would know where to take her. Just then a taxi pulled into the curb, and quickly Jenna hailed the driver, and smiled at him through the window.

He came to a halt and opened his boot, then got out and greeted Jenna as he took her luggage from her, and placed it in the boot.

Jenna asked him if he knew of a reasonable car hire business.

"Sure do! A mate of mine too!" he said, and explained the route.

"Good, that is where I need to go!" she said, then got in the back.

Jenna settled back in the comfort of the seat, and her thoughts drifted to her family. She would be twenty in four weeks' time.

Would they even remember? she fretted. *We shall see!*

She opened her handbag to retrieve her diary, then unlocked it with the key secured on a chain now around her neck. She made a mental note of directions written there on the route to the property. *Leave Blue Bay by Dover Road, travel for four miles.* she noticed.

Sitting forward a little she spoke to the taxi driver. "Excuse me driver. Could you inform me where Dover Road is please? I need to find a property named 'Oceanview'. I believe it joins that road!"

"Not a problem, that's an easy one miss. Dover Road follows the ocean. It is one of the main roads out of Blue Bay. We will go past the turnoff on the way to the car-hire shop. I'll point it out to you!" he said. "However, you turn off Dover Road to enter 'Oceanview!' There's a big entrance sign four miles down, you can't miss it!"

"Oh, thank you. I am much obliged to you mister."

"Any time, miss." came his reply.

So far things were panning out for Jenna, so she relaxed a little. She searched in her diary again. *Staff? No! I don't wish to meet them today. Maybe just my father and my mother to start, and settle in to my room. Yes, enough for one day.* she thought.

The taxi driver interrupted her thoughts as he spoke. "Coming up to the turn-off now miss. It's called Link Road. If you follow that down to a round-about, then you will see the signs for Dover Road. You will need to turn left onto Dover Road!"

"Oh, excellent, and how far is it to the car-hire shop from here?"

"Only one mile, just around the next two bends, so you haven't got far to come back to get out to the main road."

Then they arrived, and Jenna was thanking him again. It was no trouble to find her way when she hired a car. She enjoyed the ocean drive and sights, so she drove past the Blue Bay Surf Club slowly.

Oceanview the sign read up ahead, so Jenna slowed the car to veer off the main road, and drove through the portals at the entrance.

So, this is it then! she realized, as she negotiated the turns in the gravel road. *Home should be about one mile down this road!*

How alien does that sound? she thought to herself, as she tried to picture it, but nothing came to mind. Then she noted, when looking through the trees in passing that the road was now veering towards the ocean. She approached a steep incline, and when she topped the rise, she encountered the full view of it, and couldn't help but gasp at the beauty. Quickly she parked the car and ran to the edge of the cliff to look over, and out into the vastness of the deep blue ocean.

A shadow seemed to pass before her eyes. Her pulse started to pound in her temples, and she put a hand up to her forehead as she backed away slowly. *What is it?* she wondered. *What is wrong with me?* All she knew was, that she had to get away. *But from what?* she wondered. Her hands trembled, and her knees felt weak as she looked around at the vacant car parks. Apart from two rather old vehicles, one a van, the other a small, well-used sedan, the main car spaces for the residence were deserted so, she felt a little unsettled.

Hmm! I should have called father to tell him I have arrived. They must be out somewhere. *Never mind, what's done is done Jenna.*

She dug deep for her diary in her handbag and unlocked it. She found the page, and read the words which would direct her to her room, and her parent's rooms. Feeling a lot more in control and her confidence restored, she crossed the carpark to open the gate, but almost instantly she paused to look at the grounds and homestead.

It was a massive house perched right on the cliff face facing the ocean. She could only imagine what the views would be like from the top balcony. *Endless views for miles I expect, but the house is in need of some love, and care.* she realized, as she gazed at the grounds in disappointment. *If I lived here, I know it would be immaculate!*

Surely my mother can see that work needs to be done here. Why doesn't she organize it? I know my father works, but he is home weekends, and there is the staff. It is listed in my diary who works here, and where! *Hmm, staff? No! I have already made my decision to meet them another day.* So, she walked briskly across the lawn.

Jenna wasted no time locating the external staircase, and quickly climbed up to the top balcony where she walked straight across to the railing which faced the width and breadth of the ocean in all its glory. *It is so vast and majestic in size, and so much beauty to behold.* she thought as she stared beyond. Soft clouds scattered to the horizon where the sun filled them with light that shimmered in reflections across the water, and she gasped in awe. *Oh, it is so beautiful.*

Blue on blue was the water. Different colours seemingly defining the depths of the great ocean, but in and around the shoreline, she noticed where once again it changed to the softest green, making it look like an island paradise. Soft peaks of white formed upon the crest of massive waves which rode up high and then plunged down with a thunderous roar as they broke, to finally end the pantomime of their entrance by rolling calmly towards the beach, and then sank down deeply into the soft white sand, until some unnatural force seemed to be sucking them back to be reclaimed again, and the sand appeared to be fighting nature by straining to stay.

Jenna shook her head in wonder. *I might go down there later! But firstly, my room.* She walked briskly down to the end room that she knew would be hers, and turned the door knob. It seemed stuck, and she pushed hard, but to no avail, the door would not budge.

She bent down and looked at the lock. *Why is my door locked?* she wondered in annoyance. *Damn! Now what? I will try mother's room.* she decided, and went back to the other end of the balcony. She knocked on the door and called out, but no reply. Gently she turned the knob, and realized her mother's room was locked also.

Miranda heard the footfalls on the stairs outside the window. She rose from the table quickly and tried to see who it was but they had passed so she raced outside just in time to see a young girl step onto the top balcony. Commonsense told her a trespasser, and she became hesitant, but there was something familiar about the girl.

Something inside her chest squeezed as she gasped for air. *Oh, my goodness! I must find out for sure who that is!* she thought, as she backed away slowly, and opened her front door in haste, then she raced across the lawns towards the kitchen.

"Cook, cook! Are you in here?" she called, as she burst through the doorway, but found the kitchen was deserted so, Miranda went in search of Melita the housemaid, and located her in the laundry.

She breathed a sigh of relief, and spoke quickly but assertively.

"Melita, you will need to find the cook. I have an urgent job for you both, and right now, this is most important!"

Melita glared at her, she didn't like this person at all, and to have to take orders from her now was about all she could bear. "What is it?" she snapped. "What is so important that can't wait?"

Miranda shook her head. She had exhausted all avenues trying to cope with this one, and found her so rebellious.

"For just once Melita, do what you are told. I find it's becoming a chore just to have you work here, but be warned Melita Sanchez! If you continue trying my patience, I'll sack you! Understand me?"

Melita ignored her, but Miranda wasn't expecting any reply.

"I think we may have an intruder, Melita! Someone just walked up the outer stairs beside my rooms to the top balcony, now I must know who it is? I tried to look, but failed to notice in time! So, you had better get the men, and cook to go up the internal stairs with you! I think it was a young girl. I am not very certain, but a stranger no doubt. On the other hand, it could be someone we all know quite well. It is another possibility, as she looked familiar in some way!"

Melita's head flew up to stare at her face. "How do you mean, familiar? What possibility? Who do you mean exactly?" she asked.

"If it's not an intruder, then it's Jenna of course! No-one else lives here, and it wouldn't be Julia!" Miranda chuckled at the thought.

"Unless Julia is back from the dead, or her holiday away if you like! But no! Not ever would I have mistaken that awkward limp, or her camouflaged face either, that is for sure!" she laughed evilly at her own sick joke. "But Jenna? Even though she's older now, I'd still recognize her I am sure, but I didn't see the persons face!"

Melita glared at her. She didn't think that was at all funny. Her face paled as she thought of the possibility of it being Jenna Temple and the repercussions that might entail, especially with police, and further questioning. That scared her, but even more outlandish was the possibility of Missus Julia Temple's return. Her hands began to shake and her body trembled when she attempted to speak up, but Miranda Delvin was still going on, before she could utter a word.

"So, Melita, we need to know for sure who is up on the balcony. Go and find the staff, and we'll all meet at the bottom of the stairs!"

Melita was about to protest, but had second thoughts of doing that, so she hung her head, and replied. "Yes missus!" and left.

Miranda wheeled around and hurried to the living room where she sank down into the softness of the settee. *Oh my! This woman is testing me, I must get rid of her.* I will talk to Richard tonight. He said he would be late, *so I am guessing I'll have to deal with all this myself, though I may call him or leave a message if it is Jenna here!*

Frustrated, but in need of answers, she rose from her seat, then walked towards the staircase, and waited for the staff. When they had all arrived, she addressed them. "Now everyone, we must find out who is up there, so, listen carefully. Whoever it is, I don't want them to see us, so we move quietly in twos, then when we get to the top of the stairs just wait there, and I will have a quick look!"

Jenna stood rooted to the spot. She was baffled about the locked doors, and was at a loss for ideas on what she should do now.

I really have messed this return visit up! she thought. *I should have let father know I would be coming home today!* He obviously has taken mother somewhere for the day, *and that is why her door is locked.* Who knows what time they will be back? However, my room is locked also! *Has it always been locked in my absence?* she wondered. *I must have possessed a key when I resided here,* but I don't know where that would be now, it has been a long time.

Vaguely she looked out over the ocean, and she had an idea.

Hmm! It does look so inviting. I may go down just to fill in some time, and walk along the beach. *Yes, good idea, it's a beautiful day.* So, with that in mind, she set her belongings down, then walked down to the end of the balcony, and stood at the top of the stairs as she inspected the steps. *They all do look to be intact but I had better go slowly just in case.* she thought *as she was so wary of falling since the operation.* She certainly didn't want to be sent back to hospital! Doctor Wilson had cautioned her to always take it easy.

Jenna took her first tentative step down. Dark shadows instantly crept into her mind, then bright stars clouded her vision. She shook her head, simply trying to clear her mind, but then ignored them as she proceeded to the next step. Almost as if she had done it before, she began counting the steps, but at the fourth step her body froze. For some unknown reason she just couldn't take that step, as some force seemed to be pushing her back. Fear consumed her. *What is happening?* she wondered, as she tried to force her foot to obey, but something was holding her fast. It was impossible to make the next step. *She started to shake badly.* Her mind twisting in turmoil.

There was something about the steps that created fear in her as she stood on shaking legs, and she knew she would probably fall.

Jenna wavered as she submitted to the tortures of her mind.

For years Jenna Temple had lived in darkness. Deep in her mind, her past memories were blocked, but now within those shadows bright stars materialized to temporarily blind her sight, and change spasmodically though it was daylight. Then they dissipated only to be replaced by a white dazzling light which pierced her senses.

Whatever is happening to me? Jenna winced, as she lifted her hands up to her pounding temples in defense, momentarily in fright.

Distorted scenes flashed before her, and thoughts of a forgotten past long buried. Shafts of light stabbed cruelly at her eyes, and her head hurt with such ferocious pain, that it brought her to her knees. Stilled memories returned by spasms of light, and hazy thoughts. Her head ached to visualize a time in her life she'd lost completely, only now it clearly was alive as she recalled the real horror of it and she groveled on the steps in shock, struggling to rise. The staircase was now plunged into darkness but she could see clearly. As if by magic she re-lived the gruesome scene as it appeared on the beach under the steps, but what she saw would stay with her forever now, when home-life was obliterated, and darkness took over to rule her.

There was a body…cold and lifeless…dead eyes staring… There was blood…much blood…and her body trembled. *She screamed a silent scream in recollection*, but more-so when *she recognized the body*.

She shivered as she stood staring down at the mutilated body of her mother! *No! Oh no, it just can't be true! Was this real…or some cruel prank…or was it a fact?* Shock was taking over, but some influence forced her to face reality as the visions flashed before her. Her body quivered, *she started shaking uncontrollably, and sobbed with* grief.

Jenna stared around in desperation with un-seeing eyes…*There were people…*Just shadows really…Peering at her…*Who were they?*

Confusion took over, but her heart cried another emotion…

…Fear…she felt it…It consumed her…

Jenna felt threatened, and sensed the deadly danger. So, quickly, she wheeled around to access the deck to the external stairs.

Who should I turn to? Who could I trust? she wondered blindly, as she groped for each step while the tears smarted her eyes.

Should I ring my father now? she questioned herself, but for some reason she decided against that as all thoughts were racing through her mind now, and she realized. *I am in urgent need of help, and some advice!* Instead of helping me, and being honest with me, my own family! *My father, to be exact! Has obviously deceived me greatly.*

My mother is dead! Dead! She has been for some time, I fear. I know it for certain now as I have just recalled that dreadful morning. *I can remember that exact day in my past now!* As she fled for her life she started sobbing, great heart-breaking sobs, her eyes rimmed with tears that slid down her cheeks, and fell to dampen her blouse.

My father has been lying to me all this time! Each and every visit to the hospital has been filled with his lies about mother, *but why?* She realized the problem with certainty as she quickly descended the stairs, then raced across the lawns toward the car park. She tried her utmost to digest it, *to face the unwarranted deceit she had received.*

Where should I go to? she stressed. *I have no-one, except maybe the police. Should I?* she queried herself. *Yes, the police are exactly who I need to speak to because my mother was murdered!* she cried. *I know it was murder because her body was mutilated!* Not just a simple fall! *But me? I remember a step was missing and then I was falling.* Did that cause my injuries? *Hmm! Some mystery, or was it? I remember a shadow now!* I'll tell the police! Jenna reached the car, and got in quickly, not even looking back as she accelerated with haste to join the main road. Surroundings seemed familiar, so she arrived at the police station quickly, parked, got out, and then took the stairs up to the building.

Fresh tears appeared as the sergeant ushered her inside. She was hysterical, and blabbering incoherently, so he called his superior.

Miranda was at the top of the stairs when she beckoned the others to join her. They all hustled in close as she whispered.

"I am certain our intruder is Jenna Temple. An older version, but definitely her! Please look and give me your opinions but be quiet!"

She led them out onto the balcony. They all stood against a wall and stared at the girl down on the steps at the end of the balcony.

"Oh!" gasped Melita Sanchez, her voice raspy. "Tis her for sure!"

"Yep, that's her alright!" offered Paula Hastings as she frowned.

Ted Hastings shuffled forward only to gape as he peered toward the stairs. "Oh no! Have to agree, it looks like Jenna Temple to me!"

Pablo Sanchez had hung back behind the others, but Miranda pushed him forward. "What do you think Pablo?" she asked.

"Omg yes! It's Jenna Temple! I'd know her anywhere, even if she is much older now." he hung his head, and gritted his teeth hard.

"Good, that is established, a united identification. Now, what to do about it, is the question, as Richard is not here, but at work!"

They all turned to stare at the girl, each with their own thoughts.

"Look!" exclaimed Pablo. "Can you all see what is happening now? What is wrong? Now she is down on the deck, but struggling to get up. Something is dreadfully wrong with her! What is it?"

"I think I know what is wrong with her Pablo! It is simple, she has lost her memory, so it is all foreign to her, and she is confused."

"No, no! It has to be something else. Look at her now!"

Jenna turned to face them with un-seeing eyes. They seemed to be shadows staring at her, as tears streamed down her face. She was shaking, her chest heaving, and her sobbing turned to convulsions like someone possessed. Her face turned white and masked by fear.

Everyone gasped just to look upon her, but it didn't take much summing up to determine what was happening. Jenna Temple had regained some memory and they knew what that meant. She would now know her mother was dead, and may even know her attacker.

Summoned to work a case in his home town of Blue Bay where as a youngster he completed his preliminary training while joining the police force, Homicide Detective Jack Rickard sat triumphantly at his old desk to tie up some loose ends of yet another solved case before he returned to the city where he worked in his own practice.

He had come a long, long way since the days of working hands-on with Homicide Detective Jeremy Woods, and completing all the courses at university to finally obtain the all-important 2:2 undergraduate college degree. Then the learning, the tutoring by working with the great man, earnt his claim to the title, Homicide Detective.

His success was unheard of in many circles, especially in the city branch where he had honed his talents, and worked with the best.

For someone so young to make it to Homicide Detective was a gift not many achieved, but it was second nature to him now at age twenty-one. His birthday was a memorable day. He had done the hard yards, but back in his home town he was in his element to be recognized as a hot-shot Homicide Detective with accolades to earn him the tag. He knew they were all proud of him at Blue Bay Police Station, and he needed to give back a little, as they all did so much for him to dictate his life. He looked up now as the one person who had helped him most, Senior Constable Joe Jenkins, appeared.

"How is it going Jack?" he asked, as he quickly gained access to the seat opposite Jack, eased into the soft leather, and slid a file over.

Jack smiled. "All done sir! Would you like to join me for dinner tonight? I decided that I will head off early in the morning now!"

"Dinner? Maybe. But first things first. I think you might want to reconsider when you read this file and meet the lady next door. She is hysterical, and blubbering about murder no less. It is a classic case of a mystery murder. Right up your alley Detective Rickard!"

"Oh! No, you don't Constable Jenkins. I know what you are up to. I think someone here could handle the case by the sounds of it!"

"She is probably on drugs anyway if she's rambling on, or she could be just lying, they do you know! Wouldn't be the first time!"

A frown creased the constable's forehead. "That is not possible Jack, not this time. I will need you here urgently, especially now!"

Jack looked puzzled, and he stared into the Constable's eyes, but noted he was deadly serious though his demeanor seemed anxious.

"I don't get it sir. What is so important about this lady, and this case, that has you so riled up? You and the guys can deal with it!"

"No Jack, we can't! I will need a specialist for this case. You must hear me out Jack, and place your trust in me! Just read the file!"

"I do trust your judgement sir, don't get me wrong, but really? This seems a little over the top, and out of character for you. So, you do believe the tale this lady has spun sir? Is that it?"

"Definitely Jack, with all my being! So will you when you meet!"

Jack was bewildered. "How can you be so sure after only a brief meeting, and with no investigations done Constable Jenkins?"

"I am certain Jack! I know of intensive investigations undertaken concerning this case many years ago, but all proved fruitless!"

"So! It is not a new case then, Constable Jenkins?"

"Jack! Enough interrogation, you may need that later! Just read the file contents, and follow me please!" he stood, feeling agitated.

Jack shook his head. Casually he opened the file and scanned the pages of the report. *Hopeless case!* he mused. *A trail as cold, and dead as a missing body.* However! *Murder is murder, and that is my specialty!* Though it wasn't the only factor convincing him to take on the case. He visualized a deranged person claiming to have had amnesia, but now had memories enlightened to recall a dead body. But no! *It was simply a name on the report that tripped his memory*, to clinch it for him. *Jenna Temple!* Her name sprung out at him. *I'll be damned! Omg Jenna where did you come from? Does this murder relate to your brutal attack?* He jumped to his feet. "Let's go Constable!" he said breathlessly.

Jenna was talking to the officer. Her eyes were filled with tears, and rimmed red, but a commotion at the door caused them both to cease as Jack Rickard, and Constable Jenkins burst in the room.

She stopped crying to just stare at Jack Rickard, then she spoke.

"Oh! Is it really you, Jack?" she gasped. "Yes, I know you, Jack!"

Jack laughed. "I do hope so Jenna Temple, you were pledged to be my wife one day. You don't realize how happy I am to see you!"

"I'm pleased to see you too, but your wife? I am just starting to remember things so, don't jest as some things still remain lost to me, especially this place, home and family since I lost my memory!"

Jack frowned, then smiled at her. "No need to be sorry Jenna, I do understand, but what I said is true. My name is Jack Richard, we grew up together, went to school together, and were inseparable!"

"What I mean… Jenna spluttered. "This morning, I didn't know of you but now you seem so familiar Jack Rickard!" she said faintly.

He grinned. "Thank goodness for that! Now, introductions are over, do I get a hug!" he asked. "I've searched everywhere for you!"

"Oh Jack! Please don't joke. You don't know how good it feels to be able to look upon your face and recognize you, but earlier today, I wouldn't have! You see, I have had no recollections of home for years now. My lack of memory even caused me to doubt my own father's identity! However, I have just fled from our home in fear!"

She started to tremble, her shoulders shook, and the tears welled in her eyes, then slipped down her cheeks. "It was so horrible Jack!"

He pulled her into his arms and she just melted into his embrace, sobbing softly, and trying to get as close as she could to feel safe.

Jack waited until she had calmed down before placing a finger under her chin to lift her head, and looked into her eyes, then spoke.

"Do you feel up to telling me what happened Jenna?" he asked

"I will try my best, though I know it is going to be so difficult!"

"Just take your time, and if it is too upsetting you can stop!"

"Ok, thank you Jack! As I recall first of all, because my room was locked, I decided to take the stairs down to the beach, and go for a walk. It was fine at first, I even counted the wide steps, but then I couldn't proceed as I seemed to be glued to one certain step, then I couldn't move forward no matter how hard I tried. I began seeing shadows, bright white lights flashed in my head. I was frightened and something was wrong in my head, the pain was unbelievable, I have never experienced such pain, and it brought me to my knees. I was absolutely terrified as visions began to appear. I noticed a step missing. I was laying on the deck looking down at the beach below under the stairs and what I witnessed was too horrid to explain! But so very real as if it was just happening." and she started sobbing.

Jack was quick to hold her in case she fell, then helped her into a chair he had pulled out. "Some water please sergeant." he asked.

Jenna sipped the water when it was handed to her, and tried to compose herself before she continued. "It was just so dreadful that I almost passed out as I witnessed it. All my memory of that day came flooding back in an overload. I saw it all as clear as day Jack!"

"What did you see Jenna?" queried Jack.

"Why, mother of course! Mother is dead Jack and most definitely murdered because her body was so mutilated. Her head…her head was severed!" she spluttered, and she began sobbing again. "Her body parts were separate, just lying beside!" Jenna gagged, and hot liquid rose up her throat. She coughed into a handkerchief, and still crying, she added. "I recalled seeing it for real when I fell on her!"

Jack rested a hand on her arm, and stared at her. "You fell? What were you doing out at that hour of morning, and how exactly did you fall Jenna? Were you pushed over the railing, or did you slip?"

"No! I heard screams from my room, so went out to investigate. I was counting steps, but the fifth step was missing! I hovered, and swayed! I couldn't turn back so, then I fell through it. I thought I would be crushed on the rocks, but I landed on my mother. Mother was dead Jack! I will never forget her eyes staring at me!" and she started to cry. Then she lifted her head as if in recollection. "But Jack there is more! I remember a shadow! It loomed up beside me! Then I was hit violently by something hard, and the darkness closed in!"

Jack wrapped his arms around her and rocked her as she sobbed. He took a brief glance at Constable Jenkins, and shook his head.

"Just rest Jenna. I need to tie up a few things, and we will go!"

Something twisted Jack's insides, urging him to re-act quickly. He wheeled around to face Constable Jenkins "My god sir! We have a murder of the worst kind.! I will definitely be taking this case sir, and let's get to the bottom of this, once and for all!" he whispered, then grabbed a note-book from inside his jacket, and began writing.

He looked up when he was ready to speak. "Can you spare me some good men sir? We will all need to work very closely as a team, and treat this as a new investigation. I will require all old records, and forensic reports from here, and also from the City Branch!"

Constable Jenkins was gaping after Jenna's reverie. "Consider it done Jack! Bear in mind whatever you need will be at your disposal, and I'll do my utmost to obtain all records as soon as possible!"

"Excellent sir, thank you! I will also need search-warrants ready to search any premises, but when I'm ready. Can you handle that?"

"Just leave minor details to me Jack. You have my total support!"

"Thank you, sir! We commence tomorrow! Arrange a briefing at 7 a.m. with the officers you choose for me and send two officers out today to 'Oceanview' to speak with Richard Temple! Advise him to have himself and his staff available and present at 'Oceanview' in the living room next Tuesday at 8 a.m. for a new investigation. No-one is to leave the property or town until we've questioned them!"

"Consider it done Jack. We'll meet in the morning for briefing!"

Jenna was staring hard at Jack. Suddenly, he seemed a different person, and was completely taking control of the whole situation. Officers were bending to his beck-n call, and him giving orders to Constable Jenkins of all people was something she never expected! She had to know why, right now. *What is going on?* she wondered.

Jack noticed her puzzled face, and spoke gently to her. "Ah! I'm sure I know what you are thinking Jenna, which proves we have to talk! Come with me now!" he held out a hand. "You've had enough for one day. We will talk later when you recover from your shock!"

He turned to talk to Constable Jenkins. "I won't be going home to my parent's house, sir so, just call my mobile if you need me. We require somewhere safe, and private, as we have so much to catch up on, and if Jenna is feeling up to it, we have even more important details to discuss after dinner. So, I shall seek us some lodgings!"

Constable Jenkins raised an eyebrow. "Do you think that would be appropriate Jack? I mean, people may talk!"

"Appropriate or not, that is what we will do! I don't really care who talks, or thinks otherwise. We have to discuss many things! Are you alright with that Jenna?" he asked, as he looked at her.

Jenna frowned. "Well! Normally it would be Jack, and I certainly wouldn't go back home, but that is where my clothes are! I left there in rather a hurry you see! My belongings are up on the deck outside my room. I couldn't get in Jack, and mother's room is locked also!"

"Of course. Ah! I remember now!"

"Constable, you still have keys to both rooms I hope, as I will need them during my investigation? Remember you changed the locks after the incidents ages ago?" he queried.

"Yes! I do remember Jack., and luckily, I did, as they are still here in a safe deposit box. I'll go and get them now!" he said, and left.

"Just as well we decided on that Jenna, because no-one's been in the rooms since your accident and your mother's disappearance."

Jenna breathed a sigh of relief. Just the thought of others in their rooms was daunting. She knew she must have personal things there and her mother? *Well mother's room.* she recalled. *Was her life!*

Briefly thoughts of her mother's voice in her head returned. But then she realized something. *Jack just said my investigation. Why?*

Constable Jenkins came back into the room and jangled the keys in front of Jack. "Here we go people, keys are all safe and sound!"

Jack took the keys. "One other thing, sir. Jenna left her suitcase outside her room. Ask the officers when they go out to 'Oceanview' to get it and bring it to me. I'll text you where we're staying!"

"I'll hold these keys for now Jenna, I'll get copies made for you!"

Jenna stood staring at him. Suddenly she was remembering much more about Jack Richard, but suppressed the feelings of anxiety, and the million questions she had. So, she politely replied. "That is fine by me Jack! I don't plan on going back to 'Oceanview' anyway! There are far too many bad memories there now! It frightens me!"

Jack frowned. "Hmm! Maybe you feel that way now Jenna, that is understandable. I know you are stressed out, but at some point, you might just have to reconsider, as 'Oceanview' is where this new investigation will begin. Also be aware Jenna, that I will be relying heavily on your memory to crack this case. So, any minor detail will be of importance, and I am quite positive you want justice served. Anyway, we'll talk about that after dinner tonight, but right now, let's get out of here! I'll see you bright and early Constable Jenkins!"

He's assuming control again, why? Crack this case! Jenna fumed.

"We will be waiting Jack. Have an enjoyable night, Jenna!"

Jenna smiled awkwardly, but replied. "Yes, Constable Jenkins!"

Suddenly Jenna felt embarrassed. Hardly had the words passed her lips in reply to the Constable, she was so exasperated, she burst out in protest to Jack. "Enough!" she cried out. Her voice, even to herself, seemed quite hysterical. "I do apologize for my frustration, Constable Jenkins, but I must address Jack, as he seems to be hiding something!" she turned to look him square in the eyes, and spoke.

"What is going on with you Jack Rickard? You are with-holding something, I just know it! What is it I am missing here? Everything you say is very fine and well Jack but it just doesn't add up. Instead, shouldn't Constable Jenkins be heading this new investigation, and shouldn't he be asking me to attend the morning meeting to aid him in his investigation? You act as if it is you! I suspect you have some explaining to do Jack Rickard, and I am certainly not waiting until after dinner for you to do that! I want answers now!" she stressed.

That is something I did not think I would hear, but Jenna still has that fire! Jack chuckled. "Ah! It is so good to have you back Jenna!"

Constable Jenkins chuckled, and grinned at Jack. "I'm sorry Jack! I must set Jenna right from the start, and that means right now I'm afraid! I know you would much prefer to tell her yourself Jack, but you are prolonging the issue now! Are you ok with that?" he asked.

Jenna stared from one to the other in a puzzled manner. She felt they had some misunderstanding. But no, they were both joking.

Jack chuckled. "Yes, of course Constable Jenkins, if you must!"

Constable Jenkins faced Jenna, and smiled. "We will need all the help we can get so, thank you Jenna. Of course, you may attend our meeting in the morning, but it's police work, and pointless for you! But your turn will come, you'll need to recover first. However, you should be aware that this is not my investigation at all! Rather, this investigation lies solely on the shoulders of one Jack Rickard! Or, to be exact. May I present to you, Homicide Detective Jack Rickard!"

Jenna paled. Then a red flush covered her neck, and crept up to her cheeks in embarrassment, and her hands went to her mouth to stop herself screaming. "My god, I remember Jack! I can actually remember the exact time you said it. I can hear your voice clearly!"

"Something has jolted my memory to recall your exact words. I remember it was at breakfast on the balcony with my mother. You were informing us both of your plans. You specifically mentioned you intended on leaving school, and would apply for a position as a policeman then study at Uni to be a Homicide Detective one day!"

"What joy! I can actually remember that, Jack! Also, I recall more of you, and myself now, and our feelings back then!" she laughed. "Congratulations Detective, I am so proud of you!" she ran to him.

Jack laughed with her as he grabbed her quickly. They embraced, and he kissed her cheek tenderly, then he whispered in her ear.

"Thank you, Jenna! But I was determined to do it for us, for our future. A big congratulations on remembering so, I feel at last. We are getting somewhere!" Jenna's eyes flew wide. She lifted her head suddenly as the tears streamed into them, but she babbled on. "Yes. Oh yes! It was about our future. I remember it all Jack! It was to be your eighteenth birthday that day! We were going riding, a day to celebrate, and discuss our future. Oh my god, I remember!"

Jack's smile was huge. *How long he had waited to hear that?*

"You are so right Jenna! Thank the good lord you have regained some memory back, especially of us! We were separated for far too long, but we are back together again now!" but Jenna continued.

"I recall more, Jack. I was excited and couldn't sleep, as you were coming early. In the early hours of morning, I was still awake so, it was that day that I heard the scream. I think it was my mother, Jack! My mother's scream I heard! So, I slipped outside to the balcony to listen, and heard yet another scream. That is when I crept slowly to the steps. Oh Jack! That's why I fell through the steps! I was moving quickly counting them, but the fifth step was missing. Just one step down, but I couldn't stop! I couldn't stop. I fell forward into the gap down to the rocks below! I see it all so clear in my mind now!"

Jack could see she was getting agitated, and he held her at bay so he could speak to her. "Jenna, it is remarkable that your memory is coming back to you! That news is music to my ears, but the other things? We need to wait for you to recover a little before we get into that, as it will be a strain for you. This investigation will be so full on when we start. So, try to relax now! You have had quite a shock today. We have one week, so we will talk when the time is right!"

Jenna looked at him, there was so much she wanted to say. Her mind was filled with so much now, but she conceded to say. "If you think that is best Jack, then that is what we will do! However, I must say this as I just thought of it. I can only guess that the shock from the visions I had at Oceanview today, and what was revealed to me, must have triggered something in my brain, and rekindled my lost memory, for that to happen the way it did! I did not think anything like that could happen, but obviously my doctor did!"

"You see Jack. My doctor being the specialist he is in this field! Told me it would be in my best interest to return home just to see if anything changed, or if I recalled anything. So, I can only guess he was hoping something like this might happen! Because medically, they have done all that they can do for me at the clinic. It is so very strange, but I can remember most things now, even our childhood Jack! Maybe you can fill me in on the things I struggle with, just to help me remember the rest, Jack? Would you mind? she inquired.

"You can bet your bottom dollar on that Jenna! I shall help you all I can. We have a lot before us my lady, and I too, will be needing your help as well, quite a lot in fact! So, for that reason, I don't want to overload you. I must agree, you make a good point concerning your specialist! I do think he was on the right track, and had good reason to want you to return home, and luckily for you, so far, his plan is working. I for one, am pleased he convinced you as I haven't been able to find you, and I have searched for years Jenna Temple!"

Jenna looked at him "Oh, we have so much to catch up on Jack!" she frowned. "So many lost years that we have to make up for!"

"We do indeed Jenna! So, shall we do that starting now? Furthermore, it is what we should be talking about, and concentrating on tonight! Not on the case, or any other things, just on us! Our lives, our feelings, and our future! What do you think, do you agree?"

Jenna looked at him, then smiled. "That would please me greatly Jack! Just to see you again, but to remember you as well, is a bonus. Just to sit and chat about our future life makes me very excited. So, it is a big yes! I can hardly wait for this new chapter to begin!"

"Excellent!" Jack cried. "One phone-call, and we are out of here!"

He made a gesture to grab his phone, but Jenna stayed his hand.

She looked sad as she spoke. "I am so sorry you couldn't find me Jack. It must have been dreadful for you. You should have asked my father where I was, he knew! I was in a coma for some time, and then later I may not have known you, so it would have been worse!"

Jack frowned. "I didn't want to bring this up right now Jenna, and I don't want to talk more about it, but seeing you mentioned your father. I just want you to know that I did go out to 'Oceanview' specially to speak with him, and to ask where you had been sent to. Jenna, your father refused to tell me, he told me to phone in future, asked me to leave 'Oceanview' with the notion I wasn't welcome!"

Jenna gaped. "Oh my, I am so sorry Jack. For some reason I don't want to recall my father too much as he was so very strange when talking to me about mother in the hospital, and now I know why! Mother, was dead then Jack! He knew she was missing, but still he pretended she was at home. He was purposely lying to me Jack!"

Jack frowned as he thought on that, then he spoke. "Jenna, that is just so odd, sick actually! But why would he do that? I shall have to make a note to look into that, and question him on that!" and he grabbed his black notebook, and started jotting down a few things.

Jenna smiled as she looked at him. "I have one of those too Jack!" she said, as he was placing the book in his breast pocket.

"One of what Jenna?" he asked, puzzled by her statement.

"A notebook! Only I call mine, my diary!" she laughed at her joke. "I acquired it soon after my operation whilst in hospital as occasionally, I was having trouble recalling what had been said!"

Jack laughed. "Oh, I see! However, a very good idea Jenna!"

"It was the best idea, but don't you laugh now Jack Richard. It is my lifeline, as I have my life story in it if you must know. I pestered my father into giving me all sorts of information when I planned to come home, especially mother's name. Strange! I felt like someone punched me when he said her name, an eerie feel as I couldn't recall my parents, or if I had family? I wanted to know the people I knew, what school I went to, any special friends I had. How best to travel out here, directions and distances to 'Oceanview,' and to my room. So, you see I had no recollection at all of home, or the people in it!"

Jack's face was set with seriousness. "I wish I could have helped you, Jenna. It was not for the want of trying though, but my hands were tied. It must have been a nightmare for you. We can talk of it later." He pulled her close, and then as an afterthought, he asked. "Was I on the friends list, or special friends by any chance Jenna?"

Jenna frowned. "Well, that is so strange Jack, but no! Your name wasn't mentioned. I guess it was just luck that I came to the police station and you were here, because I was beginning to recall things then, and I was sure I knew you as soon as I saw you!" she said.

"Hmm!" replied Jack. "Your boyfriend, and future husband, not to mention your best friend, not on the list! Your father better have some answers when I speak to him next, and I'm guessing it will be a shock for him to see I am the Detective leading this investigation!"

"I think so Jack, and I too, want to know why he has lied to me, and deceived me in my time of need, when I needed the truth!"

Jack looked at her, and wished he had all the answers, but said instead as he looked into her teary eyes. "I can promise you one thing Jenna Temple, that I will not rest until I have found out who is responsible for your mother's death, and to recover her remains!"

Jenna blinked and the tears fell from her lashes and rolled down her cheeks. "I know you will Jack! I am so lucky to find you again!"

Jack looked serious. "The day is getting away Jenna, I must make a call to secure our accommodation! I know of a Lodge on the beach just off Dover Road. It has self-contained cabins that would suit our purpose. Your thoughts on that? We can talk when we get settled!"

Jenna smiled. "That sounds perfect Jack. Yes, make the call!"

He grinned, with thumbs up to Jenna as he secured the booking.

Jenna was so excited when they checked into the lodge. Jack had secured a two-bedroom cabin, and she loved him so for that. It had everything they would need, and it sat right at the water's edge.

Jack made them each a drink, then they sat out on the deck of the balcony over-looking the ocean. "Cheers to us Jenna!" he said.

As she leaned closer, he caught a glimpse of the neck chain she wore. "A beautiful chain Jenna, but what motif is on it, it's hidden."

"Ah! It could be the key to my heart!" she laughed, and held it up.

Jacked chuckled. "I'll be dammed, it is a key! But, why a key?"

"It is a key to my diary Jack. Just a tiny habit like my mother had! I too wear it always as she wore her mother's neck chain with green shafts of stone. It was because of this key I began to hear the voices!"

Green shafts of stone? I've heard of before! he sat forward. "Voices?"

Jenna giggled. "No, I'm not crazy Jack., but it was scary to hear mother's voice giving me directions to find a key, but I couldn't see her face. I now know I was recalling an actual conversation we had in her room a day prior to her city trip to put her affairs in order! On that day Jack, mother told me someone was trying to kill her!

Jack gaped. "Why, Jenna? What key? I must write this down!"

Chapter Eleven

They only had one week, but in that week so much was achieved. Jack had attended the briefing, and everything had been set in place for the following Tuesday. He was waiting on forensic reports and didn't have to go into the office until they came. That gave him and Jenna many hours to cram a few lost years into that time.

They enjoyed idle chit-chat and long lunches on the deck as their surroundings proved to set their mood for much reminising, and re-kindling their relationship. Jack was setting the pace with most of their conversation, steering clear of mentioning the investigation, but in his mind, the wheels were turning, and he already had ideas.

He was taking things slowly with their relationship too so as not to pressure Jenna, though secretly he had an unsatiable urge to hold her close, to kiss her, and more. He wanted to be sure it was Jenna who made the first move, then he would know she was ready.

It really came at an unexpected moment. They had just enjoyed a swim in the ocean, laughing as they ran up the sand, and his hand grabbed hers to help her, and they fell laughing onto their towels.

Jack fell on top of her, and the smile left her face. Immediately he apologized and started to rise, but she was quick to re-act as her hands clasped his and she pulled him back, then her arms encircled him. He felt her body warmth as she moved closer. When they came together the wetness of her salty lips on his was too much to bear.

He groaned as he kissed her with his pent-up passion and all his emotion and love for her went into that exchange when he held her so close to him, and she seemed to press her body in even closer to him if it was possible and all Jack's frustration seemed to disappear.

"God, how I love you, Jenna Temple!" he whispered into her ear as he nuzzled her neck, and then his hands roamed over her body.

Jenna responded by cupping his face with her fingers to kiss him longingly, her tongue teasing. She also suffered pent-up emotions, and succumbed to a wild state of abandonment to release the built-up desire and excitement overcoming her. She relished the feel of Jack's hands touching her body but it roused some panic within her as he reached her most secret parts and squeezed her breasts gently.

"I simply cannot believe I actually have you back again Jenna!" he muttered with emotion. "I won't be letting you out of my sight this time, you can bet on that my lady!" he added with certainty.

Jenna was finding it hard to restrain herself from calling out in urgency. Quickly she disengaged her hold on him to look into his eyes. "I certainly hope not Jack! Please don't ever let us be separated again!" she replied, then added with an emotional assurance in her voice. "Come with me Jack, it is time!" and she pulled him up.

Jack knew exactly what she meant but he just couldn't believe it. Now they were running across the sand hand in hand, their towels dragging behind them. At the step to their cabin, Jack scooped her up into his arms to carry her across the deck. Her head rested upon his shoulder. Then he was opening the door, and crossing the room to lay her tenderly on the bed, and bent to unclasp her swimmers.

Her top released her breasts and Jack gasped as he slid the straps down her arms. He bent over her to suckle one breast, and then the other and her nipples stood up proud as she groaned with pleasure, and arched her back. Jack squeezed her nipples gently, then traced his finger down to her belly button. He slipped his hands inside her swimmers to whisk them away, and stood staring at her beautiful naked body. He stripped off his trunks, and stood naked before her.

Jenna smiled, and reached up for him. He lay down beside her, and when their lips came together rather urgently their kiss seemed to ignite a fire in them. Jack couldn't contain his love and showered kisses on her neck and breasts then relished the feel of her salty skin as his tongue licked her belly button. Her legs fell apart to expose inner thighs as his lips nuzzled her, his tongue probed. Jenna spoke.

"Jack, please! I can't wait. Oh, please stop, make love to me now! I have an urgent need to feel you inside me, but please be gentle!"

He moved up to cover her body, then he looked directly into her eyes. He knew exactly what she meant. Jenna would still be a virgin and he was proud of that fact. "I will be Jenna, just trust me!"

"Oh! I would trust you with my life Jack Rickard!" she replied. "Just don't waste time!" She could feel his hardness thrust against her belly, and she slid her hand down to take him in her hands, and then she could feel his movements and she realized at once what he wanted so she moved her hands in sync. Their urgency mounted so quickly as she guided him into her. She stiffened, but then relaxed when she felt him inside her. However, Jenna could not contain the overwhelming spasms overtaking her body when he gently slid in further. His motion was gentle, until she felt the full length of him deep inside her when his thrust increased and she thought she must burst. She was moaning loudly, her whole-body shook, then she felt his body shudder, he gasped and fell like a dead man on top of her. Jenna was ecstatic. *If this is love, and making love? I want more.*

They lay so close together, their bodies entwined, and spent.

Jenna looked over at Jack who seemed to be sleeping. So, gently she leaned over him. "I love you! Jack Rickard!" she whispered.

He stirred, and rose on one elbow to look into her eyes. "I also love you too Jenna Temple. So much so, that it hurts!" he pulled her close, and kissed her deeply, and added. "I cannot believe after all we have been through; we have found each other again! To me, that is an omen so, I must say this." he slid off the bed to kneel down as he spoke to her. "I want to marry you, Jenna Temple, I always have! I haven't a ring to secure this ask today, but if you agree, we can shop for it tomorrow. Will you marry me, and be my wife, Jenna?"

Jenna smiled down at him. "Of course, silly! We were meant to be together, and we love each other, so marriage is the next step!"

"I am so pleased to hear you say that, Jenna. However, I want to marry you as soon as possible, while I am still in Blue Bay! As after this investigation our lives will change, and we haven't got into that fully yet. Besides, my parents live here, they will want to be at our wedding! Tell me your thoughts on that?" he asked meekly.

Jenna gasped. "Our marriage here, and so soon? It's a big ask!"

"Sooner than you may think Jenna. I would like to arrange our wedding for this coming Saturday if you will agree! My mother will arrange it for me, and we can still stay here, but as a married couple! Then we are free to get stuck into this investigation!"

"It does sound so easy! But would I have a minister, and a proper wedding dress? Who would give me away? I don't trust my father now! Besides, can we afford to stay here for an unlimited time?"

"Minor details Jenna! We will go shopping tomorrow for your rings, and your wedding dress. I will hire suits, so you have good photos, and good memories, and please don't worry about money Jenna! I am quite wealthy. I charge an enormous fee for my services! I have earnt that. Also, my father could give you away if you wish!"

Jenna gasped. "Oh my, you seem to have it all worked out Jack! So, I am saying yes! Definitely a yes! I would be so proud to be your wife, Jack. We'll work out the finer details when the investigation is over, so that is a good idea! Tomorrow will be a very busy day, but an important one. Come rain or shine, we will get married on Saturday Jack. Ha, ha! See, I am already excited!" and she laughed.

Jack laughed with her. "Thank the good lord for your decision my love, you won't regret it! I must call my mother at some point and get the wheels turning. Maybe we should go to my parent's house for dinner tomorrow night! Should I arrange that?"

Jenna smiled. "Yes, please Jack. I think that is a good idea!"

"Excellent, a done deal! We should shop for wedding invitations tomorrow as well, so we can decide who we want at our wedding and hand them out personally, or post them. Your thoughts?"

"That is a great idea, Jack. Your mother and father would like that, and I am guessing you would like to ask your work colleagues from the police force. As, for me? I don't think I have anyone to ask at all. It seems so sad really and my father has disappointed me so!"

"Yes, I do understand that Jenna, but he is your father, your choice! But I'll definitely ask a few of the guys and their wives or partners from the force. I would have to leave it up to my mother to book the church and priest, and our reception too? Where would you like to have it, there are so many lovely venues around here!"

Jenna smiled. "Do you know what Jack? I would love to have it right here! Have you seen the formal dining area inside the Lodge overlooking the ocean? It is so beautiful. It would be perfect!"

"Ah! A great choice Jenna! It's a lovely room, and it opens out to a secluded garden. We could arrange it all here ourselves, and even get the priest to marry outside if you wish. So, first thing tomorrow we will visit the manager and try to secure a booking for Saturday. No doubt the management here will arrange flowers as well!"

Jenna was so excited the next morning when they finally met up with the manager of The Lodge, Jim Sully. A middle-aged man with sandy hair and spectacles. He was very helpful, then smiled fondly at them as he checked his bookings for Saturday. "You are in luck people! Saturday is perfect for us to arrange your wedding!"

Though it was short notice, Jim Sully didn't seem fazed at all, and assured them he could cover all aspects of their day. They had a formal meeting to discuss all issues like flowers, menus, the cake and music and decided to be married by a celebrant outdoors in the gardens with a light luncheon to follow. Then they would re-locate inside to the great room for the reception, formal dinner, and music.

Jack paid the deposit, and they all shook hands, and that was all they had to do, except turn up on time. They were both ecstatic, and laughed together as they walked back to their cabin.

"Can you believe it Jack? We'll have everything all in one place and we can get dressed from here. How convenient!" she bubbled.

"Yes Jenna, it's almost as if it was meant to be! Now! While you are getting ready for the all-important shopping trip, I shall phone my mother to tell her we are coming over for dinner tonight. I think I will wait until then to inform them of our wedding. It will be good to see their reaction as we tell them, and they get the invite! Don't you think Jenna? They always loved you, so they will be happy!"

"Good idea, a surprise is nice. I do think they will be pleased!"

"I also must make a call to Homicide Detective Jeremy Woods. He is the person who trained me, and has rooms next to mine. He has access to my files, and as I am going to be in Blue Bay for some time, I will need someone to take over my work load. He'll organize that! I will ask him to our wedding, but I don't expect him to come, we shall see! Now, have you thought more about your father? Are you going to invite him? I need to know who is giving you away so I can get a suit to fit. We only have three days left you know!"

Jenna giggled. "Ok Jack, this is so magical. Three more days, and I will be Missus Jenna Rickard. I can't believe it, but it does sound good! Yes, I have thought about my father, and I guess it is only right that I should ask him to our wedding, and to give me away! However, under no circumstances will Miranda Delvin be getting an invite. I do not want her at our wedding, Jack. You must agree?"

"I do agree! You should call your father before we go out, but make it perfectly clear that Miranda is not invited! I can't believe she still lives out there! If he is coming, I'll need his measurements sent to 'Gilford's in town.' Do you remember the place right in the town center? Well, they are still there, and it is where I plan to get the suits from, and they do alterations if needed!"

"Fine, I will tell him that Jack. Maybe you could drop his invite out and put it in the mailbox so he will know the time and place."

"Yep, that is a good thought and should fix the problem so you won't have to go out to 'Oceanview,' which is good! Let your father know that's what I will do! But, remember this Jenna, it is very important if he is at the wedding! At no time in discussion should you tell him you are aware of the investigation! I would like them all to be unaware of what is to happen next week. Surprise is the best tactic! At the moment they will know, and think the police are running the investigation. It would be best to keep your memory status a secret now too, until the investigation begins next Tuesday! I spoke to Senior Constable Jenkins at the briefing regarding these topics, and that is what we decided was best. All officers have been briefed, no-one from the station will disclose a thing! What about you Jenna? Can you bend the truth a little for once in your life?"

Jenna looked seriously at him before she spoke. "Jack, trust me! I will do anything you say if it means catching my mother's killer. So, it will be difficult for me, but yes, I will be on my guard!"

He smiled. "Thank you, Jenna. A big ask, I know! Good girl!"

Richard stepped out to the patio to take the call. He knew it was Jenna calling, now he needed answers to important questions he had to ask her, since his heated conversation with Miranda Delvin.

Some time had passed since his last visit, but to his knowledge, Jenna was still being treated at the city clinic, and she was attending university. According to Miranda. *That was not so.* She was quite adamant she saw Jenna on the top balcony at 'Oceanview' recently, but from the onset of the phone call, Richard didn't get a word in.

Instead, it was Jenna who dictated their conversation. Brushing off testy questions with simple, but curt explanations as if they were needless or unimportant, and quickly got to the point of her call.

Richard became frustrated, and he fumed. He wasn't getting any satisfaction from her replies which were not realistically answering any things he wanted to know. Then, at the mention of her wedding planned for Saturday, and who she intended to marry, simply sent him into a violent rage. His temper flared as he growled in protest, saying she was far too young, and still not at all well enough to get married, and that Jack Rickard was simply not a suitable choice. But it fell on deaf ears as Jenna's anger flared when he demeaned Jack.

She told him she was well enough, and that she was of age where she could make her own decisions, and that Jack was the love of her life. She ended the call quickly by saying that his invite would be in the mail, but it didn't include Miranda. Jenna gave him two hours to inform her if he was giving her away, and the line went dead.

Richard looked at his blank phone in disbelief. *Damn me! She was stubborn as a child! But now, she's a force to be reckoned with!*

He shook his head. They had only just been told that there would be another investigation into the disappearance of his wife Julia as evidence has prompted the case to be re-opened. Himself, Miranda and the whole staff were to be interrogated, and Miranda was livid, and now this. He walked inside to face her, and break the news.

Miranda looked up from the settee where she was sitting when Richard came back inside. It only took a brief glance at his flushed face for her to realize something had annoyed him, because he had that mean look, he always seemed to get when his temper flared.

"What now Richard?" she asked. "Was that the police again?"

Richard shook his head and flopped into the chair opposite her.

"It doesn't rain unless it pours lately, Miranda. It seems you were right about Jenna being out here. I just spoke with her on the phone, or I should say she spoke to me, because I simply didn't get a word in! So, all our questions are unanswered, except for the fact that she is in Blue Bay, has been for some time I'm guessing as I was just told of her imminent plans to marry this coming Saturday!"

Miranda almost choked as she sipped a drink.

"What? You are kidding of course?"

"Nope, afraid not! My invite will be in the mailbox apparently, and I have the option of giving her away, or not!"

Miranda laughed. "Looks like you are the favourite father then! Just tell her to get someone else, and we won't bother going to the wedding either. She has a cheek that one! She is still just a kid too! How can she marry when she is undergoing treatment in a clinic?"

"I got no update on her treatment, only that she is well enough! Also, Miranda." he said, as he stared at her. "You are not invited!"

Miranda fumed. Her eyes widened as she screeched. "How dare she? She will not be dictating to me! I will go if I want to, but don't choose to, and you shouldn't either. Who is the groom anyway?"

"One, Jack Rickard it seems!"

"Oh my! This gets better and better! I thought we got rid of him!"

"I did too! That is what I am most angry about, and you are right. I won't be going to the wedding. Old police buddies will be there for sure if Jack Rickard is to be her husband. I want no part in that! I will reply by text message. I couldn't be bothered calling now!"

Jenna had just completed her shopping for a wedding gown, and was feeling excited to get everything so quickly. With parcels in hand, she hurried to meet up with Jack at the rendezvous they had planned, and she waved as she saw him there waiting for her.

He smiled and pulled out a seat for her. It was a busy restaurant but he was able to choose a seat outside in an alcove. He stood and greeted her with a kiss. "Looks like you've been busy my lady, but where is the wedding dress? Surely not in those small parcels!"

Jenna chuckled. "Ah! I knew you would want to peek at it, so I am having it delivered, just so you don't see it before our wedding!"

"I see. Guess you are right. I had forgotten about that tradition."

"Well tradition maybe, but realistically it's being altered a little!"

Jack laughed. "Well, I've been busy too. I bought the invitations, and I looked at rings. I didn't buy any as I thought you would like to choose, but something took my eye. A matching engagement and wedding ring for you, and a wedding ring for myself. So, what are your thoughts? We could go to the jeweler after lunch if you like!"

"I'd like that very much Jack! It sounds wonderful, maybe we could fill out the invitations and post them while we are in town!"

"A great idea!" replied Jack as he pulled out the invitations. "I just have to get suits organized. Did you hear from your father?"

"Oh! The invitations are very nice Jack." she said as she pulled one out to look. "Father? Well, I am not sure. I haven't heard my phone ring but I will look now." she said as she dug into her bag.

A puzzled look altered her features as she looked at her phone, and then at Jack. "Well, no phone call Jack but I have a text message. He is not coming to the wedding, or giving me away, and he told me that in a text message? I don't believe it! Maybe I was too matter-o-fact on the phone, or it could be because I didn't invite Miranda!"

Jack frowned, and laid a hand on her arm. "Don't upset yourself Jenna. It may be for the best in case someone talks about the case."

"Anyway, we will speak to my father tonight. I'm certain he will give you away. If not, then Senior Constable Jenkins certainly will!"

Jenna looked fondly at him. "I am fine Jack! Surprisingly, I feel relieved in a way. I must say things with my father have been no less than awkward of late, and I really have lost trust in him."

"I can understand that Jenna, but if you need support, you know I am here. We have a lot before us, let's not let anything spoil it!"

"Thank you, Jack. I know that, and I love you so!"

"I love you too, Jenna." he leaned over the table and they kissed.

"Now, let us eat. I'm starved! Make your selection and order the steak for me as well while I go outside to ring my parents. It looks like we will be done in town earlier than expected, so we should plan on going out to their place later. How does that sound to you?"

"Yes, perfect Jack I only need to buy a pair of white shoes, and the invitations we can start writing out after you make your call!"

"Sounds like a plan. I won't be long Jenna!" he said, as got up and walked out through the trellis of flowering miniature roses.

Jenna watched him leave, and she sat deep in thought. *Yes! I am certain we will have a happy marriage!* We communicate so well, and our love is growing stronger each day. Thank goodness I came back here when I did, *or I may never have found him again!* She thought about the repercussions that would have had on her life. A change of direction maybe, and she shuddered in dread of what could have been. As she sat her mind wandered and a sense of gloom suddenly came over her when she thought of what was to come next week, fear seemed to rise up inside to squeeze her throat.

Can I handle the pressure? Am I ready to recall what happened. I have to, I just have to for Jack, and myself. *I must face this!*

Her mother's voice seemed to whisper. *Oh, yes you can Jenna!*

It seemed almost like a plea from the grave of her mother. Jenna began shaking as she realized how it imitated her own thoughts.

Jack sauntered up beside her. His voice made her start, but then seemed to shake her back to reality to release her from her doom.

"Well, that's all sorted, Jenna. My parents will both be expecting us this afternoon, we shall stay for dinner tonight. But keep in mind Jenna, I won't be telling them about the investigation until after our wedding. Let's just concentrate on our celebrations first, is that ok?"

"If that is what you want Jack! It may be for the best!" Jenna said.

"Good, now let's get these invitations sorted, we can post them after lunch. I am sending one to Homicide Detective Jeremy Woods, and wife, just in case he can make it, and I suggest you fill one out for your father also, he may change his mind. Still, we will ask my father to give you away, and Constable Jenkins I want for my best man. I'll hand deliver his invite on the way, and ask him. Agreed?"

"Yes, Jack I agree. I have resigned myself to the fact now that my father doesn't want to be with us, or be involved on our special day, but it is maybe for the best. I will send an invitation just the same."

"Be positive Jenna! Try to think of someone you want to invite."

"There is no-one Jack, school friends I've lost track of. If anyone, it would be my specialist Doctor Eric Wilson, his wife and family. They were so good to me in my time of need. They invited me into their home to spend last Christmas holidays with them, and treated me like one of their own. We went horse riding, and Doctor Wilson helped me get my driver's license. So, we became good friends!"

"Well, there you go Jenna, send them an invite!" replied Jack.

With that decided, they enjoyed some casual conversation over lunch, and with invitations in hand, went to post them, then visited a shoe store, and walked down to the jewelers. Jenna was filled with joy over their purchase. She couldn't stop smiling as they walked across the street to 'Gilford's.' Jack's selection was matter of fact so he was fitted for his suit at once, but his father's and best man's, he selected appropriate sizes to be altered if needed and delivered.

Carol and Steven Rickard were sitting on the front porch of their weatherboard home just out of town. They had a small acreage and an orchard of which produce they sold to the local businesses, and anyone who came out to the small shop-front to purchase.

They both smiled as the car pulled into the driveway, and Jack and Jenna got out and walked up the path towards them.

"They make such a lovely couple. Don't you agree Steven?"

"I most certainly do Carol. What a turn of luck it was to throw them together again after so long." he said as he waved to them.

Carol smiled to herself. Then she was off her chair, and down the few steps in haste to greet them. She was so proud of Jack and his achievements that earnt his status in life, but to find Jenna again was simply icing on the cake for him. His mother knew that well. She knew there would never be anyone else for Jack, except Jenna.

Then she was facing them and fighting off tears as she embraced Jenna, then Jack. "It soothes my soul to see you again Jenna, and to see you looking so well and happy, is so great to see. We all thought we had lost you. Welcome to our home!" she said in earnest.

"Yes, welcome to both of you!" said Steven by her side now, and he moved forward to hug Jenna, and shake Jack's hand.

Jenna smiled at them. "Thank you, mister and missus Rickard. Finally, I am recovering nicely, and my memory is coming back to me too, but my happiness is strictly because of Jack. Just by chance, to see him again, was the best thing that has happened to me for a long time. We have much to tell you, and to discuss with you both!"

"That sounds good Jenna. I am sure you have a lot to share with us. We have missed you these past years, and so has Jack. Come! Let's all sit up on the porch, and I will endeavor to get some drinks to celebrate the occasion, maybe Jack could help me?" he asked.

Like Jack, he too was a handsome man with an infectious smile that came easy, as his deep grey eyes twinkled, Jenna noted.

"Sure thing, father." Jack replied, as Carol took Jenna's hand and led her up the steps to the porch where she seated her in a comfy chair, and sat opposite her on the settee. She smiled broadly, as her green eyes seemed to be smitten slightly by tears, then she spoke.

"You have grown into a beautiful young lady Jenna Temple. You always were so cute growing up, but now you've blossomed. I am so pleased to hear your treatment was successful. We were all so concerned for you, but then our communication link ceased!"

"Yes, I know. My father didn't help Jack at all in his struggles to find me. I apologize for that. In time I will tell you of my treatment."

Carol frowned at the mention of Richard Temple, but she smiled at Jenna to say. "There is no rush to do that Jenna. Take your time, and when you feel comfortable you may tell us then. We are just so happy you are home again! We don't wish to pressure you."

"Thank you for understanding missus Rickard. I do find it quite difficult to talk about what I have been through over the years and I guess total recovery will take some time. I just have to be patient."

Jack and his father placed the drinks on the table, and sat down, and it was Jack who spoke first. "Well folks, I guess you have been wondering where I've been. With the case completed my intentions were to go back to the city next day." he chuckled. "I was coming out here, but look who I ran into." Jack grinned as he acknowledged Jenna. Needless to say, we've had some lost years to catch up on so I secured a place for us to stay just out of The Bay. But in that short space of time, we have both made a decision, and I extended my stay for an important reason. Jenna has something for you both!"

Jenna smiled as she stood to hand over the envelope to Carol.

Carol quickly opened it, and her hands clasped her mouth as she gushed. "Oh! Steven, just look. It is a wedding invitation for us!"

"Great news! Well done you two, now we can really celebrate!"

Their smiles were a treat for Jack and Jenna to see, and they both smiled back. But for Jack, just to witness their expressions was all he really wanted, and he couldn't help but make a joke.

"I know this is short notice mother and father, but I asked Jenna to marry me before she ran off again, and behold she said yes! Can you believe that? What else could I do, but marry her quickly!"

Everyone laughed, though Carol was in tears as she said. "Oh Jack, you have made me the happiest mother. This is such great news. Welcome to our family Jenna." she said as she hugged her.

Jenna had tears in her eyes too as they hugged, and then Steven Rickard hugged her. "Welcome Jenna. I am so pleased for you both. This is one wedding I will be looking forward to. "We have to go shopping Carol." he commented, and she laughed. "If either of you ever need anything at all, just ask. I am always here!" he added.

Jenna looked at Jack in question, and he nodded. "Well, there is one favour I would like to ask of you Mister Rickard?" she uttered, as she looked into his eyes.

Steven smiled. "Fire away Jenna. How I can help?"

Jenna's eyes were downcast, but then she took a deep breath and lifted her head, "Would you do me the honour of giving me away Saturday please Mister Rickard? I'm at a loss for words to explain."

Steven Rickard could see she was at the point of breaking down, so he asked no questions, just smiled his best smile, then he replied.

"It is I who shall have the honour Jenna, and by all means. I will be so proud to walk you down the aisle, and hand you to my son. You were made for each other so, it will be our most, happiest day!"

Jenna smiled. "Thank you so much Mister Rickard. You see, my father won't be attending our wedding apparently, but if there is anyone you would like to invite, just let us know."

"My wife and I will discuss it and let you both know. It's a lovely venue you have chosen too, the garden is perfect at The Lodge."

Carol couldn't stop smiling, and she spoke up "We have been out there for dinner and the chef there is marvelous, and seeing you are getting married outdoors Jack and Jenna, you will be pleasantly surprised with the setting as it is absolutely beautiful. So, tell me how did you decide on that particular venue Jack?"

Jack frowned. "Well, I will do my best to answer that, but please understand mother and father that I can't go into full details right now, it is not a good time. But Jenna had an incident at 'Oceanview,' and it was at the police station that I run into her. She was so upset and I decided to take her to The Lodge, and hire a cabin there. That is where we have been staying. So, because we were familiar with all on offer there, we decided to hold our wedding there, or rather Jenna did. It was her suggestion! We do promise to talk to you both about what has happened after the wedding. Is that ok with you?"

"By all means Jack. Your wedding should take priority, and we know if there is anything you want to tell us, then you will do it in your own time. So don't worry yourselves about that. Now, about the wedding. Is there shopping to be done? What about suits Jack? Or a wedding dress for Jenna? Invitations, a cake? Can I help?"

Jack laughed. "You will not believe this mother, but we have it all sorted, and at The Lodge right down to the last tune at night. We will show you our rings later. My suit and Jenna's wedding dress is being delivered to us, but I need you to ring Gilford's father with your measurements and address so they can deliver it here Friday."

"Ah! I see one small problem with that Jack." said his mother.

"Which is what?"

"A little thing called tradition. You are not supposed to see the bride's wedding dress until you are getting married Jack!"

"Ah, we did think of that briefly. So, what should we do?"

"Simple! Have Jenna's dress delivered here. Steven will collect her on Friday morning and bring her here to stay for the night.

"No doubt, we will have last minute things to do like hair, and nails, and Jenna can relax by the pool that day. She will get dressed here on Saturday. I will do her hair any way she would like it done, and help her dress. Steven can drive her to the wedding venue!"

Jack chuckled, and looked at Jenna who was smiling.

"What do you think of that idea Jenna?"

"I think it is absolutely marvelous, so thank you Missus Rickard. I must say it was worrying me a little, so I accept your offer."

"Excellent! So, consider it done and we will look forward to your company, Jenna. Won't we Steven?"

"You bet! I will ring Gilford's when Carol measures me Jack!"

"Thank you both. My best man is to be Senior Constable Jenkins. I only spoke to him briefly on the way out here, and then handed out the invitations for a few mates. But, out of everyone during my work life, he was always there for me, and really it was because of him that I gained the traineeship in the city. I do owe him a lot. My position, my status now, my lifestyle really. Though I know it was me who done the hard yards, he still pathed the way for me. I won't ever forget that. He was over the moon when I asked him to be my best man, and gave him an invite for all his family. Jenna has sent an invite to her specialist and his family who were good to her also. We are not certain who will come at such short notice, so we'll see."

"Yes, I recall Senior Constable Jenkins's involvement. It is good that you come out to help him when you can Jack." said his father. "Now, sort out what else is to be done and I'll fire up the barbeque."

"Yes, I did promise him that I would help when I could, so it was lucky I was here just finishing up a case when I found Jenna." Jack looked at Jenna. "It might be an idea to call the bridal store now Jenna, and give them this address to send your dress here Friday, and then we will be done for the day, and able to relax a little."

"Good idea. Excuse me all while I make the call." she replied.

Friday turned out to be a very important day, and a busy one. As planned, they were enjoying their last breakfast together out on the deck until Sunday, when then they would be Mister and Missus Rickard, so it was an important morning to them, but interrupted when Jack received a phone call from the Manager of the Lodge.

He placed the receiver down, and spoke to Jenna. "It looks like I have some last-minute arrangements to organize with the manager after breakfast Jenna. It is only about the dinner seating, but I can handle that if you want to get ready to leave. Oh! Looks like father is here already!" he said, as he looked out the window and noticed Steven Rickard driving his car into the drive.

"I'll go out and meet him, Jenna! Then I will put the kettle on so we can have a cuppa while you are getting your things together!"

"Thanks Jack" she said as she bent to kiss him. "All the things I need are packed so I won't take too long. Pour one for me too."

"Ok, let's get moving young lady. Will see you tomorrow, Jack."

Jack stood and pulled Jenna into his arms. Their kiss was long. "I am going to miss you Jenna, don't keep me waiting tomorrow!"

She laughed. "I will try not to, but please wait for me Jack!"

Steven helped her with her things, and Jack watched as they got in the car, and he waved as they drove away. He was excited, and so looking forward to tomorrow, and marrying Jenna. *Finally, it is all happening for us, my wishes are coming true.* he thought.

His phone rang to break his train of thought. It was Gilford's. His suit would be delivered within the hour. *I'd better get a move on then. I'll just have enough time to meet with the manager.*

With the seating arrangements sorted Jack reached the cabin just in time to meet Gilford's delivery van. He grabbed his suit, as again his phone rang, only this time Senior Constable Jenkins spoke.

Jack laughed. "I just received my suit. Are you calling to tell me you received yours also sir?" Straight away he detected a strain in the Constable's voice. He acknowledged receiving his suit but said that was not the reason for his call, and he started to explain.

Jack stood still, and listened intently. A bristle seemed to shoot up the back of his neck and he shivered in expectation as Constable Jenkins mentioned that the forensic reports were back.

"I am sorry for calling today of all days, but you'd better come into the station Jack!" Constable Jenkins was saying. "These reports could be important information for you Jack as the forensic reports came from a new team at the city branch this time! Can you make it, it is rather urgent, and we must talk, especially before Tuesday!"

"Yeah, sure Constable Jenkins. Luckily Jenna just left to stay the night with my parents so, I can leave right away."

"Good, I was hoping to talk to you alone. What I have to say is not for Jenna's ears today, the day before her wedding. I'll see you soon!" he said, and the phone went dead.

Jack went inside to hang his suit up, then he locked up the cabin and left straight away. He wondered what could be so important today of all days, that couldn't wait until Tuesday, they were only reports. *I guess I'll soon know.* he thought.

He pulled into the station and just managed to get the last car-park. *It must be busy today.* he thought, as he got out of the car, and approached the entrance of the station. He spoke to a few of his mates briefly, then headed down the hall to the Constable's office. His voice called out 'enter' as soon as he knocked, so he went inside.

"Thanks for coming Jack. I'll try not to keep you too long. Pull up a chair, and have a look at these samples, and read these reports. Someone has gone the extra mile with these tests, and you are not going to believe what they found. Contrary to the initial tests."

Jack read the bold print. **Positive DNA tests for Julia Temple.**

"Well, I'll be!" he said as he stared up at Constable Jenkins. "You don't realize what this means to me sir. I can't thank you enough!"

Jack raised his eyebrows as he scanned the first page. He couldn't believe it. Three positive DNA tests for dried blood samples in sand, and also human bone chips in sand. But the last item seemed to ring bells for him. Positive DNA found on shafts of green stone.

He knew it was a significant finding and could recall them being found along with insignificant prints of covered shoes, but seemed sure Jenna mentioned shafts of green stone at some point. He stared as he inspected the delicate shafts of green stone in the case. "I have a gut-feeling these shafts of stone mean something Constable. I will discuss them with Jenna first, but tomorrow we will be rather busy, so I'll take the case with me if I can, to show her on Monday? Poor Jenna! We have one day for a honeymoon. I wish I had something planned for Sunday! Also, something is bugging me about the shoe prints, are there any photos of them I could look at on Tuesday?"

"Yes, I have some screen shots. I'll set up a projector on Tuesday for you. Now! Don't take the stones from the case Jack, as they are important evidence, and bring them in on Tuesday, understand?"

"Thanks sir! I'll take care of the stones, were they tested before?"

"They were Jack, but by a different team. They now have at their disposal a more accurate up-to- date technology test for stone, and blood samples mixed with sand! Now, as for your other problem! I may be able to help you out. I own a boat, and the island across the waters cater especially for newlyweds at the resort there. If you are able to secure a booking for Sunday, I could take you across at first light, and you could spend a mini honeymoon there. Stay the night, I will collect you on Monday after breakfast. What do you think?"

"What do I think? You are a legend, Constable Jenkins! Find me the number, and I will call straight away. I cannot believe it. If I get a room, this will be a total surprise for Jenna, so no telling! Because on Monday, poor Jenna is going to have to talk about her mother! Horrendous details, and that my friend, will be very hard for her!"

"I know Jack, I just hope she's able to do it. Here is the number!"

Jack grabbed it, and dialed. After talking to reception, a smile lit up his face, and he gave the constable a nod. He wanted to take full opportunity of activities on offer there, so he booked them in for everything, and Sunday breakfast as well, then ended the call.

He chuckled. "I hope we can get there for breakfast sir, as I have just booked it and a full schedule. Maybe leave in the early hours?"

"No problems Jack, consider it done. We will leave at 5 a.m."

"Perfect! Jenna will be beside herself, and also by the way. The manager at The Lodge told me this morning that he is giving us the bridle suite for tomorrow night as a wedding gift, and Jenna doesn't know it yet either. I'll let you know the room number tomorrow so you can collect us there. I'll pack our bags when I get back today."

"Good, then we are all sorted. I will meet you in the foyer of The Lodge tomorrow at 11.30a.m. Best of luck for your future happiness Jack. You deserve it after what you have both been through."

"Thank you, sir, and I hope you and your wife enjoy what I have on offer for our wedding day, and night! I best get going now."

Constable Jenkins extended his hand. Jack gripped it. "You've always been there for me sir, so it means a lot you are my best man!"

"It is my pleasure, Jack. I hope the forensic results help you with your investigation. I guess for you and Jenna, it starts Monday!"

"Yep, Monday will be a hard day for us! See you tomorrow."

Senior Constable Jenkins watched Jack as he turned to leave, and walk away. *He is a top bloke, that boy. I always knew that!* A great cop too, and a far better Homicide Detective. *He will turn this case on its head, that is for sure.* I just can't wait to be involved, and to assist him. But first things first. *A wedding that we thought would never happen.* I am so happy for him and Jenna. For Jack to find the love of his life again after all this time is quite a miracle really.

Things do happen for a reason! he mused.

True to his promise, Senior Constable Joe Jenkins hailed Jack in the foyer of The Lodge at precisely 11.30 a.m. Saturday morning. Jack was speaking to the Lodge Manager then they shook hands.

He looked up, and smiled at the Constable. "Well, my best man! Looking dapper too I see sir, and have to say, prompt as usual!"

"Morning Jack. Great day for an outside wedding. Must say you scrub up pretty darn good yourself. One thing Jack, please drop the sir! Joe will suffice in private, unless of course we are at the station, or certain times on the case, then call me Constable. Ok?" he stated.

"Sure, thing sir!" replied Jack in jest, and they both laughed.

"Right, let's get out there, and wait for the bride!"

Jack scanned the seated guests as he went to his place, and there he was. His huge frame unmistakable to Jack, sitting in the second row with family and Jack felt honoured. He placed one hand on his shoulder to squeeze it as he passed by, and nodded to him and his family as Homicide Detective Jeremy Woods looked up and smiled.

Just prior to noticing Jenna enter, his eyes rested on one family. *Strangers.* Jack thought, then he realized who they would be. *Jenna's guests have attended, her specialist and his family*! She'll be ecstatic.

Then Jenna was captivating his attention. She only had eyes for him. His heart swelled as she walked the garden path towards him.

He had never seen her looking so beautiful, and he smiled at her as the soft music played., and beside her his father was beaming.

Then he noticed his mother holding up her train, and he smiled. He liked it to see his mother was involved. She even took Jenna's bouquet on cue, as Jack held out a hand to Jenna, but as his hand closed around hers, he felt her trembling. He squeezed her hand in re-assurance. She smiled at him with huge green eyes swimming with tears. He grinned back, hoping a tear didn't fall on her gown.

Then the celebrant was starting the service. His father stepped forward to do his part, and Jack was placing a ring on her finger.

They were prompted to say their chosen vows, and when they became man and wife Jack grabbed Jenna, and swirled her around and kissed her deeply, much to the enjoyment from their guests.

A short pause for the signing, and some photographs, and then they were mingling with the guests under the big marque, and the photographer followed, taking shots from all angles.

Jenna noticed her specialist, Doctor Wilson and his family. She was so excited, and couldn't wait to introduce them to Jack. So, she whispered to him. "Please come with me Jack. You must meet these special people." and she tugged at his hand.

"I did notice them sitting there when I came in Jenna, and I am so pleased for you! But I too have someone special for you to meet!"

"Excellent, how exciting. I do love surprises!" Jenna bubbled. "You will have a few before this day is done my love." Jack grinned.

By now champagne was being brought out on trays, followed by trays of food for the light luncheon. Jack grabbed two drinks as they reached the Wilson's table, and Jenna hugged each person.

Fay smiled. "Jenna Rickard! I have to say that you make the most beautiful bride. You look absolutely stunning my dear girl, so full of life, but most of all. You look so happy! I am pleased to see that!"

"Oh Fay, thank you. I am so happy, and feeling well. I owe it all to my husband Jack. It means the world to me that you all came to our wedding. To all of you, Doc Wilson, Fay, Emma and Jill, I'd like you to please meet my husband, Jack Rickard. Jack they are my very special guests, you know who they are!" Jack laughed. "I certainly do. Thank you for coming, and making this day special for Jenna. I've heard so much about you all. He held out his hand. Pleased to meet you in person Doctor Wilson, Missus Wilson, and girls."

"Please call me Eric now Jack, my wife is Fay. We can drop the formalities. We were so excited by Jenna's news, we had to come and wish her well, and to check you out of course!" he laughed.

Jack didn't know if he was being serious or not, but he continued. "Well! I guess that is only fair! You have done so much for my girl, or I should say. My wife, now!" he chuckled. "I do appreciate that, but just so you know, Eric. I plan to take good care of her. We grew up together, and Jenna has always been the love of my life!"

Eric Wilson chuckled, and Fay smiled, as she liked Jack instantly.

"Don't mind my little jest, Jack." uttered Eric. "I am quite certain Jenna will tell us all about you, and I know she wouldn't settle for less. It is why we are here, to lend you both our support if we can!"

"Thank you, Eric, that does mean a lot, especially to Jenna. It was freakish luck really, running into Jenna after all this time. I lost track of where she was sent to and couldn't find her! Now, would you please excuse us, we must mingle. We have a special day planned so, enjoy the light luncheon. At the break inside we will have more time to talk then before the formal sit-down dinner and music!"

"Sounds marvelous Jack, will look forward to chatting later."

Jenna spoke. "I also! I have much to tell you Doc and I must talk privately with you! But now we have to meet the guests and Jack's tutor. Jack is a Homicide Detective now, and his mentor is here!"

"Great stuff Jack, well done, and Jenna by all means we'll talk."

Jenna felt in awe of Homicide Detective Jeremy Woods when she met him, the man who molded Jack's life just seemed to captivate an audience, and she was most interested to talk to him more later.

So, their wedding was a huge success, and Jenna was so thrilled about their bridle suit, but it was the next day which really was the surprise of her life, and the beginning of their married life. Senior Constable Jenkins was waiting in the foyer at 4.30 a.m. and whisked them away to the jetty where his boat was moored, and took them out to the Island. It was a perfect setting for newly-weds. Jenna and Jack took full advantage of this time together bonding, and relished privacy because come Monday after breakfast it was back to reality.

Chapter Twelve

Jenna sat in silence on the deck outside their cabin at The Lodge. Only one sound captivated her attention, and that was the sound of waves breaking, and the surge of the ocean as it rushed into the shore. She had heard that sound before, and her mind slipped back to the morning of her attack on the beach, and her mother's murder.

Tears welled in her eyes as the memory became vivid. *I have to do this!* Any minute now, *Jack will be wanting to talk with me. So, I must be prepared. He's been so patient with me.* she thought. *It's just that it is so difficult to realize my memories are actual fact.* I can see it all so clearly in my mind, but to explain each, and every detail is going to be heartbreaking for me, and I know it will tax me. I wish there was another way, but there is not. *I must help Jack with all I know!*

Jack watched Jenna through the kitchen window as he prepared their coffee. He could detect by her demeanor that she was already struggling. It was heart breaking to realize he must go outside and shatter the happiness they shared. He could imagine her thoughts and what was going on in her mind. *Can she talk about it though?*

He put a smile on his face as he walked outside, then placed their coffees, and cake on the small table. "So pleased to be of service Missus Jack Rickard!" he chuckled, as he sat down opposite her.

Jenna looked up at him a little puzzled, and though tears lined her eyelashes, she managed a smile. "You gave me your name!"

"Well, it is your name too now. You have the option of how you would like to be addressed. It's a personal thing, so you decide!"

"Hmm! I will have to think on that a while kind sir!" she replied. Then her face shone with happiness. "Oh Jack! Wasn't our wedding wonderful. I had such a marvelous time. So, thank you so much for all you done to make it a very special day. We will have our photos back in five days the photographer told me, I simply can't wait!"

"A very special wedding for a very special girl Jenna. I'm just so pleased I found you again to give you that wedding! It was special!"

"I simply loved your friends from the force too. But Homicide Detective Jeremy Woods, he is quite a character and his family were so nice to me. I took the time to chat with him privately in the break. He is a very interesting, intelligent man, and he speaks very fondly, and highly of you Jack, so I think you have a friend in him for life!"

"Yep, I sort of know that, as we just clicked from day one. I guess that is how I climbed the ladder so quickly. I owe him so much! But I have news too. I actually spoke privately with your specialist, Eric Wilson. Nice fellow, so too is his family. But strictly speaking, from a Detective's point of view, I really wanted to talk to him about your initial head injuries. How he would describe the injury that placed you in a coma, what set-backs you experienced after that, and what treatment was given. More importantly! What did he think caused that injury, and what weapon would be used? His reply matched perfectly with our forensic reports of a rock tested with your blood on it. So, I told him about this report, and that I was The Homicide Detective taking on your case, and also your mother's murder!"

"He was dumbfounded, as he had no idea about your mother's murder, so I had to explain what happened to you at Oceanview to jog your memory, and he did say he was hoping something would bring you out of it, not thinking it would be the recall of a murder!"

"Thank you, Jack. I couldn't face telling him that!"

"Eric also offered to make a statement in court if it was needed about your injuries, and help in any way he could. He also told me how proud he was of me personally. He admired my dedication to finally achieve my goals to become an acting Homicide Detective, to set up our future. So, you could say we covered some ground!"

"Oh my! It is so great to hear you both got on, and that he maybe can help in your investigation. He really is a very special man my doc! He helped me heaps in my recovery. I also had a talk with him much later. However, I'm a little surprised you will be investigating my accident as well as my mother's murder, Jack! Are you sure it is really necessary? I didn't realize, so, it is news to me I must say!"

Jack frowned as he looked straight into her eyes. "Your accident, was no accident Jenna! It was attempted murder! You were left for dead and obviously someone was coming back to deal with you but I think your discovery by the boy from the surf club squashed that plan, and saved your life. So, to answer you. Yes of course! I'll most definitely be investigating your fall, and your attack in detail Jenna! So, if not your mother, what did you talk to Doctor Wilson about?"

"Well, when we finally got to have a private conversation, I had to tell him of my experience at Oceanview. My reaction at the steps, and how it affected me. He would want to know about the severe pain in my head and the blinding lights, shadows forming, and my memory slowly coming back. I only told him I remembered falling through the steps to the rocks below, and where I was attacked. I just simply couldn't come to tell him the rest of the details of my mother's murder that I witnessed. It would have been too painful!"

Jack looked forlornly at her before he could speak. Then he took a deep breath and threw caution to the wind as he began.

"Jenna! You do know today is a very important day for us both, and for me to gather information, as tomorrow the case begins, so I have to be prepared. There are questions I have to ask you, that only you know. I don't plan on asking you of the vision you saw of your murdered mother initially, we can leave that until after lunch if you prefer, but more of other things that are important as well. Can you work with me please, try to give me some understanding to go on?"

He looked at her hopefully. Then she raised her head to look into his eyes. "I know it is time Jack, and necessary. I've been dreading it all morning, but thank you for understanding, I will try my best!"

"Thanks Jenna, if it gets too much let me know and we will rest."

"I will Jack. Where did you want to start?"

Jack pulled out his notebook. "We start at the beginning Jenna, the morning of your fall, and then your attack, but no need to say anything about your mother, I know parts of it already. So, we will cover that this afternoon. Are you ok with that? Are you ready?"

"Yes, Jack. I am as ready as I will ever be!"

"Good! Firstly, to bring you up to date. I know we were to meet early the next day as it was my birthday. We were going riding, and we had things to discuss, but you weren't at the gate as planned so I went up to your room. Your door was ajar, but you weren't inside. So, then I decided to check your mother's room. I found the doors opened as the lock was broken, but inside, the place was in chaos. I noticed her walking stick still there, and found that odd. Then I was worried. I searched the stables for you, but no Jenna. I went down to see your father, but the police were already knocking on his door as you had been found by a new employee of the surf club, lucky for you, as he had called the police, then an ambulance to go to the club. They took the paramedic team down to you by a sand buggy."

Jenna's eyes widened. "My goodness! I haven't been told any of this, and I can see what you mean about my accident. I was lucky!"

"You certainly were my lady. Now let's get down to it."

"Why on earth did you go outside to the deck in the early hours of morning? Would you remember an approximate time?"

Jenna thought about it first. "I am not sure of the time though I know I was still awake at 3 a.m. I know it was moonlight. I couldn't sleep because it was coming through my window, and I got up to close the drapes. That is when I heard the first faint scream so I went outside onto the deck to listen, and there was one more scream faint on the breeze, but I heard it. It was a moonlight night so I had no problem seeing as I crept along the deck to the steps, but then there was silence, and that seemed much worse, so I quickened my pace as I started to descend the wide steps, counting as I went down."

"Stop right there Jenna! I need to know more about the steps, it is very important. Are you quite certain you fell through the steps, or were you pushed down, Jenna?"

"No, I definitely wasn't pushed Jack. I would have felt that, and I didn't, besides it was moonlight, I would have seen. It was simply because of a missing step, and I couldn't stop my momentum!"

"So, which step did you fall from?"

"I fell from the fourth step into where the fifth step should be!"

"How can you be positive of that, and why count the steps?"

"You are aware Jack, there are rather a lot of steps down to the beach. They are quite wide, and it's easy to miss a step, or take two steps on one. I used to make a game of counting them as a kid. Habit really, but that is how I know it was most definitely the fifth step I fell through. It was completely missing, I could see the big gap, but couldn't stop. I hovered on the fourth step, but couldn't go back!"

Jack rubbed his chin. "Hmm! Looks like someone was eager to get rid of your mother. Maybe she was pushed, or fell through too!"

Jenna eyed him quickly. "Exactly, Jack! One step down through the gap is why I fell in the same place where she was murdered!"

Jack jotted some notes down in his notebook as he said. "This is good Jenna. I agree! You are doing well. Now! I know the steps are solid, do you know how they are connected to the railings? I should know I've climbed them many times, but we will check tomorrow!"

"I am pretty sure they all have hefty bolts, and stays as well."

"Hmm, I see. So, to remove that step would be quite a task!"

Jack started writing again before he continued. "This is important to me Jenna, about your attack. I think it is safe to say that the rock with your blood on it was what caused your injury. So! Tell me your opinion. Do you think the fall onto the rocks was what caused you to lose consciousness, and ultimately put you in a coma?"

"Definitely not Jack!" Jenna replied. "Or rather, not completely."

Jack looked directly at her. "How can you be so certain Jenna?"

Jenna trembled. Her whole body shook as she tried to continue.

Jack put a hand out to steady her. Are you feeling alright Jenna, or do you want a break, we can do this later if you like?" he stated.

She looked at him with a determination in her eyes.

"No! I must do this, so I will try to continue as best I can. Now, to answer your question. I am certain Jack, because as I was falling, I expected a big hit of landing on rocks, but it didn't come, as my landing was cushioned somewhat!" she sobbed then tears filled her eyes. "I was scrambling to get up, just to get away! I was conscious, and not badly hurt at all, only so devasted with grief to witness the scene before me of my dead mother, and in a dismembered state. I stared in disbelief, and couldn't believe my eyes. You see Jack, I fell on mother, that is what saved me! My fatal injury must have come later!" Then she started to cry. Big heartbreaking sobs which tugged at Jack's heart, and he pulled her into his arms. "Good grief! My poor darling, it's over now!" he said as he showered her with kisses.

"We don't need to talk about it again. Rest for a while my love! I have only one more question about your attack, an important one, but I will go and get us some refreshments first!"

Jenna looked him squarely in the eyes with hers filled with tears.

"Then let's get it over with Jack, and then I will rest!"

"Are you sure?"

"Most definitely. Let's get it all out now!" Jenna replied.

"Ok! We know you saw your mother, and it was moonlight, and the fall didn't cause your final injuries but something else obviously did Jenna! Did you see anyone, or can you explain it more to me?"

"I was finding it hard to see clearly. My heart was breaking, tears filled my eyes, making it hard to identify things as I was crying so much. But then suddenly, something blocked out the moonlight!"

"Do you mean you were plunged into darkness? How, by what?"

"Yes! It was a shadow, Jack. It moved to block out the moonlight right next to me. I was so confused I couldn't see. Then came the hit to my forehead. It must have been the rock you spoke of, as it struck me so hard, I fell down senseless. But Jack! That was the last thing I remember, until I woke in hospital in the city some months later!"

"Woah! My poor love. I will have to fill you in later as to what happened to you prior to that, and after. But right now, I need you to concentrate hard, tell me more about this shadow. Do you recall how you first saw the shadow? Did you have to look up? Or look down at it to see it? Was it large in size, or small?" he queried.

"Definitely large in form to block out the moonlight. But also, I felt I had to look up at it after I had briefly sensed it by my side, and realized then it was a shadow. A shadow of a human form Jack!"

A crease formed on Jack's forehead. "Hmm!" he said as he began writing, then asked. "Did you recognize any mannerism, Jenna?"

"Sadly no! Sorry Jack." Jenna replied." It happened so quickly!"

"Not to worry, we will stop now Jenna, and I will order lunch."

Jenna placed her hand upon his arm, and stared at him with eyes that were swimming with tears. "Jack, please! We must continue while I am thinking about it. I don't want to resume after lunch!"

Jack's brow creased as he spoke to her, and lifted his eyes to meet hers. "Jenna. It's just that the next line of questioning will be quite in depth about your mother, are you sure you can handle that?"

"I can only try Jack. Just be patient with me, and let us be done with it, or I may not be able to continue. So, order lunch, and when it arrives, we will stop, but we must cover everything in that time!"

"As you wish my love!" he replied and rose from his seat. Then, as an afterthought he smiled, and asked. "What say I order seafood and a bottle of bubbly to celebrate your courage Missus Rickard?"

Jenna smiled for the first time. "I do so love it when you address me like that Jack, and yes please. I would like that very much!"

"Good, I'll make the call to order for a bit later, and we'll begin."

He walked inside with his phone in his hand, and Jenna watched him go. *Thank the good lord I have you, Jack!* she thought.

In no time he was back and placed a drink down on the table for each of them. "This is an appetizer for what is to come." he smiled. "Lunch is ordered, I just need to grab something from inside, so he went back inside. When he came back, he had with him a small box. He placed the box on the table, then sat down opposite Jenna, and immediately opened his notebook and he flicked through the pages until he found the right place, then looked at Jenna, and smiled.

"What is in the little box?" asked Jenna curiously.

His brow creased again. "That my love will hopefully be my last question for you. So, be patient. First things first, so let us begin. I have things written down that we must discuss. You have told me some, but I need to know more about voices you heard, and a key?"

Jenna frowned. "Hmm! The voices? I began hearing voices in my head in hospital after my operation when I got my lockable diary!"

"Somehow, it was the key that started it all when I held it at first to unlock my diary, and the voice told me to find a key. Strangely, I knew it my mother's voice! I don't know why, but she seemed to be giving me instructions. I tried hard to see her, but no vision of her would form. It was freaking me out at first, and I thought I was going crazy, but for some unknown reason I didn't want my doctor or nurse to suspect anything unusual was happening to me because they were monitoring my memory. But why I hid that from them, I don't know! I just felt it should be kept as my secret."

"I never fully understood the voice or why I was hearing it until I returned home and experienced the attack on the steps and the jolt of my memory returning in an overload. Then I realized the reality of it was so simple. All the instructions I heard from the voice in my head was really of an actual conversation I had with my mother on the day she came home from hospital. Her injuries were extensive from the horse fall, but healing! So, you see. Subconsciously, I was witnessing a memory recall way back then, and didn't know it!"

"My goodness, that is amazing Jenna. I feel so proud that you could work it out. However, do you remember that conversation?"

"Word for word, Jack! It is in my mind as if it was yesterday!"

"Excellent! Will you recall it for me. I think it has vital clues!"

"My pleasure Jack, and you are correct. It does have vital clues. One being a key. I remember I must find a key in mother's room!"

"Oh! The key. It is of importance after all? So where is it?"

Jenna smiled. "You may want to hold that thought a while Jack, as we need to back-track a little. There is more you should know!"

"You see, it all started the morning of father's guests stop-over. I had problems that morning with Pablo at the stables arguing with mother on how she wanted her horse saddled. Pablo didn't seem to realize, and didn't want to know she was his boss, the person who paid him, not my father who had hired him. That puzzled me a lot!"

Jack frowned. "Just one minute Jenna if I may butt in. Was it only Pablo who treated your mother this way?" he asked.

"Well no. Mother constantly got into arguments with all the staff members! For some reason they didn't think they had to answer to her. All of them were rude to her, and treated her very badly. It got worse after the fire that left her disfigured, and with mood swings."

"I see! Interesting." he mused, thinking on that for a while. "But it was your father who hired the staff. So, he was their boss after all, is that it? I guess it seems a logical reason, it is his property also!"

"Jenna looked directly at Jack. "Well, not exactly Jack. Firstly, all staff were hired by my father but under authorization from mother. 'Oceanview,' as a whole estate, including land, house and contents, stables, stock, the outbuildings, belong solely to my mother, passed down from her parents. The estate has been in mother's family for many decades. Father signed a contract on their wedding day and an indemnity clause was added as usual, to relinquish all his rights to any ownership of 'Oceanview.' Be patient! I'll tell you the rest!"

Jack stared blankly at her. "Hmm, ok I will try! I do recall being told similar, by Constable Jenkins. Who would have thought? But, being the husband or next of kin he would be owner in the event of your mother's demise! This could alter things dramatically so, who knows what all the staff were informed of by your father when he hired them, or what promises he made to obtain their total loyalty!"

Jenna frowned. "Ah, not so! Patience Jack!" and screwed up her face. "But you have me there. That is something I would never have thought of. However, now you mention it, I can see where it could have had repercussions for my mother, causing trouble with staff."

"I'll try to be patient, sorry! But exactly Jenna, your mother was kept in the dark, who knows what else. Carry on the recollection!"

Vaguely Jenna tried to regain her thoughts? "Oh yes! Another thing was quite strange the morning of mother's horse accident!"

"You see. There was not only friction with Pablo that particular morning Jack because when mother and I left the stables we noticed Miranda Delvin going over there unattended. To us both, that was not acceptable, especially for a guest. Why go over there alone?"

"Hmm! Miranda Delvin did rub me the wrong way. I know her husband died in a somewhat untimely car crash, didn't he? I may need to look into that. Did she cause any trouble at Oceanview?"

"Most definitely Jack. You will see how, as I reveal it all to you."

"Now, we come to the day mother returned from hospital after her fall. I had left her room open to air out, and we were to meet on the deck for breakfast after I had checked on it with Paula the cook. When we sat to eat breakfast, mother was livid. She had just caught Miranda Delvin snooping around in her room, and ordered her to leave her property. She did not like, or trust Miranda Delvin at all!"

"You might be interested to know also, Jenna. When I drove out to visit your father to ask him for any information about your health or your whereabouts, he refused to help me, and sent me away, but that is when I overheard him and Miranda arguing. Miranda was cursing about keys not fitting, that she'd never find the will now!"

Jenna frowned. "Oh! How devious! I did tell you mother caught her red-handed. I bet she was searching for mother's will then!"

"You can bet on it, Jenna. So, obviously, it wasn't the only time Miranda tried to get in the room then."

"Oh, I think you may be correct! Now, you must know mother's thoughts on that day Jack! She was quite adamant, and swore to me her girth strap had been tampered with that morning. She insisted someone, either living, or working at 'Oceanview,' was trying hard to kill her! Two accidents seemed suspicious to her! This, prompted her to inform me that after breakfast, we must have an important discussion in her room! Yes, quite sinister, also it's the conversation you want me to recall and quite detailed. Be patient, and take notes.

Jack gaped at her. "Hmm! The plot thickens. I do need to hear of the conversation you had with your mother, and to explain why you were hearing her voice giving you directions. However, if it is detailed, we may leave it until after lunch, as I still have one more important question to ask you." *Then he was staring hard at her.*

"Jenna, this will be tough for you but it must be done I'm afraid!" and he pushed the small box towards her. "I promised you that this will be my last question for today, but a very important one I feel. I just need to know if you have ever seen the contents inside this box before? Please don't touch or pick up any of the contents inside they are vital information and possible clues to your mother's murder!"

Jenna stared at the box as if it was about to reveal a poisonous snake, and she shivered as Jack slowly opened the lid, then pushed the box closer towards her. Her scream was a heart-breaking thing to witness, her voice incoherent as if she had been bitten by a snake.

Her whole-body shook, and her hands trembled uncontrollably as the tears filled her eyes. She pushed hard against the table, then blindly knocked over the chair in her quest to escape. She stumbled, and screamed again as visions filled her head. So, sobbing her heart out, she groped a way through the doorway to flee from the deck.

Jack was up and after her in a flash. *He knew it was too much.*

He found her laying across the bed where she threw herself in exhaustion. She was till sobbing, so, he sat down beside her gently, and reached for a whisp of hair that covered her face, then tenderly kissed her cheek. A hand went to her temples where he massaged in hope to soothe her, and his other hand caressed her shoulder.

"Jenna!" he whispered into her ear. "I am so very sorry my love! Please forgive me?" he pleaded, as he gently rolled her on her back and showered kisses on her face until the sobbing ceased. His lips found hers and to his astonishment her response was with urgency.

Jenna's reactions became quite amorous as she returned his kiss.

Her fingers of one hand curled in his hair, the other trailed down his back, then around his waist where she un-zipped his trousers. But her mouth was seeking his with a wild abandonment he hadn't seen in her and with a fiery passion. He groaned as she took him in her hand, then his hands roamed her body, caressing her gently.

Their lovemaking was exhausting so, they lay entwined, neither able to move, but both relishing the feelings of love for one another.

It was Jenna who spoke softly first. "Oh, Jack! I love you so!"

"I love you too Jenna, more that you will ever know!" he replied.

"They are the shafts of green stones from my mother's favourite necklace Jack! A beautiful piece her mother gave her that matched her eyes. She wore it always except when she swam or bathed." she whispered. "Of that I am quite certain Jack!" then she sobbed again.

Jack pulled her closer to his chest, and covered her lips with his.

"Hush baby, I know! Thanks for being so brave, it's over now!" he said, as he looked into her eyes swimming with tears. "One more thing I need is a photo of that necklace if you have one, so I can be certain? Also, if your mother always wore it, then it would be safe to say she was wearing it when she was murdered! Is that correct?"

Jenna had no more words left. She simply nodded her head in agreement with him to acknowledge his question, then cried again.

"Good girl, thank you. We stop now as lunch will be here soon!"

As if on cue the doorbell rang, and Jack smiled. "Right, let's settle down and have a well-earnt rest Jenna." he said as he walked to the door, and opened it. Their lunch was on a trolly, so he thanked the steward and wheeled it in. "Shall we eat outside Jenna?" he asked.

Jenna lifted a lid and gasped. "Oh! That does look fabulous. Yes Jack, let us eat outside please, I do so love the view of the ocean out there. But I am not certain we should open the champagne yet as it might fuzz my memory. I do take it, you still want me to recall my conversation with mother, don't you?" she queried sadly.

"I do Jenna, but only if you can manage it. I don't want to cause you any more grief, you have been through too much. But not now! We rest now, and recover first, then we shall see how you feel later, but you made a good point about the Champagne. So, I'll just make us both a drink to have with our lunch for now, then much later, if we can get it all done, we will celebrate big time. Would you like to wheel the trolly outside? I shall bring everything else we need."

"Yes, I could do that." she replied softly.

He watched her take the trolley. She was trying to be brave, but her face was a ghostly mask. Her bottom lip trembled, and sadness gripped his heart for what he had put her through. He waited until she was seated outside then grabbed some things from the kitchen, and went to join her. He noticed the sun was still high in the sky, and its rays shone down on their seated area, and for the first time that day he noticed a hint of a smile on her lips as she relished the feeling of it on her face, and her sadness seemed to wilt a little.

"Ah! What a great spot in the sun Jenna. Pity we can't stay here forever, but let's enjoy it while we can." he said when he sat down. "Now, we have a great selection of seafood here. So, enjoy. Cheers!"

A strange look appeared on her face as he looked at her, holding up his glass. "No home!" she said weirdly. "I have just realized that we have no home, Jack!" her voice seemed to crack as she spoke.

Jack laughed. "No, but we'll get one as soon as this case is over!"

Jenna looked at him sadly. "Something so very important, but we haven't even taken the time to discuss it?" she questioned him.

Jack could tell by her face that this was very important to her, so, he chose his words carefully. "Well, no we haven't as yet Jenna, but we shall get to that discussion in due course! Just try to be content here for now, and we will work it all out. In case you have forgotten already, it has been pretty full-on since we united once again, and our discussions have been rather on another line of thinking, so first things first. However, with our whirlwind marriage, and guests to cater for, it has been a busy time. We need this place here so I can handle the workload involved in this case. I hope you understand that? I need your total support, but I want you to be happy too."

"That's just it, Jack. I do understand! But believe me when I say that I would be happy living anywhere with you. But really, I guess the time hasn't come for those discussions about a home as yet. It just hit me hard when I realized it. Do you know, we have wedding gifts unopened, because we haven't got a home to put them in!"

Jack chuckled. "Well, Jenna! That is one easy problem to solve. How about when we are done for the day, we sit down to open all our gifts. It will be a memorable time for us! Would you like that?"

Jenna's smile lit up her once sad face, and she gushed out a reply.

"My dearest Jack. Yes please, a great idea. You are so amazing!"

"I do try." he joked. "Now, let us eat wife, I am starving here!"

Jenna laughed for the first time that day. "In that case, I concede. Homicide Detective Jack Rickard!" and they both laughed.

Jack was pleased he could get Jenna back on track as they had a lot to accomplish before even thinking of house plans. *Who knows how long it will take to get a result on this case. It is a raging monster!* he thought. *However, I do like the way things are shaping up.*

Their lunch was incredible, their banter soothing. So, slowly Jack saw the lines of stress and fatigue slipping away from Jenna's face.

It was an incredible day, the warmth from the sun caressed them and the ocean tempted them. So, they even managed to fit in a swim before showering, and getting seated once more for their final talk.

"Well, this will be a breeze after what we have already covered Jenna. How is that memory of yours?" Jack queried.

Jenna didn't hesitate to reply, and to Jack that was a positive.

"I think I am good Jack, and yes this will be much easier."

He smiled at her to give her courage. "Good to hear! But firstly, I must commend you, Jenna. Your recollection has been excellent so far, I am so very proud of you. You do not realize how much you have helped me already. Slowly but surely, a plan is forming! Now! Let us get started so we can unwrap our presents." he chuckled.

Jenna smiled, and chuckled too, then she was serious. "Where to begin? Hmm! Best I tell you something else first! For it was the day after our conversation. My mother requested that I take her to the train station so she could catch a train into the city. She intended to hire a well-known solicitor there known for his discretion to create a new will, and to put all her affairs in order! She didn't trust a soul here, especially not my father after his infidelity she became aware of when he openly moved Miranda into 'Oceanview.' She wanted them both off her property, it is in her will! She planned on opening a post office box in my name that day. Which by chance Jack, is why it's vital I must find a key. It is a key to the post office box containing a copy of that will, the solicitor's name, and deeds for Oceanview!"

Jack was silent, trying to process it all. It was the part about the deeds which confused him. "Most of that is understandable I guess, under the circumstances, but why give the deeds to you Jenna?"

Jenna looked directly at him. Gone were the tears, just a look of determination instead spread on her face as she replied in earnest.

"Ah Jack! Mother was very devious. Now I understand why. So, I am as determined to see it through. I know of her plan for the new will. It would state one name only. 'Jenna Temple,' as sole owner of 'Oceanview' effective when I'm eighteen, and why I get the deeds!"

"My god! Now I realize what you were getting at, as you will be the sole owner of 'Oceanview,' and not your father. But you will be twenty soon! So, that solicitor hasn't acted! He hasn't done his job!"

Jenna laughed. "Well at least someone hasn't forgotten it is my birthday soon! Thank you for that Jack. How time has got away!"

"It certainly has Jenna, but your birthday, I would never forget!"

Jenna pondered on their conversation a while, then added. "On the contrary Jack, you will be pleased to know this solicitor is doing exactly what mother requested of him. We went over it together, and that was her plan in case I couldn't take over at eighteen. Once again, she was correct! But I think you will find that her assets, and all monies would be frozen at any time something happened to her. Her bank was to get a letter from this city solicitor's firm to put that plan into action. I haven't been here so, I am not sure of that, but someone is paying the bills for 'Oceanview' for it still to operate!"

"You are correct Jenna. I remember Constable Jenkins bringing that up. That is why he changed the locks on the two rooms as your father had taken control, and was obviously paying the bills to keep all the staff on. But the particular time I mentioned that I overheard Miranda arguing with your father about the keys not fitting, and the will! I think it would have been when your mother's assets were frozen! Wow! Your father is going to be absolutely ropeable when he finds out you are the sole owner, and they have to vacate!"

"Hmm!" Jenna pondered. "That is going to be unpleasant, and difficult if I know my father. He'll fight me every inch of the way!"

Jack looked squarely at her. "Not so Jenna. If my guess is correct, this solicitor of your mother's will dictate the turn of events!"

"Do you think so Jack? I couldn't stand trouble, or a court case."

"Most definitely, Jenna, you will see! However, I can't guarantee there will be no court case. What say we leave it up to your mother's solicitor when we find this key. Now to the final piece of the puzzle! Please, let it be now Jenna. This all-important conversation!"

Jenna smiled. "I trust your judgement, Jack. Plus, as it turns out. It is an all-important conversation Jack, though a little strange!"

Jack stared hard at her. Then a curious look graced his face when he questioned her. "How so, Jenna? Why would it be strange?"

Jenna laughed. "I hope you see the funny side Jack through the absurdity of it. You see, Jack. Mother was quite paranoid when we entered her room for this discussion. She was totally convinced someone was trying to kill her, and hell-bent on getting her affairs in order, but so meticulous in her protection of me. The secrecy that I had to abide by so she could give me vital details, was to the point of ridiculous. She said not to confide in you, just to keep it secret!"

Jack frowned. "I see, but to the point of ridiculous? How so?"

"Well Jack, Mother said she would create a treasure hunt, a quest to obtain the all-important details I would need in finding the key!"

Jack laughed. "Are you serious, Jenna?"

"Deadly!" she replied, and he knew that look on her face.

"Ok then. Do we have any clues? Can you remember that?"

"Clues? Hmm! I think I can recall them. If not, we are in trouble!"

Jack was starting to get frustrated. "Ok Jenna. Let us start at the beginning with the voices. What were your mother's instructions?"

Jenna smiled. She knew now how clever he had become. "Hmm! A good idea Jack. Better get your notebook, and pen ready. My first experience involving my mother was soon after my operation when I bought a lockable diary, and I had questions for my father about people and places so I could recall them from the diary. I asked my father for my mother's full name, and when he told me I felt like I had been punched in the chest. I knew that name Jack! I jumped in fright the first time I heard her voice in my head saying." *Remember, you must find a key Jenna!* "Another time she whispered." *Right here is my favourite place in the whole world Jenna!* "Then, once again." *This is the oldest book I own, but one you must remember, Jenna.*"

" Lastly. *You will know when you turn eighteen the time is right!*"

Jack was writing as quick as he could. Jenna was on a roll and he didn't want to miss anything. When he finally caught up, he looked up to say. "Very scary for you Jenna! However, did you cope?"

Jenna's smile was awkward. "At the time, Jack. I thought I was losing my mind, but somehow from deep inside I sensed it was my mother's voice so, after a while I became used to it. Though, what a relief to finally realize it was an actual conversation I was recalling."

"Yep, it is strange how the mind works. Right, let us move on to when you went to your mother's room. What did she say, or do?"

"Well, the first thing I recall is commenting on her orchids, and the view from her window seat. That is when she spoke. *Right here is my favourite place in the whole world Jenna,* remember that!"

"We covered many topics regarding her will, and her plans to go to the city. The necessity to hire a meticulous lawyer there, and that she wanted secrecy so things would go smoothly for me to take over the property. She was quite meticulous and adamant of that!"

"Then she was explaining her plan and the secrecy needed. That it must be done her way to protect me, and I knew the conversation was becoming serious. *You will know when you turn eighteen the time is right!* she spoke. Then ambled down to the bookshelf where she plucked a book from its home to hold it up. *This is the oldest book I own, but one you must remember, Jenna! Two things are vital to recall, this book, and my favourite one!* This is your quest to search for what I leave you!" *Remember you must find a key, Jenna.*

"So many words. Are they all clues Jenna?" questioned Jack.

"I am not sure Jack, but I guess we will find out just how difficult mother's quest is when we proceed to search for the key. However, she did go to great lengths to conceal everything, and to keep it all a secret, even her trip to the city. So, keep in mind that she wouldn't want anyone else to unravel her clues, so I am guessing it would be about topics that only I personally would know more about!"

"Hmm! Hopefully Jenna, otherwise we may be chasing our tail. Is there anything else of importance that you can think of Jenna? Anything at all that may be helpful to me!"

Jenna racked her brain before answering. "Not that I can think of right now Jack. I believe we have covered it all, but I will think on it some more just in case. It is just a matter of sifting through for clues, then living with myself for my stupidity!"

"Whatever do you mean by that, Jenna?" frowning as he asked.

"Only one thing still hounds me, and I can't stop thinking about it, as the fact of the matter is this. My mother knew she was a target for murder, and I didn't take her seriously!" she said regretfully.

Jack folded his arms around her as she cried. "Jenna! You can't take the blame! Don't be so hard on yourself, you weren't to know!"

Then he smiled at her, and attempted to cheer her up. "Think on the good things you have achieved Jenna, and be more positive, as no-one could have foretold your mother's fate. However! Good god Jenna, your memory is so precise now! I really think you are cured my love, and that is worth a huge cheer. Do you realize it is because of you and your recollection, that I now sense a new plan of attack forming in my mind, one that will stand them all on their toes!"

Jenna smiled fondly at him. "Oh, my goodness! Really Jack? That all does sound quite ominous. I can't wait to find out. But yes, you may be right about my memory, as I feel in total control now, and I have surprised myself. So, I guess some celebrations are in order!"

"Ah! Good to hear. Let's open that bottle of champagne, and unwrap our presents. We have had a big day, and thank you Jenna!"

"You are welcome, Jack. To be honest, I am pleased it is over!"

He grimaced. "Ah! Not quite, Jenna. It is just beginning. I hope you are up to it, but now it is imperative you must find this key to the post office box in the city. So, getting you out to your mother's rooms seems first priority on my list so you can begin the search for it to obtain the solicitor's name, and his details to contact him. I am finding each time we talk my plans are changing but for the better."

"Well, I guess tomorrow is another day, but an important one!"

"Exactly Jenna. That's the spirit. Come tomorrow morning I will be going very early to the station to talk over things with Constable Jenkins, and to look over some slides he has for me. However, I will be telling him how I plan to handle this case now. As initially, I was going to tell the officers to handle the interviews and questions, but now I have much more pressing duties for them to do tomorrow, and besides I prefer to hold private interviews with them all in their homes, maybe later in the day. I think that will shake them, as they won't be expecting that. I must keep them all guessing Jenna! So, if everything goes to plan with Constable Jenkins then he will make certain that the house, and estate is vacant for us to go out to. Then I will be coming back here for you so I can take you to your mother's room to search for the key. Do you think you are up to that Jenna?"

Jenna smiled. She was just beginning to realize how professional Jack was going to be with this case. "Yes, Detective Rickard! I will feel more comfortable if no people are there so, I will be ready!"

"Good girl Jenna, just be positive. We will just take one day at a time! But keep in mind that I will be with you all of the time, and I promise not to leave you alone at any time. However, if we find this all-important key tomorrow, then that will be a huge bonus. If not, then we will go back the next day, and the next, until we find it. Are you happy with that?" he queried.

"Yes Jack, I do know you will be by my side, but I don't want to keep you from your investigation just to baby-sit me!"

"Don't you worry about that, Jenna, that won't happen. Once I have seen the slides at the police station, and briefed the officers, Constable Jenkins, myself and the men will leave for 'Oceanview.' I'm bound to have more questions for the Constable on the beach, and I need to see for myself certain things before I can give my men final instructions. So, rest assured, Jenna. I will have searched the crime scene before I come to collect you. My job will be done!"

"From that point on, it will be up to the officers that Constable Jenkins have at my disposal to do what I ask of them!"

Jenna gaped. "Hmm! It does pay to be a Homicide Detective!"

Jack chuckled. "Well! I suppose it does have some advantages. I don't have to do the hard yakka, my officers will do that. However, my plans must be spot-on, if I am going to give them a direction of where we are heading with both cases, and what outcome I would expect to get. They will be carrying out a lot of searching for clues, and I have to create a picture for them, and prompts of what we are looking for, so they have a goal to work towards. I have given a lot of thought to both these cases and agonized with ideas endlessly!"

Jenna stared at him, and for the first time she could see tiny lines etched in his brow and realized the stress he was under so, she said.

"Oh Jack! You must forgive me for worrying you over petty things. Now I have only this minute realized, the weight you must have on your shoulders with such an important task ahead of you!"

He smiled at her tenderly. "Do not think for one moment lady, that your time with me is petty! To be frank with you, I must admit that it is due to my talks with you which have turned the wheels in motion in my head. I do think I have an excellent plan of attack for both these cases. So, Jenna! I must compliment you my love for your strength, and grit. As you have given me so much more information than it would have taken me weeks to accumulate. So please, I will hear no more of the negative talk from you Missus Jack Rickard!"

Jenna laughed. "Well, only if you say so sir!" she replied, as she pulled him close to her, and his lips found hers. Their kiss was long, and so tender, and Jenna was gasping when she pushed him away.

"I guess you could say that it is not so bad at all to be scolded."

"Cheeky girl!" said Jack as he smiled. But Jenna became serious as she stared into his eyes. "I am so very proud of you, Jack Rickard! So proud you made Homicide Detective. I hope you realize that!"

Chapter Thirteen

It was a perfect day, and Jack felt a spring in his step as he crossed the carpark to the entrance of The Police Station. He had mixed feelings but the positives were leaping out at him so, he was hoping some of his hunches would be right, or it was back to square one.

He strolled down to the board room first because that was where Constable Jenkins said to meet him and sure enough as Jack walked through the open doors, he was there setting up the equipment.

"Morning Constable!" Jack said. "Thanks so much for coming in so early. How is it coming along with the set up?"

Constable Jenkins looked up, and smiled. "Just about have it all done for you Jack. Maybe ten minutes more, then I'm ready to roll!"

"Excellent, thank you. I will go down to the kitchen and get us some coffee. This may take a while, as I only want to do this once!"

"Yep! Good idea. I'll have it all sorted and listed by the time you get back, and then we will start. How did your talk go with Jenna?"

"Better than I expected Constable. She has given me a new line of thinking. As a matter of fact, I will need you to set up a new file!"

Constable Jenkins eyed him, then he grinned. "Ah! I thought you may say that so I have taken the liberty of creating a new file on paper, and on the computer. You only have to ok it, and it is ready to go! I knew exactly what to call it seeing it was the birth of your first solo murder case here at home! It is the first of its kind here in Blue Bay Police Station, and everyone is chuffed about that. Can't say how proud we are of you Jack! We all hope we get the privilege of working with you again someday!" he said instantly and opened a drawer to pull out a red file, and slid it across the table.

This was no ordinary file Jack noticed as he looked at the leather-bound red file with embossed gold letters on the front reading.

Homicide Detective Jack Rickard…Resident Detective/Blue Bay
'THE RICKARD FILES'

"My god, you don't do anything in halves Constable!"

"I simply love it, and can't wait to use those pages. A big thank you, and to the guys so much for this gesture! I will thank the boys personally." then he laughed. "What if I didn't like it, Constable? It is printed in gold. Don't you think that is a little presumptuous?"

Constable Jenkins laughed too, and replied. "Not at all Jack! It's called, I think… *Being switched on to your partner's likes and dislikes.*

"Think about it Jack. In many years to come you will be a legend. Every-one will remember Homicide Detective Jack Rickard! As that file will live on after you. We are creating history today!" he joked.

"Well! Let's create a good one, starting with this!" he said, as he placed the small box down on the table. "I know of one important entry my file will have! I obtained from Jenna positive ID on shafts of green stone from Julia's necklace. So, one strike in our favour!"

Constable Jenkin's eyebrows shot up in surprise. "Oh boy, that is great news, and a huge bonus to this case Jack. Well, done!"

"Sure is. So, we'd better make the outcome of this case a winner! Now, I'm off to get the coffee, be ready to start when I get back!"

Constable Jenkins saluted him, and a wide grin spread across his face as he replied. "Right, you are then Detective Rickard!"

Jack's chuckle as he left the room made Constable Jenkins smile.

They don't come any better than that boy. I am so proud to have had a hand in his success. *I only hope he can succeed in getting a positive result in this case,* where others before him have failed.

Jack returned to the semi-darkness of the room, and he set the tray down on the table, and poured their coffee. "Looks like you are ready to roll Constable. But it's almost like movie night in here!" he exclaimed, as he set their coffees down on the desk.

"Yep, the darkness will give you a better viewing, it is all good to go Jack, so let us begin." he paused a minute as he looked up at Jack's face to add. "Please keep in mind Jack, that these slides were taken as soon as I visited the crime scene. So, that is before I got the officers down to the beach. However, I must say that I found these findings insignificant to the investigation because all the tracks in the sand seemed to be masked as if all the shoes had been covered, and there were no prints of any shoes to be seen. So unfortunately, I don't hold much confidence in what I have to show you Jack, I'm sorry. These slides are the only evidence of any footprints down there to date because all this evidence was lost when the team came down and practically dug up the whole beach."

"That is alright Constable, I understand, but we will sort it. Just so we don't waste time I will inform you where I want you to look for footprints if you have them. This is important! If you can isolate these prints so we can enlarge them, I want to look at prints going from the body to the steps, and under the steps. Any prints around the body, also leaving the body, and I need to know which direction they went! That is very important. If you took slides of prints going up the hill to the carpark, include them. Is that possible Constable?"

"Yes, it is possible as I have them all listed, and notes included."

"Good man." replied Jack. "About how long do you need?"

"Oh, not long. Now you have given me specific areas it makes it easier. Give me fifteen minutes, and I should have it all in order."

"Ok, good. How many men did you organize for me today?"

"I have informed ten officers to wait in my room for you Jack."

"Thank you, Constable! Ten, is a good number for what I need. I will just duck down to inform them of today's proceedings just to save us time, then they can prepare to get ready for when we are done here. Did you get the search warrants for me?" Jack asked.

"Yes, Jack, all done. We have search warrants for the 'Oceanview Homestead,' the stables, and the residence cabin on the grounds for Paula and Ted Hastings where they reside, and also for the home residence of Melita and Pablo Sanchez. Is that all you wanted?"

"For now, Constable. Thank you so much, we are a good team!"

Constable Jenkins laughed. "We are indeed Detective Rickard!"

Jack smiled, then left to go down to address his men. Today was a big day, he had so much for them to do. He hoped it went well as the trail he was about to follow was as cold as the dead body laying somewhere yet to be discovered.

True to his word, the Constable had actual pictures on the screen when Jack returned. "Ah! At last. Which scene am I looking at sir?" he asked, as he sat down. Can we zoom in if we need to?"

"These are of footprints around, and from the site of the murder scene we feel, as it was where the majority of blood was found, and affirmative! If you want to zoom in I can, as I now have that feature on this projector. However, Jack! Keep in mind that you will only see indentations in the sand, no actual footprints to speak of really!"

"Oh! But they are actual footprints, Constable! If you concentrate you can see clearly their shape, and the size of the footprint! Zoom in on the murder scene first for me please, and scroll slowly!"

Constable Jenkins looked up from his projector to stare at Jack.

He had a puzzled look on his face when he spoke. "Yes of course!" he muttered absently then set the dial on the projector to enlarge.

"Do tell? Why are we looking for shapes, and sizes, Jack. How will that help if we don't have a print from shoes to identify them?"

"Ah! That's the tricky part sir. But all is not lost, we still have the outline of the print so we can determine the shape of it, and if there are any irregularities in the tread, and the size is most important to determine what size shoe or boot we are looking for!" Jack replied.

Constable Jenkins shook his head. *Why didn't I think of that?* he wondered, then looked at the concentration on Jack's face in awe.

"Yes, of course Jack!" he said, and moved the slide across slowly.

"Hmm! Just pause now! Do you see that sir? Two distinct prints close to the murder scene. One made from a very large boot I would say, it is embedded deeper into the sand than the smaller print."

"I am so sorry, Jack, but you have lost me. I see nothing! Are you certain that is what you are seeing?"

"Most definitely sir. I have learnt to read these types of prints on slides before. Now, if you would carry on with the rest, please." he said, and reached in his pocket for his notebook, and made an entry.

"Yes, quite amazing Jack if I may say so!" stated the Constable.

"All in my training sir. I was trained by the best!" replied Jack.

"I can tell! Now we leave the scene heading towards the steps!"

"Stop!" called Jack. "Go back to the last one at the murder scene, and enlarge it more!" and Constable Jenkins did as he was asked.

"Hmm!" said Jack. "That is interesting. I can make out toe prints embedded in the sand. Do you see that, Constable. It is a bare footprint. Do you have another slide of that so I can look further?"

"I don't see it at all Jack, but the other prints that go back, head up the hill or towards the dunes. I can show you them, if you like?"

"Dunes, what dunes?" queried Jack.

"Oh, some parts at the base of the cliff were called the dunes."

"Hmm! I see. Ok! Try that please, Constable."

On the first slide Jack called a halt. "Stop! There it is Constable!"

"A full foot-print, only now the emphasis is on the heel, as if the person is going backwards. That is so strange. Next slide please?"

"Ah! Stop there. I see the bare foot-print clearly. However, why is the smaller shoe-print further back? Next slide please? Ah! Ah! We have both prints now, but the larger boot print is so very close to the bare-foot print. "OMG! I think I know what that is Constable!

Constable Jenkins looked up in surprise. "Really, Jack. What?"

"Jenna told me of a shadow that blocked out the moonlight. We are looking at the boot-print of Jenna's shadow sir. I am certain of it! Also, I will bet my career on it that the person with the large boot-print is Jenna's attacker, the person who attempted to murder her, and could possibly be the murderer of Julia Temple!"

"Oh, my god Jack. This is a huge finding."

"Yes, it is sir! We must press on. So, more slides going to the rock wall please! Can you remind me to check out those dunes today?"

"Yep! Sure will. Now there are several more slides, but only one could possibly be a shoe-print heading towards the wall or dunes."

Jack looked carefully at the slides as the Constable slowly moved them across. Hmm, only the smaller shoe-print. Ok, what next, sir?"

"Back to the prints heading to the steps, and under the step."

"Ok! Roll it." said Jack. "Stop! I recognize that print. I know for sure it is the same larger boot-print we just saw at the murder scene. Note how the left foot rolls a little to the inside with a step. More!"

"Oh! Now I have two prints going towards the steps. Where did it come from? It is the other print almost out of the screen, which is different to the other two. See that? It is another print. Enlarge it!"

"I will try, but I don't see it." said the Constable in frustration.

"This shoe is not covered sir. It is a flat soled shoe with no tread or heel! Which means I see three people at the crime scene sir!"

Her Mind SCREAMS MURDER

Jack looked up quickly, a concerned expression on his face. "Are you sure the shots were taken before anything was disturbed?"

"Of that, I can be certain, Jack. I specifically took them myself."

"Ok, thank you sir, a relief. It is most important to my findings." and he jotted something in his notebook. "Ok, continue on!"

"Right, this is more of just under the steps, Jack."

"Hmm! The same two prints. Remind me when we go out there to have a good look at the fifth step, Constable! Jenna told me it was the fifth step that she fell through to the rocks below. I will need to examine it thoroughly, especially look at the bolts, so bring tools!"

"I will Jack." replied Constable Jenkins who was already lost.

"Now, are there any shots of them coming back the same way?"

Constable Jenkins moved a dial. "Well, yes! But only one print."

"Show me?" asked Jack. "Where did the other print go, go back!"

"Stop, sir! See just at the edge of the screen the other print goes towards the beach. Ah! The boot print too. Why is that I wonder?"

"Well! If that was me trying to replace that huge step, Jack. Then I think I would need some help!" the Constable offered.

Jack stared at the Constable. "What do you mean, sir?"

"Well! Just an idea, I mean. Those steps are wide and awkward. I'd need some help to get it up top and to hold it as I put bolts in!"

Jack laughed. "You old dog, but you are a legend, sir. Of course! That is why the prints headed for the beach, just to access the steps to go up and secure the step. Can't thank you enough Constable!"

Constable Jenkins laughed too. "Just pleased I could assist in this small way Detective Rickard!" and they both laughed.

Jack was smiling, but still making notes in his book, then he said.

"We are getting there, Constable! We only need to view slides of footprints leaving the murder scene, heading towards the exit up the hill. I know there may be other prints involved, it's the only exit. However, we know what prints to look for now, don't we sir?"

Constable Jenkins looked straight at Jack, and laughed. "Only if you say so Detective Rickard! But please, don't rely on me!"

Jack chuckled. "You have proved to be rather a worthy partner, Constable. So, I shall include you in any discussions in future!"

"I can only try my best, Jack. Now here are your last lot of slides. A lot of traffic going that way. So, do you see the prints you want?"

Just scroll slowly sir, and I'll keep looking. Yep, stop there! I see the larger boot-print and the smaller one behind it but not the other footprint of the flat soled shoe with no heel, or a tread, and no bare-foot prints either. But I am almost positive the bare-foot prints are Jenna's, as she left her bed to go outside to the deck that morning. I will ask her about that later. Ok! Just to be quite sure, show me the rest, then scroll through them all one more time. But we must move fast now. I have to give the men their orders, tell them to make their lunches, today is going to be a long one! Then we go to 'Oceanview,' and onto the beach where I can check out a few things before we go inside. It is imperative that I do that before the days, proceedings!"

"Ok, Jack. I'll be as quick as I can. Focus now, and I will scroll."

Jack stared at the screen until the last slide was shown. "Yep, all good sir, we can quit now. I have got more than I really expected. So, I'll meet you down in your office when you're done?" he asked.

"We have a good two hours to search the beach, plenty of time!"

Constable Jenkins looked up. "Yep! We got through that rather well actually. All is going to plan, and I will be right behind you."

Jack walked into the Constable's office, and was in the process of greeting his men when Constable Jenkins entered. "Good, we are all here now, so, I can be very specific about the strict orders I want followed meticulously. It is a very important day for us all. We now have evidence of murder to re-open the case of Julia Temple, and reasons to investigate an attempted murder on Jenna Temple!" The interest from the officers intensified as he began to outlay his plan.

As he faced all the diligent listeners Jack new then he had a good team. "Right guys. This is your schedule, and all-important tasks today, searches and interviews. Just remember, when we go inside for this meeting they will be expecting interviews so, no-one can leave the premises until we have told them what is happening! We will all go into the house together, so you must wait in the carpark for a short while as Constable Jenkins and myself have a couple of pressing things to check out on the beach first, but we we'll return. I must point out something specific so, take notes please! I cannot stress this enough and the importance of it. *Just be very thorough with your searches today, but only search for the items I asked you to look for!"*

"Keep your phones handy as I have sent photos to you of the necklace, we are looking for so you can all identify it. If you find anything that is relevant, take photos, wear gloves and bag it as evidence! Just one more thing of importance! I will require four officers to search the Homestead at 'Oceanview' but not the two rooms upstairs of Jenna, and her mother, Julia Temple. They are both the rooms at each end of the top balcony, and they are both locked. I will need two officers allocated to search the cabin on the premises where Paula the cook, and husband Ted Hastings reside."

"Another two officers for the stables so, take Pablo Sanchez over there as he runs the stables, but don't let him take anything when he leaves to join the two officers escorting him and Melita Sanchez to their home residence! Also, at the close of the meeting, make sure you stay with the workers whose premises you are allocated to search. They will all be informed to vacate their homes prior to the searches. So, nothing must be taken from the premises only phones, wallets or bags, and they can return back home at 5.00 pm, to wait on my attendance for interviews. So, while you're waiting for us, work out teams who is going to search where? Do a time schedule for me for interviews to advise them! I'll be in Julia Temple's room!"

Jack looked around the room and concentrated on the faces of his men. They were quiet, but looked as if they had taken his orders on board seriously, and they looked a likely lot.

"Any questions team?"

"No sir!" they all said in unison.

"Great, then let's get this show on the road. Good luck to you all. I think we are going to need it to crack this case. Ready Constable?"

"Yes Detective, I'll just get some tools!" answered the Constable. "I will ride with you today, Jack, and Jack!" he added, as he moved closer to face him. "Best of luck Homicide Detective Jack Rickard! Three cheers for the Detective, men, and good luck to all of you!"

The room was filled with cheers, and Jack felt quite humbled as he replied. "Thank you, guys, but let's hold the cheers until we win this thing, we have a long way to go!" Then he moved to shake each officer's hand, also to Constable Jenkins. "Thank you, sir." he said.

All was quiet at 'Oceanview' as they all stepped out of the police cars in the car-park. "This is it team, we should be about half hour at least I think, but you have your instructions so, wait here for us!"

"Yes Detective!" came the replies.

Jack, and Constable Jenkins wasted no more time, and quickly grabbed their gear and when they reached the well-worn path, they started the descent down the hill towards the beach.

"Shall we check out the steps first Jack?" the Constable asked.

"Yes please, sir. Let's get that out of the way." replied Jack.

As they walked along the beach, they finally reached the rocky area. Jack took notice of the high-tide marks amongst the rocks just under the steps. "There are so many rocks down here. I can't believe Jenna survived the fall. She was one lucky girl, that's for sure!"

"You might be mindful of that when you see where the fifth step is, Jack!" chuckled the Constable, as he forged a way up the incline to access under the steps, then pointed up to the fifth step.

Jack held a hand up to shelter his eyes from the sun, and looked up. "Hells bells! Are you sure that is the fifth step Constable?"

"It sure is Jack, but you can check it out when we get up there!"

"I don't mean to be skeptical sir, but I will have to just to satisfy my curiosity, as that step is way too high up. How would anyone replace that big step from down here? Even if you stood on top of the rocks, you wouldn't reach it." he sat on a rock deep in thought. *A ladder?* he questioned himself, but ruled that thought out when he imagined all the things required to take up the hill to the carpark.

Constable Jenkins muttered. "As I said before Detective Rickard, I think help would be needed for that task… his voice trailed off as he stared at Jack's face, so deep in concentration.

"Hmm!" Jack mumbled. "Something just doesn't add up! If that didn't keep nagging at me, then I could almost picture it, Constable, but which-ever way you look at it, I think you may be correct. What we have is two sets of shoe-prints leaving here to access the steps that lead up to the Homestead. Looking at it from down here, this has to be a massive effort to replace that big step. It looks very wide, and would have to be quite heavy, especially if it was taken up the steps. I think it would take one with lots of strength, or stamina, or more likely two of them or another way? What is your opinion sir?"

"Same as yours I think, except there is no other way! It was either done under the steps by way of pulleys, but that would be more to carry, or it was taken up top. What is it that is nagging at you, Jack?"

Jack looked at him as his concern seemed to etch lines in his face.

"Just the simple fact is this. If this job is so strenuous, then why isn't the other person helping? Why stay here at the murder scene?"

Constable Jenkins looked surprised. "Strange you should think of that. Are you sure there was a third shoe-print, Jack?" he asked.

"Most definitely sir of that I'm quite sure though now something Jenna said comes to mind. What say we go up and have a look, sir?"

"Sure, let's go. Fill me in on that later when we do our thinking!"

As they walked up the steps Jack remembered almost jumping to reach the next step some years ago, and now it seemed more of an effort, but finally they reached the top and he looked back down.

"Interesting prospect, Constable. Let's look at that fifth step."

He looked closely at the big bolts on the steps as he descended, but when he looked at the fifth step, something seemed different.

"Take a closer look at those bolts Constable. What do you see?"

"Well, the bolts are rusty on most and well screwed in, but the fifth step? Hmm! I don't see rust around the outside of any bolt."

"Exactly sir! Get those tools out, I want to try something!" and he leaned over the side to look underneath. "Excellent, the bolts are only screwed in from the top as the base is a solid metal plate. Well, I'll be sir. You are not going to believe this!" he said excitedly.

"What is it Detective?"

"Those huge wide steps have a hollow in the middle section!"

Constable Jenkins raised an eyebrow as he said. "Are you sure?"

"Yes, I do think so, but when I unscrew these bolts, I'll dismantle the step and check it out. If that is so? You know what that means?"

"Well! My guess is the step would be much lighter, easier to lift."

"Exactly sir. Quite ingenious really. So, to carry one from down on the beach up to here is very strenuous, but not so for two. Hand me a solid screw-driver, we will try to un-screw another step first."

Jack kneeled to the task at the first step, then Constable Jenkins handed him the screw-driver. He tried to un-screw the first bolt but it wouldn't budge, so he put all his strength from his shoulders into the next effort. "God damn, but these bolts are so rusted, they won't move. It would take an electric drill to remove them as they haven't been moved for many, many, years. Let's try the fifth step." At the fifth step, Jack checked it. "Looks like the steps sit in a timber ledge, clever!" When he attempted to unscrew the bolts, they came free.

Jack laughed as he stood to stretch. "Guess it's safe to say that the bolts in the fifth step have been removed in recent years, but just think on this Constable. For them to be removed, then it would take the use of an electric tool, maybe re-chargeable, but still. Who-ever removed them must have known these steps well, and that the bolts were too rusted to remove by hand. So, this leads me to believe that someone living here loosened the bolts previous to the murder!"

Constable Jenkins shook his head, as he said. "I think you are on the button there, Jack. Great thinking my boy, great thinking!"

"Thank you, sir. Finally, I feel confident in what we have to do. Let's check out this step just to make sure. He lifted his end of the step up, and grinned. "Ah! It's heavy, but not too heavy, but from down there too heavy for one, even with the inside hollowed out!"

They both stood and chuckled as Constable Jenkins slapped Jack on the back. "Good work, Jack. Who would have thought of that?"

"I guess it makes sense really, seeing the steps are so high, they would need access to them for repairs, but all credit to the builders of 'The Homestead,' don't you think, Constable?"

"Yes! Think you are right Jack. I also think Jenna was right in the telling of her story. It was definitely the fifth step she fell through!"

Jack stared at The Constable. "Yes, sir! It is good to get that conformation, but Jenna was also correct in saying her mother's body was mutilated, and decapitated because I realize now why the third person stayed at the murder scene with the body. It was to chop her up, and bag her. So, rather than a body, we are searching for body-bags! Let's replace the step and we'll check out the wall and dunes!"

"Yes, we must! My goodness that is so gruesome, and incredible of you to work it out Jack. I must say our research has borne fruit."

"Most definitely, but we'll see! Quick now, down to the beach!"

Constable Jenkins led the way up past the dangerous rocks, and the high-water line. "This is the base of the huge cliff-face here!"

He pointed further down. "The dunes used to start down that way though, if I can recall!" he paused abruptly to look back at Jack. "Though, I am fairly certain it was somewhere around here where we found the last shoe-print, and I took the shot, Jack" he said.

Jack moved closer to the rock wall, then with his hand he felt the rough surface as he walked along. "Covered in moss! Why would shoe-prints head this way? To what purpose? Where did they go?"

Constable Jenkins looked a little abashed as he spoke. "So sorry Jack, but I don't know that. They are all the photo's I took. Because, when the shoe-prints had no tread on them to identify, I am afraid we lost interest in them as there was other pressing things to do."

"So, the dunes weren't searched at all, Constable?" he asked.

"Well, no, I'm afraid not! There was nothing to see anyway."

"Why are they called the dunes then? It just looks like a wall."

"I believe local people say there were caverns or passage-ways beneath the masses of sandstone, but as I said, there was no way to check that as there seemed no access from here. It seemed pointless to waste time. Sorry, we weren't interested in the cliffs anyway!"

Jack kept walking along the rock face. "Caverns, passage-ways or hollows, but where?" he muttered "The locals would be correct, don't you think Constable, if they say there were caverns here?"

"I am not so sure Jack as we couldn't see any evidence of that."

"Right, you are sir. Then let's save some time as you head down that way, and I'll search up this way. Look for anything that may have lodged in the rock-face to block a gap or entrance!" said Jack.

Constable Jenkins shook his head. *Does he never stop thinking?* he questioned himself as he bent to the task of rapping the rock wall and kicking pieces of sandstone in frustration. Then suddenly his fist seemed to disappear into the wall, and he jumped in fright.

His face paled as he scraped away more sandstone, also pebbles and debris, as it fell from the hole! Then a big gap could be seen.

"Jack! Hey, Jack!" he called out. "You had better come and look at this here! I think I have found something. Well, a hole at least!"

Jack's head flew up with excitement, then he jogged through the sand to reach the Constable. "Oh, good work sir. Get the tools out!"

Soon there was sandstone flying all around them as they both attacked the rock-face with hammer and chisel, and huge pieces of sand- stone fell out to make a wider opening. Jack called a halt, and stood back to grin at the Constable, then he spoke.

"Well, I'll be! That gap is large enough to squeeze through now, and seems to open out behind it. I wonder if it's one of the so-called caverns the locals spoke of, or just a cave-in of the actual sandstone? How long has it been hidden? I guess in your search here years ago it would have seemed a natural gap, maybe even filled with debris so it didn't look like an access so, you ignored it! Over time in wind and rain it's been concealed by debris and sandstone pebbles."

"It could well be, Jack. Thinking back on it, I do recall the actual cliff-face had wide gaps in the sandstone. We ignored it as it looked like part of the wall. As I said, we weren't interested in the cliffs."

"Hmm! You do realize that this alters things dramatically today, sir. I must leave nothing to chance, and no stone unturned here!"

"What are you saying, Jack? What do you plan on doing?"

Jack looked hard at the Constable, then spoke. "I won't rest until we investigate this gap in the cliff-face further, sir! I think it is just as important as the search of the resident's premises we planned on today. Just think on this a while Constable? Light would have been fading fast as according to the boy who found Jenna, it was close to daybreak so, whoever was here would be afraid of being seen! Time would've been an issue for the murderer. A body to dispose of, or body-bags to bury, and a hill too steep to climb. No sir, I am certain Julia Temple's remains are somewhere down here!" stated Jack.

"Hmm! I do get your point, Jack. I feel a little foolish now!"

Jack looked at the constable sternly. "Don't feel that way at all sir, things have a way of changing to alter the scene of a crime. Only now I need your assurance on how I plan to proceed today. It's vital to search the premises today, and the beach, and do the interviews."

"Maybe I could search only the premises of all the workers today who reside either at 'Oceanview,' or their homes. Then resume our search the following day of the remaining rooms, the kitchen, and other areas inside the 'Homestead', also the stables and yards. Your thoughts on that, sir? Any further suggestions to add?"

Constable Jenkins shook his head, and smiled. "Not at all, Jack! As a matter-of-fact, I think you have a great plan, all down pat!"

Jack smiled. "Excellent, then let's get moving sir!" he replied. "We have time to inform the men of the changes, and still make the appointment time at The Homestead. Thank you so much for your input, sir. We have achieved so much, and sometimes it's good to have a second opinion, and have someone as a sounding board!"

Constable Jenkins chuckled. "If you say so, Jack. Though, now I think on it, you changed tack on all my ideas anyway!"

Jack laughed. "Well, at least I had your opinions to work off, sir!"

They both laughed together as they reached the path, then they climbed the incline to the carpark, and Jack turned to the Constable and added, as a grin spread his mouth wide. "One other thing sir. Would you baby-sit this lot for me while I work with Jenna today?"

Constable Jenkins grinned back, but answered seriously. "It will be my pleasure Jack, so consider it done!"

"Thank you for that sir." he stated, then addressed his officers. "Well team, Constable Jenkins and I, had a very fruitful visit to the beach. So much so, I have decided to alter our plans a little as far as our searches go today. We still search the cabin on the premises at 'Oceanview,' where Paula, and Ted Hastings reside. So, I need two men there, and the residence of Melita and Pablo Sanchez, another two men there as well. However, inside the Homestead itself, we shall only be searching Richard Temple's, and Miranda Delvin's quarters today, and no other rooms inside so, I need two men there. I also want two men for a search of the grounds, front and back. We will vacate all premises for our searches, if you have times allocated for those people for interviews, let them know at the meeting. So, when they return to their homes, I will be there to personally hold their interviews. As of tomorrow morning, at 8am sharp, our task is to search the remainder of the rooms inside the Homestead, and also down at the stables, and yards. However today, I have a new search for two men to do!" he looked squarely at them all.

"There is a widened gap in the rock-face of the sandstone wall that we discovered on the beach down towards the steps. So, I want it searched thoroughly. I think you'll find that a hammer and chisel is all you will need to chip away at the sandstone, because that is what we used. So, you may need to add them to your equipment. If you need me at all during the day, I will be with Jenna in the end room of the top balcony opposite the stairs. No need to report there to me today, if there are any findings at all, bag them in the usual way, take pictures, and we will discuss them back at the station!"

Jack looked around at the intense faces, then asked. "So, are we good team? Does everyone know their job for today?"

They all nodded, and replied. "Yes sir, Detective!"

Jack smiled. "Good, then let's get this show on the road. Refer to Constable Jenkins for any questions, he will be with you all today, and he will take the two men down to the beach who are allocated to search the gap in the wall and dunes, to show them where it is!"

He beckoned them to follow, and Constable Jenkins fell in beside him. "Just a thought, Jack, but if you want to create an element of surprise with Richard Temple, hang back, and I'll introduce you!"

Jack laughed. "You old devil! I love it sir, that will rock him!"

They all walked through the gates and across the lawns together. At the front doors Constable Jenkins took the lead, then opened the doors wide to allow his officers through then they followed him down to the living room where Constable Jenkins rapped once on the door and led his men inside, but Jack purposely lagged behind.

"Good morning, all. It is a pleasure to see you all in attendance. Thank you everyone, for that. However, we have a slight change of plans for today. I have in my possession warrants to search the said premises, grounds and surrounds of 'Oceanview!' We also plan to search the residences of permanent residents and staff here, to cater for the new investigation we have a Homicide Detective in charge, who will explain the proceedings to you!" said Constable Jenkins.

Richard Temple rose from his seat with an angry scowl gracing his face as he retorted in protest. "This is an outrage! I won't stand for this invasion of privacy so, what is the meaning of this? We were all told we were to assemble for questioning on the missing person case so, why would you need a Homicide Detective for that? Which one of you is this Detective? I want to place a formal complaint, this is an insult to my integrity, and a home intrusion!" he stated.

Constable Jenkins smiled. "Of course, Mister Temple, so pleased you asked. Allow me to introduce the Detective in question, all the way from the big city no less!" he stepped aside as Jack entered the room. "I give you Homicide Detective Jack Rickard!" he stated.

A hush fell on the room, as the workers fell silent, then gaped at each other. All, except for Richard Temple who laughed out loud, and sneered at Jack. "Is this some poor excuse for a joke?" he asked.

Jack moved forward. His face became serious as he spoke. "I do assure you Mister Richard Temple this is definitely no joke! Rather, a homicide case in process so, abide my instructions! Residences are to be vacated for two days from 9.am-4pm to assist officers in their search. I will personally conduct interviews in your homes today!"

"I will have no two-bit college kid give me instructions!" replied Richard. "By what authority do you have that right Jack? We have no murder investigation going on, my wife is missing that is all!"

"Excuse me Detective Rickard!" interrupted Constable Jenkins. "If you could hold your reply, I must address Mister Temple!"

"As you wish, Senior Constable!" offered Jack.

Constable Jenkins focused on Richard Temple's face, and stared into his eyes. "Just to clarify this once, and once only Mister Temple. To show some respect it would be appreciated, and appropriate to address the Detective, as Homicide Detective Rickard in the future, Mister Temple!" he said, in a voice of authority. "Back to you sir!"

Jack nodded, and made a notion, and the Constable handed him the papers. Jack's eyes blazed as he spoke. "On the contrary Mister Temple, this is no missing person case of Julia Temple, it has now become a murder investigation due to recent findings. Also, I will be now investigating the attempted murder of Jenna Temple (now, Jenna Rickard!)" Gasps could be heard from the workers. Jack eyed Richard carefully as he frowned. "But my authority is this, Mister Temple! Court Orders with search warrants from a most reputable institute!" he waved the papers at him. "My order of status, also my station well earnt by many years of study under the best Homicide Detective this Country ever produced so, I earnt my tag! That is the authority I have bestowed on me, Mister Temple! It is called law!"

"My court orders are from a judge, and allow me to investigate this murder case in any way I see fit. Search warrants for in-home residents of the 'Oceanview' estate, surrounds and workers homes. If by chance you rebuke these orders Richard Temple, I'll have no alternative but to arrest you, and you'll go to jail for obstructing justice and hampering this investigation! I would suggest you take a seat, and follow my orders like the others. Do I make myself clear Mister Richard Temple?" Jack asked most threateningly.

Richard Temple's jaw had dropped, and he raised an eyebrow as he glared at Jack Rickard. *Hmm! How the pup has fully grown now?* he puzzled secretly. He frowned as his face became grim. He said not one word as he sat down, but his eyes never left Jack's face.

"I take it you are in agreeance, and you will co-operate with my officers? Is that correct Mister Temple?" asked Jack.

"Yeah, sure!" came the disgruntled reply from Richard Temple, then quickly he corrected himself to say. "What I meant to say was. Yes of course, Homicide Detective Rickard!" he added with a smirk.

Jack eyed the room as he suppressed a smile. Satisfaction was so sweet, but so too would it be to solve this case. *I must not relent!* he thought, as he stared at each person in a new light. *I am certain my murderer is here.* he pondered. Only one person smiled. But he could see it in all their eyes, feel it in their demeanor, even sense what they were thinking. *This is very different as we will be interrogated!* and they would be right! *Was it fear that masked their faces?* He felt that he could almost smell it. *It should be!* he mused. *I am on a mission so, my plans are, to be ruthless, and unrelenting in my search for justice.*

"Excellent. So, we move on! My officers will give you all specific instructions that must be followed. Your commander in charge will be Constable Jenkins. Jack looked at Constable Jenkins and smiled.

"Take it away sir! You have control now so, let the proceedings begin. If you need me at all today, then you know where I will be. Just schedule a meeting at the station for after interviews today, and we shall go over all our findings, and our plans for tomorrow!"

"Yes sir, consider it done. I will organize that with all the officers later, Detective Rickard." commented Constable Jenkins.

"Good man." replied Jack. "Thank you all for your attendance today everyone!" he uttered, and saluted as he walked towards the doors, then disappeared into the hallway. He was deep in thought, but was really excited about the next step. He was to pick up Jenna.

Chapter Fourteen

Jenna sat cross-legged on the settee. "I just don't know Jack! Now, I am confused, I'm so sorry. I really thought this would be easy!"

Jack looked at her tenderly. "Nothing is ever easy Jenna, maybe I can help you!" He pulled his notebook out, and flipped through the pages. "Ah! This is it, your conversation with your mother!"

Jenna stared at him in amazement. "You have it written down?"

Jack laughed. "Of course! I don't do interviews without purpose, so let us re-start. Was your mother's room familiar as you entered?"

"Yes, the same as it used to be, except a few things out of place!"

"Ok! Think back to the voices saying to find a key! Your mother arranged a treasure-hunt to find a key here in her rooms! Correct?"

Jenna looked at him in frustration. "Well yes, Jack! You know it is, but we have been over that. Isn't it all a waste of time?"

"Not really Jenna as we have overlooked something important! My entry here says you commented on her orchids as you walked in, and said she had told you this!" *Right here at the window setting, is my most favourite place in the whole world, Jenna!* "Is that correct?"

Jack looked at her, and he knew she was getting frustrated. Bear with me Jenna, as later we will be laughing at this tiny hiccup."

Jenna smiled at his patience and persistence but said dryly. "You say that now Jack Rickard but from where I'm sitting it's not likely!"

"Ah! Ye have little faith my love so, let's continue. We are in your mother's room, but do you recall all your mother's instructions?"

Jenna frowned. "Don't be daft Jack! You know I remembered my mother ambling down to the end of the book-case and saying to me as she plucked a book out. *This is the oldest book I own Jenna, but one you must remember,* as there will be no paper trail to prompt you!"

"Well! I done that. I plucked it from its home, and here it is! So, I did recall, Jack!" she cried, as she held the book up once again. "It is *The Tale of Two Cities.*" then frowned again. "Not that it helped me at all to remember, as there is nothing inside it. I didn't find any clue, or a scrap of paper even so, we are stuck now Jack!"

"Show me the book please Jenna?" he said so she handed it over.

"Hmm! The edges are very tattered, and torn so, it is quite old indeed. But so too will the pages be I am guessing, and he opened the book, then very slowly so as not to rip a page, he turned each page over very carefully in his search for something, anything odd.

He looked up to ask Jenna. "Did you check every page, Jenna?"

"Well, I flipped through it, but didn't actually go page by page, as I thought a note would fall out of it, and it didn't!"

"This tells me two things, Jenna. We have the right book, but we are going about it wrong. No note is going to fall out Jenna, if your mother was so devious and hell-bent on secrecy. We'll search page by page first, just to make sure. Carefully he turned the numbered pages, and inspected each one, but there was no evidence of any instructions in any of the pages. As he turned the last tattered page, he thought the book was going to fall apart, and he stared at Jenna.

"This book is so delicate, but we must inspect the jacket covers!"

So, he turned the book over, and then back again very carefully. "Hmm! Do you notice any difference from the front cover of the jacket compared to the back cover, Jenna?" he asked inquisitively.

"It looks the same to me, Jack. The book has a jacket, though it does look very well worn, but no evidence of any note with clues.

"Just take particular interest in the jackets if you would, Jenna. See how the flap of the jacket cover comes free from the first page, but the back cover, what do you make of that?" he turned it over.

Jenna took the book from him. "Oh! I see what you mean, though I think with old age the back jacket flap has stuck to the last page!"

"Either that, Jenna. Or is has been purposely stuck!"

Jenna stared at him. "Do you suspect it was Mother?" she asked.

Jack grinned. "I am beginning to think so Jenna, and I'm starting to believe things you have said to describe your mother are proving true. Put the kettle on, would you please?" he asked.

"At a time like this, and you want coffee?" Jenna stated.

Jack laughed. "No, not coffee! Though seeing we are boiling the kettle, we may as well have a cup if you want, as I think this could be a long process! You see, Jenna, if we are to release the jacket flap from the last page without destroying it, we shall have to steam it open, otherwise the jacket may crumble, and any note with it!"

"Oh! I see. My goodness, Jack. You really have learnt a lot!"

"I guess I have Jenna. Now, I will put this book in the light from the open window. When the water boils, just bring the kettle over!"

Jenna made their coffee, re-boiled the kettle and took it to him.

"Thank you, Jenna!" he said, then he gently held the back jacket cover over the steam. As they watched, the jacket flap lifted up, and Jack paused, pulling the cover away. "We will wait a few minutes before we continue Jenna so, let's drink our coffee."

"Do you think the flap can be released intact, Jack?"

"I'm not sure, Jenna. We can only try!" replied Jack.

Gently, Jack teased the paper from the jacket, but some of it was still stuck. "We'll apply a little more steam please Jenna, then let it sit before I try again. That is about all I can do, or I will ruin it."

Jenna boiled the kettle again, and once again Jack held the flap over the steam, but this time he sighed with relief as it separated.

Jenna laughed. "Oh! Well, done Jack!" she exclaimed, but then her face fell in a heap as she realized. "But there is no note, Jack!"

"Damn! What a waste of time that was!" However, inquisitively Jack gently lifted the jacket cover. "Good heavens! How this stayed in one piece is beyond me?" he muttered as he carefully opened the flap that was stuck. "Hello what's this then? There is printing under here. You have to see this Jenna as it looks like double-dutch to me!"

Jenna stood up to lean over Jack's shoulder ready to decipher. GOTV3P243 "What the hell is that? It looks like some code! I have no idea what that means, Jack I'm sorry. Surely this was not written by my mother? It can't be our note, as I don't understand it at all!"

"Something tells me that it is, Jenna!" he flipped through pages of his notebook. "Ah, yes! You told me this, if you recall...That your mother went to great lengths to conceal everything, to keep it all a secret, even her trip to the city...You said to me... *Keep in mind, that mother wouldn't want anyone else to unravel her clues,* if they stumbled upon them. *So, you assumed the clues would be on topics, that only you personally would know more about!...* "Do you recall?"

Jenna stared at Jack flipping through pages in his notebook, and when he read out what he had found there, she was dumbfounded.

"Really, Jack? Was all that written down in your notebook too?"

Jack chuckled. "That and lots more, all about the cases, Jenna!"

"You amaze me how thorough you are Detective Rickard!"

Jack laughed. "If you say so, Jenna but I'm convinced this is your mother's message left for you, a beginning to your treasure hunt. A little difficult so to speak, but the first clue in a search for the key!"

Jenna gaped at him. "Then, I am afraid the search will end here, as I have no idea what those letters, and numbers mean, Jack!"

Jack stood, and held out his hand. "Come, Jenna, we both need to clear our thoughts so, let us call it a day. Somewhere along the line, we have missed something important, but we will work it out. We'll go back to the Lodge to have some lunch. What do you say?"

Jenna took his hand, and spoke. "I think you may be right, Jack. My head is hurting, and I can't think straight right now!"

"I did notice Jenna. So, we leave it until later. I have important interviews arranged for me this afternoon, and then much later, an important meeting with Constable Jenkins, and the officers back at the station to discuss the days findings and our plans for tomorrow. So, I might be late getting back for dinner. We could order dinner to have in the room if you like? I think that will be the best idea, but I will call you and let you know approximately what time I should be there, but you can order for yourself earlier if you are hungry."

"Yes, a good idea, Jack, however, I'll wait for you, just call me!"

"Ok, sounds good. Expect a call from me about 7.30pm, and you can order then anyway. That will give you more time to relax, and clear your head. Tonight, we will talk more about today's events."

"Will do, let's get out of here, please Jack."

"One thing more, Jenna. Do you want to see your room?"

Jenna looked at him, and her face was strained as she replied. "I just can't do it, Jack. Maybe tomorrow but now I just want to leave."

"Yes, I understand fully Jenna. This must be all so stressful for you, so we mustn't rush things. If you are not coping any day, just tell me because tomorrow is another day, and I don't want you to think you must continue, and be overloaded with anything. Ok?"

Jenna smiled at him. "Yes, thank you for understanding, Jack. I thought I would be more help to you today so, I'm disappointed in myself actually. I wish there is at least one thing I could help with!"

Jack looked at her, then quickly flipped through his notebook. "Well, seeing you asked my lady. There is this small thing, but very important just the same if you could answer one question for me?"

"Of course!" replied Jenna. "What is it, Jack?"

Jack was turning pages in his book. "Ah! Here it is. I knew I had to ask you something important, but so much has been happening today, I haven't had the chance to ask you. Something come up at the station this morning when we were going through the slides. I wanted to ask if it is not too confronting to you. Do you recall if you wore shoes or any footwear the morning of your fall, and attack?"

Jenna didn't hesitate. "Of that I can definitely help, Jack! I know for sure that I was bare-footed, as I had climbed out of bed to close the drapes when I heard the scream, and went straight out on to the balcony, then down to the stairs so, no. No footwear, just bare feet! Why would you ask that, Jack?" she queried.

Jack smiled. "That is so good to hear so, I can confirm that now!" He made a mark in his notebook, and looked up at Jenna. "Funnily enough, Jenna. I detected your bare footprints on quite a few slides this morning, and had to confirm it was you! So now, I can almost picture a scene. I will need to elaborate further when more evidence comes in, but I am pretty certain I saw the shadow you mentioned, or rather, the prints of the person who cast the shadow on to you!"

Jenna hands clasped her mouth as she gasped. "Oh, Jack! Do you know this is an awesome finding? Thank God, I remembered!"

"So pleased you did too as your shadow could be the murderer!"

They left by the side staircase, and when they reached the lawns, Jack looked around. All was quiet in The Homestead so he guessed the workers, also Richard and Miranda were gone. Only his officers doing their jobs searching the rooms. *It will be interesting to see if we get any findings today.* he thought to himself. *Hmm!* But more so, the beach. *He had a feeling churning in his gut about the dunes.*

Richard Temple's face had a fierce scowl as he answered a knock on the door to his rooms himself, and flung the door open wide.

Homicide Detective Jack Rickard, and Senior Constable Jenkins stood on the threshold awaiting entrance, one officer stood outside.

"Better come in, but make it quick officers. It is almost dark, and I am a busy man! We have had enough interruptions to our lifestyle today with officers combing through our belongings while we had to vacate, so disgraceful! This is a pointless interview, and you both know it! I have nothing more to add to my statement on this case. So, get it over with quick smart!" he grumbled in a grumpy attitude.

Constable Jenkins stepped forward. "Looks like I have to remind you again Mister Temple! This is a new investigation! Any original statements will be added to, or simply replaced by new statements, and anything removed from your lodgings will be returned if they are not part of our ongoing search for evidence. Also, to remind you that we are not all officers so, please address us accordingly. This is Homicide Detective Jack Rickard, please address him as such, and to you I am Senior Constable Jenkins. For your information again, this is no initial interview, but rather a current interview, and a new investigation for evidence in the murder of one Julia Temple, your wife and for the attempted murder of your daughter, Jenna Temple. I would have thought, that you of all people would co-operate with us! Detective Rickard will take over now, and he stepped aside.

Jack noticed Missus Miranda Delvin seated towards the back of the room. Except for a puzzled look on her face, she seemed quite at ease, and wore her trademark smile. He recalled that smile from the initial meeting in the living room. She was the only person who had managed a smile during that meeting, he thought that odd.

Miranda simply stared at this young kid who had now become a man to be reckoned with. *A Homicide Detective too, no less!* thought Miranda, and a puzzled look crossed her face as she watched him.

His demeanor was relaxed, though his face seemed set like stone as he spoke in a deep voice filled with persistent authority, but the worst was his green eyes boring straight into Richard Temple's she noticed, *and Miranda flinched in fright as he addressed her.*

"You may leave these rooms immediately please Missus Delvin! This is to be a private interview, and quite extensive. I would advise you go to the kitchen for refreshments, an officer will assist you and bring you back for your private interview in your quarters!"

"Oh! You startled me Detective Rickard. I was deep in thought!" tinkled Miranda as she rose elegantly from her seat. "Anything to oblige Detective!" she said, and smiled as she swayed towards him.

"This is outrageous officers we usually dine together!" protested Richard. "Just wait a while please Miranda, and I will sort this out quick smart!" and he turned towards Jack, and roared. "This time is not acceptable at all. Just get out, and come back another time!"

Jack hadn't forgotten the humiliation he suffered last time here. He clenched his teeth as he tried to suppress his anger against the impertinence of the man, but he continued to speak placidly.

"Mister Temple, a reminder. This is a murder investigation, anything you say or do, is to be recorded as evidence in a court of law!"

"Constable, make notes please!! he stressed as he turned to him. Constable Jenkins replied. "I am way ahead of you Detective. I have made notes, and recorded all conversations since our admission!"

"Thank you, Constable! Now would you ask our officer outside to accompany Missus Delvin over to The Homestead, please?"

"Will do, sir!" uttered the Constable, and he walked outside.

Richard Temple's face flared with pure hate as he stared at Jack.

Jack smiled. "Well, Mister Temple. We can do this the easy way, or the hard way. Either you co-operate, or suffer the consequences. Your choice? A little more than you gave me when last I was here, when I all I needed to know was Jenna's whereabouts!" he stressed.

Richard's blood boiled. It was bad enough having him for a son-in-law, but now as a Homicide Detective taking full advantage of his position, was a bitter pill for him to swallow. His little dig didn't go unnoticed either of their last conflict here. But this time, he had no way out so he had to co-operate, but he thought to himself. *Your time will come Detective Jack Rickard!* Of that, *you can be certain!*

"Ask away then!" Richard said offhandedly, and took a seat.

Jack smiled as he circled the room. He had no intentions at all of sitting, but rather thought that he could maintain his authority most professionally standing, then he spoke out. "So, tell me about your staff, Mister Temple? Their employment status, their attitudes etc.,"

"What?" snapped Richard. *To watch him prowling around the room* seems bad enough, *but what has this line of questioning got to do with anything?* Richard asked himself. "I thought this was to be a murder investigation, not a positions vacant interview?" he quipped.

Jack smiled. "Clever, Mister Temple. Just answer the questions, if you wouldn't mind. In the long run, it will save us time! You did want to dine, didn't you?" Jack added, as he stared into his eyes.

Richard scowled at him as he replied. "That is too much to talk about now, and I have had a long day, and I haven't eaten. Besides, you know the staff who work here. They have been here for years!"

Jack frowned. "I also have had a long day Mister Temple, and I haven't eaten dinner either, but my dinner will be much later than yours. I have conducted interviews since 3.30pm today. Yours will pass quickly if you co-operate, and Miranda Delvin's interview will be my last for the day. So, let's do what needs to be done, the longer you drag it out, the longer we will be here, and I may have to come back for a second interview, and I am sure you would love that. So, as this is a new investigation we will start from scratch. Things are never the same as they were years before so, whether or not I know your staff is irrelevant. So, I want to know all about your staff!"

"If it is too much as you say, then write it down, and then give it to Constable Jenkins while I am interviewing Missus Delvin. Or, I could use a tape recording if you wish? Most interviews are taped!"

"I guess I could write it all down then." replied Richard.

"It is good to see you co-operating Mister Temple! I must stress though, I want to know everything about them, the good and the bad. Any past arguments, and your relationship with them all!"

Jack pressed the record button, then looked squarely at Richard before changing tack. "I am a little confused Mister Temple. Please explain your relationship with Missus Miranda Delvin?"

Richard looked angered. "That is of no concern to you Detective. My private life is just that, private! So, you don't need to know!"

"On the contrary Mister Temple, it is within my rights to ask any personal questions about any potential suspect especially when the said person Miranda Delvin, has been living here for many years, and believe me, everyone who lives or works here are suspects!"

Richard looked uncomfortable as he spoke. "I guess we have an arrangement." he offered.

"Hmm! A long-term arrangement from what I can see, Mister Temple. Are your sleeping arrangements in sync also?" he queried.

Richard raised his voice. "I don't have to tell you that!"

Jack chuckled, and replied. "I think you just did Mister Temple!"

Richard was getting heated as a flush of red marks crept up his neck, and he tugged at his collar, trying to breathe easier.

"Yes, I do remember you bringing Miranda to 'Oceanview' even though your wife was here!" Jack prattled on. "Frankly, I found that odd Mister Temple. It was after Miranda's husband was killed! Oh, that is a recall!" Jack stated. "I must remember to look into that!" he dug into his pocket, and jotted down a reminder in his notebook.

"Is there anything else you would like to say of Missus Delvin? What she means to you? Her relationships with staff? Anything?"

Richard was finding it hard to concentrate. He knew he was being taped, and if he lied? Well, it would only take one person to tell.

"Well, I guess we have a certain relationship." he stammered.

Jack smiled. "How would you describe her?" he asked.

Richard was so angered by all of it. "God damn it, I don't know. Bubbly, friendly, extremely clever, talented and very beautiful!"

"Hmm! Quite a package. Sexy too I bet!" countered Jack.

"Damn sexy!" Richard had it out before he could stop himself.

Jack chuckled. "What did your staff think of her?"

"Oh, the staff rarely had much to do with her." Richard lied.

Jack frowned, then flipped through his notebook. *Hmm! Yes, here it is.* "According to my interview with Melita Sanchez, she says that Miranda Delvin runs the household at 'Oceanview,' and with an iron fist. She describes her as controlling, bossy, so over-bearing and very devious. She says that woman is the devil! Big statement!"

Jack raised his head to meet Richard's stare. "Your thoughts on that Mister Temple? Would you care to elaborate?"

Richard laughed. "You can believe the staff all you want but they are all low-class people, and that will be in my report about them!"

"I see! I will expect also in that report, a detailed entry regarding specific times of your movements and of course your whereabouts on the morning of the said attack, and murder! That will be all!"

"An officer will accompany you to the house during Miranda's interview. Jack opened his phone to make the call to his officer, and at the same time looked at Richard's shoes. *Hmm! Interesting shoe, a loafer, and large too! Where have I seen that type of shoe?* he pondered.

"Ok, rules! You must be out by 8.30am in the morning! All areas of 'Oceanview' are out of bounds as of now. Officers will patrol the premises all night to ensure that, tomorrow our search resumes.

Jack stared directly at Richard with his green eyes blazing! "You knew your wife wasn't coming back, didn't you Mister Temple?"

Richard was startled. His face flushed showing the anger he felt at himself for being side-tracked and to be caught off-guard. He wasn't expecting more questions so, he stuttered, and stammered before stammering in reply to the Detective's leading question.

"Well, I... You see, I... As time went on..."

"You were having an affair weren't you Mister Temple? If Julia came back, it would spoil things, wouldn't it? She'd be in the way! But you knew she wouldn't be back so, she wasn't missed, was she? Jack felt Richard faltering and took the opportunity to push him.

"She was a monster! Damn it, of course I didn't want her back! Yes, I was having an affair, lots of them. However, with Miranda it was different. *Richard was rambling now.* "Miranda is so special!"

Infidelity! Hmm! "Maybe Julia had her reasons to doubt you after all Mister Temple. It was so convenient with Julia out of the picture, wasn't it? I wager you wanted to be rid of her so badly to allow you and Missus Miranda Delvin to live, and run 'Oceanview' together, didn't you? How cozy it has all worked out for you!" stated Jack.

"You are damn right I wanted to be rid of her! Julia was a living night-mare. We hadn't shared the same bed for years. I hated her!"

Jack gulped. *My god does Jenna know?* "Hate, is a big word Mister Temple, and sides with revenge, or retribution! I'll now refer to my earlier question. *You knew your wife wasn't coming back, didn't you?"*

Suddenly a change overcome Richard Temple as if waking from a dream. He wore that obstinate look again, his eyes weren't glazed over now and his chin jutted out as he stared defiantly, then a smirk graced his face as in a deep voice, he spoke. "Real fancy words! But sorry, you have it wrong Homicide Detective Rickard. I hated my wife Julia, enough to not want her back, but I didn't murder her!"

Jack eyed him. "Interesting! But once again, you eluded the exact answer to my question Mister Temple! You lied also to deceive your daughter by thinking Julia lived. That's all!" he pressed stop record.

Miranda Delvin breezed into the room. She nodded to Richard at the door, but made a bee-line straight towards Detective Rickard.

Her smile preceded her, and somehow it lit up the dim room.

"That was a very long interview Detective Rickard!" she stressed as she stood in front of him. "I do hope you are ready for me, and I hope Richard hasn't answered all the juicy questions!"

Jack could have laughed, but instead he took the time to study her. *Miranda is either very clever or a really good actress.* he thought as he looked her over. *Immaculately dressed, she had an awesome figure, a beautiful face and a smile to die for. Yes!* She is a very beautiful woman! I agree. His eyes shifted to her feet to be instantly disappointed.

So tiny! Her shoes are so very small, too small! I almost would have bet otherwise. How interesting! he lifted his head, and their eyes met.

Hers seemed to be pools of purple, and he smiled as he said.

"Take a seat please Miranda. I am ready for you now. I hope you don't mind, but I record all interviews! It cuts out the paperwork!"

Her laugh was a tinkle, and Jack shook his head as he smiled. He didn't expect anything else. *This interview will be very interesting.* he thought as he looked at her, but it was difficult to focus on her face when her breasts were bulging out of her blouse. He knew this type of woman. Cunning, devious, manipulative, and so very clever not to disclose anything to incriminate themselves. *Was she this type?*

She was smiling that sweet smile as if butter would not melt in her mouth. *Or, maybe she is as innocent as she seems!* he thought.

Jack pressed the record button. "Ok, Miranda, now we proceed!"

"Tell me about your husband, and your relationship with him?"

Immediately the sweet smile disappeared from her face and now that tiny worried frown appeared on her forehead as her face paled, but then miraculously she recovered to be obstinate in her reply.

Miranda stared at him defiantly. "I'm not sure I understand that question, or the relevance of it either Detective Rickard!"

Jack knew he had hit a nerve, and he fought back a smile as he replied. "George! Your husband. He was killed in an untimely car accident I believe. I'd like to know of your relationship, what you did together at home? Whether or not you helped George at all around the house, all that!" he stated as he studied her. Her hands were in her lap now, and she twisted, and twisted a handkerchief.

She looked at him directly. "George was the love of my life, so it upsets me to talk about him Detective. But yes, we always did many things together, whether it be at home or elsewhere."

"You lived on a very dangerous cliff as I recall, so I imagine the road would have been quite precarious." Jack questioned.

Miranda laughed. "Not to George, it wasn't. He knew that road like the back of his hand. It was hard to believe he had an accident on that road. He must have been tired, and veered off the road!"

"I see! Do you recall who maintained his car at the time?"

"Why, George of course! He never trusted anyone with his car, he did all services himself at home, it was always in tip-top shape!"

"Very wise when you must negotiate that road every day. Did you ever help him? Was he a man to teach a woman about cars?"

Miranda's laugh was a tinkle. "Yes of course, silly! Just prior to his accident he explained car maintenance to me on how to check brakes, change oil and stuff. George was very thoughtful like that!" she dabbed at her eyes with her handkerchief as if to wipe a tear.

"Thank you, Miranda. Didn't mean to upset you, so we will drop that subject. "What is your relationship like with the staff here?"

Just the change in tack threw Miranda a little, but surprisingly once again he was amazed how quickly she recovered composure.

"Oh, I think I have a solid relationship with all the staff here. It was hard at first, now I have gained their respect." said Miranda.

"Really? That is good." said Jack, wanting to keep some things to himself. "Hassles would be a pain as you've lived here for years!"

"I am a curious one, but why is that, Miranda? Tell me how you originally come to move to 'Oceanview' in the first place, and also why you have stayed so long when you have a home of your own?"

Miranda looked squarely at him. *My god, but he is so devious.* But I must persist, *though he keeps changing tack.* she told herself.

Miranda smiled her best smile before continuing.

"Well, Detective. As I recall, I think it was after George passed in the car accident, and Richard came out to the house when I was so devastated that he told me to pack my things, and come out to live at his home!" she grabbed her handkerchief to dab at her eyes.

Jack smiled at her. "That was so very thoughtful of him. Why do suppose he would do that Miranda when his wife still lived there. Did Julia Temple agree with that arrangement?" he queried.

Miranda was so taken back that she stuttered her next words. "I well I...I guess... I...don't really...know that, he didn't say. He was sorry for me, he was just being kind, I guess. But he must have talked to his wife, though they didn't live together you know. So, it really wouldn't matter, would it? It is Richard's home 'Oceanview' so, I think he could do what he liked! Don't you agree?"

"I think it matters a great deal. I know it would to me if it was my home, and my wife moved someone else in!" Jack stated. "But you do know it is not Richard Temple's home, don't you, Miranda? Yet he let you stay, simply by being kind to you. Is that correct?"

Miranda was feeling harassed, and her face paled. "Yes, I said that!" she snapped. "Richard told me it was his home!" she added.

"So, after many years is Richard still being kind to you by letting you live at 'Oceanview?' How would you explain that, Miranda? I am a little confused. Or was your relationship with Richard Temple more personal than you say in the beginning and more-so now. So, how would you describe your living arrangements?" Jack queried. "Before you reply, keep in mind we have searched your quarters!"

Miranda felt un-well. Her face was pale and she was feeling faint. This had never happened to her before. Usually she was always in control, but now she sat quivering in her seat, not knowing what was to come next. Detective Rickard hadn't even got to the murder yet, and it was making her nervous. His questions were like bullets fired from a gun. She was feeling the pressure, and felt threatened.

Miranda looked at the Detective and knew that she couldn't lie. *What had Richard told him?* she wondered, before she answered.

"Yes, Detective we do have an intimate relationship, and did so at the start. We share the same room if that answers your question!"

Jack smiled. "Well, part of it, Miranda, thank you. However, the important one about 'Oceanview' is unanswered. "You do know it is not Richard Temple's home, don't you, Miranda?" he repeated.

"I already told you Detective that Richard said it was his home!"

"Hmm, yes you did, but I have reason to believe you know that 'Oceanview' does not belong to him!" is that correct?"

Miranda twisted in her seat, her face was not a happy one, and Jack knew he was pushing her buttons when she snapped at him.

"That is all I know, Just, what Richard told me, and that's that!"

"How odd. So, you didn't receive a letter from a solicitor's office to say 'Oceanview' belongs solely to Missus Julia Temple? Richard, telling you of an indemnity clause in papers they signed for their marriage arrangement? A city firm would have a copy! At the same time, you got a letter from the bank saying her assets were frozen!"

"No! We didn't get any letter from any solicitor!" she screeched.

"Jack looked at her to reply. "Strange, Miranda! But I know that isn't true! See, I happened to be outside your rooms and overheard you and Richard discussing both letters. I went there in desperation to find out about Jenna's health and her whereabouts, and I wanted her father's help, but I wasted my time as he refused to give it!" Jack stood to acknowledge the interview over, but glared at her to add.

"I also heard you arguing about the locks on the rooms upstairs being changed, you were angry with Richard for letting the police do that when you wanted to search for Julia's will. Why Miranda? Why search for Julia's will if she wasn't deceased but only a missing person? You knew she wasn't coming back, didn't you Miranda?"

Miranda's mouth widened as she gaped at him. She was at a loss for words. These were incriminating accusations and they were so true as she recalled the incident. *What will I say?* she worried.

Her forehead was crinkled by several deep frown lines now, and she struggled to answer, then a thought came to her, and she smiled that sweet smile. "Well, Detective Rickard, it was like this. I caught Richard out in a lie about his wife and the estate, and I wanted proof he was telling the truth, and only her will would state that!"

Jack shook his head. *This woman is so unbelievable. I really do think she is capable of anything.* he thought to himself, but didn't bother to pursue her lies. Instead, he looked at her sternly, and spoke.

"I will require your house keys for the cliff property. I wish to conduct a search there tomorrow. I would appreciate you not going up there until I say so, you may get them for me now! That is all!"

Jack pressed stop record, and walked around the desk to wait.

Miranda opened her mouth to protest but then thought better of it. She left her seat, and went into the bedroom. When she returned, she glared at him as she slapped the keys into the Detective's hand. She was going to offer him some clever quip, but Jack got in first.

"Just remember Missus Miranda Delvin. The next time you may be questioned it could be in a court of law! In there, you must swear to tell the truth, the whole truth, and nothing but the truth! Just a thought to leave you with, and he turned on his heel and walked to the door where he paused and turned to say. "A reminder, Miranda Delvin, the top balcony is off-limits to you, and Richard, and these premises will be patrolled by police officers all night. Thank you!"

Constable Jenkins was waiting outside the room, and he spoke to Jack when he got closer. "Good, we are on time Detective! How many officers do you want left here tonight sir?"

"Yes, all done! I will need one officer up on the top balcony, one over at the stables and one at the entrance to the house. Better leave another two to relieve them during the night. Find them all a room where they can take turns sleeping. Just make sure out of the five officers left, they are from the areas that we searched today because we must go over details with them at the station tonight during our meeting. We can inform the others in the morning what is decided. I will go out to the car and wait for you, Constable. I want to process the interviews I had today before we leave for the station."

Constable Jenkins nodded, and spoke. "Right, I will get the men sorted, and we will be off. I'll meet you in the car-park, Detective!"

Jack was already thinking as he nodded, and walked away. *The Sanchez residence? Hmm! Melita Sanchez* is a very dominating one. So strong in her body, and will, *a tough nut.* Very outspoken with her answers, *rebellious even.* Her shoe size is medium, flat-typed shoes with a thick tread. *Pablo the son lives with her,* and he seems so very intimidated by her. *Could it be he is afraid of her?* If so, could he be intimidated easily? *I must test that tomorrow!* He seems very timid, an anxious type. He seemed on edge all through the interview. At one time he looked like he was going to lose the plot. So, yes. A very nervous person, easily broken I feel if he was pushed. *He definitely was hiding something it seemed.* There were lots of stops and starts to his answers. He wears medium sized joggers with rigid soles.

Paula and Ted Hastings were an odd couple. Ted, he was the silent one who spoke hesitantly with his head hung low. He was tall, and lean, but Paula was tall also and a very large, hefty woman. *Paula was the dominant one, defiant,* her answers were copy-book. He wore solid work- boots, steel capped with a tough rigid sole and laced up tight.

Though, strangely enough, Paula wore boots also, but a different type of boot not an outside work-boot like Ted's. They were smooth and laced up also, *but more emphasis was on the very thick sole,* probably to support her weight. It must take a toll on her working long hours in the kitchen so, it would be tough on her legs and feet *and a solid, cushioned boot would be required. Hmm! Interesting findings there.* Then there was Richard, and Miranda. A lot of questions to be answered there. Richard wore loafers. *Why? How strange.* Maybe they were his house shoes, not his work shoes. His foot was quite large unlike Miranda's very small one. *That was a bit of a shock to see.*

Jack sat in the car and pondered on it all. A few things just didn't sit right with him. *It will be interesting to see the other findings.*

Constable Jenkins tapped on the car window on the passenger side, then opened the door. "All set over there, Detective, and our five officers will meet us at the station." he said, as he sat in the car.

"Good work, Constable. I am anxious to see what they have for me. It's been a long day, and I am starving. Oh! I must call Jenna first, and tell her to order. What do you think sir? Maybe another hour's work at the station, and then a re-cap in the morning?"

"Yes Jack. That sounds fine to me!"

"Good! I will call Jenna now, and let her know that." Jack dialed, and spoke to Jenna, a quick call, but then he told her he had to go.

"We decided today we would order in the room tonight, sir. So, it will be great to just go home, relax and eat. Jenna didn't cope too well today, sir, we had to quit, and achieved nothing really. It may be a long night as we have some things to go over after dinner!"

"Just take it easy with her, Jack. It must be so terrible for her to try and recall things that she would much rather forget about."

"Yes, I am aware of that, and I can actually pinpoint the triggers now, which is good. I know how far I can go. I will go gently with her, sir. But so far, she has been remarkable, her memory is fine!"

Jack walked into the room, and they were all waiting for him. He smiled but didn't take a seat as he addressed them all.

"First of all. Thank you all for today. A big job I know, but I hope someone has a result for me. However, one more day to go. We will start with the dunes. I am most interested in the findings there. Who was there?' he asked, and an officer stood up. He handed Jack his report, and spoke. "It's not what you wanted, Detective, however, tomorrow with the proper equipment we should be able to push in further. We chipped away the sandstone, and did make it a wider entrance, but inside there had been a cave-in, and a lot of rubble to get rid of. We couldn't see well either, it was dark in there because the cave entrance that we could just make out, was almost closed. We need shovels, a means of getting the rubble away to dispose of, and we need lighting, then we'll have a chance to search further!"

Jack was disappointed, but nodded to the officer. "Can you help arrange that equipment for tomorrow, Constable Jenkins?"

"I may have to ask the surf club if we can have access to a sand buggy and trailer, the rest is an easy fix, Detective."

"Excellent, thank you! Now guys, Richard Temple and Miranda Delvin's rooms please. What do we have from there, anything?

An officer stood, handed his report over, then placed a box on the table. "No sign of the evidence you wanted, sir, only old shoes!"

"Shoes? Let's see what we have!" Jack stated, as he opened the box. He looked quickly knowing most of them were Miranda's, and hers were too small for what he was looking for. Then his hand fell on a larger one, and when he turned it over, he blinked in surprise. *The same shoe as Richard was wearing today, a slip-on loafer, but a very old one.* This one is worn thin with scuff marks, the leather is marked and scratched, *the inner sole has had sand inside it as if he wore them down to the beach.* He held them up. "Where were these shoes found? Bag them as evidence, and send the others back!"

"Those shoes weren't in the wardrobe, but rather tucked away under the staircase cupboard as if to be discarded!" said the officer.

"Hmm! Good work. Now, who was at the Hastings residence?"

An officer stepped forward with his report. "We also didn't find anything incriminating, Detective. We just packed what shoes we thought you may want to see, and he placed a bag on the table.

Jack looked in the bag. Straight away he identified Ted's work-boots, and looked them over. The others were all boots in the bag, all different types of boots. He pulled them all out, and turned each pair over to look at the soles first, when suddenly he gasped. *Well, I'll be!* he mused. *Interesting, looks like my work is not yet done!*

"We'll keep all these boots so, bag them please officer!"

"Now, the last for the day. The Sanchez residence." His officer was standing, ready to hand the report. "It was a similar story for us, Detective. No crucial evidence so, we packed some shoes!"

"Good." said Jack. He identified Pablo's riding boots, but it was the joggers he was interested in, and also Melita's flat-typed shoes with a thick tread. "We can bag this pair!" Jack stated. "Now, about tomorrow! No-one is allowed in the house while you search. Sort it out with Constable Jenkins, who is going where? Constable, a word please?" Jack moved over closer. "I want two officers at the stables. I'll be upstairs with Jenna, but I want you to pick Pablo up and take him over there. Ring me and I'll come over to observe his reactions. I believe he can be intimidated. So, I want to lean on him a little and pressure him with some direct questions. I have a key to Miranda, and George Delvin's house, and I want it searched. Especially look if there are security cameras? If so, I want any tapes of footage from the day before George's accident, check the date. Thank you, sir!"

"But right now, some things are on my mind, bugging me! If you could set up the projector maybe tomorrow, and bring up the beach slides again, I must see them. I think it may prove important!"

Jenna was preparing nibble's for an entrée as he walked in. "Oh! You're just in time Jack. Dinner will be ten minutes they tell me. I'll prepare us a drink." and she began pouring them. "So, tell me? What of the results today?" Jack frowned at the question. He pulled her close to wrap his arms around her, and kissed her deeply.

"That bad hey?" she inquired, and laughed as she stepped back.

"Well, not a total loss, some possibilities maybe. We'll see! I have a lot of thinking to do, but not now! Firstly, I want to shower before our dinner arrives, change into something comfortable, have a few drinks, and maybe just chill out with you! With no talk of the case!"

"Sounds good to me, off you go then. I may change also!"

Jack strolled in, a big smile on his face and dressed in a tracksuit.

A knock came to the door, and Jenna opened it wide to let the waiter wheel the trolley in. She thanked him, then turned, and said to Jack. "Dinner is served, sir. Shall we eat outside?"

"Perfect, Jenna!" Stars lit up the sky as the very last rays of the sun dipped below the horizon, and the moon rose up in all its glory. So, they sat for hours enjoying some idle banter, then Jack's whisper broke the spell. "Better call it a night, Jenna! I have notes to go over for tomorrow, and a need to lie down. You could read for a while?"

"Good idea Jack, come on!" she said as she pulled him up.
All was quiet. Jenna was locked deeply in a book and Jack searching his notebook, and making notes when suddenly he paused. "Hmm! These words seem different to what you said this morning, Jenna!"

"What words?"

"This first entry of your conversation with your mother. "The first part you got ok… the next bit reads… "Two things are vital to recall! This book, and my favourite one! Is your quest to find a key!" Jenna sat upright quickly. "Mother's favourite book of course! As if I'd forget it! What was the code, Jack?" He replied. "GOT V3 P243." Jenna jumped out of bed. "I know what it is, Jack. I know! I know!"

Chapter Fifteen

Jenna was excited, and couldn't wait to get out to 'Oceanview.' It was only 6 a.m. in the morning, but she was insistent they should buy breakfast at a take-away on the way there. Jack only had time to grab coffees, and bacon and egg rolls on the way.

All was quiet at The Homestead as they walked silently across the lawns to the entrance where one of his officers stood watch.

"Morning Detective Rickard! Missus Rickard!" said the officer. "All is good here, and no-one tried to enter the house."

Jack smiled. "Good work officer! Would you let us in the house, as we want to take the internal stairs up to the balcony. Jenna, and I have some important work to do in her mother's room, but I will be down later as I have to go over to the stables for an interview!"

"All good, sir, follow me inside." he said, and unlocked the door. "You will find another officer up on the balcony, sir so, I will leave you at the stairs. He will assure you of your privacy." he added.

"Thank you!" said Jack as he ushered Jenna through the doors, then they took the stairs up to the balcony, and walked to the end.

Jack opened the doors to Julia Temple's room, then he stood aside while Jenna passed through. He closed the doors, and flicked the light switch on inside, deciding they may be able to see much better, but Jenna wasn't concerned at all. Instead, she was already making her way towards the bookcase. He chuckled as he pulled the drapes across, and light filled the room. "Should we eat first?"

"Oh, no! I couldn't yet Jack! Let me at least find an answer to the clue we have. He looked at her face first, set in that obstinate way she had, then spoke. "As you wish my lady!" and sidled up beside her. "So, what reasoning do you have for the code GOT V3 P243."

Jenna looked at him, and smiled. "Ah! My mother knew I would remember. This is her favourite book from a series which I bought for her." Jenna answered, as she walked down the line of books. "I know the book, but just can't remember exactly where it was!"

"So, decipher the code for me, and I will help you look!"

Jenna looked at him, then spoke. "GOT is the name of the book series. 'Game of Thrones.' V3 means 'Volume 3' P243 is Page 243."

Jack laughed. "Oh, how clever your mother was! A great series too! I started reading them when I was studying at university!"

Jenna gasped. "Oh! Look Jack. Here they are!" and she plucked Volume 3 from the shelf. Immediately she fanned the pages until she reached page 243. As she opened it a note fluttered to the floor.

Jack reached down and picked it up for her. "Well done, Jenna!" he said. But as he watched her reading it, he noticed the deep frown was forming to crease her forehead. "What is wrong, Jenna?"

Jenna lifted her head, and her deep green eyes were clouded by pools of tears. As he watched she blinked, then they slipped from her eyelashes to her cheeks, and fell down to dampen her blouse.

He pulled her close to hug her. "What is it my love?"

Jenna handed him the note. "All I can say Jack, is that my mother is testing me to the point of ridiculous! She left me this crazy poem!"

Jack chuckled. "A poem? But don't be too hasty, Jenna. It must have some point to your quest!" but Jenna was quick to reply.

"You may laugh Mister Jack Rickard, but I would like you to tell me the meaning of it? If it is indeed part of the quest... Because, my dear husband... I do not have a clue!... So, we are stuck again!"

Jack smiled as he looked at the note, and began to read out loud.

The Quest: The ocean beckons, just like a ship at sea
Simply remember where the boards do shrink
From this endless view, a luncheon spree
So, food and beverage I think
No time to dwell, as deep in the bowels, a quest awaits
Seek it with purpose, then we will share one final cheer
From my most favourite place.

When he had read it all, Jack looked up at Jenna to say. "It is no poem, Jenna!" he chuckled. "But a riddle in fact. Another ploy from your mother for you to figure!" he laughed. "I must say, I give her credit where it is due. Surely you must give an 'A' for effort?"

Jenna's eyes blazed. "Don't you dare make a joke of this, Jack! It is no laughing matter as mother is testing me to the limit and I begin to wonder if she was insane when she did all these secrecy things?"

Jack felt sorry for her, and he put an arm around her. "No, Jenna, not insane, but very clever! She was making sure only you would find the key, and the way I read it is this. It is her final good-bye!"

Jenna's eyes filled with tears. "Oh! Jack. Do you really think so?"

"I do! Read the last two lines. She is talking about the key when she says. *Seek it with purpose*. The purpose is to find what she left for you like her will, deeds to 'Oceanview,' the solicitor's name, and contact details. *Then we will share one final cheer from my most favourite place*. Is your mother saying good-bye! Is how I read it!"

Jenna's eyes widened. "How is it I don't think like that? You are far too clever Mister Homicide Detective. I must concede you're right!"

Jack grinned. "If you say so my lady, I dare not argue? Now, shall we start the riddle at the beginning, it's usually the best place?"

Jenna laughed. "Ok, but let me try!" *The ocean beckons.* "Well, it certainly does from here!" and, *like a ship at sea.* "I can relate to that too! We often seen ships on the ocean. But the next part. Hmm? Not sure." *Simply remember where the boards do shrink* "Any ideas?"

"Well, Jenna. When she says *Simply remember* It makes me think you know the boards shrink! So, if not on a ship? Then where?"

Jenna laughed. "I don't believe you, Jack. It is here in this room!"

Jack looked at the floor, and it was all timber, board flooring, and he laughed. "So, the boards in here do shrink?"

"Definitely! Mother was always complaining about the creaks."

"Ok, well done! Now the next part is straight forward, or is it?"

From this endless view, a luncheon spree

So, food and beverage, I think "Your thoughts on that, Jenna?"

"Well, when mother and I admired the view here it was usually at lunch time, and we used to sit right here at this table setting!"

"Ah! Ah! Now you're getting the hang of it, Jenna. I believe your mother is directing you to this table setting. However, the next line is intriguing! Almost like your mother doesn't want you to linger!" *No time to dwell, as deep in the bowels a quest awaits seek it with purpose*

Jenna gasped. "Of course! She doesn't Jack! I know what she meant, *deep in the bowels* is under these creaking boards!" and began pulling the table and chairs away to roll back a mat. As she tugged at a gap in a board, it came free, and there tucked in a corner was a tiny box.

Jenna lifted the lid. "Yes!" she cried in elation, as she spied a key and a note. "Oh no mother please!" she wailed as she read. *Where I travelled to, look for No 16.* She slumped in the chair to try and work it out, but stood quickly. "Oh, my! City Central Station. Box No 16!"

Jack smiled. "Great job, Jenna. Your quest is complete, but now we must trace the source of the key, that means going to the city!"

Jenna stared strangely at him. "Go to the city, but when Jack? Do you really mean right now? What about the case?" she queried.

"Definitely, as soon as possible, Jenna! If we leave as soon as we can, then we might get an appointment with your mother's solicitor today, cross fingers! Providing this elusive key fits the No 16 postbox at City Central Station!" he laughed. "Or, I guess your mother may have had the last laugh with another trick planned for you!"

Jenna frowned. "Oh my! I dread the thought, Jack."

"Ok, this is my plan. I'll drop you off at The Lodge, as it is vital, that I go into the Station before we can leave. Constable Jenkins and the officers will be preparing for the day, and I want to change the order of things today. We may stay overnight in the city, as I would like to catch up with Detective Jeremy Woods at some point if he is free. Maybe dinner, or drinks even. You will have to pack a bag for us Jenna so, some nice clothes for us both. What do you think?"

"Yes, I can do that, so consider it done. It will be nice to catch up with him again. I do hope we are able to get an appointment to see this solicitor of mother's today, but what is the urgency, Jack?"

"Well, if you recall Jenna. Once a statement goes out from police to any link about an impending murder investigation well, all hell will break loose here. Your mother is listed as missing and a murder investigation is a whole new ball-game. So, having said that, I want to warn Constable Jenkins not to declare it yet while the case is on, and the solicitor, well I want to speak to him about it. He will know when he meets you that there has been a change in your mother's circumstances, and I want to ask him to hold off sending any letters to the police, the bank, or to your father, as I don't want any of them at 'Oceanview' to be scared off, and try and fly the coop before I can solve this case, and solve this case I will, Jenna! Very soon too!"

Jenna was amazed. "Really, Jack? Can you tell me anything yet?"

"No, I can't do that Jenna. I have to be absolutely certain first!"

Jack arrived at the station early and no-one was there. He walked to his room and sat at his desk to update his new file. He tidied up his entries, then locked it away, just as the Constable walked in.

"Well, you are the early bird, Detective. That is good, as we have a lot going on today. Let us hope for a productive search today!"

"Good morning, Constable. Well, the reason I am here early is to speak to you about today before the team arrives. Something rather urgent has come up that can't wait. I want to alter today's format!"

"It must be important Jack so, what change of events came up?"

"You won't believe it. Jenna, and I had a huge breakthrough this morning at 'Oceanview' in her mother's room where we endured an ordeal of a quest, or rather a treasure hunt, her mother requested of her!" Jack chuckled. "This all came about when Jenna's memory was awakened at 'Oceanview' on the day she returned. She used to hear voices in her head, but later realized it turns out to be an actual conversation she had with Julia on the day before she went missing. So, all along it was her mother's voice giving her instructions!"

"My goodness, Julia Temple thought of everything, poor lady! She certainly knew someone was out to get her, but a clever lady, hell-bent on having things in order. So, what was the quest she set?"

"That is an understatement, sir. You won't believe what we went through, but I haven't got time to go into detail this morning, but tomorrow I will. The quest she set was a search to find a key. A very important key that Julia Temple hid up in her room. A key to a post-box that she set up for Jenna in the city, and inside it will be the all-important solicitor's name and contact details, and surprise! Deeds, to 'Oceanview,' with a copy of Julia's latest will to confirm Jenna as the sole beneficiary of the entire estate, 'Oceanview!' That is what her mother told her the day Jenna put her on the train for the city!"

"Jenna's memory recall was outstanding. She was able to recall taking her mother to the train station so her mother could board for the city to employ a solicitor to handle her affairs. Yes, the solicitor from the same firm who informed you of Julia's assets to be frozen when listed as a missing person. Now Jenna will finally know the solicitor's name. Talk about clever, Julia Temple was meticulous!"

Constable Jenkins raised an eyebrow. "My goodness, such great news. However, someone won't think so! One Richard Temple!"

"Exactly!" said Jack as he eyed the Constable seriously. "Hence the urgency to go into the city today. It is vital I get to speak to the solicitor so, if we locate the post-box we'll ring for an appointment. I also want to stress the same issues with you sir! I can't afford at this stage of our investigation for anything to rock the boat to scare our suspects off and that could definitely happen if Julia Temple's status suddenly changes from being a missing person's case, to a murder investigation, and that would only come from you sir if you send out updated information! Then all hell will break loose! So, I am asking you to please to hold off, sir. A big ask, but a vital one!"

Constable Jenkins rubbed his chin as he realized he had almost done that last night. "Hmm! Detective, you have only just caught me in time, one more day it would have been done. But rest assured I have your back, Jack. We are in this together, and we can't afford a solicitor breathing down our necks, wanting people evicted from 'Oceanview' who are prime suspects, if he gets a letter of a murder investigation. No, that won't be happening on my watch!"

Jack smiled. "I knew you would say that, thank you, sir! I only hope that the solicitor is as understanding. Now, let us sit down. I need some important changes made today, sir, so make a list!"

Constable Jenkins grabbed a pen and paper "Fire away!"

"Firstly, cancel the house search for today, but have two officers staying there to guard entrances. Richard and Miranda may use the kitchen if accompanied by an officer. Tell him searches will resume tomorrow. If he kicks up a ruckus at all just throw him in the clink!"

Constable Jenkins chuckled. "That, I'd love to do Jack!"

Jack chuckled too. "Ok next! Cancel the stables search, but keep one officer on watch. Don't get Pablo in today, rather inform him you will drive him in for a second interview with me at the stables, 8.00am sharp and use your warrant to find another shoe he wears?"

"On the subject of shoes. I can't stress enough the importance of this! Get an officer to take these shoes down to the beach, and run some tests for me! He handed the Constable the shoes, and told him what he wanted. Now to the beach search! Continue it today if you can access the surf club vehicle, and trailer you need, but tell the officers only to get the rubble out today! Once they get to another opening or gap stop all work as I want to inspect that tomorrow. Also, it's a go ahead with the search at Miranda Delvin's house! Tell everyone it is all hands to be on deck at 6.30 am for a briefing in the morning. Also, have the projector and slides set up ready for me, sir. I'll be here at 6am. Is that satisfactory for you Constable?"

"Constable Jenkins smiled. "It sure is Detective. It is a pleasure to see how you work. A man on a mission so to speak!" he offered.

"Thank you, sir. Now, I must move, and go to collect Jenna on-route for the city. Jenna is packing us a bag to stay overnight, we'll leave well before daybreak. Jack stood, and they shook hands."

"Good luck, Detective, have a safe journey. See you at 6.00am!"

"That you will, sir!" replied Jack. He turned to leave and quickly disappeared through the door out of sight, to walk down the hall.

Jenna was ready to leave when Jack pulled into their carpark so, she quickly got in the front seat beside him. She smiled, and spoke.

"Cross fingers it goes smoothly today, Jack. I have everything we need. I am rather excited about what we'll be doing in the city!"

"Actually, me too. My only concern, your mother's solicitor! By rights he should get notification of your mother's change in status from missing person to murdered but the Constable is holding off!"

Jack looked straight at Jenna just to stress a point. "You do know, Jenna that if we get an appointment to meet him today, firstly you will need your proof of identity when you introduce yourself, so he will know who you are, and introduce me as your husband to start. Then it will be entirely up to you Jenna, to tell him your story about being in a coma, then losing your memory. Explain what happened to you at 'Oceanview.' How your memory was restored to recall a scene on the sand of your mother's dead mutilated body! You were witness to that so, your mother was not missing, but murdered!"

"So, you must officially inform him that at this time a murder investigation is in process at 'Oceanview!' Can you do that?"

Jenna stared across at him. "Are you quite sure I have to do that, Jack, couldn't you explain it to him? You are so much better at it!"

" No, not a good idea, Jenna! You must think of it like this now. Once you are introduced to the solicitor, he will immediately know that his job is almost done. All that will remain, is for him to transfer everything over to you, and abide by your mother's request in her will, and that is to vacate your father, and Missus Miranda Delvin from 'Oceanview,' which we don't want to happen at this particular time until the case is complete. So, Jenna, I suggest you stand firm, take the upper hand against him, or he will try and overrule you."

"Remember, you must take control in place of your mother. You will be the client who gives him all instructions from now on. Then say, I am the Homicide Detective on the case. I'll take it from there!"

Jenna smiled, then she replied. "Now that you have explained it in detail to me, Jack. I know I will be confident doing it your way."

"Thanks, Jenna. I knew you would be ok, but we must do things correctly so there is no mis-understanding between both parties. I just hope we can find that post-box!" Jack chuckled.

"Oh, it won't be a problem, Jack. I have been there with mother."

"Well! That's great news, so we'll sit back to enjoy the trip now!"

Richard Temple was livid, and stormed into the room. His face reddened as he cursed. "Damn it all, Miranda! I just arrived home, and some officer escorted me to the door. This morning, they wanted to escort me to the kitchen just to get a coffee so, I didn't bother, and got one at work. Now we have a problem about dinner. There is no staff to cook or serve, and I sure as hell aren't doing it!"

"Hello to you too Richard! It seems to me that lately you're doing more cursing than anything else. Don't I deserve any attention?"

Richard looked at her, and his heart melted. "Damn it, Miranda, but I am so sorry. I guess things are getting on top of me. What with the intense interviews and searches and now we are under guard. I don't like it! He moved towards her, took her in his arms and kissed her longingly. Hello, my love and please forgive me?"

Miranda leaned backwards and her eyes seemed glazed over as she spoke. "Hmm! That is better Mister Temple, however I haven't had it so easy either. Quite frankly, I am still trying to recover from my interview with Detective Rickard. I don't usually get fazed by much, but his line of questioning got under my skin. Just between you and I, Richard Temple, I can tell you I was a little rattled!"

Richard stared into her beautiful eyes. "I would like to say you will get over it, but in all honesty, I must say that I also was taken off-guard by his way of questioning, but realistically so, to the point where I said things I shouldn't have. He is just so damn matter-of-fact, and seems to refer to other subjects that have no relevance just to side-track you. So yes, he does tend to have a way to confuse the mind. How did he get to be so smart? I hate to admit it, but he is!"

Miranda chuckled. "Ah! Finally, we agree on something Mister Temple, how grand. However, I must say this Homicide Detective certainly does merit the tag he boasts. A force to be reckoned with, I fear, but I will have you know it is not only you getting into strife with him, Richard, as Detective Rickard plans to search my house!"

That floored Richard. "Your house? Damn his cheek, he has his feelers out everywhere. What interest would he have in searching your house, how would that benefit him. So, what are his terms, do you meet there, or how does he get access to your property?"

Miranda looked away for a second to compose herself, then she automatically replied. "Well! It was at my interview with him that he told me not to go out there, and demanded my house keys. So, I had to hand them over to him, I believe officers will be there today!"

"Damn it all, get ready to go out Miranda. I have had enough of being here." then as an after-thought, he asked. "What of the staff, Miranda? Have you seen any of them, or heard anything?"

Miranda looked up at him. "I haven't seen any of them, as they are not allowed at 'Oceanview' or come to work here, but I did have a phone-call from Melita just a while ago. I had given her my mobile number ages ago luckily so she could call me any time about our washing and cleaning our rooms, but she sounded very agitated!"

"Agitated, what about? Is everyone going crazy?"

"As she spoke on the phone, her voice quivered. I knew she was shaken about something. It was then she told me they had a visit from Senior Constable Jenkins at the police station, who drove out to speak to Pablo to inform him to be ready to be picked up early tomorrow morning by the Constable himself as he was being called back for a second interview, but at the stables with you know who! The Constable also had a warrant for a further search of the house!"

"Quite frankly, that worries me! Out of everyone at 'Oceanview' who is a suspect in this case, why pick on Pablo?" she asked. "Pablo knows too much and that is a concern if he doesn't shut his mouth!"

"That does it, Miranda! Let us get out of here right now!" replied Richard. "We need to talk privately, and I'll have to get the number off you to call Melita and Pablo Sanchez. Someone has to be abrupt with them, and set them straight. I'm guessing that has to be me!"

It was a quick trip into the City, no unnecessary stops, and traffic was minimal as Jack drove towards Central Station.

Jenna couldn't sit still on the seat beside him. So much depended on the outcome of today, and quite frankly she was concerned. In despair she took a quick glance towards Jack and was just about to speak when he placed his hand over hers, and squeezed.

He knew how nervous she must be, and he tried to reassure her.

"Try to calm yourself Jenna, and believe that by the end of this day everything will be alright. You will see, just have faith!"

Jenna attempted to smile but her lips were instead rather twisted as she replied. "I am trying my hardest to, Jack, but the closer we get to a result, the worse I am becoming. My nerves are so bad!"

"Well! I would suggest, rather than dwell on the outcome here, just think of the ordeal you have been through over the years, not to mention the pain, just to get to this point. That should cure any nerves. You've been through the worst, and the best is yet to come!"

Immediately Jenna smiled as she looked at him to reply. "I thank God every day for you Jack Rickard, you are my sounding board, my rock! You seem to have all the answers to my many questions. I am so lucky to have you in my life again. I love you so very much!"

Jack looked across at her, then he smiled. "I also love you Missus Jenna Rickard. I have done all my life so, to actually find you again, and make you my wife has made me the happiest man. Now, let's not dwell on the negatives. See that tunnel just up ahead, that is our pathway to positivity. It is from that moment on that many things will change dramatically to alter our lives and our future. You must believe that. It is our destiny, Jenna, and together we will succeed!"

Jenna was in awe of his way of thinking. It re-assured her, and she replied. "Guess I just needed reminding Detective Rickard so, thank you for the insight. I am excited as your words soothe me!"

"Ah, we have an agreement. Good, I see the exit to the car-park."

Traffic seemed to emerge from everywhere once they exited the tunnel and the City Central Station car-park was no exception when they entered, but Jack calmly persevered until he had maneuvered the car around towards the lifts, and began looking for a car-park.

"Keep an eye out for a car-park not too far from the lifts, Jenna. I'll just keep going around. Wow, how lucky. I am sure that's a park in the next row. Can you see it better than me, Jenna?"

Jenna strained her neck to look, and exclaimed. I think you may be correct. Right next to that red car. Is that where you are looking?"

"Yep, that's it, well that wasn't so difficult after all." he chuckled.

Jack parked the car and they took the lift up to the ground level and were overwhelmed instantly by the hustle and bustle of the city and Grand Central Station as they walked out into the throng.

"What now, Jenna?" Jack asked. "I have been to Central Station many times but wasn't exactly looking for post boxes. Do you have any ideas which way to go, if not we could be looking for hours."

Jenna laughed. "Well luckily Jack, when I was much younger, I came here with my mother a few times. In those days she used to have a personal post-box for when she stayed in the city sometimes. So yes, I know the way. We need to take the escalator up to the next level, and we will find them down a laneway just on the right."

Jack stared at her strangely. "You do realize you're talking about your childhood, Jenna? So, am I wrong to suggest this, or does that mean your memory is totally restored?" he queried.

Jenna smiled. "I do think so Jack. I can recall things back to when I was very small and of you and I as kids. It's a great feeling, as now I have a sense of belonging by knowing my past, and who I am!"

Jack put an arm around her. "You don't know how that sounds to me Jenna. I am so happy for you. You see we have such special memories, and it would be a shame if that was taken from you."

"Rest assured Jack. I remember it all and I am thankful for that!"

Rows and rows of post-boxes lined the walls of the laneway and Jenna stepped forward eagerly to search for number 16. She left Jack behind as she hurried along and was almost at the middle of a row when suddenly she stopped. "Come quickly, Jack!" she called.

She dug deeply down into the pocket of her handbag where she kept the important key, and said a silent prayer that it would open the box as she inserted it into the slot. Her joy was expressed with a squeal as she turned the key, and she was staring at the open box.

"It opened, Jack! It actually opened, and there are lots of folders here, help me!" she cried as she started passing them out to Jack.

He struggled to contain them in his arms but then noticed Jenna had no interest in them, discarding them one by one, and continued looking. "What are you doing, Jenna, why not open some of these?"

"Something is missing, the dates are wrong, but there are more!"

Jack was puzzled. "What is it you are looking for, Jenna?"

"A letter penned to me by the solicitor when I turned eighteen!"

"How would you know it is here, as that was some time ago?"

Jenna looked at him. My mother told me that her solicitor would pen a letter to me to this post-box when I turned eighteen simply to inform me that I am the new owner of the property 'Oceanview.' It is how mother wanted it, Jack, and she planned it meticulously so I would have no problems concerning ownership, because she knew father would fight any will, and her bank was to be notified by the solicitor as well. The letter will be old, as it would have been sent after my birthday that's why I'm looking for old post-dated letters."

Jack just gaped until he was able to reply. "You had ownership of 'Oceanview' from the age of eighteen, and no-one knew?"

"Pretty much!" offered Jenna matter-of-factly. "An appropriate quote from mother, is." Jenna laughed. *I never joke about money or of my estate Jenna!* she told me. "Oh! Look Jack!" she exclaimed, as she fingered a letter. "This is it, the date fits. I think it is the letter, Jack!"

Eagerly, Jenna opened the envelope, and when she saw the logo on the letterhead of the letter, she gasped. "Yes, this is the firm, Jack, and her eyes roamed to the signature. This letter was penned by a solicitor in that firm. One, Miles Cartright! He can only be mother's trustworthy city solicitor, and she began to read it out loud.

"It is just as mother said it would be. One of those folders should contain a copy of her new will, and he will have the original. Also, a copy of the deeds to the house that he will be holding for me!"

She passed the letter to Jack and he scanned the page. "This will save a lot of hassles getting an appointment with him, Jenna as your date to meet him is long overdue. This letter is your calling card! When you phone to ask for an urgent appointment today, use it!"

Jenna smiled. "I most certainly will, Jack, now I have this letter! On another note, could we go somewhere private to have breakfast. I am starving! Besides I need fuel for the fire before I call his office!"

Jack chuckled. "A good idea, Jenna now that you mentioned it, we haven't eaten all trip so I too will enjoy breakfast, and I know just the place so, let's go back to the car. I will call Detective Woods once you get an appointment time set, just to see if he is free at any time today to meet up with us. I like how things are shaping up."

"I do too, Jack. This trip has been really worthwhile so far."

It was a dimly lit tavern he took her to, and he selected the alcove seats off the back wall in the corner, and instantly a waiter came to serve them. Jack ordered drinks, and asked for a menu.

"Hmm! Cozy." offered Jenna with a smile. "But drinks, Jack?"

"Just the one, Jenna to soothe us. I'll order coffee with our meal."

"You're the boss, Mister Homicide Detective." she chuckled.

Jack grinned at her. "Only if you say so my love." he said. "Oh, by the way, you probably didn't take any notice where I parked out back but there are motel rooms upstairs if you wanted to stay here the night? It would save a lot of travelling around the city by car!"

Jenna couldn't believe things were going so smoothly. "Exactly, Jack. Staying here will just be perfect. We could use the room as a base, and catch a cab to wherever we need to go. By the look of this menu." she said, looking it over. "They have more than enough to cater for our meal requirements, should we wish to eat here!"

"Yep, I agree so, a good idea."

They talked small talk during breakfast. Nothing of the case, or of their hunt for the key and postbox. Simply, both of them enjoying the subdued atmosphere to experience their own thoughts.

Jack was first to break the spell. "If you are ready, Jenna. There is a private room down the aisle where you could make your phone call from, and I will secure us a motel room, and settle the bill!"

Jenna smiled at him as she stood. "Wish me luck!"

"You won't need luck my love, just confidence in your ability to get the job done. I will come down there when I am finished here!"

"I wish I had the same faith you have in me, Jack. I'm nervous."

"You will be fine. You are a Rickard!" he smiled at her.

Jenna giggled. "That I am Detective." she said and left him there.

Jack shook his head as he watched her walk down the aisle. *God damn me, but she doesn't realize her own capabilities.* She has far more resilience than me, is so much more determined than me, but still doesn't realize her full potential. *It may have something to do with her being in charge as a child,* she doesn't see challenges, *just does the job.*

He stood up and walked over to the counter to make his room booking and settle his account. *Hmm, maybe I should talk to her about that another time when things settle down. Jenna really needs to know.*

He followed the path she took down the aisle, absently thinking about her. He entered the private room just as she was saying thank you then ended the call. She looked up, caught his eye, and grinned.

"Piece of cake!" she said, and chuckled.

Jack laughed at her. *He really didn't expect otherwise.*

They sat together in a booth and Jenna relayed her conversation.

"I think I must have opened a pandora's box, because as soon as I mentioned mother's name, and mine, there was much excitement in their office, and the solicitor himself took over the call, Jack!"

"Goodness, well done Jenna."

She looked directly at Jack as she spoke. "Apparently everyone was on alert to notify him if I called, even if it has been some time happening. You see Jack, mister Miles Cartright is not any ordinary solicitor. He is mother's best friend's grandson, specifically selected to do this job for mother years before. Which is why she trusted him explicitly as his grandmother made the arrangements for them to meet. He is a very pleasant person to talk to, he was so relieved I contacted him. We have an appointment to meet at 11.30am today."

"Excellent Jenna. I will just contact Detective Woods, and see if he can meet up this afternoon? Then he had a thought, and asked.

"Did you tell the solicitor about your mother, Jenna?"

"No, Jack I couldn't, not over the phone. I will tell him later."

"Good idea. Now, just give me a second and I'll make my call."

Jenna was doing some research on her phone when he returned.

"How did the call go, Jack. Did you talk to him at all" she asked.

"Yep, but today is not a good day for him, and tonight he has to attend a dinner. Best he could do was meet us later for drinks."

"Oh, that might suit us better, Jack. Where are we meeting him?"

"I told him to come here, seeing we are staying here. I guess it is as convenient a place to get to as any. Now, I will just order a cab to pick us up. What area is the place we are going to, Jenna?"

"Right in the heart of the city. I think it is the main street. Here is the letter with the address, do you know it, Jack?"

Jack took the letter and glanced at it. "Yes, I have been there. That section of the main street is a thoroughfare. Lots of tall skyscrapers and shopping malls." he stood. "I'll order that cab now."

"Cartright and Co Solicitors the red-lettered sign read on the huge glassed building. Jack and Jenna stood at the entrance below of the double-doored entrance feeling dwarfed by its presence as they strained their necks to look up at it.

"Hmm! I smell money, Jenna. If the building is any indication, then it is a very successful practice, no doubt."

Jenna nodded. "I agree, Jack. It is certainly impressive. Let's go."

They both pushed on the revolving doors, and walked through together into the entrance, then hand-in-hand across the tiled area towards the lifts. There, Jack looked at a placard on the wall listing all the partners of the firm. He smiled at Jenna as his finger rested on one name. "Miles Cartright. Level 7 Room 1. Top floor, no less!"

Jenna smiled at Jack. "He might be the senior shareholder in the company, the building does bear his name after all."

"Yep, it looks like it." said Jack, as he pressed the button for the lift. When they stepped inside, he spoke. "Just remember our talk, Jenna. You are the boss, so take control or he may try to!"

"Something tells me that is not going to happen, Jack. Having learnt that he is the grandson of mother's oldest friend, then I am more inclined to believe he will only be too pleased to help us."

"Yeah, I see your point, but just be wary. You've got this, Jenna!"

Jenna smiled at him just as the lift reached level 7 so, she reached over to kiss his cheek. I shall be fine, thank you dear husband."

Jack pulled her closer to press his lips on hers just as the doors opened. They parted with a chuckle, and then stepped into the hall.

"There you go, Jenna. Room 1 Miles Cartright, and it's 11.10am!"

"Perfect timing." commented Jenna. Then she made her way to the reception desk to check in, and Jack sat in a chair to wait for her.

Jack noticed the receptionist make a call when Jenna left her, and Jenna had no sooner sat down when the door to Miles Cartright's room opened, and a young man was striding out towards them.

Jenna stared at him. He was tall, and immaculately dressed but seemed to be quite muscular to fill out his fine suit as if he worked out. He was younger than she imagined, his jet-black hair seemed to imitate the colour of his highly polished black shoes then her eyes shifted to his face. He wore a huge grin spreading across his almost, baby face, his hand was outstretched as he stood before her, and Jenna looked up into the softest grey eyes she had ever seen.

"Jenna, Jenna Temple from 'Oceanview' at Blue Bay? Allow me to introduce myself. I am Miles Cartright, we spoke on the phone. I can see you are definitely Julia Temple's daughter, Jenna! You bear a huge resemblance to her besides, my mother has photos of you as a child, the years have treated you well Jenna now you are older."

Jenna smiled as she looked up at him to reply. "Good morning, mister Cartright, and thank you. Yes, I am Jenna Temple. Though I am recently married so I am now Jenna Rickard and I am so pleased to finally meet you. This is my husband, Jack Rickard."

Jack stood, and they all shook hands.

"Come, come to my room please Jenna, and Jack. We have much to discuss, and he ushered Jenna across the floor, then opened the door to his rooms. Take the seats up close to my desk please people, and Jenna, no more Mister Cartright. Please call me Miles!"

Jenna smiled at him. He was doing all he could to make her feel welcome so she began to relax, and spoke. "As you wish, Miles!"

He looked at them both before he spoke. "As you know Jenna, I am Ethel Cartright's grandson as I briefly explained on the phone. However, her relationship with your mother goes back many years to their youth. They have always been great friends and have kept in touch even though your mother was at Blue Bay. She introduced me to your mother who had great concerns for her safety so many years ago and grandmother was very concerned to hear about your mother's disappearance. She still lives, but she is a little frail now!"

Jenna squirmed in her chair. *Here it comes!* she thought, as she felt Jack squeeze her hand in reassurance, so she looked at Miles and smiled before she spoke. "Miles, I am so very grateful to have the opportunity to discuss my mother's misfortune with someone who actually knew her and your grandmother knew her as a friend. That pleases me, and I would like to visit her one day if possible."

"Definitely, Jenna. I am certain she would love to see you. I shall give you her details before you leave so you can contact her some time. However, like me, we would both like to hear any updates on the whereabouts of your mother as it has been some time now. Julia Temple gave me strict instructions should anything happen to her, and I have followed them religiously. So, I consider my job almost done. She has paid me generously to make sure everything goes smoothly for your take-over at 'Oceanview,' and the property was signed over to you when you turned eighteen. I did try to contact you, but you seem to have disappeared. So, you will find copies of all the paperwork concerning her will, the ownership transfer of 'Oceanview' into your name, all done by me and sent addressed to you at Post Box number 16 in Central Station. I have a key for you."

"There are just two more orders I must complete. One is to clear all trust funds with the bank, and two. Remove two people from 'Oceanview.' Your father Richard Temple and Miranda Delvin. I do hope it doesn't cause you any stress but it is an order. Your mother was quite adamant about this, and it is stated in her will, Jenna!"

Jenna couldn't help but feel the irony of it, that Miles had a key to Post Box 16, when she had just been through hell to find it. She could feel the tears fill her eyes, and Jenna could barely see as she tried to focus on Miles's face to thank him. "I am so sorry, Miles but this is very difficult for me. I have the worst news to tell you, but to do that I must first tell you what happened to me, where I've been. Would you mind bearing with me for a short time while I explain?"

Miles stared at her, and couldn't help but wonder what could be so bad, but he answered. "Of course, Jenna, you go right ahead."

Jenna gulped, and began by telling him about the attack on her down on the beach at 'Oceanview,' the repercussions that caused her to end up in a coma, and her length of time spent in hospitals.

"Oh, you poor girl. I had no idea. I am so sorry for going on!"

Jenna stopped him curtly with a hand. "You weren't to know, Miles, how could you? Only now, I have the worst part to tell you about mother and what really happened to her. You see, I now have proof of that since returning to 'Oceanview.' Because it was there, I experienced a devastating mental breakdown which resulted in my memory returning to me in an overload." So, she explained how it suddenly happened to her. The gruesome discovery as the visions were revealed to her, and what she witnessed on the beach below of her attack, and of her murdered mother with a mutilated body.

Miles stood. "My god, Jenna that is sad, devastating news. Are you sure about this. I mean good god, what do your doctor's say?"

"Well, they expected it to happen at some time, so they were not concerned but relieved that finally I had some answers to my life. Admittedly, to see my mother like that was not what I expected to go home to. But yes, real enough to warrant a Homicide Detective!"

"Homicide! A murder case then? Julia Temple was murdered then, not a missing person? My god I haven't been notified by the police. This changes things. I have my orders from Missus Temple."

Jenna tried by telling him she would be taking over her mother's interests, and would take on his employ for any further work, but then she broke down and began sobbing, deep sobs from the heart, and Jack put an arm around her. He looked sadly at Miles Cartright, and asked. "Would you mind if I took over now Miles? I think that Jenna has had enough now. I am the acting Homicide Detective on the Julia Temple case. We are looking at murder of the worst kind!"

Miles looked every bit as devastated as Jenna, but he summoned a reply. "Yes, yes of course Detective, do carry on!"

"Very well!" replied Jack. "I do know you have obligations to Julia Temple, Miles. But considering the circumstances, I think it is best you cut all ties, and work with Jenna from now on. You have done the job Julia asked you to do with an exemption of vacating 'Oceanview.' On that subject, I would like to formally apologize to you on behalf of Senior Constable Jenkins for not notifying you of the murder status. My fault actually. I asked him to hold off because I have many suspects in that household, and to remove them at this vital time could jeopardize my chances of success in the case. So, I do hope you will agree with me, and hold off also, as it is in the best interest of solving Julia Temple's murder. What do you say Miles?"

Miles looked at Jack. All he saw was a dedicated Detective trying his best to solve the murder of his grandmother's best friend.

"Yes, of course I have your back Detective. Please bring them to justice. I'll wait further instructions from Jenna. Is that ok, Jenna?"

Jenna smiled for the first time as she looked at him. "Thank you so much Miles. Mother would have been proud of you!"

"Thanks Jenna! I guess you have a deal, Detective!" he added.

Jack also smiled for the first time. They had jumped one hurdle.

"You have no idea what this means to both of us, Miles. I am so close to solving this case, I can smell it. Just to have your support means a lot to us. Rest assured that you will have many business dealings with Jenna in the future. Like mother, like daughter you know, and Jenna will turn to you first when she is in need of your services, or even as just a friend to chat with. I know she will visit your grandmother, so maybe you could join us at her home when we arrange it. That will give us a chance to keep you up to date!" Miles smiled. "Thanks Jack." he said, as he put a hand on Jenna's shoulder, then spoke softly to her. My condolences to you Jenna!"

"Your mother was a great lady. She will be sadly missed, but my grandmother will be heartbroken when I break the news to her as your mother was a very dear friend to her. So, Jenna Rickard, if you ever need a friend at any time, I am here!" he said sincerely.

Jenna looked up at him as the tears flooded her eyes. Quickly, she attempted to dab her face with a handkerchief as she replied. "I don't have many friends, Miles. I have been out of circulation for so long now, but I would like that very much. I will be in touch, and Miles, thank you very much for being so understanding, and tell your grandmother I will contact her when this case is over."

"I will, Jenna. I will tell my secretary to give you her details on the way out. If you wait out there, I will get you all your paperwork. Deeds to 'Oceanview' in your name and the original current will of your mother's. Thank you both for coming in to meet with me. It was a pleasure to meet you Detective Rickard, and good luck with the case. I take it you will keep me informed?" he asked.

They all stood, and shook hands. "Definitely, Miles. I must thank you for working with us. I am pleased we met! We will be in touch. I am sure Jenna will have instructions for you in the near future."

Miles smiled. "Of that I am sure, and quite frankly, I can't wait to work with her, the apple does not fall far from the tree, Jack." he chuckled and faced Jenna. "You are much like your mother, Jenna."

Jenna smiled. "Thank you, Miles. I guess she has taught me a lot.

Miles walked with them to the door. "Best of luck, Jenna and be strong. That is what your mother would expect you know."

Jenna smiled. "Of that I am quite sure Miles, thank you!" They sat waiting in reception while Mile's secretary checked her files to pluck one out, and walked over to hand Jenna a note bearing Ethel Cartright's address, and contact details. Jenna was thanking her as Miles breezed through the door. "Here you go Jenna, all signed and sealed. All your existing assets, and you are a land owner, no less!"

In the cab on the way back to the motel, Jenna sat very quietly. Her thoughts roamed to her mother. Her misgivings flooded to the forefront of her mind. *Oh, my, how I wish I could have helped her.* Jenna's heart cried out for help. *I didn't realize the seriousness of it.*

She started sobbing softly, and tears rolled down her cheeks.

Jack pulled her into his arms. "What is it, Jenna? I thought you would be happy after that visit. So, what are you upset about?"

"Oh Jack!" she sobbed. "I just can't get it out of my mind. I keep going back to the morning in mother's room when we were having that discussion. I really didn't take her seriously Jack. Why didn't I, why?" she wailed. "I am such a dreadful daughter for not listening to her, as she was quite adamant that someone wanted to kill her!"

"Jenna, that is not true, you are not so, please don't say that! You cannot blame yourself, and you must realize that fate has a way of playing out regardless of our input. Please listen to me, and put it behind you now, as there was nothing you could have done. Will you do that for me, and focus on our future?" he lifted her chin with a finger and their eyes locked as he stared deep into her misty eyes.

"Oh, Jack. I am so sorry. I guess you are right, and I will get over this feeling in time. I just feel so sad, but I will focus on our future!"

He smiled. "Good girl. Now what say you freshen up for our visitor when we get back to the motel as he can't be far away!"

Jenna met Jack in the lounge. She had changed, applied a little make-up, and her face beamed as she noticed the big man walk in. She was excited to meet up with him, and squeezed Jack's hand.

Homicide Detective Jeremy Woods appeared as if he owned the place as he weaved a path towards them, and pulled out a chair. He pecked Jenna's cheek. "Greetings, Jenna!" he stated, as he extended his hand to Jack, and his voice boomed. "So great to see you both!"

"So good to see you again Detective Woods." replied Jenna, and Jack added. "It's great to see you sir, so pleased you could meet us!"

"Wouldn't have missed it for the world. I must say that you both look well! So, tell me all now. How is this case coming along Jack, and pray tell, when do I get you back?" he chuckled. "The team are anxious to swap notes with you, any chance you can call in?"

Jack grinned. "Not this time, sir. I hope my temp is doing, ok?"

"I guess you could say he is keeping his head above water!"

"I see, but come tomorrow at first light, we are out of here! We had a rush trip to the city to find a key that Jenna's mother left for her, so we could meet up with her mother's solicitor, and we had a meeting this morning, all is good there. Long story though so, I will have to elaborate more next time. Jenna has been helping me with the investigation, and her memory recall has shed a new light on a lot of things so, I am at the crucial stage of my investigations, and have given specific instructions to the team. I am hoping to obtain big results when we get back in the morning. So, maybe in another week, or two even, would tie it all up I'm hoping, sir!" offered jack.

"Hmm! So soon. You have been busy Detective, but remember this is the nitty, gritty part, Jack so, don't forget the golden rule!"

Jack grinned. "How could I sir, when you always remind me, and I know what it is! To never forget to expect the unexpected sir!"

Homicide Detective Jeremy Woods chuckled at Jack's statement, and he looked at Jenna as he spoke. "You do see what an excellent student I had, Jenna? He never forgets anything I say! Even to this day he remembers lessons and tutoring I gave him from way back! I'm so pleased you are getting involved and that you have regained all your memory. That has got to be the biggest outcome to date."

Jenna smiled. "It certainly is Detective Woods, but working with Jack, I can see exactly what you mean. He has learnt so much from you, and his study, I can almost sense a different person. He has a certain way of thinking that is beyond me. I am so proud of him!"

"Ah, Jenna, and so am I. That is a gift that not many possess!"

Jack was up at 3am. He didn't sleep too well as the excitement, and questions filled his head, he just had to get on the road. So, he made them some coffee, then woke Jenna. "Jenna, wake up now love. We have to get going, and get out of the city before the peak hour. Drink your coffee and we will stop somewhere for breakfast."

Jenna stirred. She felt she hadn't had enough sleep, as they had talked for ages with the Detective the night before, and then Jack, and herself had sat outside and re-capped the events of the day. She swung her legs off the bed and stretched. "On my way, Detective." she remarked as she headed to the bathroom and then returned to sip the scolding coffee. "It's still dark outside." she said to Jack.

"I know. I couldn't sleep anyway, so may as well hit the road. It is a very important day today. I am going to wait until we reach the lodge before I shower and change, and I'll be alert for the day."

"Yes, I will do the same. Jack. Just pack up, and let's go."

Getting through the city at such an early hour was a breeze so Jack stopped at the next roadhouse where they relaxed and chatted over breakfast. "So, what is your plan today, Jack?" asked Jenna.

"Ah! One important day, Jenna. A lot is relying on the tasks I set for my officers before I left. So, let's cross fingers I get some results. Having said that we have a long strenuous day in front of us all."

"I will be going into the station very early as I want to update my file. I have a new one now, a special gift from Constable Jenkins, and he has named it. 'The Rickard Files.' Embossed in gold letters too no less on the front cover. I enjoy using it as it jogs my memory."

Jenna nudged him. "Nothing is too good for the local hometown Homicide Detective Jack Rickard" she joked. "But seriously, Jack. I am so very proud of you, and it does look like it to me that everyone else is also. It was very nice of the Constable to do that for you. I am guessing he wants you to come back to 'The Bay' again soon!"

Jack chuckled. "Of that, you can be sure of, Jenna!"

Chapter Sixteen

It was just breaking day when Jack pulled into the police station. He shook his head as he noticed a light on inside. *I don't believe it!* he thought, as he walked up the steps, and unlocked the door.

But I just bet Constable Jenkins is here already.

"Hello there!" he called, as he walked briskly down the hallway towards the light and entered the room, and sure enough there he was setting up the projector. "Good morning, Constable." he said.

Constable Jenkins was startled, and looked up. Then he laughed.

"Good morning, Detective. Looks like you couldn't sleep either. I have much to relate, good news too! I expect one hell of a day!"

"Sounds promising, but first things first, sir. I want to do some work on my file, and go over a few things to refresh my memory as I have some important issues today. It won't take me long."

"All good. I am still setting up your slides for later. So, how did the trip to the city go? Any luck with the solicitor?"

Jack smiled. "We got lucky. Turns out the solicitor is a grandson of Julia Temple's oldest, and dearest friend from way back!"

eedless to say everything went smoothly. Now, Jenna is the sole owner of 'Oceanview,' and the estate! Actually, she was at age eighteen, but no one even knew! Her mother was smart hiring this particular solicitor, he knows his job well so, everything was ready for Jenna really, and all of the staff in the office were so pleased she had come forward to contact them as no one knew how to find her. Also, we met up with Detective Woods, and had a great afternoon with him. He sends his regards, and says you are due for a visit."

Jenna and I were a little frustrated by what lengths her mother went to just to protect her so, I can tell you it was a huge relief to finally find that post-box that the key fit, when we got to the city!"

Constable Jenkins laughed. "I'll bet! Julia Temple was always a clever lady. So pleased the trip was successful, now down to work!"

"Yep, I will be back in a while." replied Jack as he left the room.

It was 6.10 a.m. as Jack walked back into the boardroom. "Just bring up the shots of the prints under the steps, heading towards the beach sir! We will start there when we get back. I will go down and unlock the front door, and meet you down in your office!"

"No problem, Detective. That won't take me long!"

All Jack's team were waiting at the front door when he got there.

"Morning, guys. Come on in, then head down to The Constables office, I will meet you all there." he said, as he opened the doors.

As the officers assembled in the room, Jack looked around at the beaming faces. *Hmm! Am I to assume that there are good tidings?* He purposely waited until Constable Jenkins joined them, and then he spoke. "First of all, I want to thank each, and every one of you for the input you have had on this case. I know I set hard tasks for you while I was absent, I am just hoping some of it bears fruit. Having said that, I would like to advise you all that my rush trip to the city with Jenna was a huge success, and assets accumulated for the case. We caught up with Detective Woods too, so he sends his regards!"

They all clapped, a couple of cheers, and grins from ear to ear.

"Thank you, men!" said Jack. "Now down to business so, who would like to report first?" and one hand shot up quickly. "Me! Ben Jeffries sir, and my partner John Firth!" offered the officer, and they stepped forward. "We had the task of searching Miranda Delvin's house. There was nothing that you were interested in there, and we searched it thoroughly. However, I must say sir that you hit the nail on the head when you adopted the idea of looking for surveillance cameras. We found four external cameras, Detective. We also found the computer that operated them, and were able to view the tapes. You won't believe this, sir but we have convicting evidence, a huge find. Shall I set it up for you on the computer so you can view it?"

Jack stared at the young officer. "You bet, officer Jefferies, thank you both for your work. Good job. Let's all take a look at this first!"

They lined up behind officer Jefferies, and watched as the eight shots came up side by side. "I've set it up to take step by step shots of the scene on the tapes, sir, but there is more if you require them."

"Excellent work Ben. Now walk me through what you see!'

"Thank you, Detective." said Ben proudly. "As you can see, the first take is of Miranda Delvin leaving the house by the front door."

"One moment officer Jefferies. I need the date and time?" Jack said, as he pulled his notebook and pen out of his pocket.

"Easily done, sir. The date is on the top of the screen and the time also. I have checked with Constable Jenkins and it is the day before George Delvin's untimely accident that caused his death!"

Jack's forehead creased until it was a deep frown, then his eyes focused. "Great work guys, interesting, but the next shot please?"

"It gets more interesting Detective, now you see Miranda Delvin enter the garage. Take notice of what she's holding in her hand!"

"I'll be damned if it isn't the special tool for cutting brake lines!"

"You got it in one Detective. Look at the next shot I'll enlarge it!"

Jack sat down, and pulled his chair close. The shots were so clear he was impressed by the quality. Then, as he watched the slow motion as Miranda Delvin lifted the bonnet of George's car, and as Ben zoomed in, Jack could clearly see Miranda use the tool to sever the brake lines. "Oh, my god!" he gasped. "This is excellent work, guys. You have both excelled here!" he turned to Constable Jenkins.

"You do know what this means Constable Jenkins?" he stated.

"I certainly do, Detective Rickard! I am just waiting for your orders. So, how do you want to do this?" he queried.

Jack thought about it first, then turned to the Constable. "This is a separate issue, so let's not confuse it with the ongoing case, even though I still think Miranda Delvin has had a hand in the demise of Julia Temple, but we can add other charges later. No Constable, we act immediately! The charge is manslaughter with definite intent to murder. George Delvin didn't run off the road from being tired, or didn't miss a turn as believed. His brakes failed because the brakes lines were cut so, eventually he had no brakes at all to stop. I believe the tapes are enough proof to put Miranda Delvin away for a long, long time, and to charge her with the murder of George Delvin!"

The Constable nodded his approval. "Precisely, Detective!"

"Good!" said Jack. "As soon as we're done with the slides in the boardroom you may take both officers, Ben Jeffries, and John Firth with you to 'Oceanview' to make the arrest., Constable Jenkins!"

"As you wish Detective Rickard." answered the Constable.

Jack acknowledged both officers. "You men have done your job, and a good one I might add, so wait here for Constable Jenkins!"

"Yes sir, Detective Rickard, thank you sir!" they each replied.

Now he looked at the rest of his team, and spoke. "Now another important issue gentlemen. The Dunes, who had that task today?"

Two officers stepped forward. "Officer Tom Hurley and Officer Jim Pitt." said Tom. We also had a huge breakthrough Detective!"

"With the help of Constable Jenkins securing all the equipment needed, we found it easy to remove all the rubble, and chip away the existing sandstone, then take it away. That's when we realized your hunch was correct Detective, for at the back there was a small entrance, an opening, or old cave even, if you like. We were able to fit through it, and we could see all the ground had been dug up in there. What we need to do now, is find out why? That would mean digging up the whole floor area in that entrance Detective!"

Jack smiled. *Hmm! So, bitter-sweet!* he thought to himself, then he grinned broadly, and spoke to the officers. "That is exactly why we are here men. Great work, both of you so, no need to wait. Go back down to the beach, and get the job done. If there are any findings, I will be at the stables at 'Oceanview' at 8.00am. We have a search on there and I have an interview, so, please bring any updates over to me there as soon as you can. So, off you both go, and good luck!"

"Yes, sir Detective!" they both replied in unison, then turned on their heels, and headed straight towards the door.

Jack watched them leave. "You have excellent officers Constable Jenkins. Now, whilst on the subject of the stables. Would you collect Pablo Sanchez for his interview after the residence is searched, and have two men ready to search the stables. We will finish here soon!"

"I'm way ahead of you for once Detective Rickard! I've already decided to do that sir, and two officers are out there!" he chuckled.

Jack smirked at him, and chuckled. *Cheeky Devil.* he thought, but said instead. "I would expect no less from you Constable Jenkins!"

All the men had a smile, or added their laugh to the comradery.

"Ok, all jokes aside now guys! I need to view results of the shoes taken from Richard Temple's residence? An older pair of loafers!"

"Well, it was me sir, officer Jim Evans." he took a step forward. "I used both shoes to make tracks, then took close-up pics, and they were clear, so I tagged the shoes, and prints identically!"

Jack shook his head. "You know, any one of your officers could make Detective one day sir, if you steer them in that direction!"

Constable Jenkins chuckled. "Well, you may be pleased to hear, Detective Rickard. Since your success we've begun such a program specifically for talented, up-and coming potential candidates!"

"You have?" remarked Jack in surprise. "Well done, Constable!" He eyed officer Evans. "In that case, Officer Evans. How would like to accompany me when I compare the slides in the boardroom?"

"Would I? Oh, could I Detective, how exciting? Yes, I would love to accompany you so, thank you Detective!" replied the officer. He stepped back leaving the shoes on the table, but now he grinned.

Jack scanned the room. "Now! This could be the most significant find for prints guys. If the officers in charge of boot prints from Ted and Paula Hasting's boots, could you step forward, thank you!"

"Officer Bill Canes, Detective, my partner officer Dale Hendy!" Bill said, as they stepped up to the desk to place the boots down.

"Now men. I hope you covered the boots before making tracks?"

"Definitely Detective, that was my job!" said Dale. "I used thick cling wrap, and when Bill took the shots, they came out perfect!"

Jack eyed them both. "Great choice guys! Jack lifted up the boots and could see they were tagged. "Good work, but did you label the pics you took with identical numbers as the boots? It is important!"

"Most definitely Detective. We followed all your instructions!"

"Then I thank you both. Having said that I think you both have earned to join us when we compare slides. Your thoughts on that?"

Both Officers seemed glued to the floor, but Bill focused first. "No need to think Detective Rickard, it would be an honor for us!"

Jack smiled. "In that case men, come along to the boardroom, all of you, and bring the respective boots you had, thanks again guys!"

Constable Jenkins smiled. *Typical!* "It is so like Jack Rickard to share his knowledge with them!" *Such a great Detective he's become.*

Her Mind SCREAMS MURDER

They all assembled silently in the board room, and Jack asked them to find themselves a chair while he explained the procedure.

"Firstly officers, we will be viewing slides that Constable Jenkins took at the crime scene some two years or so, ago. Long past now! These prints incorporate two different styles of shoes. One covered to hide the tread, and one not covered! One is a boot, one a loafer! Just one thing these tracks have in common is the direction they are heading! Both are under the steps, but heading towards the beach! Why? I have my own theory on that! So! Which shoe, or boot print is a match to prints you have here? Slides do not lie. Having said that I want officer Jim Evans to join me first, followed by Bill Canes, and Dale Hendy. Stand behind me all of you. I will ask questions!"

Constable Jenkins nodded to smile knowingly. *I'm so pleased they have this opportunity.* I had my own chances, but each time I was lost in the wake of Jack's brilliance. *I hope my team fare better.*

The officers seemed to float across the floor, their chests puffed out with pride. They all looked at Constable Jenkins as Jack spoke.

"If you could bring up Jim's prints first, and align them with the older prints, please Constable?"

"Doing it now Detective. I must say the pictures are so clear!"

"Excellent! Now Jim, just take a look at your photos, and tell me if they compare at all with any of the older prints, and if so. Why?"

Jim moved closer to the screen to compare the slides carefully. He took his time, then looked over to Jack, and exclaimed. "I really think the shoe-print in front of the other boot print, matches the one I tested at the beach sir, though I can't be sure. My reasoning is that, I didn't cover this shoe, it had no tread, and I believe the older print of the similar shoe was not covered either. Just a flat soled loafer!"

Jack smiled. "Jim. That is a great assumption and you are correct. We are looking at both the slides of the flat soled loafer that was not covered, and team. That loafer belongs to Richard Temple!"

Jack looked first to Constable Jenkins, and then to his officers. "You all must realize the facts don't lie. Can I safely say Richard Temple was at the scene of the crime, do we all agree on that?"

One by one the officers voiced their agreement, and Constable Jenkins replied to Jack. "You can be sure of that Detective. Brilliant work!" then addressed the men. "I must stress that particular print was only half a shoe-print when Detective Rickard first picked it up on the slides. It doesn't show anywhere else at the crime scene, only from the steps heading to the ocean! Care to elaborate, Detective?"

Jack stood to offer his opinion. "It is my belief after seeing proof, that it was Richard Temple who helped carry the missing step up the steps to put it back in place. That is why his prints leave under the steps and head towards the beach, to access the balcony steps. I ask you, could that make Richard Temple an accessory to murder?"

They all gasped at the reality of it.

Jack held up a hand. "However! Let's not get ahead of ourselves here, as our main issue is this! *Who was the murderer?* Our task is to find that out. Please, come forward Bill, and Dale! You had the task of re-creating the covered boot prints from two pair of boots. One pair are Paula Hasting's boots, the other Ted Hasting's, taken from the Hastings residence. This is most important for you to know, that the larger covered boot prints not only followed Richard Temple's prints, but were found at the crime scene, as well as the place where Jenna was attacked. But which boot? Would you both look carefully at the slides to compare your findings with the older prints, men?"

"If you would please, Constable. I would like the print following Richard Temple's first! Then the prints under the steps, and finally the crime scene, and also beside Jenna's bare footprints!" he added.

"Bringing them up now, Detective!"

"Right officers. Older prints of a covered boot, as opposed to the covered boots you took pics of. Do any pics match the older prints?"

"Let us look at the print following Richard Temple's towards the beach first, and please don't guess, this is most important!"

Both officers leaned in to look closely at both slides. *Something seems odd about that print Detective!* said Bill. *I can't be sure!* said Dale.

Jack chuckled "Hold that thought, Bill! Now look at prints of our old slides under the steps, at the murder scene, then at Jenna's side. Does anyone have similar prints. Do we have a matching boot?"

Bill looked confused as he scanned the prints. *What's bugging me?* "Mine looks similar in some shots, but *not others! Could I have a match?"*

Dale shook his head. "I don't think it's mine, sir." *I have no idea!*

"Not to worry guys, it's all a learning process. Let me enlighten you. Back to the first old slide, the print following Richard Temple. Which foot? Left or right, do you think made that print gentlemen?"

Bill was frustrated. *"Never thought of that, it could be the right foot?"*

Jack grinned. "Your thoughts, Dale?" *I definitely have no inking, sir!* stated Dale, as Bill stood bewildered, and confused.

"Ok listen up. But let me tell you, one of you has the answer. The reason you couldn't identify that print is because it was made by a right foot so, if you expected a left foot, it wouldn't be there! But you'll know the reason you could identify some of the other prints. Turn over your boots to look at the soles, and you will know why!"

Both officers gaped, but turned the boots over. At once Bill started. *Of course! the prints alternate. I was looking for the odd one, the left boot.*

"Nothing to see here, just a very thick covered sole." said Dale.

"What does that tell us, Bill? Is it why the prints looked odd?"

Bill grinned. "I'm embarrassed to say I think so, sir! Please explain!"

"You will see no markings made by a right boot-print! Where-as the left foot shows a definite roll in-ward of the boot. It is repetitive in all our print findings at the specific sites. So! Whose boot, is it?"

"God damn, I think I know. Mine has a big dent in the left sole!"

"Yes Bill! I believe you know our possible attacker, and murderer!"

Both officers just stared at Detective Jack Rickard, but it was Bill who muttered. "I don't understand your logic, Detective. Why say possible attacker, and murderer? I think you just proved whose boot was sighted under the steps and heading towards the beach, beside Jenna, and the murder site!" commented Bill in confusion.

"To me, that is a little confusing as well." remarked Dale.

Constable Jenkins looked at both his officers, and chuckled.

"That's precisely why you study to be a Detective, officers!"

"Care to elaborate, Detective?" he asked, as he eyed him.

"Well men, the law is a strange thing sometimes, and the actual proof needs to be some hard, undisputable evidence. So, to put it in perspective for you. Yes! We have real evidence, and we even know the owner of the boot who made those tracks, to be our would-be attacker, and murderer. But in a court of law, it is not enough!"

"Not enough! What more could there be, Detective?" asked Bill.

"So much more! We need actual proof of a person committing these crimes by some footage, or sighting. Photos of the murder or another source. So, you see men I am back to square one! But not to worry as I have a few tricks up my sleeve yet. I just need it to play out my way! You see officers us Detectives never give up! There is always a loop-hole, the only trick is how to find it!" he chuckled.

They all laughed, but both officers wore a frown now, as they could not see any result in the near future, and both had their own concerns as to how Detective Rickard would proceed from here. *It had been a monster of a case but now, still no end in sight!* But as they both gaped at Detective Rickard's face. *He obviously didn't think so.*

"Ok, back to the grindstone men, and thank you for your help. There were some good answers there. Now, I'd like you to get out to 'Oceanview' as soon as you can. We must get the Homestead searched, and the grounds at the stables. Just leave the inside of the stables, and the office until I am there, please if you would!"

Jack watched as they talked briefly to Constable Jenkins to get their respective orders, and then they were on their way. He turned quickly to The Constable, and beckoned to him to take a seat.

He stared into the Constables eyes. "So close, sir. So very close! Just today? So much is riding on today but if things pan out for me, we are going to turn this case on its head, sir!" he stated.

Constable Jenkins shook his head. "We are?" he queried.

Jack laughed. "Yee, have little faith my friend!"

"Ah! I have all the faith in the world in you, Detective. But me? I feel as if the boat left long ago, and I was in it!" he laughed.

Jack laughed with him. "You judge yourself too harshly, sir. You are the best off-sider I have ever had!" he stated.

"All I can say to that is. Your other off-siders must've been bad!"

They both chuckled, then Jack looked serious as he spoke. "Let's do this, sir! We are a great team. So, let's do it, and then some!"

Constable Jenkins sensed his determination as he looked at him. He could detect it in his eyes. They were so vivid, and very alert as they smoldered, and darkened to a deeper green. *He knew for sure in that instant, that Detective Jack Rickard was never going to quit.*

Jack however, was on another tack trying to put a plan together.

"What would you say if I went to pick up Pablo for his interview instead of you, sir? I think it may serve as a scare tactic, and to scare him is what I must do as I am sure I can get under his skin. Besides, you already have one important task to do first up. That is to arrest Miranda Delvin. So, are you ready to go out to 'Oceanview' sir?"

Constable Jenkins pondered on the question, but then answered.

"Firstly, Jack. I'm definitely ready to go and make the arrest. So, I'll pick up my men from my room, and we will leave. Something about that woman just didn't sit right with me, and poor old George was a good bloke. Only, I have another possibility for you to think on. I rather think it more professional if my officers collect Pablo!"

Jack looked like he was weighing up his best options and then he smiled, and spoke. "You know I think you are correct! Yep, the two officers searching can bring him! I have paperwork to do while waiting for you to come back to the station, then when you are free, we'll go to 'Oceanview' together. I may need your help anyway!"

Constable Jenkins chuckled. "I may just mark that on the wall!"

"What are you talking about?" asked Jack, but chuckled too.

"My win! My first win against you, Detective! Surely that must merit a mark on the wall! Now, what was the help you needed?"

Jack laughed. "Yeah, I guess you got me there. Now, I have been thinking that I must get all this interview taped. I was wondering if you could follow me during the interview, and record it for me?"

"That would be my pleasure, Detective. We have unexplained issues that we need answers for, and I am hoping I will hear that."

"Ah! There will be that, sir. Pablo Sanchez won't know what hit him, and by the time I am finished he will be begging to be locked up. That boy is hiding something, and I aim to find out what!"

"Well, I have seen you in some tricky situations but you always seem to pull through so, I guess I am in for a treat, Detective!"

"That you are, sir, but now it's time to do what you have to. So, good luck.!" said Jack as the Constable stood and they shook hands.

"You bet. I'll arrange for the two officers to collect your guest for maybe when we are ready to leave here later. It's just a phone call."

"Sounds perfect."

"Oh, by the way Detective?" queried Constable Jenkins when he faced Jack. "What's our plan for Richard Temple, he may be there?"

"Let that be for now sir. For a conviction, I will need just a little more, and I don't want to interfere with his movements because he may try to contact someone. Could we could bug his quarters?"

Constable Jenkins chuckled. "Yes, Detective consider it done. I must say you're pulling out all the stops, you are a cunning one!"

Constable Jenkins started to walk away, then as an afterthought, he turned to grin. "I rather think this task is to my liking, Detective. It is why I became a policeman, to see justice done. So, I love it when the law punishes criminals with just rewards, don't you Detective?"

Jack smiled at him. "I think that every time I close a case, I have been successful with, sir. There really are no words to describe that feeling, a massive sense of achievement, a fulfillment even. That is when I am proud to be a Homicide Detective, proud I achieved my dreams. So, yes. It definitely is the reason why I love acting for the law, sir!" he said. "Now get going or we will never crack this case!"

"As you so demand, Detective Sir!" then he turned, and walked briskly towards the door. One wave, and a smile, then he was gone.

Jack shook his head at the Constable's humor and he smiled. He was so very lucky to have had the privilege to first meet this officer, to have him as a boss, and his tutor. As Constable Jenkins not only shaped his career, but had become his very best friend. He walked down to his office and opened the locked cabinet, and his hand fell on the 'Rickard File.' He had so much to write in it today so, he sat eagerly at his desk and grabbed his notebook to refer to his notes.

Time passed, and he was still working when he heard the chaos down the hall. He knew what it would be when he heard the high-pitched screaming coming from the interview room. He rose to get up to peer through the windows and he could see Miranda Delvin, mouth wide open screaming all kinds of invective at the officers.

This was a side of Miranda Delvin he had not seen before. Gone was her brilliance to communicate. Her seductive, perfect image of a woman's beauty that won many hearts, and gone was her astute mannerism, her standing of how she held herself to proclaim her as untouchable, unreachable, and unpredictable. There was simply no comparison now as he stared upon her distorted face which became an ugly face in defeat as she screeched out lies trying to save herself.

Miranda and Richard had been chatting while indulging in a cup of coffee prior to Richard leaving for work, when interrupted by a loud knock on the door. "Who could that be at this hour?" she stated as she rose from the table to go and answer the door herself.

"Probably one of those damn officers with some new demand. I will be pleased when they leave here." Richard said, as he frowned. Most of their conversations these days was of what was happening at 'Oceanview,' even down on the beach. They both felt threatened and their mannerisms were defensive now towards each other, and starting to show a strain on their relationship. They were both edgy and argumentative with each other. It was all pretty much full on, all the searches, and impositions on their privacy was taking its toll.

There were so many questions, endless questions of their where- abouts, their movements until their wits were shaken. Richard was struggling with questions about Julia Temple and his daughter, Jenna Temple, now Jenna Rickard. *That name was starting to irk him, and he rued the day Jack Rickard returned to Blue Bay as a proven Homicide Detective.* But what annoyed him more so, if anything, was the simple fact… *That Homicide Detective Jack Rickard was so damn thorough at his job.*

Miranda opened the door wide, and standing there was Senior Constable Jenkins, and two of his officers. She detected a change in their demeanor, an aloofness almost and something seemed to twist her insides. A premonition maybe, but she had learned to trust her gut, and assumed at once that something was not right as she stared at their grim expressions. She immediately turned and beckoned to Richard, who rose from his seat to come and stand beside her.

"Miranda Delvin?" stated Constable Jenkins sternly.

"What is it this time, Constable?" Richard retorted loudly as he interrupted them to take over the conversation, and his face took on a viscous scowl when he fronted Constable Jenkins.

"That would be Senior Constable Jenkins to you Mister Temple!"

"I would appreciate it if you address me as such in future!"

"Whatever!" quipped Richard.

"My visit today, is to address Missus Miranda Delvin, not you. So, step aside Mister Temple, and make way to allow us to enter!" and he beckoned his officers to step forward.

"Now hang on just a minute. I haven't exactly asked you to come in!" offered Richard, getting annoyed now.

"That is irrelevant to this visit Mister Temple. Step aside please, we are all here on police business! Officer Jeffries, if you would do the honors at once!" he stated, and beckoned to his officer to enter.

Richard pushed his frame forward to block his way. "Now hold on just one minute. What honors? What the hell is going on here?"

Officer Jeffries took a step towards him to stare before speaking. "I am here to make an arrest Mister Temple! I advise you to remove yourself from my path, or I will arrest you also for interfering!"

"Missus Miranda Delvin, step forward!" urged the officer. Miranda jumped, her hands trembled as she listened to her name being called, and the knot in her gut twisted, threatening her. Then her face paled as the following words altered her life forever.

"Missus Miranda Delvin you are so charged with the murder of George Delvin. You have the right to remain silent, anything you…. Suddenly the room spun as she listened to her rights being read to her, but when she spied the hand-cuffs her eyes could barely focus any more so, she wheeled around quickly, and fled from the room.

Richard Temple's face darkened in temper as his blood rose up his neck threatening to choke him. "What is the meaning of this, are you all crazy? Murder? You have it wrong officers, it is a mistake!"

"It is no mistake Mister Temple! We hold solid evidence against Missus Miranda Delvin, and she will have her say in court! You are obstructing justice and this is a police arrest, so stand aside please!"

"Follow her Jeffries!" called Senior Constable Jenkins.

Jeffries took chase, but was quick to return saying. "She's locked herself in the bathroom, sir! What do we do now?"

Constable Jenkins looked exasperated as he replied. "Well! You break the door down and make the arrest Jeffries, and pronto too. I want this tidied up quick smart! Do I make myself clear?"

"Yes sir, right away sir!" replied officer Jeffries.

Richard stepped forward. "This is preposterous Constable! You won't be breaking any door down in this house!"

Constable Jenkins reached for the hand-cuffs in his pocket and pulled them out. "This is your last chance Mister Temple! Your very last warning!" Then he beckoned to his other officer to step closer.

"Escort Mister Temple out to the front balcony officer Firth. Use these to cuff him, and arrest him if he causes more ruckus!" he said sternly as he gave him the hand-cuffs, then eyed Richard Temple.

"Come along now Mister Temple." said the officer, as he placed a firm hand under Richard's elbow, and urged him to move.

Richard glared at Constable Jenkins as he shook his arm free of the hold officer Firth had on his elbow, but he went along with him just the same to the outside balcony, then he paced up and down.

What the hell is happening? he wondered. *No doubt this is the doing of Detective Rickard.* His blood boiled at the thought as all the yelling, and cursing heard from inside, became closer. An officer appeared in the doorway. His face was contorted, and his hand was bleeding profusely. He almost had to drag Miranda outside because she was fighting him every inch of the way, clawing at his eyes, scratching his face as she cursed him with a new set of invective. She had bitten his hand so hard her teeth hit bone. Almost at once blood spurted into her face, but she held onto the doorway so he couldn't budge her. Miranda Delvin was not giving in easily, she was ferocious and was still kicking and screaming as Constable Jenkins and his officer stepped in to contain her, and they all dragged her away to the van.

Chapter Seventeen

Oceanview was all a-buzz as officers crawled in every nook, and cranny to carry out an intensive search. Jack was proud of them for their input, and faith in him. *I must not let them down, nor Jenna either!* he thought as he walked across the lawns of the 'Homestead' with Constable Jenkins beside him, and headed towards the stables.

Jack took a quick look over his shoulder and caught a glimpse of Richard Temple pacing along the verandah, still accompanied by two officers. If the scowl on his face was any indication of his mood as he glared at them, then he was livid, he knew something was up.

"Richard Temple does not look at all happy, Constable! Did you manage to bug his quarters, sir?" he whispered to the Constable.

"Because if he is going to contact someone, it will be today!"

"He wasn't impressed when we charged Miranda, but she fled to lock herself in his bathroom. My officer had to break the lock to hand-cuff her and finally remove her from the premises. I managed to fit one bug in his phone, and another in his bedroom during the chaos so, that should do the job, Detective!" said Constable Jenkins.

Jack grinned. "I can't thank you enough sir, but how do I receive any notification of any calls he makes?"

"Simple, I get a red flag notice to my phone!"

"You do?" Jack chuckled. "How clever. Is anything there yet?"

Constable Jenkins chuckled too as he faced The Detective. "Now don't be too anxious Detective Rickard. Just give the man time, for at the moment, I don't think Richard Temple can see past Miranda's arrest. He was furious, but to the extreme point where I was forced to warn him to back off, or I would arrest him for interfering in her arrest. He looks a little deflated now, don't you think, Detective?"

Jack looked over his shoulder once again. "Yes! Richard Temple looks as though he would rather be in another place right now!"

"Exactly! So, let's get over to the stables and organize the officers and then prepare for your interview with Pablo!"

Richard Temple had seen enough. He shook his head and slipped through the doorway to disappear inside where he slumped on the couch. It didn't look good, and his face paled as the sensation of fear over-whelmed him. He sat there trying to digest all that was happening and he started running his fingers through his hair as if instead he should pull it out by the roots. *Why George? George Delvin of all people?* George had stuck by him through the good times, and bad. *He was my best friend, and my business partner.* he thought. *Until Miranda James appeared on the scene!* He tried to think back to those times, and knew that George was easily lead. However, now with this latest evidence piled against Miranda, *finally I can see the light. Miranda James played George Delvin just as she is playing me now*! But, murder? *Could Miranda James/Delvin commit murder?* he wondered.

Well maybe not directly, *but in-directly she could if it meant getting her own way.* Was she devious at all? Oh yes! *She was definitely that!*

He tried his hardest to recall many things she had said to him.

Once, Miranda had told him straight to get rid of Julia, his wife. Now he was second-guessing her actual meaning of that, because at the time he wasn't sure so, he queried her, and she laughed it off. But he knew now that way back then she was planting ideas in his head.

She was extremely clever. Oh yes! Obviously, Miranda had it all mapped out, *to make sure she never veered from her plan.* he realized. Then, out of no-where he recalled that her first husband had fallen overboard whilst they were on a cruise ship, and was lost at sea. *Could Miranda have had a hand his demise too?*

Oh no! What have I done? "What the damn hell have I done?" he screamed out loudly. His own voice alien in his ears, as he rose from the couch drunkenly, and paced the room despairingly. Suddenly, he stopped dead in his tracks, as Miranda's laughter echoed clearly in his ears, and her words describing an incident with Pablo about Julia's girth-strap and how she'd black-mailed him. *Yes, blackmailed him!* Even though she was a partner to the main damage caused.

It was the day I invited the staff out to stay at 'Oceanview' when Julia encountered the bad fall down at the horse jumps. *Yes! That in itself was a gross intention to murder for certain, and she had a hand it that*! As that accident, *was no accident* and it could have been fatal, but with a great fight, and a great medical team, Julia Temple had survived.

Oh yes! Miranda James/Delvin had everyone's measure, and she had convinced me that Pablo would do anything I wanted after that. *Whatever I asked of him he must obey me, or else he would be exposed.* So, Pablo was grossly intimidated, threatened and blackmailed by her. *But I also grossly used that against him in the worst possible way!*

"Pablo!" he screamed out. *"You were played by her too! We all were!* Only I was too blinded by her beauty to see it! *What a fool I was!"*

She will pay for this.

"God, damn it where is his number? I must call Pablo pronto! I must look out for number one. I won't go down for this. No way!"

Jack smiled as he looked ahead, and could see two of his officers waiting outside the doors to the stables. "It looks to me as if they are all organized, sir. Great team of men you have Constable!"

Constable Jenkins stared up ahead, and was pleased to note his orders were followed. "Yep, they would make any senior, proud!"

"Right, this is it, sir! Let's make it happen!"

"You bet Detective Rickard!" said the Constable.

As they arrived at the stables Constable Jenkins received a phone call to say his officers had collected Pablo, and were on their way.

"Great timing Detective Rickard, our guest is on the road now!"

"Perfect! Just enough time to set up! Then get this search done!"

"It will happen Detective, be patient. We'll achieve an outcome!"

A good one I hope! pondered Jack. "I felt sure there'd be another pair of his shoes somewhere?" he whispered. Only now, The Constable was about to address his men so, Detective Rickard stepped aside.

"Greetings team!" The Constable said as they neared the stable doors and he shook each officer's hand. "If you have any updates, or any reports, now is the time to make Detective Rickard aware!"

Jack stepped forward to greet them and they both acknowledged him, and one officer reported. "Good morning, Detective Rickard. Everything is as you ordered. Two of our officers are searching the grounds, and we are waiting for our orders from you for inside!"

"Good men! Now, don't wait for The Constable and myself to get prepared, we'll grab one of you later. Begin the internal search immediately of the entrance, stables, and Pablo's main office! We will be out back. This next order is important. If there are findings at all you have permission to interrupt us at any time. Is that clear?"

"Yes sir, Detective Rickard!" both officers said in unison and left. Then Detective Rickard heard a definite ding. "What was that, sir?" Constable Jenkins grabbed his phone. "The call has been made, sir!"

The Detective laughed. "So, the plot thickens, you old devil!"

"Though, we'll have to keep it for later now Constable Jenkins! As time is of the essence right this minute! I guess you could call it, cutting it fine, but who knows? It may be our savior later this day!"

"I must agree Detective, let's pursue what we started out to do!"

"Good, come along sir, and we will find our place of attack!"

They strolled through the stables amidst the din now created by officers filing through anything and everything trying to unveil any piece of evidence, and similar was happening in Pablo's office.

"Where are we heading to, Detective?" asked Constable Jenkins.

"I think out back will be best for starters. I want to make it feel casual to him, because after that phone-call I'm expecting him to be just a little on edge!" *Somewhere out of the way, and private."* Detective Rickard was thinking as he surveyed the area they just walked into, and looked to the corner. "Ah there! That will be perfect, sir. It looks like a tack room but clear access to the outside so, plenty of light."

"Could you grab one of the men to set it up for us. We will need two tables and three casual chairs in that corner? Have him set you up in the very corner with a table and chair, and the other table out in the center with two chairs facing the outside, savvy? Maybe place some hay bales around to make it feel relaxed. I'm going to wander outside, let me know when it is done. Also, ask one officer to direct our guest out here when he arrives! Oh! Have him grab a kettle, and the necessities' for making coffee, tea etc., if there is any! Maybe a small table or bench next to a power-point would be good!"

"Yes savvy! Consider it done, Detective!"

"I'm trying to set a scene Constable. First impressions are vital!"

"Yes, I get it Detective. You think of everything!"

"Well, hopefully, or we're in trouble! Oh, I guess I ought to tell you this now. Make sure you record from the minute he walks in. If we move from this area, then follow!" He looked at the Constable seriously. "Thank you for everything, sir, you've been my rock!"

Senior Constable Jenkins looked the Detective square in the eyes. He smiled at him, and replied. "You know Jack, I have been waiting for just the right time to tell you this, but I am guessing this is it. So, I must say it has been an absolute pleasure for me to work beside you on both these cases, as your standards are second to none. It makes me proud to see how far you have come since you were but a boy! So, a position with Homicide Jeremy Woods was an excellent choice for you, but you grabbed the chance with both hands. I do admire that in you, Jack! So, congratulations for making the best of an opportunity because now you are a man to be reckoned with. A brilliant Detective, and you do deserve all the accolades bestowed upon you. This is one thing I'll savior for retirement, the memories I shall have of this time will live with me forever, Jack Rickard!"

Jack chuckled, because if he didn't, the tear that was threatening to fall from his misty eyes, would then disclose his gut feelings. He felt choked up with emotion, but it was not the time. He needed to be tough, so he laughed it off by saying. "Trust you by getting all sentimental on me Constable, but let's not get too carried away. A job still has to be done, and we need to focus. However, thank you sir for your kind words. I too will always remember our time here! Now, back to the order of things. Is there anything else we forgot?"

Constable Jenkins responded as if nothing had been said. "Well, maybe. I had a thought of when I'm recording. Should I jot down his expressions when you ask him about certain people, or places?"

Jack laughed. "You know what sir? You really never cease to amaze me. What a great idea! But will you have time?" he asked.

Constable Jenkins laughed. "Probably not, but I may just put my shorthand skills to work. Seems like a good chance to try that!"

Jack laughed, and shook his head. "A man of many talents you are sir, now get things moving, I am going for a quick look outside!"

"Yes, Homicide Detective Jack Rickard!" the Constable saluted.

Melita Sanchez stood threateningly in front of her son, dark eyes blazing, her hand raised high. Then came the slap, a loud crack against his cheek, forcing his head to twist sideways from the sheer power in her muscley arm. *"Get a grip, boy!"* she cursed.

Pablo was standing paled-faced in the living room not knowing what to do, or how to stem the feelings of doom since receiving the phone-call full of murderous threats from Richard Temple. He was shaking so badly when the unexpected hit come, and he rocked on his feet from the force of his mother's attack. Such venom he heard in her voice. *There would be no help from her!* he thought, as he rubbed his cheek. He had no-one to talk to, and no-one to advise. *Pablo knew he was in way too deep, and had* no-where to go, no-where to hide, and the tears ran down his cheek as his body trembled.

"They'll be coming to collect you any time now so, pull yourself together! You're a weakling, that's for sure but you better liven up!" She prodded him. "Are you even listening to me, Pablo? This is so important! Just stick to what we discussed!"

He looked at her through bleary eyes. At this particular time, he felt hate for his mother. She had put him in a situation that was now irreversible, but he replied to avoid her wrath. "Ok!" he muttered.

"You tell them nothing, Pablo!" his mother spat at him. "Just act ignorant, that shouldn't be too hard for you. Give nothing away at that interview with Detective Rickard, either. So, tell him nothing, and stand your ground! You hear me, boy? You better get your facts right, or there'll be trouble for you right here!" she raised her hand.

"Yes!" he whispered, as his head hung low. Her threat seemed paltry, but he knew it was the life-sentence he endured all his life. But they were all ganging up on him, he couldn't take much more.

Just then, there was a knock on the door. Two officers pushed it open, and one spoke. "Our search is complete Missus Sanchez! So, come with us now and we will take you to your interview Pablo!"

Pablo sat forlornly in the back seat of the police vehicle looking out the car window as the trees flashed by. Somehow, he figured that the trees and scenery, resembled his life in a way, just like the passing of time, and he could relate to that. He really wished that he could have his life over and be like a tree, to sprout a shoot, and regrow. He sighed deeply as a feeling of doom blanketed him.

"Almost there, Pablo!" said the officer who turned around in his seat, as if he could read his mind.

Pablo didn't speak, just kept looking out the window until they reached the rise and the car-park came into view and he shuddered. Then the driver was parking the vehicle so very close to the edge of the cliff on his side, and the visions plagued him of what might be happening down there, he knew officers would be there. Then an officer got out, and went to his side of the car and opened the door.

"Come along, Pablo, just a short walk now!" he stated. Then he walked beside Pablo to the gate, and across the lawns, and the other officer trailed closely behind them.

Pablo watched as officers seemed to appear from no-where, all searching the grounds, and obviously inside The Homestead. Then they were at the gate. He ambled along on legs like jelly, down the familiar track to the stables. More officers greeted them at the steps, and he was escorted though to where his interview would be held.

"Homicide Detective Jack Rickard looked up as the officers, with Pablo beside them, entered the tack room. Pablo's eyes widened in surprise as his thoughts raced. *This doesn't look like an interview room.*

Constable Jenkins, sitting in the corner, noticed his expression at once, and made his first shorthand entry, then he pressed record.

"Ah Pablo! Come in, come in!" said The Detective with a hint of a welcome in his voice. "Thank you, officers, we shall speak later!" He waited until they left the room before he uttered. "Don't mind Constable Jenkins, Pablo. He will be recording our talk today!"

"Please take a seat here with me, Pablo!" the Detective said as he ushered Pablo toward the table and chairs in the center of the room. Maybe some water to start, Constable before we all settle."

"Yes Detective, right away sir." The Constable said, and went to get them a water jug and glasses, and placed them on the table.

Pablo took his seat, still baffled by the treatment. He expected to be in trouble or that he would be harassed, so he relaxed a little.

Detective Rickard noticed that. *Good! I will proceed in caution.* he decided. "Well Pablo, thank you for coming in! Today I have some pressings issues that I would like to discuss with you. Some may be pleasant, and some not! But it is not my aim to upset you, rather I would hope you can provide me with some honest responses as I have been away for some time so, I am not familiar with you all. Could we discuss the people who work and live at 'Oceanview'?"

Pablo looked at The Detective. He had a kind face, *and he didn't see any problem with just talking,* so he said. "Yes sir, Detective!"

"Excellent Pablo. Firstly, I would like to talk about the Hastings couple. I believe they live on the premises, is that correct?"

"Yes sir, Detective. They both live in the cabin here!"

Jack pulled out his notebook. "Just to make sure I don't miss anything important Pablo. Now, let us talk about Ted Hastings! His role at 'Oceanview' his interests and his manner. Is that, ok?"

"Yes sir, Detective. Ted Hastings is usually a quiet person, and keeps to himself. He is the handyman, and grounds person here!"

"Excellent, thank you, Pablo. Does he own a car?"

"Yes sir, Detective. He owns a white van. Both of them drive it!"

"How would you describe your relationship with Ted?"

"Well sir, Detective. We work together a lot on the grounds, and venues. He is a kind person, always helpful. We get on rather well!"

Jack held up his hand. "Before we continue on, Pablo. You may drop the 'sir!' 'Detective,' will do for the remainder of our talk, ok?"

Detective Rickard made a show of writing in his notebook then he looked up at Pablo who sat with his hands on his knees, and he looked relaxed, so he continued. So, Pablo, shall we press on?"

Pablo tried to smile, something he hadn't done in a while and it came out a crooked wry smile, but he replied. "Yes Detective!"

"Good! Now to Paula Hastings, Ted's wife I believe. Could you tell me her role at 'Oceanview" her interests, and her manner?"

Jack noticed Pablo clench one trembling hand. "Yes, Detective. Missus Hastings is Ted's wife, and cook here at 'Oceanview.' I don't know about their social life, they work long hours, well we all do!"

"Yes, I could imagine, Pablo! So, tell me how would you describe Paula Hasting's manner, and your relationship with her?"

Detective Rickard noted Pablo's hands trembled as he clenched one into a tight fist. When he replied, his other hand wavered when trying to stress a point. *Something about Paula Hastings upsets him. I wonder what?* He stared at the Constable who raised his eyebrows.

"Paula Hastings can be abrupt, and quick to cut you down. She is extremely bossy, a very rough, domineering person most times!" The reply surprised Jack so, he asked. "Did you get on with her?" His hand wavered. "I didn't have to get on with her, mother did!"

Detective Rickard surmised that previously he was struggling when the tell-tale hand wavered. *He was sure Pablo had something in common with Paula Hastings.* He wrote in his notebook then moved on. "I see! It is your mother who works with her mostly, correct?"

"Yes, Detective, that is correct!"

"Can we discuss your mother now, Pablo? What her role is here, describe her manner, and your personal relationship?" he noted immediately one hand clenched into a fist, the other fist went to his mouth, and Pablo seemed anxious before he could summon a reply.

"Mother is the housemaid and also a waitress at 'Oceanview' so, she works closely with Missus Hastings, especially at functions!"

With an updated notebook the Detective asked. "Do you drive?" Pablo was caught off-guard with a change in the questions, and he stammered a reply. "Well… no Detective. I don't have a license!"

Detective Rickard chuckled. "Why on earth not, Pablo? You are of age, so how do you get to work each day?" he queried.

Pablo frowned as this was not his favorite subject, he sighed. "Mother says I don't need a license because it's too expensive for me to get a car, and we can't afford it. So, I ride my bicycle everywhere!"

"Your mother has a car you could drive if you had a license!"

"Oh, no. I couldn't. No, mother would never let me do that!"

Detective Rickard looked at him carefully. *He looks very unsettled, scared even. Why?* "You must earn good wages Pablo, don't you?"

"Yes, Detective but mother takes all that. 'For my keep' she says but she allows me spending money!" then came his awkward smile. *Spending money?* Jack winced. *For goodness sakes!* "Are you happy to live at your mother's house, or would you rather your own place?"

Pablo's fist clenched. "I can't do that Detective, my mother won't let me, she gets too angry if I ask, besides I don't have any money!"

"Your mother has money, your money! You should be aware it is wrong of her? Must you always do as your mother says Pablo?"

"Yes, sir Detective, always!" replied Pablo as he hung his head.

"Just how angry would she get if you didn't, Pablo? What would she do? Tell me if you would, if you regard her as a violent person?"

Pablo's hands trembled, and his face was flushed as he tried to reply. "My mother, yes…she'd throw things…I…She'd get so…yes violent…she is too strong for me…She…no, I can't argue with her!"

"I have to ask, but has your mother ever struck you, Pablo?" Pablo's face paled as he looked up. "Yes Detective, I get beatings!"

"Would you have proof Pablo?" queried Detective Rickard. "Yes Detective!" Pablo's eyes filled with tears as he lifted his shirt. When Jack spied huge welts, he said. "This sickens me to the core, Pablo!"

Homicide Detective Jack Rickard rose from his seat. His face was marked by a fierce scowl as he raised his voice "Enough Pablo! Good god man you must know this is unacceptable behaviour from your mother! Why take beatings, why live in fear! Do something!"

Pablo began shaking, then he sobbed. "I have no-one, no-one can help me. No, I cannot do a thing Detective, if I want to live that is!" A look of disbelief marked The Detective's face as he spoke. "Are you telling me you will be seriously harmed by your own mother?"

Pablo could barely speak, and his body trembled as the words tumbled out. "Ye..es sir, Detective, tha..t is what I am saying!"

The Detective placed a hand on his elbow. "Come Pablo, we are getting out of here. Just give me a minute to address my Constable!"

Pure fury was evident in Detective Rickard's eyes as he turned to face Constable Jenkins. "That is a wrap for now Constable, stop recording! I can't go any further until I speak privately with Pablo. This boy is strung as tight as a guitar string and if I push him like I was going to, he is going to snap. No, I must find out what else he knows, and firing questions is not going to cut it. His mind must be spinning as he has major problems, but there is more he is involved with and I aim to find out what. We'll break for an hour or so. Please assist me by babysitting the officers, sir. I'll take the recorder out in case. Get someone to get coffees out to us, and order some food in!"

Constable Jenkins glimpsed Jack's eyes as he passed the recorder over, and realized the words from that conversation were bugging The Detective, big time. He had never seen such anger in his eyes before so, he said. "Right sir, I understand. You can count on me!"

"Pablo and I will go for a short walk, *and sir!*" he whispered. "*It is now a good time to check out the phone-call message of Richard Temple's but do it in private.* I will need that information when I get back!"

"You got it sir! I will walk out to the carpark." said the Constable.

"That's good, thank you, but keep the other officers out of here!"

As Jack turned to leave a disturbance at the door distracted The Detective, and he looked up just as two police officers burst in.

"Hold up one second Detective Rickard!" one of them called out when he noticed The Detective about to leave the room."

A deep frown creased The Detective's brow and he held up a hand immediately to stop them. "Not now!" he said firmly, and signaled to Constable Jenkins to intervene.

"But Detective, the officer persisted. You said to interrupt you if we found… "I said NOT NOW! Deal with this Constable Jenkins!"

Constable Jenkins was quick to intervene. "Come along men. We must leave The Detective for now as he has some pressing issues to deal with. You will all get your say, just a little later. Let us go back to your search area, and you can show me your findings for now!"

A look of relief passed Jack's face as he acknowledged Constable Jenkins, then walked over to Pablo to place a hand on his shoulder.

"All sorted Pablo. So, now let's go outside, the sun is shining and I noticed the horses in the first paddock. We can discuss them if you wish? Keep in mind that this will be a casual conversation, Pablo. I'll only record if I need to but we won't be discussing the case, ok?"

Pablo looked up quickly in surprise, relief evident on his face.

"Yes Detective, that will be ok. I love to talk about the horses!"

"Good! We have an hour. In that time, we have food ordered, so then we will eat but someone will bring a coffee out to us soon."

Homicide Detective Rickard did not miss Pablo's smile as they ventured out to stand side by side at the rails of the paddock fence.

"So, tell me Pablo. Why are the horses up in the first paddock?"

A concerned look crossed Pablo's face, but still he replied "Well Detective, since we were laid off, I just had to go out and bring the horses in so I can give them extra feed, and keep an eye on them!"

"Hmm! So, I gather you rode your bike here each time Pablo?"

"Yes, I ride my bike here every second day Detective Rickard!"

Jack looked over at the horses. "Such beautiful horses Pablo, I can see why you are so attached to them. They are very good stock!"

"Only the best stock is purchased here!" said Pablo proudly.

The Detective's brow creased with an idea entering his mind. "I might set up the recorder Pablo as there are some things I am not sure of and you may happen to mention them. Is that ok with you?"

Pablo smiled as he looked at The Detective. "Yes sir, that is ok!"

"Good!" said Detective Rickard as he grabbed the case, opened it, and set the recorder up on a post. "It is just if we need it, Pablo. However, I have one question on my mind, and he pressed record.

"Would you know who purchases livestock for 'Oceanview'?"

Pablo frowned. "Well, I never really thought about that before so, I am not certain, but I guess it would the owner of the property!"

The Detective smiled. "Well, I am guessing you must mean Julia Temple, is that correct? It wouldn't be Richard Temple, would it?"

Pablo's face paled and his hands trembled at the mention of Julia Temple, and Richard Temple as he tried to summon a reply.

Detective Rickard was quick to notice. "Take your time, reply at your leisure. You do know who owns 'Oceanview' I take it Pablo?"

"Ye…es Detective!" he spluttered a reply. "Well, I know now, but we assumed it was Mister Richard Temple, as he told us that!"

"So, who set you on the right track of that information, Pablo?"

"Jenna Temple, Detective!" tears rolled onto his cheeks in reply.

"Was it the same day Julia Temple had a horrendous horse fall?" Pablo's body shook with his reply. "Ye…es, Detective Rickard!"

Detective Rickard's eyes darkened as he asked his final question.

"You know more of Julia Temple's accident, don't you, Pablo?" Pablo hung his head, tears flowed as he said. "Ye…es Detective!"

"Thank you, Pablo! Enough for now, let's walk a while. I would like to be the one to help you. I could protect you if you let me in!"

Pablo looked at him with unseeing eyes. "You would help me?"

"Definitely! But I can't help if you aren't completely honest. I can see your stress Pablo, so you must reach out for help. You are being treated poorly at home by your own blood, your mother! By being brutalized you are taken for granted and severely victimized, who knows what else? There are people who can help in these situations, Pablo. I sense you know more about these cases than you are saying Pablo, the truth will come out, it always does you know! I'm willing to help you but my hands are tied if you don't open up right now!"

Pablo looked at The Detective for a while before he spoke. *He had no-one else.* "If you help me Detective Rickard, what do you want?"

Finally! thought Jack. "This is the deal, Pablo! When we resume to record after lunch, I will ask you only one question! If you answer that question honestly, then for us both to concrete a deal I would expect a full confession from you immediately! I will want to hear all you know concerning Julia and Jenna Temple, and of any others involved. I'll support you to the best of my ability, but a judge will determine the severity of your involvement. Understand Pablo?"

"Yes sir, Detective Rickard. I do understand!" muttered Pablo, shaking his head and the tears fell. "But where would I start? It is so bad, so awful, a…nd I've done ba…d things I don't want to talk about. "Why help me? How could you help me Detective?"

"We will take it slow, Pablo and have breaks. Providing you give me all the information I require in full detail! You must elaborate on the one question I ask you and I must know about Julia Temple's horse fall! You did say you knew more! Also, the attack on Jenna Temple if you have any details! If you do that, then we will act. My officers will remove your belongings from your home immediately. You will be placed in Protective Custody in a safe house until the hearing, and you will be a key witness in court at the trials of Julia and Jenna Temple! I will do everything in my power to speak up for you, Pablo and hope that is enough to sway the Judge's mind!"

Jack looked straight at Pablo. "I hope you understand that?"

Pablo stared back at him. "Yes, sir Detective. I realize that!"

"Good! Your mother will be brought in for questioning about her treatment of you, so you must make a detailed statement! Also, I will need photos of your injuries, Pablo. So, I will ask Constable Jenkins to take those today, if you agree to that? Then it is a simple matter of pressing charges against your mother!"

Pablo's eyes flew wide, and he looked so scared. "Press charges, against my mother? Oh! I can't do that, she will kill me, Detective!"

"Precisely! That is why you must do it, Pablo, to stop the abuse!" offered Detective Rickard. "She won't be allowed near you anyway, and your safe house will be guarded. So, do we have a deal, Pablo?

Pablo's body shivered as he sobbed. He thought long, and hard about it, but finally knew the Detective was right. He had no-one, he was in far too deep, had done terrible things and could go to jail.

"Ye...es Sir Detective Rickard, we have a deal!" he stammered.

"Good man!" offered Detective Rickard.

Constable Jenkins followed the two officers who headed straight for Pablo's office adjacent the stables. At the door he paused to survey the small room. Pablo's desk had been pulled out from the wall, a mat pulled back to expose a hidden trap-door, gaping open to reveal a storage space underneath, but it was Pablo's desk which urged him to move closer where four items sat on top.

Intrigued, Constable Jenkins walked up to the desk, his officers right at his heels. "Care to explain the contents you have here, men? Is this your find, officers?" he queried as he turned to them.

"Yes sir, Constable!" replied Officer Bill Cains who had stepped forward. "You will be amazed at what we have discovered, sir!"

"Let me be the judge of that, officer. You may open them now!" Officer Cains tugged at the strings of a bag to tip out some clothing.

Immediately interested, The Constable stepped in for a closer look, and the officer handed him some gloves. "Thank you, Cains!" he said offhandedly, as he donned the gloves to pick up one item. He looked up. "Pablo's clothing and someone else's, all stained!"

"Yes, we expect so, Constable!" Cains said and turned to another bag to reveal the contents as a worn pair of sneakers as they fell out.

Constable Jenkins eyes flew wide. *The missing shoes!* he realized. *Medium, well worn, old even, but heavily stained. Detective Rickard will love these.* He eyed a bag, and one boxed item. "They are?" he asked.

"Ah! The ultimate prizes!" said officer Cains as he offered them. The Constable grabbed the bag at once and out tumbled a Hatchett, so heavily stained that he gasped. He took the box and unclasped the catch. Inside sat the beautiful, yet stained green stoned necklace with missing stones, owned by Julia Temple. He grinned broadly.

"Well done! Now we have all the missing pieces! Great work!" Both officers beamed in reply. "Thank you, Constable Jenkins!"

"You are both most welcome! However, it does not stop here men! Take many pictures of all these items, send them to me, and to Detective Rickard. Bag each item separately, label them, also box them! This is so very important! You have hard evidence here! So, then pack them up all together in a bigger box and guard them with your life! My plan is now to get them directly to forensics for stain testing as soon as possible. However, I must get Detective Rickard's approval first so, just do what I have asked while I go out to speak to him. If I get an ok, I think it would be best if you drive to the city immediately, and get the tests done there, and don't let these items out of your sight! Do you both understand the importance of this?

"Yes sir, right away, sir!" replied Dale Hendy as he stepped up to take the pictures, then they both started repacking the items."

When I return, I will walk with you to the carpark. There is one more thing, I must do there! Get it all sorted now, I will be back!"

Constable Jenkins walked quickly through the rooms and stables to the outside area where their interview took place and headed straight outdoors into the sunlight. He noticed Detective Rickard and Pablo strolling back towards him, chatting like old friends.

Detective Rickard looked up to see him waiting outside, and he bent down to speak softly to Pablo. "It looks like Constable Jenkins wants my attention, maybe some direction for our men. Would you excuse me for one second, Pablo? Just wait at the railings as I won't be too long, and I'll ask if our coffee is being sent out to us! We will continue our conversation then if you like!"

Pablo nodded. "Yes, of course Detective Rickard, that is ok!"

"Good man!" replied The Detective as he left him, and walked towards where Constable Jenkins stood. "Ah, Constable. You need instructions I guess, so how can I help?" he inquired.

Constable Jenkins moved so that his back was to Pablo down at the railings, and he spoke softly. "They found it all, Detective! You can trust me when I say that, I mean it all! If you are happy just with viewing the photos later, my plan is to have them drive to the city asap with the evidence for testing, but I need your approval, Jack?"

Detective Rickard kept a straight face though his heart thumped madly in his chest as he spoke. "By all means, Constable, the sooner the better!" he said off-handedly. "Get some coffee out to us, and get on with it!" then whispered. *"We've minor discussions on certain topics to complete, but I have him onside, and I've cut a deal! He'll talk!"*

Constable Jenkins smiled. *Always the professional* he thought as he said. "Good! I am on my way, your coffee will be out soon, and food is on its way. Shall we resume the interview in half an hour?"

"Yes, please Constable!" Jack said, smiling as he walked away.

The Constable was quick to return to his men and pleased to see everything finalized in his absence. "Good work team! One of you, take coffee out to The Detective, and Pablo, and check on the food!"

"But you two." he pointed to his officers. "Follow me now, out to the carpark with your precious cargo. I'll walk with you to your vehicle, and will give you final instructions before you set off!"

As they walked across the lawns, Constable Jenkins checked his phone, then spoke up. "Great, I have received all the photos of our evidence officers, thank you for that as Detective Rickard is happy to view them later. Now, listen carefully men! When you arrive in the city, send me a message, and when you are returning. It is most important that I know that, but more urgent is the test results! There will be an officer in charge at forensics, so I request he personally phone me with the results! It is urgent, tell him that, and at no time let this evidence out of your sight, and make sure you get a written receipt for the items and a case number. We have a very important interview in half an hour, so I want you guys gone as soon as we reach the carpark. Got all that? Any questions?"

Bill Cains and Dale Hendy looked seriously at The Constable, and Bill replied. "You can rely on us sir. We know how important this is, and we will urge them to do tests immediately if they can!"

He watched them put the evidence in the boot, get in the vehicle to drive away. He grabbed his phone to access a flagged recording and listened intently as Richard Temple's voice came on loud, and clear. Though he was ranting and raving and cursing Pablo for his stupidity, throwing death threats his way, Pablo replied meekly, and so clearly intimidated. *The Detective will have a field day with this!*

"Hold up, Constable!" a voice called as Tom Hurley topped the steep hill to the carpark. "We've an urgent situation in The Dunes!" Constable Jenkins stopped dead in his tracks. "What is so urgent?"

"We have uncovered a body, sir! Or part of it, at this stage!"

"Well, I'll be! Great work! Go back to tape the area, don't leave the site or touch anything! Give us thirty minutes for an interview, then call the morgue and coroner! We'll meet you all at The Dunes!"

Slowly, Pablo took his seat. His eyes then darted from Homicide Detective Rickard to Constable Jenkins who had just walked in and nodded to him as he passed on direct route to speak with The Detective. "Are you ready to begin, sir?" he asked, then added so softly. *Twenty minutes only, then we must be down at The Dunes, sir!"*

At the mention of the Dunes, Detective Rickard's heart pounded so hard, he felt it difficult to keep a straight face as he replied.

"Yes, Constable Jenkins. Take your place, and let us begin!"

The Constable also had a straight face as he nodded and replied to The Detective. "As you wish, sir!" and made his way to his desk, sat down, then he pressed the record button.

Homicide Detective Rickard looked hard at Pablo, and asked. "If you are ready to begin Pablo as promised. I have but one question!"

"Who murdered Julia Temple, Pablo? Elaborate if you would!" So, as predicted, the interview was to begin. But Pablo sat frozen in his seat as he winced. *I just have to do this!* he chided himself. *I must do it!* His whole body churned with emotions as tears welled.

Detective Richard noticed, and placed a reassuring hand on his shoulder. "Take your time, Pablo, but realize how important this is to you! Simply recall the events as truthfully as you can remember!"

Pablo looked at The Detective, and knew that he was right. *If the others pin it on me, I am a dead duck. No! This time I stick up for myself!* He nodded to Detective Rickard and tried to compose himself, then slowly and agonizingly painful, Pablo Sanchez began describing a scene on the beach under the steps at 'Oceanview.' He named Julia Temple's murderer, and the fatal Hatchett blow that took her life.

Detective Rickard nodded. *Hmm! I have the exact footprints of the murderer's boots.* "Just one question, was anyone else involved?"

Pablo hung his head, but he named the others involved.
Then Detective Rickard frowned. "I don't like to interrupt Pablo! But I must question the fact that you didn't mention your mother!"

"Was your mother involved at all with Julia Temple's murder? Also, now might be the right time to tell of your involvement too!"

Pablo looked straight into the Detective's eyes. "Mother? No, sir! Not at all! I can see now how mother played it smart so she would not be charged, even though she engaged a huge role in the murder with Miranda Delvin and Richard Temple! It was all about money with her, Detective! Richard Temple had promised us all shares and dividends in Oceanview so, she was making sure he kept his word. They black-mailed us all, and had a hold on each of us for different occurrences. You see, it was Paula Hastings who caused the stove to explode when Julia Temple was disfigured years ago, and Ted helped cover it up! Though it didn't go undetected by my mother."

"She reported it to Richard Temple to keep him onside. He knew then to what lengths he could push them. He threatened to expose them both so, they were beholding to him. We were all pawns, Ted, Paula Hastings and me, but when Miranda Delvin arrived on the scene it was the beginning of my nightmare! She black-mailed me, threatened to tell police lies of the horse accident, then convinced Richard Temple I'd do anything he asked. I was in their grips, and mothers also. She flogged me, used brute force to make sure I did exactly what they asked me to do at the beach so, I had to obey!"

"Hmm! Leave it there. Pablo, we will get back to your statement! Instead, I'd be interested if you continue on with the events leading up prior to, causing the horse-fall accident of Missus Julia Temple?"

Pablo nodded. Then as if in a dream, began recalling events that led to Julia Temple's accident. The phone call from his mother, her order to cut the girth strap, then Miranda Delvin's final act added to his causing the fatal fall. Her cunning concealment of evidence, her involvement convincingly hidden led to blackmail, she had him in a corner. She and Richard Temple used the advantage by making him obey, or be exposed as the guilty party of Julia Temple's fall.

Detective Rickard and Constable Jenkins exchanged glances, but The Detective didn't comment, he simply asked Pablo directly.

"Would you proceed to your part in the murder now Pablo?"

Pablo's face paled at the blunt question. However, now the time had come to explain his involvement in Julia Temple's murder, he felt sick to his stomach. Visions swamped him, and he really didn't think he could re-live it again. For so long he had been pretending it didn't happen, but the nightmares hounded him for many years.

It was at that particular point he broke down. His body doubled over in sheer agony as his eyes brimmed red with tears. His words became incoherent as he stammered and stuttered, trying to relive again gruesome details he had for so long been trying to forget. His whole body shook uncontrollably at the realization of what he had been forced to do. What he had done was monstrous, unforgivable, evil even, and he couldn't cope anymore. His face became distorted in anguish and disgust as the bile rose up in his throat.

Detective Rickard raised his hand. "Stop recording, Constable! Get some water here, and organize coffee, while Pablo goes to the restroom to wash and refresh! Go and have a break now, Pablo!" Thankfully, Pablo rose gingerly from his seat. "I think I will do that, Detective!" he said, with his head bowed as he tottered away.

Jack waited until he had left the room, then his eyes flew wide. "What is going on, Constable?" he asked. "Tell me quickly!"

"Our officers found parts of the bagged body in The Dunes, Sir!"

"In fifteen minutes, they will be contacting the Morgue and the Coroner to meet you down there! Two officers have left for the city with evidence found in Pablo's office. *Stained clothing, the missing joggers, a Hatchett and the elusive necklace, sir! We have it all, Detective!*"

"Excellent work Constable and the team! But, the Hatchett, what a find! It was the murder weapon according to Pablo's confession!"

"Yep! No doubt that will be proved later after testing!" said the Constable. "Also, I listened to Richard Temple's taped phone call, clearly undermining Pablo Sanchez, blackmailing him with murder threats even, and laying blame on Miranda Delvin, you'll love it!"

"Excellent Constable Jenkins! It is all happening today!" *he chuckled.*

Constable Jenkins smiled. "Ah! But it's not really new to us, is it Detective? Just about everything that has eventuated was predicted by you at some stage, Detective Rickard. With each and every scrap of evidence painstakingly sourced, it set us on the right track, gave us direction to all avenues you covered. I am proud to witness your tenacity, and unbelievable Detective work! If I may say so, sir?"

Jack chuckled. *The Constable is at it again.* "Compliment accepted sir. So far, it is panning out nicely so, I guess I did something right! But now, the crucial part is yet to come, and we need to wrap it up!"

"Yes, Detective, we have not completed our task yet, any plans?"

Jack's eyes glazed over as he stared at him. "I think so, sir. I am going with my gut! I know now what this boy has got to tell us! He has gruesome tidings to tell so, it's not going to be easy on him. He's already struggling! This confession of his will, seal it for us. Don't miss a thing, and have paperwork ready for him to sign. I must be precise, but thorough to complete the interview in time! But now I'm thinking a different approach is needed here because he can't take much more. So, bear with me. I hope I make the right call!"

Constable Jenkins looked up quickly but noted he was deadly serious so, he replied. "It is your baby after all Detective Rickard!"

Detective Richard smiled. "Knew you'd say that! When we're done, get his body pics taken, then have two officers on stand-by to whisk Pablo away to the station to make his statement, and to press charges on his mother, then on to the safe-house. I will view all the evidence, and listen to Richard Temple's recording before we go to The Dunes, thanks sir!" he said in finishing as Pablo appeared.

Detective Rickard smiled at him. "Ah! You look refreshed, Pablo. Take your seat, and we will continue, but with a different plan. I sense your stress, and don't want to cause you any undue pressure so, if you are open to direct questions and answers, rather than have you relive your involvement, I only need a yes, or no to questions.as you will be required to elaborate in court! You realize that, I hope?"

Pablo looked relieved. "I know Detective so, ask the questions!"

"Good! Who made the brutal attack on Jenna Temple?"

Pablo's eyebrows shot up at the new line of questioning, but he replied, naming the attacker and the type of rock used to attack her.

The Detective nodded. *Hmm! Once again, I have the exact same boot print to confirm that, and also the rock used to knock her senseless.*

"Why was Jenna down there, Pablo? Why was she attacked?"

Pablo's eyes filled with tears "Jenna wasn't to be there but she fell through the step! A fall that could have killed her, but she fell on her mother. I pleaded for Jenna to be spared, to no avail. She was a witness so my plea fell on deaf ears, then a beach-buggy showed!"

"We found Julia Temple's bagged body severely dismembered! Her necklace, murder weapon and items stashed in your office!"

"You have?" screeched Pablo in disbelief, as he began to sob.

"Are you the one responsible for dismembering Julia Temple's body, Pablo? Then to bag her dismembered remains and bury her?"

"Ye...ess sir...I'm so...oo...so sorry, but they forced me to do it!"

"Who forced you, Pablo?"

He was shaking badly as he replied. "I had no say in the murder! Richard Temple, Miranda Delvin and mother forced me to do it!"

Detective Rickard's eyes darkened as he asked. "Who ordered the death of Julia Temple, Pablo, and the attack on Jenna Temple?" Hate filled Pablo's eyes. "Richard Temple, Detective!" he spat. "He ordered Julia Temple's murder! Jenna no, as she wasn't to be there!"

"I see!' said The Detective! "That'll be all, wrap it up Constable!"

Chapter Eighteen

Jack almost gagged as they painstakingly lifted the final bag from its resting place in the dunes and placed it in a large, tough, body bag. He watched Julian Dent, a superior from the morgue as he took charge. So meticulous at his job, he didn't seem to notice any odor.

Jack looked around at the remaining bags. They all seemed to be there but he wouldn't know for sure until Julian done his job at the morgue and laid them out. He noticed a sand groper, on loan from the Surf Club, on stand-by to load the bags and get them up the hill.

"Detective Jack Rickard?" the voice queried next to him.

"Yes! That would be me." replied Jack. "Who is asking?"

"I am the coroner!" he held out his hand. "Mason Dell. I will be accompanying Julian with the transfer of the body to the morgue. I will be present for the identification of the body." he added.

"Well met!" said Detective Rickard as he offered his hand. "Meet my accompanying officer, Constable Joe Jenkins. Everything is in order for the transfer so, I will leave you in his hands while I return to notify Jenna Temple, the deceased's daughter, of our discovery!"

Constable Jenkins moved forward to greet the coroner. "Hello Mason, we have met before!" he said as their hands met. "I will follow you to the morgue. Who do you need to identify the body?"

The coroner smiled. "Yes, I remember meeting you, Constable on many occasions actually. We seem to meet in unlikely situations. Now for the identification of the body I will need a next, of kin. So, the deceased's daughter would fit the bill!" he turned to ask Jack.

"Is that possible Detective Rickard?"

Detective Rickard frowned as he thought of that situation, then he spoke. "Well Mason, I am not really sure Jenna will be up to doing that, I would have to ask her once I've told her we found her mother's body. You see, she has just recently regained her memory! She was in a coma for a long time, but on returning to 'Oceanview' it triggered something in her brain and her memory returned. She has had a horrific time with the disclosure of seeing her mother's dead body on the beach, and remembering her attack at the same time which caused her to be in a coma. Failing that, would I be able to identify Missus Temple? I am her son-in-law. Jenna is my wife!"

"Oh! How dreadful for the young lady. See what she says first, and if she is unable, then by all means, you can identify the body!"

"Ok, then that is what I will do. I will go and see her now. Thank you, Mason. When will you be ready at the morgue?"

Mason rubbed his chin. "Better give us a couple of hours, or I could call you if you prefer, Detective Rickard."

"Yes, that would be better if you call me. Jenna and I have a lot to talk about." he turned to Constable Jenkins and spoke. "Would you give Mason my mobile number sir, and are my instructions being carried out at the station for Pablo?" he asked.

"Will do, Detective, and rest assured everything is being taken care of as we speak. You go and spend some time with Jenna!"

"That is reassuring, a load off my mind. See you at the morgue!"

Australia! Murmured Jenna to herself as she watched an array of colour that the sun dispersed as it streamed through the trees and onto the deck where she sat. It moved to the western side now, high in the sky. *Beautiful beyond belief!* she thought. *How lucky we are!* She moved her gaze out over the water, her eyes mesmerized by the bright sunshine dancing on the ocean, and playing tricks upon the waves as they rolled in to the beach. She sighed.

We really have a lot to be thankful for, I guess! Life goes on, after all!

Suddenly, she felt so sad. She had lost her family. Not only her mother, but her father too. She knew that now. It was a gut feeling.

Despair washed over her. She hoped that she was wrong though something kept telling her otherwise. She spent a lot of time alone while Jack worked hard trying to solve the case, and her mind had wandered. She had imagined every case scenario, but always came back to the same conclusion. She desperately wanted Jack to tell her otherwise. Today was a big day for him she knew, he had said that.

Jack had raised the bar so high that his expectations were matter-of-fact, well to him anyway. He was always positive in his decisions and had a nose for the mysterious, he reveled in it, and had become an outstanding Homicide Detective. She was so proud of him.

She moved her fingers up her arm, so warm to touch as the sun played on her skin. Her body had tanned since moving to the Lodge as every day she was outside on the deck, or in the water. She loved staying there, but once again it beckoned the question. 'Where should we live?' she worried. She thought of 'Oceanview.' and shuddered.

Jenna didn't even hear Jack approach her! She was so lost in her thoughts, and it wasn't until he spoke that she lifted her head.

Their eyes met and she knew. His green eyes had darkened with concern but had a cloudy look of satisfaction she had come to know.

"Oh, Jack! You startled me." she said to him.

A frown creased his brow. "We must talk, Jenna!" he uttered.

Jenna looked at Jack seriously before she spoke. "It is over, isn't it, Jack?" she said matter-of-factly.

Jack was shocked. "You mean a finale to the mystery of both cases?"

"Yes, of course Jack, both the cases!"

"I have solved both cases, Jenna. It has been a big morning!"

"Then why aren't we shouting with glee?" she asked.

"Because, I bring sad tidings. Things you won't want to hear!"

Jenna frowned, but replied. "I have steeled myself for this moment, Jack so, don't worry about protecting me. Nothing would surprise me now, and I am sure I have already seen it in my vision anyway!"

Jack smiled awkwardly. *My god, but this girl is tough, what spirit she has.* He knew then, to sugar-coat it, would not be the way to go.

"Once again, you are right, Jenna!' he said as he sat beside her. I am going to give it to you straight, we shall discuss everything ok?"

"Much better, Detective Rickard!"

Jack realized now that he should have known. One thing that he always loved about Jenna, was her strength, he nodded at her quip.

"We found your mother's deceased body this morning, Jenna! She had been murdered, dismembered, then buried in the dunes!" Jenna's eyes brimmed with tears so, angrily she wiped them away.

"You knew all along Jack, thanks for persisting in finding her!"

"Yes, I did in my gut, Jenna. I only had to prove it, I guess! You were spot-on with your vision of her murder at the steps. But no thanks are needed. I had to do it for us both! Do you think you are up to writing out a statement of your visions and I can get it typed up so you can sign it. All the more evidence will be to our benefit!"

"Yes, of course. I'll get to that later. So, I guess it's all about proof! Do you have that proof Jack, do know who murdered mother?"

"Yes, Jenna. I now have solid proof, all the evidence and a signed confession! So, yes. I know your mother's murderer now and your attacker, the person who put you in a coma! It is the same person!"

Jenna searched his eyes. "Just tell it as it is, Jack! I can handle it!' Jack winced. "Ok, Jenna. But just know I made so many promises I didn't think I could deliver at one stage. Surprisingly there was no outsiders to this murder, only 'Oceanview' staff which is sad to say, and though this morning was tough mentally, we discovered many findings and got a solid confession so, you could say we got lucky!"

"Who murdered my mother, Jack?" Jenna queried in frustration. He stared at her. "I am so sorry, Jenna. Of course you want to know! So much to tell you, but I am grabbing at straws to try and relate it, as both cases proved more involved than we thought! *This must be hush, hush!* Your mother's murderer was Paula Hastings the cook!"

Jenna's eyes widened. "Paula Hastings? Are you positive, Jack?" "Positive! I have boot prints, fingerprints and confession as proof!"

"But murder, Jack? Could Paula really hate mother so much to murder her? So, my attack. Was Paula responsible for that also?"

Jack reacted. "Sorry, Jenna but yes! Though you were simply in the wrong place at the wrong time and unfortunate to fall through the step. Paula was the shadow you spoke of, who used a large rock to knock you senseless, just as Billy Faraday on his first day's work at the surf club was in a sand buggy was coming down the beach.

"Luckily for you, as Paula didn't have time to finish the job. We believe now they intended to come back to do just that, but when they returned you were gone. You were unconscious so, Billy rang an ambulance, and organized the sand groper to transport you up to the carpark, then to hospital. I guess you owe him your life!"

"Yes, definitely Jack. I must visit him. My goodness, Jack I really had no idea! I am so sorry for hassling you. It sounds as if it was a nightmare trying to figure it out. However, I did sense at the very onset that you relished a mystery, and would never give up. You've reached the pinnacle of your career Homicide Detective Rickard!"

"Yes, I love being a Detective! Be assured, Paula Hastings will pay!"

Jack grimaced. "However, now it's time to discuss the nitty-gritty of it and what tougher things are to come for both of us, Jenna?"

Jenna frowned. "What tougher things, Jack?"

A shadow fell over his eyes as he replied. "I am so sorry, Jenna, but two things are of importance right now. The first is, the coroner needs your mother's body identified. He told me if you were not up to it, then I could do that. So, do you want me to go and do that?"

"Certainly not, Jack. This is my mother so, I must do this for my own satisfaction, or closure if you like. I'll see it through to the end!" Jack shook his head. *Why did I expect any different reply.* he wondered as he spoke. "Of course you will, Jenna because you are so brave."

"Not really, Jack. But I will do what I have to do!"

"Yes, I know. When I get a call from the coroner we will leave."

"Ok, I'll be ready. Now what is the other thing of importance?" Jack lifted his head so that he met her eyes, he loved her eyes. Only, now they would be saddened by these new tidings. "It's about your father, Jenna." he said hesitantly.

Jenna felt her stomach sink. *This is it*. she thought and she asked. "What about my father, Jack?"

"Please understand how sorry I am, as I have to order his arrest!" Her eyes brimmed with tears, and Jack put his arms around her. "I wish there was some other explanation, Jenna. But there isn't!"

She took sanction in his arms only briefly, then lifted her head.

"I'm ok, Jack. Somehow, I knew something wasn't quite right. In hospital he was avoiding all conversations concerning my mother. He even arranged for me to write letters to her, how gross! I sensed he knew more about mother than he was telling me. So, he actually deceived me by making me believe she was still alive! I will never forgive him for that. What is his arrest for, Jack?" she queried.

Jack frowned. "Paula Hastings may have held grudge enough to murder your mother with a hatchet, but there's a twist to this case!"

"What do you mean by, a twist?" queried Jenna.

"With further investigations, evidence and a signed confession, we believe it was your father who ordered your mother's murder!"

"Oh, my goodness! I wasn't expecting that. I knew in my gut he had to be hiding something, but murder? How could he, whatever possessed him to order mother's murder, Jack?"

"Well, Jenna. We are certain Miranda Delvin put the thoughts in his mind. However, he was the one who gave the order. As this case has unfolded, we discovered there was gross blackmail happening with the staff, not only from your father, but from Miranda Delvin also. I am betting Miranda's influence swayed him. She hasn't been questioned, but it will come out, just you wait and see!"

"I find it hard to believe, though deep down I know it's true!"

"Are you alright, Jenna? Because when we go back, I must order your father's arrest as well as the others! It has to happen today!"

"Yes, Jack. Trust me, I'll be fine! Just get it all finished with. Now, on a lighter note, I made us sandwiches, and put in the fridge. No doubt we have other things to discuss. I've done a lot of thinking!"

Jack could not believe her composure, but he replied. "Ok, then. We will pause for now. I'll put the kettle on, or would you rather a drink, Jenna? Then, while we eat, we can discuss your thoughts!"

"Yes, I think it is time Jack. Maybe I will have a small sherry first to settle my nerves, and a coffee with our food. What about you?"

"Ok, but not for me! I will be working, so maybe this afternoon I can join you. Do you want to stay outside?"

"Yes, please Jack. I do love it out here."

"Right then, stay here and I will bring it out to you!" he said, and disappeared inside.

Jack served their lunch from the tray. As he sat down, he placed the sherry before her. What subject is our discussion on?" he asked.

Jenna's eyes softened as she spoke. "Our life, Jack!"

His eyes twinkled. "Hmm! My favourite subject!" he offered, Jenna smiled for the first time, and sipped her sherry.

"Would you like to go first?" she finally asked.

He looked seriously at her. "Firstly, Jenna. Think on this. If you have further questions about the case, your mother, or your father, then let's address that before we move on, agreed?"

"Yes, Jack! Once again you are right, because a couple of things are nagging me. One is hard to ask but who was it that…that…dis…

"Your mother?" asked Jack, guessing her question.

"Yes, Jack. Thank you!"

"Your mother's body was dismembered by Pablo Sanchez!" Jenna eyes widened in surprise. "No, it can't be right, Jack. He was not a violent person, he couldn't do that, could you be mistaken?" Jack looked at her sadly. "No, Jenna. Pablo confessed to doing that, but he did say he was being blackmailed and was ordered to do it!"

"Was it Pablo who confessed about the murder and my attack?"

"Yes, Jenna and others involved from 'Oceanview' were named during the interrogation I taped, and later got a signed confession!"

"Hmm! So, the murderer wasn't an outsider, but a staff member at 'Oceanview.' I could see Miranda Delvin stooping to blackmail!"

"Yes, you are correct, Jenna. Though it was your father who gave the orders. Miranda Delvin was not on the beach on the night of the murder, but your father was, and he had a hand in the plans!"

"How do you know that, Jack?"

"Because, my love. I found his footprints under the steps leading to the deck. It was your father who helped replace a missing step!" "That was confirmed by Pablo's confession so, that makes him an accessory to murder, as well as the person who ordered the murder. Your father will spend a long time in prison I would imagine!" Jenna's face drained, but she persisted. "One other thing just isn't right, Jack. My mother's necklace? It should have been with her!"

"That was Pablo's mistake. He couldn't face burying something so beautiful so, he kept it. We found it this morning where he hid it under the floorboards of his office in the stables. Your mother was wearing the necklace on the night of her murder. He confessed to taking it, along with it the murder weapon, and some other items."

"Really, you have mother's necklace?"

"Well, yes Jenna. Though at the moment it is in the city!"

"I don't understand, why is that, Jack"

"I sent it to forensics in the city with two officers this morning for testing. It is evidence, Jenna. So, every-thing we found is vital evidence. If I get the results I need when the tests come back, it will close the lid on this murder case, the court case a mere formality!"

"My goodness, but you are thorough Detective!"

"I aim to please Missus Rickard."

Jenna smiled. She loved it when he called her that. She moved next to him. "Seriously, Jack. I am so proud to be called Missus Rickard!"

"I should think so." he chuckled, and took her in his arms. Their kiss was long and passionate. "I love you, Jenna!" he whispered.

"I love you too, Jack!" she gushed, and sighed.

"Right, if that is all about the case, let's move on. I am going to get a call soon from the coroner soon, and we will have to go to the morgue for the identification. Are you up to that?"

"Yes, Jack. "However, there is one more thing I need to ask?"

"What is that, Jenna?"

"Mother's necklace, I would like to have it. Is that possible?"

"Yes, of course it's possible. Though you may have to wait until the trial is over. It is vital evidence, Jenna!"

Jenna frowned. "I thought you might say that, Jack." she replied.

"You look disappointed, Jenna. Why?"

"It's just that I wanted to arrange mother's funeral soon, and I was hoping to bury my mother with her necklace on!"

Jack looked thoughtfully at Jenna before he spoke. "You know, Jenna, if I can get the necklace witnessed early enough during court proceedings, I may be able to take photos of it for presentation after that. I would have to get permission from the judge."

"That is an idea, but how long before you get a court date, Jack?"

"I don't expect it to drag on too long, Jenna. So, I'm hoping for an immediate date. Though, I can't make any promises about the necklace yet, and besides we need to get on with our plans."

"I understand, Jack. You do what you have to do. I imagine you should have some idea in a week, wouldn't you? I too need to get on with our lives. I just want it all to be over."

Jack rubbed his chin in thought. "I think I should have some idea in a week, yes. Now, let's put that behind us and talk of our future. You mentioned earlier that you have done a lot of thinking. Let's chat briefly on that and tonight at dinner, we can discuss details."

"Good idea. One thing that is in the forefront of my mind and is constantly annoying me, is this. Where would we live, Jack?"

"Good point! Obviously, we both have work or study in the city. We could commute from here if you wanted to live at 'Oceanview?'

Jenna's eyes widened. "No way, Jack. I could never live there, and I never want to go to 'Oceanview' ever again!"

"Well, you certainly have been thinking Jenna but are you sure?"

"Positive, Jack. 'Oceanview' holds many bad memories for me!"

"I completely understand, but you are the sole owner now so, maybe you should sell it, or rent it out. What are your thoughts?"

"I can never sell 'Oceanview,' Jack!"

"Why not? What is stopping you?"

"The simple truth is, that it is mother! I propose to bury mother at 'Oceanview,' as I know that is where she would have liked to be buried with the rest of her family there, and yes Jack. We have our own cemetery, though a little secluded. 'Oceanview' can't be sold!"

"I see, Jenna! Then that is what you must do! But what to do with 'Oceanview' is proving to be a quandary. Any thoughts?"

Jenna smiled as she looked at Jack's worried expression. Then she spoke confidently. "Definitely, Jack! I have thought long and hard about many things and came to a final decision, if you agree?"

"You have? Excellent, Jenna, no doubt about you. Let's have it."

"I have decided to contact Miles Cartright to ask if he would be interested in setting it up for me. I know what I want to do. I must hire three people. Two, a permanent live-in position for a couple, man and wife, who would manage the whole enterprise. I want to turn it into a Getaway Resort, boasting lodgings, meals, trail rides, functions, that sort of thing. Maybe a bus with tours of the area and wineries. I would need to hire a stable boy to care for the horses and guest's requests and arrange settings for functions in the marque!"

"I agree, what a marvelous idea. I think Miles will take it on. But, the horses? Wouldn't you want to keep your horses, Jenna?"

Jenna looked straight at him. "No, Jack! I do not want one thing from 'Oceanview.' I will leave the horses there for guests. Also, I would like my room and my mother's rooms all packed up and the contents put in storage in the city somewhere for now. Maybe one day I will look at them. All Miranda Delvin's things to be boxed up and gone, and my father's rooms packed up and stored. I want a clean slate for any decorating I decide. Besides, I do think Miles will be sending letters to Miranda and Father to vacate them anyway."

Jack was astonished. "My goodness Jenna. Everything I have been worrying about, you have taken care of in one sweep. You are incredible, and your resilience is quite remarkable."

Jenna chuckled. "If you say so, Mister Rickard. So, all we need to talk about is where we will live, and what our future plans are, and I already have a few ideas to put on the table for discussion!"

Jack laughed. "I'll just bet you do Missus Rickard!"

Jenna laughed. "You know me far too well, Detective! Shall we continue our personal plans now, as I have no more questions?"

"How about we stop now, and continue tonight during dinner?"

"Yes, that is a better idea so, I might go to get ready now, Jack!"

"Good, that will give me time to get my thoughts in order, as I have a big afternoon, besides I expect a call from the coroner soon!" Jenna placed a kiss on his cheek in passing, then Jack watched her through the glass as she walked through the doors to the kitchen and into the bathroom. *Will she crack?* I will have to watch her very closely. *It's a big ask, after all she's been through.* he knew. *To have to identify your dead mother is not something anyone would like to do."*

Jack rose from the table and was pacing outside on the deck just as his phone rang so, he stood at the railing to take the call. He listened to the corona, Mason Dell as he explained, then sat down to wait for Jenna. *They were waiting for her.* Mason said that Julian had done his job and the body is waiting for identification. He sat pondering the case, the outcome and what he yet had to do. It had been a monster but to crack it was so rewarding and he thought on that. *I guess to me it became personal and I just had to do this for Jenna.* She had lost years of her life, and lost her mother in the process.

Then she was standing before him smiling, her green eyes were sparkling and picking up highlights from her dress. Her dress sense never seemed to amaze him as he gazed at her outfit for this all-important day. *She is prepared to say goodbye to her mother* he realized now, why the importance to identify the body, and he understood. He looked at her face, so serene, so beautiful and his heart pounded.

"All set, Jack, are you ready?" she asked offhandedly.

Jack stood and smiled as he took her in his arms and kissed her.

"Oh, you do have a way to get to me, Detective!" she chuckled. He laughed. She was showing such a brave face so, he hoped that continued. "Yes, all set, got the call and they wait for you, Jenna!"

They drove to the morgue in complete silence, each with their own thoughts. At the back entrance to the morgue, Jack drove to the double red doors to park near where Constable Jenkins stood.

"Looks like the Constable is chomping at the bit." he joked. "Are you all set, Jenna. If you want me anytime, I will be at your side."

"Thank you, Jack. Yes, I am ready so, let's get it done!"

"That's the spirit." he said, he got out and went to open her door.

"Good morning, Constable!" Jack said as he neared him.

"Good morning, Detective. Morning Jenna, good to see you!"

"Thank you Constable Jenkins and you also." replied Jenna.

"Just a quick word Constable. I am not sure if we will have time to talk later so, if not. Please make the necessary arrests after the identification when you get back and I will meet you at the station!"

"Yes, sir. Detective Rickard. That will give me great pleasure!"

"Good man." said Jack as he rapped on the door.

Almost at once the double doors swung open and Mason Dell stood there to greet them. "Hello Mister and Missus Rickard, please come in. Morning Constable." he said and stepped aside. Then he ushered them down the long hallway and into a brightly lit room.

"You know Julian Dent, of course?" he asked.

"Yes, I do." said Jack, and stepped forward to shake his hand. "Julian, meet my wife, Jenna, she will do the identification!"

Julian smiled. "Nice to meet you, Jenna. Come this way please!"

"Thank you." offered Jenna, and both her and Jack followed.

Jenna paused as the table filled her view and her eyes smarted. Quickly she brushed a tear away then she stepped forward to say.

"Thank you, Mister Dent. I will proceed if you would?"

Julian slowly lifted the sheet from the body and folded it back. Jenna stiffened as her mother's face came into view. *They did a good job* she thought. Until she bent to kiss her mother's face and a scent of makeup filled her nostrils, and she knew what was under that.

She lifted her head as the waves of nostalgia filled her senses. She put out a hand to steady herself as she faced her mother's body and the bile rose in her throat threatening to choke her. She felt sick, but steeled herself to say one final goodbye. "Goodbye mother, rest in peace!" she muttered. She lifted her head to look at the coroner with a deadly pale face. "This is my mother, Julia Temple, sir!" then she was scrambling to find her feet, trying to get out of there.

Jack was quick to notice and was beside her quickly to take her arm to steer her to the door. He waved a goodbye to the mortician and the coroner and could hear their voices behind him in unison.

"Thank you, Missus Rickard, thank you Detective." they called.

They only just made it to the outside double doors when Jenna started to retch, and Jack steered her to the garden bed. He held her long hair at the back to aid her, as he gripped her firmly and waited.

Constable Jenkins caught his eye. "I'll be off, sir. See you later!"

Jack uttered not one word, instead he waved to the Constable. Then he reached for a handkerchief to hand Jenna when she stood.

"Thank you, Jack." she said shakily as she took it from him.

"Are you ok?" he asked.

"Yes, I will be fine, just get me home please!"

Jack put an arm around her waist. "Come along then, my love."

It wasn't until they reached the lodge that Jenna spoke. "It was terrible, Jack. I kept seeing mother's body all bloody and mutilated as I last saw her. However, one thing came to mind when I looked at her. Clothes, her own clothes for her funeral. I would like to have her clothes from 'Oceanview' before her things are packed up. If I tell you what I need, would you do that for me?"

"Of course, Jenna. So, you are adamant about not going back?"

"Definitely Jack, I have to move forward from here."

"I see that. Well, today was a step forward. I am proud of you!"

Jenna smiled for the first time. "Thanks, my love, you are my rock!"

Chapter Nineteen

Lights twinkled in the garden, creating an inviting mood as they looked through the dining room windows of the Lodge.

Jenna smiled. "I am really going to miss it here, Jack. It has been our home away from home, and I have enjoyed every moment."

"It has been that and more, Jenna. We have memories here now. I noticed that management have our wedding photo in the foyer now. I guess you could say we are treasured guests, but we'll come back, Jenna. Any time we have to return to Blue Bay we will stay here. Besides, I would like to visit my parents from time to time."

"Yes, of course. I guess we won't be far away at all."
Jack smiled. "So, does that suggest you want to live in the city?"
Jenna grinned. "Well, not so much in the city, but in the vicinity. A few things have come to mind when we arrive at that discussion!"

"Well, let's do it. We did say we would discuss our future plans tonight at dinner. Besides you said that you had a few ideas to put on the table, Missus Rickard." Jack chuckled. So, fire away. Tell me all your ideas, and we will discuss them all!"

Jenna laughed, but then got deadly serious. "You see, Jack. I want the impossible. To live a country life in the city would be ideal!"

Jack rubbed his chin before replying. "Ok, brilliant. I think I get your meaning. You would like to have access to the city, but live in a country environment, with maybe horses even. Am I correct?"

"Exactly, Jack, but with an ocean view also, I do so love the sea!"

He laughed. "Are you sure that is all you want, Jenna? However, I can relate as I too, love the ocean. Just to be able to walk on a path to our own private beach would be marvelous. Don't you agree?"

"Oh, Jack. Definitely my thoughts. I am so pleased we are on the same page. I guess after seeing Doc and Fay Wilson's property, it tore at my heartstrings. I want a real home like that."

"Ah, so you want our home to be on an acreage?"

"Yes, most certainly Jack. Just think of the possibilities."

"Well, I am trying to keep up however, a few possibilities come to mind. We buy land on the ocean just out of the city. We stock it with the horses we need, you could bring yours from 'Oceanview?' Then we build our home, or, we buy an existing ocean property."

"That sounds wonderful, except for one thing. My horses. I do not want anything from 'Oceanview' and that includes my horses."

Jack raised an eyebrow. "I know you've said that but can you be sure, Jenna. They are blood stock, all of them. Irreplaceable really."

Jenna shook her head. "Maybe, but we can buy our own blood stock if you want, Jack but the horses stay with 'Oceanview.' I only want what I asked to be packed up and put in storage."

"I guess you've pondered on many thoughts, Jenna. I hope our future discussions are as easy to sort out. We have our ideas set."

"Well, not quite, Jack. We need a place to live while we do this."

"No problem. I own an apartment in the city. We could live there while we are looking at property. What do you think?"

"That would be perfect, let us begin there if you agree?"

"Sounds perfect, Jenna. We do negotiate well!"

Jenna laughed. "Yes, I think we do Detective Rickard. So, now we are back where we started and to complete your job by winding up these cases, and the trials. Any idea how long that will take, Jack?"

Jack thought for a while. "Can't give you any idea yet Jenna, until I speak with the judge and set a court date, that could be tomorrow."

"In that case, I have an idea. I could go to the city by myself and arrange a real estate to show me some rural property while you are in the process of tying up both cases, your thoughts?"

"Well, I suppose that would be a start as I don't know if I can get away to look at property. I'm going to be flat out until the end."

"Yes, I realize that, and I don't want to jeopardize your work by taking you away. I could go myself by train to the city and stay at the apartment while I'm looking. I would also like to visit Miles and tell him of my plans for 'Oceanview.' It is right after all he has done. If anything comes up that I think is a good purchase I can get photos to show you, or failing that, I can come back so we can discuss it."

"Yes, Jenna. I think that is an ideal plan. It will also give me full concentration on the job ahead. I have to have my wits about me as we are in the final stages now, and the most important part! Also, you catching up with Miles is a great idea. Yes, you should go."

"Excellent! Then I shall leave tomorrow!"

"So soon?"

"Well, I guess, come tomorrow your mind will be elsewhere and besides I would like to catch up with Miles first before the weekend as I want to advertise the positions available at 'Oceanview' I would carry out interviews for those positions, maybe here at The Lodge? Can I rely on you to arrange for my rooms to be packed up from 'Oceanview' and I'll arrange a storage unit close to the apartment."

"Hmm! Yes, a good idea. You must get the ball rolling for there. You've thought of it all." he chuckled. "Be assured I'll do the rest!"

Jack watched her as she boarded the train, then she turned to face him. Her long auburn hair fell all around her in a mass of curls, and she smiled that wonderful smile that captured his heart, as she gave him a wave and disappeared into the carriage.

He turned to leave, but on impulse he looked back and there she was, leaning out the carriage window and shouting out to him. He could barely make out what she was saying but realized she said. "Check your pocket!" So, he felt in his pocket, and sure enough he pulled out a note. "I love you Mister Rickard!" it read. Then below was a list of clothing she wanted for her mother's burial. *Poor Jenna* he thought. *She thought of everything down to the last detail.* He smiled, waved and called out. "I love you too, Jenna!" then she was gone.

Jenna reached her window seat and sank down with a sigh. *So much has happened* she thought as her mind wandered over the past weeks. Her immediate issue was to make an appointment to visit Miles Cartright and she picked up her phone to dial the number. Miles's secretary's voice came through load and clear, and Jenna was pleased to be remembered. They chatted briefly, then Jenna ended the call with a 12 am appointment secured for that day.

Perfect she thought. *One more call and I should be set.* The train left the station and rattled along the tracks on-route for the city as Jenna dialed a number for a Real Estate close to Jack's apartment. She was put through to a Sales Representative for Rural land and Property so, she introduced herself. They chatted briefly as she explained her requirements, then was surprised when he said he could show her several properties or land available along the ocean front. He could show her some land available as soon as this afternoon so, Jenna booked an appointment for him to pick her up at the apartment at 3 pm today, and she gave him the address.

She sat back in her seat feeling satisfied with her appointments but the prospect of looking at land was churning up her insides.

She was excited. This was a new chapter in hers and Jack's life and she wanted to relish every part of it. She thought of Jack and at once she was reminded how they were thrown together after many years apart. She had so much to be thankful for, but her life would not have been complete without Jack in it. He was the only person she had ever loved, and marrying Jack, somehow made it all right.

Jenna sighed. She felt the tears spring into her eyes and then roll down her face, and she quickly wiped them away. She wasn't sure if they were happy tears or if they were for the loss of her mother.

She decided that instant her mother's funeral would be special, and she grabbed a notebook from her bag to jot some things down.

With the miles slipping away, she became familiar with the roll of the carriage and busily worked on all her notes for Miles. So far everything was going to plan. *Just one thing.* she realized. *Lunch? I will not have time for lunch when I arrive in the city, or on reaching the apartment either before going to my first appointment.* Then she thought of the dining car and she looked at her watch. *Good, I can fill in time until the dining car opens and have a snack there.* She pulled out a book to read for a while, sometimes catching a glimpse of the countryside changing through the window as it flashed by her. The train was just approaching the suburbs on the outskirts of the city when she rose from her seat to weave her way through the carriages to the dining car. It looked like everyone had the same idea, and Jenna walked to the very end before she reached a vacant table.

Quickly, she grabbed a menu and ordered a light lunch with a coffee, and sat down to read again until in no time at all her order was ready and she approached the counter to collect it.

She looked out the window as the train passed through various stations on-route to The City Central Station.

As Jenna finished her lunch and they pulled into Central Station, Jack was sitting in a meeting with the Judge at the courthouse.

Judge Riley was known as a cagy old man. Through many years of service, he had steeled himself to cope with any situation. His grey eyes beaded as he listened to Jack presenting his case and pleas then he looked at him directly, making eye contact before he spoke.

"You do realize I hope, Detective Rickard, that no case is cut and dried until the court hearing, and all witnesses are exhausted. This is not the city you know!' he mumbled.

Jack knew he was in for a struggle. He was up against a cranky old codger for a judge, who was old-school, and would not accept his knowledge of the law and the evidence he had as proof to tie these cases up quickly. The judge says. *Facts must take their course in this investigation* he thought. Well, then let them, *but if we drag on for another week, the outcome will still be the same.* God help the ones who get charged by this judge, he will lock them up and throw away the key. Jack controlled his demeanor to reply with a neutral tone.

"As you wish, Judge Riley. However, you will find my evidence solid, and my confession honest and to the point so, whether it is in the city or in the country, my investigation has been thorough, no stone was overturned and my outcome would still be the same."

"That may be Detective Rickard but it must be proved in court."

"I do realize that Judge. I thought I would save you some time by doing all the ground work I have done, and get a quicker result."

"We shall see Detective!" said the judge.

"Can I ask again of the necklace Judge? Your decision on that?"

"As it is with all evidence Detective Rickard, it must be available in court so, the necklace should accompany all evidence!"

Jack was getting frustrated. "Ok, then what time frame do you put on these trials, Judge?"

"That, I won't know until all evidence is exhausted and all the witnesses are heard in a court of law, Detective Rickard.

"Judge Riley, can we set a court date now, it is long overdue?"

Judge Riley looked at Jack over the rim of his spectacles and spoke. "Hmm! Let's jot it in for three weeks from today."

Constable Jenkins, who had been sitting quietly at the back of the room, shuffled his feet and stared at the judge in disbelief.

Jack held his protests, he knew they would fall on deaf ears so, he stood and stated briefly "Well, I guess you have it all mapped out so, thank you for your time today Judge Riley." and he leaned across the table stretching out his hand.

Judge Riley was not expecting that however, he attempted a hand shake. Jack's grip was strong and purposeful, and he winced as their eyes met. Jack's eyes had darkened to a deeper green.

Jack felt the sweaty palms of the Judge's limp handshake, and he added. "We shall meet in court, Judge Riley." and he turned to exit the chambers. "Come along please Constable Jenkins, we have much work to do!' he said as he passed him at the doorway exit.

"Ah! You go to the car, Jack. I will be just a moment."

Jack looked up. "Right, you are sir, I will wait in the car." Constable Jenkins waited until he heard his footfalls on the stairs and then he approached the Judge. "Good morning, Harold."

"Joe, good to see you. How can I help?"

Constable Jenkins stared at him "Better rephrase that to more like. How I can help you, Harold?"

"What do you mean, Joe?"

"You gave the Detective a real run-around, Harold!"

Judge Riley chuckled. "Yes! I did, didn't I. Can't stand those would-be Homicide Detectives from the city who think they can come out here and run things. Yes, I just put him in his place!"

Constable Jenkins frowned. "He is no would-be Detective, Harold. More like second-top Homicide Detective in the state, maybe even Australia. He honed his skills as apprentice under the guidance of the great Jeremy Woods. Also, Jack is a local boy, not from the city!"

Judge Riley was so taken back that his glasses slipped from his head. He grabbed them quickly, but looked up at the Constable.

"What's that you say, Joe. What do you mean he is local?"

"Just that, Harold. He was born and bred here, and his parents still run the orchard out of town. I picked him up as a kid when I was first involved with this case many years ago. Not to mention that my skills for handling a case like this was simply not up to par back then, not after what I have just experienced as I have worked alongside Jack on this Murder/Mystery case of Julia Temple and her daughter, Jenna and I have never seen the like! Jack performed his preliminary training right here in Blue Bay as a police officer."

Judge Riley was speechless, he could only gape at the Constable.

"Jack is exceptionally thorough but ruthless as well, and a great negotiator which only stems from his expert training. He has a real nose for getting to the bottom of a mystery, and you would never believe what I've seen him do in these past weeks. No, Judge, this time you have judged badly, and I simply had to set you right!"

Finally, Judge Riley found his voice. "Oh! What a bumble. I am sorry, Joe, I never checked him out. A local boy too, and I treated him so badly. How can I ever re-coup from that?"

"Harold, I think you'll find Jack Rickard to be, not only a brilliant Homicide Detective, but a great listener and also one who forgives. I would suggest we get together for dinner, but entirely up to you."

"Of course, Joe. A level playing field and a social evening. I shall call my Country Club for a reservation for tonight. Say at 7 pm, if you could persuade Jack to attend. We must tie this up before this case begins, and I mean to offer him and immediate court date and also tell him that he can cross-examine if he wishes to!"

Constable Jenkins chuckled. "I think you will find that Detective Rickard plans on doing just that Judge, regardless of your tongue in cheek. Tonight at 7pm it is, I will confirm. Must go now, thanks!"

Constable Jenkins smiled as he left the room and took the stairs two at a time, then made his way across the carpark. By the time he reached the car, he had a huge grin on his face.

"What's up with you, Constable, and why the big grin? It wasn't exactly a good meeting and you look like a cat that ate the canary!" Constable Jenkins laughed now. "Well, you could say that is a great way to sum it up. However, ye have little faith, Detective."

Jack frowned. "What faith, and in what?"

"Well, in me of course! How does a private dinner tonight with the Judge sound to you, Detective Rickard?"

Jack's head lifted so he could meet the Constables eyes. "You old dog, you! What have you been up to, Constable Jenkins?"

"Hmm! Just setting the record straight. Let's get moving and I will fill you in on the details on the way to the station!"

Jack laughed. "So, the judge is ready to deal!"

"You could say that. He has changed tack now he knows you grew up here. Strange, he told me he neglected to check you out!"

"I see, anyway I wasn't too worried, one call from Jeremy Woods would have sorted him out. Now, things of importance before we get to the station. Jenna left for the city to meet with Miles Cartright and to look at real estate. As soon as I get confirmation from Miles about 'Oceanview' and the people he wants removed from there according to Julia's will, then we can act. I will need Richard and Miranda's rooms all packed up, and The Hasting's belongings from the cabin all put in storage. Also, the stables cleared of any personal things of Pablo's. Everything must be out of there as Jenna plans to turn 'Oceanview into a Getaway Resort and wants it vacated."

"Jenna doesn't dwell on things, does she? What an idea, I can't believe she is facing things head on. You have to hand it to her!"

"No, she doesn't at all, Constable. I admire her tenacity but she thought long and hard about 'Oceanview' to come to this decision."

Arriving at the station, they both left the vehicle and walked close together across the carpark, talking as they went.

"So, Constable Jenkins, finally! At last, I can smell the finish line. I hope the judge is more co-operative tonight so we can tie it up!"

"I have a feeling he has seen you in a different light, Detective."

"Good news to hear, but I'm not holding my breath. Now, how are our guests? Did all the arrests go according to plan?"

"All in lock-up, Detective. Richard Temple gave us a hard time, but we were expecting that. I too hope the judge is lenient, we need an early court date but it's Pablo I am more worried about!"

Jack stopped. "Why? What do you mean, Constable?"

"Well, if we get an early trial, we can hold the others until then, but Pablo is becoming restless. I guess he is feeling locked up in the safe-house, which he is. However, he keeps asking questions so, the longer it goes on, he may begin second-guessing his confession."

Hmm! I've been thinking the same thing, Constable. Think I will lean heavy on the judge and explain that to him. It may sway him! However, I will visit Pablo anyway as he just needs reassurance!"

"Good idea. I'll call the judge to confirm. Is Jenna calling today?"

"She said she would call sometime today. I am hoping she will get an appointment with Miles today? I need a letter from him."

"That we do!" offered the Constable. "What are your plans?"

"I am going on the assumption of a positive meeting tonight, so I shall structure my course of action for cross examination in court. Can't afford to miss a thing. I will be going through my notebook, making notes and updating my journal, what about you, sir?"

Constable Jenkins smiled. "Paperwork and more paperwork, Jack."

Jack laughed. "Ok, let's meet up for lunch, say about 1.30pm?"

"Suits me fine. Until then, we play the waiting game."

Jack smiled. "We do indeed, but come this afternoon we will shine. Make sure the officers are ready, we have much to do, Constable."

"Oh, my officers are ready, Detective. They wait your orders."
"Excellent. Will catch you later, I have much to do." Jack said as he waved and walked to his office and unlocked the door. He walked across to the windows and drew the drapes aside. Immediately, light filled the room. Then he sat at his desk, notebook in hand.

It was hours later when Jack looked at his clock and decided his work was done so, he checked his emails. One was from Constable Jenkins with an attachment of forensic reports. Quickly he opened it, then he grinned. *Now I have it all, what good timing*! An email from Miles Cartright caught his eye. *Thank you, Jenna.* he thought, as he eagerly read it. Miles's instructions were crystal clear. Jack breathed a sigh of relief and copied in Constable Jenkins, giving him the go-ahead to instruct his officers to act now. He pressed copy and two pages spat out. He was folding them just as his phone rang.

"Hi Jenna! Must say you are quick off the mark. I have an email from Miles. I assume you secured an early meeting with him, and he has acted promptly. Is he on board for the Getaway project?"

"Hi Jack! Yes, I knew it was important for you to get an email. He is sending a letter also! Miles is all for my idea at 'Oceanview!'"

"Good, but the email has helped us get things done today. I have a second meeting with the Judge tonight as our first meeting went tail up. He wasn't going to listen to reason, but thanks to Constable Jenkins we have secured a dinner meeting with him at his Country Club tonight. How goes the real estate? Any prospects there?" Jenna sounded disappointed. "Sadly, no Jack. I saw three blocks of rural land but they were either too hilly, or not grassed enough."

"Never mind, chin up as tomorrow is another day. Something will turn up. I must go now, lots to do. I will call when I have more news!" Jenna replied, and he ended the call.

Jack sat going over his notes one more time, then his mind turned to his preparation for the all-important meeting with Judge Riley.

The Country Club was dimly lit and had a prestigious feel to it as they entered and were ushered to a private room where Judge Riley sat. "Good evening, gents, please take a seat and we will get right down to it. He searched Detective Rickard face, then added.

"I considered your requests Detective in this overdue case. My apologies for my quick assumption, I do hope we can start over?"

Jack chuckled. "Hmm, a start over? You know Judge Riley? I am extremely partial to start-overs. Many of my greatest achievements have stemmed from a start-over. As a Detective, there comes a time, a missing clue or that vital piece of evidence only found when you start over. I too, am in agreeance to start over. Though I am sure we would have resolved our differences for the sake of Julia Temple!"

Judge Riley gulped. "Yes, of course, Detective, a reputable lady. I believe her daughter wants to make the funeral arrangements. So, Detective I cleared my schedule. Your court date starts tomorrow. Once you present the necklace, you may take photo's so Jenna can have it. You will have one week Detective. I trust it's enough time?"

"Jack nodded. "That is plenty of time, Judge and thank you!"

"No thanks needed, send me the funeral details. Now, let's eat!" Just like that Detective Rickard was thrown into the world of Crime, of law and order and bringing criminals to justice, and that was his specialty, and Jenna was arranging a funeral and viewing property.

At the close of day two, she called. "You won't believe this Jack. I saw a block of rural land to die for, you must see it! So, how goes the trials, is there an end in sight? I booked the funeral in Monday!"

"Sentencing begins on our short day tomorrow. Book in a 2 p.m. viewing of the land, I will drive up. What of after-funeral plans?"

"Well, nothing yet as I can't go to 'Oceanview!' I just can't, Jack!"

"Oh, I see! Should I ask my parents to arrange the wake, then?" Jenna sighed in relief. *Bless you for that, Jack.* "Yes please, can you?" She paused...*Sentencing is so soon*...Her father's face came to mind.

Epilogue

Jenna observed the lady as she walked up to the pulpit. She was quite elderly now but still sprite enough to negotiate a few steps.

It was only fitting Ethel Cartright was that special one chosen to speak of her mother. She was her oldest and dearest friend after all.

Ethel witnessed the open casket, then smiled down at her friend. As she faced the congregation and commenced to unravel her story of when Julia Temple, and herself spent their college years together, Jenna felt as if she was talking about someone else. Ethel continued by saying they both had grown up living a sheltered, privileged life with their well-to-do families who were both property owners. So, their lives were prestigious beyond any belief for that era and it was the happiest of times to remember. "In remembrance Julia!" stated Ethel, as she stepped down to place a single red rose upon her chest.

Why is it my mother never spoke of her youth? wondered Jenna. She was hearing another side of her mother's life so long forgotten, and felt blessed to be a witness to the words spoken about her today, by her best friend Ethel Cartright. Then Jenna finally realized why her mother possessed such statute and poise, why she was so correct. It was simply her upbringing and her youth, things Jenna knew so very little about, and Jenna suddenly felt proud, and finally at ease.

She felt humbled by the dedication of Homicide Detective Jack Rickard her husband, who not only solved a complicated murder case by detecting the murderer and accomplices, but also recovered her mother's remains so she could provide a burial she so deserved.

Now Jenna knew her mother, Julia Temple, could finally rest in peace.

Acknowledgements

A special thank you to my family for their continued support
To my friends, and supporters, thank you for your trust in me
There have been many great moments that I will always treasure

www.ingramcontent.com/pod-product-compliance
Lightning Source LLC
Chambersburg PA
CBHW022025290426
44109CB00014B/756